The SPORTS RULES Book

HUMAN KINETICS
with Thomas Hanlon

Human Kinetics

Library of Congress Cataloging-in-Publication Data

Human Kinetics Publishers.
    The sports rules book / Human Kinetics with Thomas Hanlon.
        p.   cm.
    Includes bibliographical references (p. 369).
    ISBN 0-88011-807-5
    1. Sports--Rules.   I. Hanlon, Thomas W.   II. Title.
  GV731.H85   1997
  796--dc21   97-27774
                                           CIP

ISBN: 0-88011-807-5

Managing Editor: Alesha G. Thompson
Assistant Editor: Erin Sprague
Copyeditor: Donald F. Amerman, Jr.
Proofreader: Sara Wiseman
Graphic Designer: Judy Henderson
Graphic Artist: Francine Hamerski
Photo Editor: Boyd LaFoon
Cover Designer: Jack Davis
Illustrators: Sara Wolfsmith and Tim Offenstein
Research Assistants: Jodie Gardner, Tammy Frye, Robin Pruitt, Vickie Bierman, Jennifer Mitchaner, Amy Carnes, Lynn Marshall
Printer: United Graphics

Human Kinetics books are available at special discounts for bulk purchase. Special editions or book excerpts can also be created to specification. For details, contact the Special Sales Manager at Human Kinetics.

Printed in the United States of America   10 9 8 7 6 5 4 3 2 1

Human Kinetics
Web site: http://www.humankinetics.com/

United States: Human Kinetics, P.O. Box 5076, Champaign, IL 61825-5076
1-800-747-4457
e-mail: humank@hkusa.com

Canada: Human Kinetics, Box 24040, Windsor, ON N8Y 4Y9
1-800-465-7301 (in Canada only)
e-mail: humank@hkcanada.com

Europe: Human Kinetics, P.O. Box IW14, Leeds LS16 6TR, United Kingdom
(44) 1132 781708
e-mail: humank@hkeurope.com

Australia: Human Kinetics, 57A Price Avenue, Lower Mitcham, South Australia 5062
(08) 277 1555
e-mail: humank@hkaustralia.com

New Zealand: Human Kinetics, P.O. Box 105-231, Auckland 1
(09) 523 3462
e-mail: humank@hknewz.com

Contents

Contributing Reviewers

Alpine Skiing
John Yacenda
Ski and Snowboard Instructor

Angling
Johnna Pitts
BASS, Inc.

Archery
Skip Phillips
National Archery Association of the United States

Australian Football
Jack Halbert
South Australian National Football League

Badminton
Paul Pawlaczyk
USA Badminton Association

Baseball
Bob Kuenster
Baseball Digest

Basketball
Jim Haney
National Association of Basketball Coaches
of the United States (NABC)

Biathlon
Max Cobb
U.S. Biathlon Association

Bowling
Bill Vint
Bowling Magazine

Boxing
Steve Ross
USA Boxing

Canoeing & Kayaking
David Harrison
Canoe & Kayak Magazine

Cricket
Max Shaukat
World Cricket League

Cross-Country Skiing
Linda Johnson
U.S. Ski Team

Curling
David Garber
U.S. Curling News

Cycling
Edmund Burke
Cycling Science Communications

Diving
Ron O'Brien
U.S. Diving National Technical Directory

Equestrian
Liz Hoskinson
The American Horse Shows

Fencing
Mark Tebault
U.S. Fencing Association

Field Hockey
Karen Collins
U.S. Field Hockey Association

Figure Skating
Karin Kunzle-Watson
Former Professional World Champion

Football
Mel Pulliam
American Football Coaches Association

Golf
Cliff Schrock
Golf Digest

Gymnastics
Dwight Normile
International Gymnast Magazine

Handball
Vern Roberts
U.S. Handball Association

Ice Hockey
Joe Bertagna
American Hockey Coaches Association

Judo
Judy Jeska
United States Judo Association

Karate
Pat Hickey
USA Karate Federation Secretary

Lacrosse
Keith Maynard
Lacrosse Magazine

Modern Pentathlon
Charlie Kiley
U.S. Modern Pentathlon Association

Netball
Pat Taylor
International Federation of Netball Associations

Orienteering
Tom Renfrew
Director of Sport and Outdoor Education
University of Strathclyde, Glasgow, Scotland

Racquetball
Otto Dietrich
U.S. Racquetball Association

Roller Hockey
Mike Scarr
Roller Hockey Magazine

Rowing
Susan Lezotte
American Rowing

Rugby Union
James S. Russell
USA Rugby Football Union (USARFU)

Shooting
Randy Moeller
USA Shooting

Soccer
Jim Cosgrove
U.S. Youth Soccer Association

Softball
Merle Butler
Amateur Softball Association of America

Speed Skating
Don Kangas
Amateur Speedskating Union of the United States

Squash
Phil Yarrow
Dunlop/Slazenger National Advisory Staff

Swimming
Phil Whitten
Swimming World

Synchronized Swimming
Margo Erickson
U.S. Synchronized Swimming

Table Tennis
Azmy Ibrahim
U.S. Table Tennis Association

Tae Kwon Do
Rod Speidel
Tae Kwon Do Times

Team Handball
Michael Cavanaugh
U.S. Team Handball Federation

Tennis
Ed Weathers
Tennis Magazine

Track & Field
Pete Cava
Media Information Officer
USA Track & Field

Triathlon
Chris Newbound
Inside Triathlon

Volleyball
C.C. Sandorfi
Volleyball Magazine

Water Polo
Jim Linehan
U.S. Water Polo, Inc.

Water Skiing
Ben Favret
Bennett's Water Ski School

Weightlifting
Lyn Jones
U.S. Weightlifting Federation

Wrestling
Bob Johnson
Amateur Athletic Union

Yachting
Robert MacArthur

Special thanks for an overall review of the book to

Barry Mano
Publisher, *Referee Magazine*
Founder, National Association of Sports Officials

Introduction

Remember making up rules as a kid with your peers for the games you played? If some rules didn't work so well, you'd change them—sometimes in the middle of the game—and try again. Fun, but not very practical beyond the limits of a backyard or sandlot.

In organized sports, such rule-making creativity and spontaneity won't work. Each sport needs a consistent set of guidelines that apply, with only minor variations, across all competitive levels and all geographical boundaries. These guidelines, however, quickly become a detailed and mind-numbing list of "Official Rules" that few can comprehend and only those who are paid to officiate bother trying to learn. Not fun and not very practical for most of us.

Because rules are necessary, but are almost always presented in too much detail to apply, we saw the need for a new approach. *The Sports Rules Book* features the fundamental rules for 54 sports. The hard-to-understand terminology is gone leaving a reference that provides a concise understanding of essential rules and procedures. In our attempt to develop a rule book that was more fun to use without sacrificing accuracy, we

- sifted through the sport's current official rules book and pulled out the rules that are essential to administer, appreciate, and understand the sport—for the administrator, coach, physical education teacher, player, and fan;
- presented those rules in clear enough terms that someone new to the sport could gain an understanding and appreciation for the procedures and rules; and
- designed the book so that it doesn't look or read like a typical rules book. We opened up the pages, included artwork and sidebars, and made the material easier to move through.

We also attempted to design each chapter in a way that would most benefit you. First we provide a brief **introduction** to the sport, often including its origins, its objectives, and, when appropriate, the types of competitions within the sport. Then we give an overview of the sport's **procedures**—how the contest begins, how it proceeds, and major checkpoints along the way. We then provide a list of **terms** that will help the reader understand terminology that is often unique to the sport or that has significant meaning. We also describe and provide a diagram of the **playing area**—field, court, or course—including markings and dimensions. We include a short section on the **competitors** themselves, including how competitions are categorized by age and weight brackets, when appropriate. We briefly describe the **equipment** and note any special regulations regarding its make or use. For 18 of the chapters, we provide significant rules **modifications** based on age or physical disability. We also describe the **officials** who are in charge of the competition, and in some cases provide drawings of common officials' signals. Finally, we list the **organization** that provided the rules for the chapter, and in many cases we also list other organizations that administer the sport.

A word here about the sources of rules for this book: In some cases, these governing bodies are international; in other cases, they are United States governing bodies. Both levels of governing bodies are devoted in part to standardizing the rules of play for their sport. If you need more in-depth rules, we suggest you contact these governing bodies. We list addresses and phone numbers at the end of each chapter. Comprehensive officiating rules and information for most sports can be found by writing to the National Association of Sports Officials, 2017 Lathrope Avenue, Racine, Wisconsin 53405. Or call them at (414) 632-5448.

In order to accommodate an international audience with measurements for each sport, we have used the commonly used measurement for each sport within the text and diagrams of that chapter. We have also provided a small conversion chart in the diagrams and a larger conversion chart here in the introduction of the book that will help each person go from English to metric measurements and from metric to English measurements.

The Sports Rules Book is not meant to be complete in its coverage of any sport. It is meant to provide the basic rules and procedures of a sport and to be practical, understandable, and concise, without sacrificing the essentials. We trust that *The Sports Rules Book* will meet your needs in these areas and will be a useful reference for you.

Measurement Conversions			
English to metric		Metric to English	
Multiply	by	Multiply	by
Feet	.3048006 m/ft	Meters	3.280833 ft/m
Feet	30.48006 cm/ft	Centimeters	.032808 ft/cm
Inches	2.540005 cm/in	Centimeters	.39370 in/cm
Inches	25.4000 mm/in	Millimeters	.0394 in/mm
Miles	1.60935 km/mi	Kilometers	.62137 mi/km
Ounces	28.349527 g/oz	Grams	.0352740 oz/g
Pounds	453.5924 g/lb	Grams	.00220462 lb/g
Pounds	.453592 kg/lb	Kilograms	2.2046223 lb/kg
Yards	.91440183 m/yd	Meters	1.093611 yd/m

Sources: C.R.C. Standard Mathematical Tables, 12th Edition, Chemical Rubber Publishing Company, 1959.
Information Please Almanac Atlas & Yearbook, 50th Edition, Houghton Mifflin Company, 1997.

To convert:

Start with the measurement with which you are dealing. Multiply by the appropriate conversion factor using all the decimal places. If there is more than one choice of conversion factor, use the one that is closest in comparison (i.e., pounds and kilograms rather than pounds and grams, or feet and meters rather than feet and centimeters). In general, round the answer to the same number of places after the decimal you had in the original number. For example, to convert 99 pounds to kilograms, look under "Pounds" in the English to metric column where it specifies the conversion in "kg/lb". Multiply 99 lb by .453592 kg/lb and the result is 44.905608 kg.

Common conversions

10 meters = 32.8 feet

100 meters = 328 feet

500 meters = 1,641 feet

10 feet = 304.8 centimeters

100 feet = 30.5 meters

10 inches = 25.4 centimeters

10 centimeters = 4 inches

20 millimeters = .79 inches

50 millimeters = 2 inches

10 inches = 254 millimeters

10 kilometers = 6.2 miles

5 kilometers = 3.1 miles

5 miles = 8 kilometers

5 ounces = 142 grams

100 grams = 3.5 ounces

5 kilograms = 11 pounds

500 grams = 1.1 pounds

100 pounds = 220.5 kilograms

20 yards = 18.3 meters

10 yards = 9.1 meters

Alpine Skiing

© Claus Andersen

Accounts of Alpine ski competition date back to the 6th century. Skiing competition began on a broader scale in the early 1800s; the sport was introduced to America in the mid-1800s by Norwegian immigrants. Early skis were made of wood and were laminated; by the early 1900s skis had become shorter. By the 1940s Alpine skis took on a more versatile shape; today's skis offer many shapes and lengths to accommodate different styles of skiing, racing, and snow conditions.

Alpine skiing consists of several disciplines, including downhill, slalom, giant slalom, super-giant slalom (super-G), parallel, team, and speed competitions. Competitions may be held in individual events or in combined events (e.g., a downhill and a slalom).

The source for rules for this chapter is the Fédération Internationale de Ski (FIS), which is the international governing body for skiing.

PROCEDURES

The following procedures are common to all Alpine events.

The *starting order* is determined by FIS points: the 15 best skiers go in the first group. Skiers without FIS points go in the last group. In competitions with two runs, the starting order for the second run is determined by the results of the first run; the skier in 15th place goes first, 14th goes second, and on down until the first goes 15th. From 16 on, skiers go in order.

Skiers in downhill, giant slalom, and super-G competitions start at intervals of 60 seconds. Slalom competitors start at irregular intervals, going at the starter's command. Ten seconds before the start, the starter calls out, "Ten seconds," and then counts down each second beginning at five. The starter then gives the start command; an automatic start signal is often used. A competitor who does not start within five seconds before and five seconds after the official start time is usually disqualified.

To correctly *pass a gate*, the competitor must pass across the gate line with ski tips and both feet. If a competitor loses a ski without committing a fault, the tip of the remaining ski and both feet must pass the gate line. The gate line is the imaginary shortest line between the gate poles. In parallel slalom, the gate passage is correct when both the ski tips and feet pass the outside gate markers in the direction of the turn. If a competitor misses a gate, he is disqualified.

The *finish area* is wide, with a gently sloped outrun that is completely fenced in. The finish line is marked by two posts or a horizontal banner. Competitors must cross the finish line on both skis, one ski, or with both feet (in case of a fall at the line). The time stops once any part of the competitor's equipment or body crosses the line.

TERMS

A **blocking pole plant** is a forceful placement of the ski pole's tip in the snow to slow progress.

The **edge angle** is the degree of angle between a ski's edge and the snow; a greater angle creates greater resistance to the pull of gravity.

An **edge set** is the equal edging of both the inside (uphill) and outside (downhill) skis to create a momentary or permanent stopping of one's progress.

Edging is the combination of edge angle, ankle, knee, and hip angulation, pressure and weight distribution, and steering that influences the degree of skidding of the skis while turning.

A **flat ski** is one that is not edged.

The **inside ski** is the one that's inside the arc of the turn.

The **outside ski** is the one that's outside the arc of the turn.

A **pole swing** is the preparatory movement of the pole forward that precedes a pole plant or pole touch; it's often used as a timing device for turning in rhythm.

A **sideslip** occurs when the skis slide sideways, under control, down the fall line.

A **sidestep** occurs when a skier lifts one ski and moves it sideways away from the other ski, and then moves the other ski next to the first ski to re-form the original parallel position.

DOWNHILL

The vertical drop for men ranges from 500 to 1,100 meters; for women, from 500 to 800 meters. Men's courses are marked with red gates; women's courses have either red gates or alternating red and blue gates. Gate width is at least 8 meters.

The course must be free of large stones, tree stumps, and similar debris. Courses through wooded terrain must be at least 30 meters wide.

Competitors are required to take part in official training on the course, which takes place on three separate days before the event.

A downhill event may consist of one run or two runs. If the event has two runs, those runs take place on the same day.

SLALOM

Vertical drop for men's courses ranges from 140 meters to 220 meters; for women's courses, from 120 meters to 200 meters.

Gates alternate in color. Each gate must be between 4 meters and 6 meters wide. Men's courses have 55 to 75 gates, with exceptions allowing for as few as 52 and as many as 78. Women's courses have 45 to 65 gates, with exceptions allowing for as few as 42 and as many as 68. Successive gates must have at least .75 meter and no more than 15 meters between them.

At major competitions the course has a gradient of 20 to 27 new degrees. It may reach 30 new degrees in brief portions of the course. The course includes a series of turns that the competitors should be able to complete rapidly. The course must be at least 40 meters wide if two runs are set on the same slope. It must contain both horizontal (open) and vertical (closed) gates, as well as one to three vertical combinations consisting of three or four gates and at least three hairpin combinations.

The slalom start takes place at irregular intervals; on the starter's command to go, the competitor must begin within 10 seconds. Competitors take two runs on two different courses; usually both runs are taken on the same day.

GIANT SLALOM

The vertical drop for men's courses is 250 to 450 meters; for women's courses, 250 to 400 meters.

A giant slalom gate consists of four slalom poles and two flags. Gates are alternately red and blue and are between 4 meters and 8 meters wide. Successive gates must be no greater than 10 meters apart. The course must be at least 30 meters wide and should present a variety of turns.

A giant slalom competition consists of two runs. The runs may be held on the same course, but the gates must be changed for the second run. Both runs are usually held on the same day.

SUPER-G

The vertical drop for men's courses is 500 to 650 meters; for women's courses, 350 to 600 meters.

A gate consists of four slalom poles and two flags; gates are alternately red and blue. They must be between 6 meters and 8 meters wide from inner pole to inner pole for horizontal (open) gates, and between 8 meters and 12 meters wide for vertical (closed) gates.

Men's courses have a minimum of 35 gates; women's courses have at least 30. The distance between the turning poles of two successive gates must be at least 25 meters. A super-G course is undulating and hilly with a minimum width of 30 meters. The competition consists of one run for each competitor.

PARALLEL EVENTS

A parallel event is a competition where two or more competitors race simultaneously side by side down two or more courses that are as identical as possible. Competitions typically consist of 32 competitors, paired off as follows: 1st and 32nd; 2nd and 31st; and so on. (These placings are based on previous races.)

Each match consists of two runs; the two competitors change courses on the second run. The competitor with the lowest total time on the two runs advances; the other is eliminated. The second round also consists of two runs. Eight skiers from this round advance to the quarterfinals; four advance to the semifinals; and two advance to the final.

The vertical drop is between 80 and 100 meters. Each course has between 20 and 30 gates; the run-time of each race should be between 20 and 25 seconds. The first gate is between 8 and 10 meters from the start.

The difference between the competitors' time—not each competitor's total time—is recorded at the finish. Difference is recorded in thousandths of a second.

PARTICIPANTS

Competitors must wear ski brakes to compete in official trainings and competitions. Competitors in downhill and super-G events must wear crash helmets.

Competition is classified according to age; see table 1.1.

Table 1.1: Age-Group Competition	
Classification	Age
Children I	11 to 12
Children II	13 to 14
Juniors	15 to 18
Licensed competitors	15 and older
Masters A (men)	30 to 54
Masters B (men)	55 and older
Masters C (women)	30 and older

EQUIPMENT

Poles are either *rigid* or *flex-poles*. Rigid poles have a diameter of 20 millimeters to 32 millimeters and have no joints. They are made of a non-splintering material, such as plastic, and when set, they must project at least 1.8 meters out of the snow. Flex-poles have a spring-loaded hinge; they must be used for all competitions except downhills.

Slalom poles are red or blue and carry a flag that matches in color. In giant slalom and Super-G competitions, two slalom poles, with a banner between them, comprise one half of the gate; a like pair of slalom poles comprises the other half of the gate. A turning pole is that pole in paired poles that is closest to the skier's line of travel in the gate. Turning poles for slalom, giant slalom, and Super-G must be flex-poles.

OFFICIALS

The chief of race controls the event and the officials. The chief of course is responsible for course preparation. The chief of timing and calculations coordinates the start and finish officials. The chief gate judge supervises the gate judges. The chief steward is in charge of safety precautions and keeping spectators off the course. A jury oversees adherence to race rules.

MODIFICATIONS

Following are some major modifications for children.

Only children 13 and 14 years old may take part in a downhill competition. The maximum vertical drop is 400 meters for both boys and girls. Courses may have no jumps, sharp curves, or other special difficulties. For maximum vertical drops and number of gates, see table 1.2.

Table 1.2: Children's Drops and Gates			
Classification	Event	Vertical drop (maximum m)	Number of of gates
Children I	Slalom	140	32 to 45
Children II	Slalom	180	38 to 60
Children I	Giant slalom*	300	15% of vertical drop, ± 3 gates
Children II	Giant slalom*	350	15% of vertical drop, ± 3 gates
Children I	Super-G	250 to 350	25 to 10% of vertical drop
Children II	Super-G	280 to 400	28 to 10% of vertical drop

*One run only

Adapted from International Ski Federation 1995.

ORGANIZATIONS

American Ski Association
P.O. Box 480067
910 15th St., Ste. 500
Denver, CO 80202
303-629-7669

U.S. Skiing
P.O. Box 100
Park City, UT 84060
801-649-9090

Angling

Courtesy of BASS Anglers Sportsman Society

During the last 10 years, bass fishing has enjoyed phenomenal growth. According to Department of Interior studies, more than 30 million Americans go bass fishing; 650,000 of those are members of the Bass Anglers Sportsman Society (BASS). The society held its first event in 1967; today it has more than 2,800 local chapters.

BASS conducts various tournaments throughout the year, ranging from grassroots events to its most prestigious event, the BASS Masters Classic. The Classic is comprised of 35 fishermen who advance from qualifying series, plus five regional federation representatives. The rules in this chapter were supplied by BASS.

PROCEDURES

Tournament waters are off limits to fishermen 21 days prior to the first day of the competition. Fishermen may receive no advice or assistance from others during the practice period immediately preceding the first day of the tournament.

Competitors may not use VHF marine-based radios, CB radios, or any other device to locate or catch fish. They also may not use grippers in landing bass; all bass must be caught live and in a conventional sporting manner. No dip nets or gaffs are permitted in the boat. All bedding bass must be hooked inside the mouth and verified by the partner before being unhooked. Snatching or snagging fish will lead to disqualification of that day's catch.

Contestants must leave from and return to the official checkpoint. The penalty for being late to the checkpoint is one pound per minute. If a competitor is 15 minutes or more late, he receives credit for no catch that day. Boat partners must remain in sight of each other, and of each other's catch, at all times in order for the catch to be scored.

Pounds and ounces are scored for the following bass: largemouth, smallmouth, spotted, redeye, and shoal. The limit is five of the above species and varies each day, unless the state limit is lower. Bass not measuring the official length result in a penalty of one pound deducted from the total score. Bass must be kept in a properly aerated livewell. Bass that are dead when checked result in a four-ounce penalty. Ties are resolved in a sudden-death fish-off.

WATERS

Tournament waters are established by the tournament director. Competitors may fish anywhere on the tournament waters except within 50 yards of another competitor's boat that was first anchored or secured with the trolling motor out of the water.

COMPETITORS

A competitor may participate through invitation only. Each competitor must be a member of BASS and must be at least 16 years old. Competitors must wear *life preservers* when the boat engine is operating. Failure to do so results in disqualification. Competitors also will be disqualified for the use of alcohol or of drugs that were not prescribed by a physician or purchased over the counter.

EQUIPMENT

Competitors may use only one *casting, spincasting,* or *spinning rod* and *reel* at any one time. The rod may be a maximum of 8 feet long. Other rigs may be in the boat, ready for use. Competitors may use only artificial lures; no live bait or prepared bait is allowed, with the exception of pork strips, pork rinds, and so on.

A boat may be 15 feet or more in length. Its horsepower may not exceed 150. When the engine is operating, a driver must be in the driver's seat. The boat must have a livewell space to maintain the limit of catch by both fishermen using the boat.

OFFICIALS

The *tournament director* is in charge of the competition. Tournament officials are used at the official checkpoint and to weigh the fish.

ORGANIZATIONS

Bass Anglers Sportsman Society
P.O. Box 17900
Montgomery, AL 36141
334-272-9530

Archery

© Mary Langenfeld

Archery's roots stretch back to the days when bows and arrows were used to kill game and enemies. The sport of archery grew from the king-mandated practice in England of those who fought for their country; tournaments began to spring up in 17th-century England. In the United States, the first archery club was formed in Philadelphia in 1826.

The object in archery is to score the highest number of points by shooting arrows into a target that is marked with rings worth various points. The rules for this chapter come from the International Archery Federation and from the National Archery Association of the United States, which is the sport's national governing body.

PROCEDURES

Archery can be contested individually or in teams of three. A competition consists of an agreed-upon number of rounds, or *ends*. An end is a series of either three or six shots. The shots are taken at a target with five concentric color zones. An arrow landing in the target can score anywhere from 1 to 10 points.

For an end consisting of three arrows, an archer has two minutes to complete shooting. For an end of six, a maximum of four minutes are allowed. In case of equipment adjustment, such as changing a bow string, additional time may be granted. Archers shoot in rotation, and can shoot from either the longest to the shortest target, or vice versa.

Scores are entered for each arrow, with the score being called out by the archer and checked by competitors. The number of arrows shot and the distance depend on the archer's classification; see table 3.1.

Shooting

Archers shoot from a standing position, without support, with their feet either straddling the shooting line (one foot over, one foot behind the line), or both feet on the line. When a signal is given to begin the time limit, archers can raise their bows and shoot. If archers shoot either before the signal to start or after the signal to stop, they forfeit their highest scoring arrow for that particular end. (In team competition, the highest scoring arrow for any member of the team—regardless of who committed the foul—is forfeited.)

A spent arrow is not counted as a shot if the competitor can touch it with her bow without moving her feet from shooting position, or if the target face or buttress blows over. The judges may compensate for lost time in such cases.

Shooters can receive no advice or instruction while they are on the shooting line, except to correct faulty equipment. (However, in the Olympic team event, the three teammates and the coach may talk to each other while one is on the shooting line.) Shooting takes place in one direction only.

Scoring

Scores are checked by competitors, and, if assigned, by scorers. The score is determined by where the shaft lands in the target (see figure 3.1). No arrows are touched until the archer completes the end. At 90 meters, 70 meters, and 60 meters, scoring takes place after every end of six arrows. At 50 meters and 30 meters, scoring occurs after every end of three arrows.

If the shaft of the arrow is touching two colors, or a dividing line between two scoring zones, the higher value is awarded. Unless all arrow holes are marked when scored, subsequent arrows bouncing off or passing through the target will not be scored. However, if an arrow does pass through the target or bounce off another arrow, and its mark can be identified, it scores however many points it would have, had it stuck in the target.

An arrow that lands in another arrow receives the same points as the first arrow. An arrow that deflects off another arrow and lands in the target receives the points awarded for that portion of

Table 3.1: Arrows and Distance			
Classification	Number of arrows	Distance (m)	Target face (cm)
Men (18 and older) and Intermediate boys (15-18)	36 ea 36 ea	90, 70 50, 30	122 80
Women (18 and older) and Intermediate girls (15-18)	36 ea 36 ea	70, 60 50, 30	122 80
Junior metric round (boys and girls under 15)	36 ea 36 ea	60, 50 40, 30	122 80
Cadet metric round (boys and girls under 12)	36 ea 36 ea	45, 35 25, 15	122 80

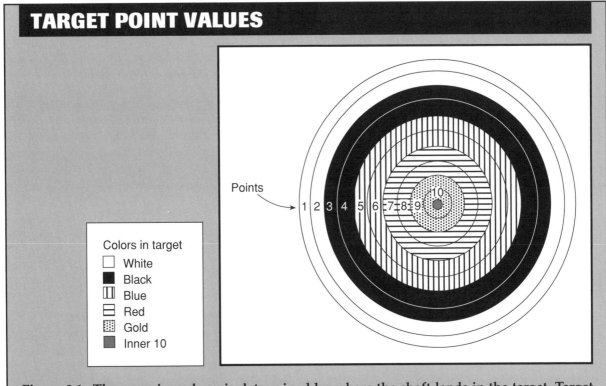

TARGET POINT VALUES

Points
1 2 3 4 5 6 7 8 9 10

Colors in target
☐ White
■ Black
▥ Blue
⊟ Red
▨ Gold
▨ Inner 10

Figure 3.1. The score in archery is determined by where the shaft lands in the target. Target point values are shown on the above target.
Adapted from FITA Fédération Internationale De Tir à L'Arc 1994.

the target face. An arrow that rebounds off another arrow scores the point value of the arrow it struck as long as the damaged arrow can be identified. An arrow hitting another target does not score any points.

TERMS

An **end** is a series of either three or six arrows for each archer.

A **gold** is an arrow that lands in the center of the target. The outer portion of the gold is worth 9 points; the inner portion, 10.

A **round** is a series of ends—the total number of arrows that each archer shoots in the competition.

RANGE

The shooting range is divided into lanes and is laid out so that shooting is done from south to north. Each lane has lines at right angles be-

tween the shooting line and the target; a lane can contain up to three targets. Males and females are separated by a clear lane of at least five meters.

A waiting line is set at least five meters behind the shooting line. No more than four competitors may shoot at one target. Each buttress is numbered and set at an angle of about 15 degrees from vertical. The distance is measured from the ground directly below the gold of each target to the shooting line. The center of the gold is about 130 centimeters above ground.

EQUIPMENT

The *target* is made of straw mat or other material and has a target face of canvas, paper, or cloth. The *target face* has five concentric, colored zones arranged from the center outward as follows: gold, red, light blue, black, and white. Each color is divided by a thin line into two zones of equal width, resulting in 10 zones of equal width. Diameters for 122- and 80-centimeter target faces are shown in table 3.2.

Table 3.2: Target Faces		
Target zone	122 cm face (cm)	80 cm face (cm)
Inner 10	6.1	4
10	12.2	8
9	24.4	16
8	36.6	24
7	48.8	32
6	61.0	40
5	73.2	48
4	85.4	56
3	97.6	64
2	109.8	72
1	122.0	80

Adapted from FITA Fédération Internationale De Tir à L'Arc 1994.

The target face is supported on a *buttress,* which is at least two centimeters larger in diameter than the target face itself. Any portion of the buttress that can damage an arrow is covered. A *bow* consists of a handle (grip), riser, and two flexible limbs ending in a tip with a string nock. A single bowstring is used; an adjustable arrowrest is also allowed. No crossbows are allowed. A bowsight or bowmark is permitted, but only one or the other may be used at one time. A bowsight may not incorporate any magnifying lens or electronic devices to aid in sighting.

Arrows of any type may be used as long as they do not cause undue damage to the target faces or buttresses. An arrow consists of a shaft with a head, a nock, fletching, and, if desired, cresting.

Finger protectors, such as tips, gloves, or tape, are permitted, but they cannot include any device that aids in holding, drawing, or releasing the string. Field glasses may be used to spot the arrows.

OFFICIALS

Officials include a competition director, director of shooting, and judges.

ORGANIZATIONS

American Archery Council
604 Forest Avenue
Park Rapids, MN 56470
218-732-3879

National Archery Association of the United States
1 Olympic Plaza
Colorado Springs, CO 80909-5778
719-578-4576

National Field Archery Association
31407 Outer I-10
Redlands, CA 92373
909-794-2133

4

Australian Football

© Adelaide Advertiser/Ray Titus

Australian football was originally developed as a game unique to Australia, incorporating elements of rugby with some aspects of Gaelic (Irish) football. It quickly evolved into a fast, rough, and free-flowing sport. The first official match was played in 1858 in Melbourne; the game was initially devised as an off-season training regimen for Australian cricketers. Today, Australian football is played by more than 500,000 players at the senior, junior, amateur, and school levels. It was a demonstration sport at the Melbourne Olympic Games in 1956.

Two teams of 18 players each (plus 3 interchange players each) attempt to score *goals* (six points) or *behinds* (one point). The most points wins. If a game is tied at the end of regulation, it is a draw; there is no overtime. The information for this chapter came from the Australian Football League and from *Australian Football: Steps to Success*.

PROCEDURES

Play begins with the field umpire bouncing the ball in the center circle (see figure 4.1 on page 17) so that it is up for grabs. Until the ball has bounced, no player may enter the center circle, and only four players from each team are allowed in the center square.

Except for when a behind is scored and when a ball goes out of bounds, possession of the ball is continually contested. The ball is advanced by kicking it, punching it, and running with it; throwing it is not allowed. A runner must dribble the ball (bounce it or touch it to the ground) every 15 meters. Catching a kicked ball in the air that has traveled at least 10 meters allows a player to take a free kick, without the risk of being tackled.

A game lasts four quarters, each consisting of 20 minutes of actual playing time; there are no timeouts. Players are freely interchangeable at any time; each team has three substitutes. A *runner* conveys messages from the coach to the players in the game. This message bearer must stay away from the ball but can stay on the field as long as necessary.

Teams change ends of the field at the end of each quarter; the maximum break between the first and second quarter is 3 minutes. Halftime lasts up to 20 minutes, and the maximum break between the third and fourth quarters is 5 minutes.

TERMS

The **backmen** are the six defenders across the full back and half back lines on a team's defensive half of the field.

Ball up is the term that describes when the umpire bounces or throws up the ball to restart the game after a stalemated scrimmage.

A **behind,** worth one point, is scored when the ball passes over the goal line after being touched or kicked by a defender, when it hits a goal post, or when it passes over the behind line without touching the behind post. A behind is sometimes called a *minor score*.

The **behind line** is the line drawn between a goal post and behind post.

The **behind posts** are the two smaller posts 6.4 meters outside the goal posts.

The **boundary line** marks the boundary of the playing field. The ball must go completely over the line to be out of bounds.

A **bump** occurs when a player uses his hip and shoulder to knock an opponent out of position. A bump is legal if it occurs within 5 meters of the ball and is not in the back or above the shoulders.

A **center bounce,** made by the field umpire, occurs in the center circle at the beginning of each quarter and after each goal.

The **center circle** is 3 meters in diameter; it is where the umpire bounces the ball. No player can be in the center circle until the umpire has bounced the ball (or thrown it up, if conditions are too wet to bounce it).

The **center square** is a 45-meter square in the center of the field. Only four players from each team can be in the center square for a center bounce.

When a player **drops the ball,** a free kick is given to the tackler.

A **drop punt** is the most common kick used in Australian football. It travels end over end backwards.

Followers are a team's ruckman, ruck rover, and rover.

A **footpass** occurs when a player passes to a teammate by kicking.

A **free kick** is awarded for a variety of offenses (see "Free Kicks").

A **goal,** worth six points, is scored when the ball is kicked over the goal line without the ball touching any player or a goal post.

The **goal line** is the line drawn between the goal posts.

The **goal mouth** is the area directly between the goal posts in front of the goal.

The two **goal posts** are 6.4 meters apart. A ball kicked between them scores six points.

The **goal square** is the rectangle measuring 6.4 meters by 9 meters in front of the goal posts from which the ball is kicked off after a behind is scored.

Handball is the term that describes the method of striking the ball with a clenched fist while holding it stationary with the other hand. This is also known as a handpass.

When a player **holds the ball** after being tackled, without disposing of it legally in a reasonable amount of time, a free kick is awarded against him.

Interchange players are a team's substitutes. In senior football a team has three.

A **mark** occurs when a player catches a kicked ball in the air, and the ball has traveled at least 10 meters and not been touched by another player.

The **oval** is the playing field, usually between 110 meters and 155 meters wide and 135 meters to 185 meters long.

The **pockets** are the areas on the field close to the behind posts.

A **rocket handball** is a handball that spins end over end backwards in flight.

A **runner** is a person who carries messages from the coach to the players during the game.

Shepherding occurs when a player uses his body to block an opponent from the ball or from a teammate in possession of the ball. Shepherding farther than 5 meters from the ball is illegal.

A player **stands the mark** where his opponent has been given a free kick or marks (catches) the ball to ensure that the opponent does not play on and has to kick over the mark.

A player can **tackle** a player with the ball by grabbing him above the knees and below the shoulders.

A **throw-in** occurs when the ball has gone out of bounds. The umpire throws the ball in over his head toward the center of the ground.

A **torpedo punt,** or *screw punt*, is a kick that spirals the ball through the air.

A **tumble pass** is a handball that tumbles end over end forwards.

A **turnover** occurs when a team loses possession of the ball to the opposition.

BALL POSSESSION

A player may hold the ball for an unlimited time if he is not held by an opponent. If a player with the ball is held by an opponent, he must immediately either kick the ball or handball the ball. The hand holding the ball must not move excessively; the motion is that of a quick punch.

A player lying on the ball is considered to be in possession of it.

A player running with the ball must bounce the ball or touch it to the ground every 15 meters. When a player catches a kick that has traveled at least 10 meters in the air without being touched by another player, he has the choice of playing on immediately or kicking the ball from where he received it.

Within 5 meters of the ball, a player may push an opponent in the chest or side or otherwise block the player's path to the ball (when he himself does not possess the ball). This technique is called "shepherding."

SCORING

A ball kicked between the two larger goal posts without being touched is a goal worth six points if it does not touch a post or a player. A *behind*, worth one point, is scored when

- a ball passes between a goal post and a behind post;
- a ball hits a goal post, no matter whether it passes between the two larger posts or rebounds back onto the field;
- a ball is carried over the scoring line between the goal posts; and when
- a ball is kicked or forced over the scoring line between the goal post and the behind post.

To score, the ball must completely cross the goal line.

RESTARTING PLAY

After a goal is scored, the field umpire restarts play by bouncing the ball in the center circle, just as he did at the start of the game. Play is also restarted in these situations:

A team scores a behind. A player of the defending team kicks off from the *kick-off square* in front of the goal.

The ball goes out of bounds. If the ball bounces out, the umpire throws the ball over his head toward the center of the ground. If the ball is kicked out of bounds on the full (without first bouncing the ball in the field of play), the opposing team receives a free kick from where the ball went out.

No player in a pack can gain clear possession. The umpire bounces the ball where a scrimmage has occurred and play has stopped.

BALL OUT OF PLAY

The ball is out of play and the clock is stopped in these situations:

- *A team scores a goal.* The clock starts when the ball is bounced to restart play.
- *A team scores a behind.* The clock starts when the ball is kicked in.
- *The ball goes out of bounds.* The clock starts when the umpire throws the ball back into play, or when the team receiving a free kick returns it into play. Note: If any portion of the ball is on or over the boundary line in fair territory, it is still in play. A player can be out of bounds and in possession of the ball, but if the ball is not out of bounds, play is not stopped.

FREE KICKS

An umpire may award a free kick against a player either with or without the ball. A player takes the kick (or handpasses) where the infringement occurred, unless a player is fouled after he has disposed of the ball. Then the kick is taken where the ball landed. Infringements against a player with the ball may be called for

- not disposing of the ball within a reasonable time when held (tackled) by an opponent,
- not disposing of the ball with a kick or a handball,
- kicking the ball out of bounds without it bouncing or being touched by another player,
- deliberately forcing or carrying the ball over the boundary line, or
- running farther than 15 meters without bouncing or touching the ball to the ground.

A free kick is also awarded when any player

- grabs or tackles an opponent above the shoulders or below the knees when the opponent has the ball;
- pushes an opponent in the back, charges an opponent, or trips or attempts to trip an opponent;
- bumps or punches an opponent trying to catch a kick in the air;
- shepherds an opponent farther than 5 meters from the ball; or
- enters the center square before the ball is bounced to restart play.

A 50-meter penalty is called against a player following a free kick if the player refuses to stand on the point indicated by the umpire, deliberately wastes time in returning the ball to the player who is to kick, holds the player who is to take the kick, or runs over the mark before or as the ball is kicked. If a ball is kicked back into play by the defending team after the attacking team scores a behind and the ball goes out of bounds without any player touching it, the attacking team receives a free kick. When a player has been infringed upon, the umpire can choose not to award a free kick if the player or a teammate in possession of the ball has an advantageous position. The umpire can call "Play on" immediately, and play continues. If the player infringed upon is injured, a teammate may take the free kick. This call is at the umpire's discretion.

FIELD

The field is oval-shaped, usually between 110 and 135 meters wide and 135 to 185 meters long (see figure 4.1). *Boundaries* are marked with white

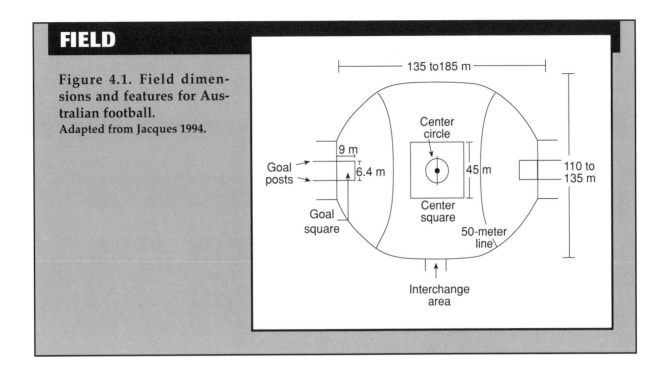

FIELD

Figure 4.1. Field dimensions and features for Australian football.
Adapted from Jacques 1994.

lines. The *center square* is at midfield, measuring 45 meters square. The *center circle* is in the middle of this square; it measures 3 meters in diameter and is bisected by a lateral line extending 2 meters on either side of the diameter.

The *goal square* is 9 meters long and 6.4 meters wide. It is directly in front of the *goal posts,* which are set 6.4 meters apart on the boundary line and are at least 6 meters high. Two *behind posts,* each at least 3 meters high, are set 6.4 meters from the goal posts. The posts are padded up to 2 meters.

Many fields have two *50-meter lines* drawn in semicircles 50 meters from the center of the goal line, to give the umpire a point of reference for marking off 50-meter penalties, and to give spectators a means of assessing the distance of kicks for goal.

PLAYERS

There are five general lines of play, with three players in each line. The remaining three players are the *followers,* who roam the whole ground, following the ball. These players are the *ruck, rover,* and *ruck-rover.*

The lines of play are shown in figure 4.2. Note, however, that players are free to move anywhere on the ground.

EQUIPMENT

The *ball* is made of leather—tan or reddish brown for day games, yellow for night games. Its length is 27 to 28 centimeters; diameter, 16.7 to 17.3 centimeters; and circumference, 72 to 73.5 centimeters by 54.5 to 55.5 centimeters. It weighs between 446.6 and 496.2 grams.

Uniforms consist of numbered guernseys (jumpers) with or without sleeves, socks, and *shoes* with "sprigs," or cleats. No padding is worn, but *mouthguards* and soft, protective *headgear* are allowed.

OFFICIALS

Three *field umpires* control the game. Each controls about a third of the ground. Two *boundary umpires* judge when the ball is out of the playing area. Two *goal umpires,* one at each end of the oval, judge the scoring of goals and behinds.

MODIFICATIONS

The following modifications are made by many junior leagues to encourage younger players' development:

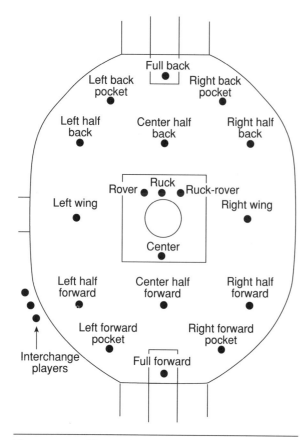

Figure 4.2.   Lines of play for Australian football.
Adapted from Jacques 1994.

- The number of interchange players is unlimited.
- Players may bounce a ball only once before disposing of it.

- Players may not soccer the ball off the ground.
- After scrimmages the contest is restarted by throwing a ball up between two players of about equal size.
- Tackling is not permitted in younger groups.
- The players who may score are limited, and scoring must take place within a certain zone.

ORGANIZATIONS

Australian Football League
c/o Great Southern Stand
Melbourne Cricket Ground
Brunton Avenue
Jolimont VIC 3002
03 9654 1244

South Australian National Football League
Football Park
Turner Drive
West Lakes SA 5021
08 8268 2008

Western Australian Football League
P.O. Box 275
Subiaco WA 6008
09 381 5599

5

Badminton

© Claus Andersen

A form of badminton, with players kicking a small feathered shuttlecock, was first played in 5th century B.C. in China. The game derives its name from its introduction in England in 1873 at a country estate called Badminton. By this time players were using rackets, and the shuttlecock was put into play after each point by servants (this is where the term "to serve" comes from). Badminton was introduced in America in the 1870s, grew in popularity in the 1920s and '30s, and became a full-medal Olympic sport in 1992.

Badminton is played by either two or four players. The object is to score points by hitting a shuttlecock over the net and into the opponent's court so that the opponent cannot return it over the net and in bounds. The rules for this chapter were supplied by the United States Badminton Association, the national governing body for the sport.

PROCEDURES

Games are played to either 11 or 15 points, with the highest score winning. Women's singles are played to 11 points; all other games are played to 15 points. A match is the best two of three games. Play is continuous from the first serve to the end of the match, except for a five-minute break between games two and three. Before a match, the winner of a coin or shuttle toss, or spin of the racket, chooses between serving or receiving first, or on which end he will begin.

Serving

The server faces the net and stands inside the service court on his right. The receiver stands inside the service court on his or her right side (diagonal from the server). Partners may stand anywhere as long as the receiver's view of the serve is not blocked. In doubles, only the receiver can return the serve. If the serve hits, or is hit by, the receiver's partner, the serving team scores a point. Once a serve is returned in doubles, either player may return a hit; partners do not have to take turns in hitting the shuttle.

When the server's score is even (0, 2, 4, and so on), the server stands on the right side. When the server's score is odd (1, 3, 5, and so on), he or she stands on the left side. In doubles, when the serving team's score is even, the players are in their starting positions; when their score is odd, they switch positions.

The receiver may not move until the server hits the shuttle. A server commits a *fault* and loses his serve if he misses the shuttle, if the shuttle becomes stuck in the net on the serve, or if he serves incorrectly. The server must

- keep part of both feet stationary on the court while serving (as must the receiver, while receiving serve);
- be totally within the boundaries of the service court, touching no lines;
- hit the base of the shuttle first;
- make initial contact with the shuttle below the server's waist;
- have all of the racket's head clearly below the hand that holds the shuttle at the moment of contact; and

- serve in a continuous motion (i.e., no faking).

Only the serving side can score a point. In singles play, if the server scores, she moves to the other service court side and serves again. If the server does not score, her opponent gets to serve.

In doubles, if the serving team scores, the server switches service court side and serves again. If the serving team loses the rally, the partner serves from the other side. If the serving team loses that rally, the opponents gain the serve. If they win the rally, the server switches service court sides and continues to serve.

At the beginning of a game in doubles play, the team that serves first gets only one turn at serving. From then on each team serves as previously stated. In doubles, each time a side gains the serve, the first serve is made from the right service court.

A service court error is made by a player who serves out of turn, who serves from the wrong side of the court, or by a receiver who is standing on the wrong side of the court when the serve is delivered. If a server or receiver is on the wrong side and a rally is played, the play stands if the person who made the mistake loses the rally, in which case the players will not correct their positioning. If the player who made the mistake wins the rally and the error is discovered before the next serve, the play is a *let* (it doesn't count) and the positioning is corrected. It is not a fault if the serve hits the net, as long as it crosses the net and lands within the receiver's service court.

Shuttle in Play

The shuttle is put into play by the server and remains in play until it

- hits the floor,
- hits the ceiling or outside the court,
- hits a player or a player's clothing,
- hits the net or post and drops on the hitter's side, or
- gets stuck in the net or suspended on top of the net.

The shuttle is not in play when a fault or let occurs.

Scoring

If the score is 9-9 or 10-10 in women's singles, or 13-13 or 14-14 in any other play, the side that reaches that score first can choose to *set* or *not set* the game. If the game is set, the score goes to 0-0 and the side who scores the following set number of points shown in table 5.1 wins.

Table 5.1: Badminton Scoring				
Score	9-9	10-10	13-13	14-14
Set points	3	2	5	3

A side in a 9-9 or 13-13 game may choose not to set, but if the other side reaches 10 first in a 10-10 game, or 14 first in a 14-14 game, that other side may choose to set. The side that wins the game serves first in the next game. Either player on the serving team can serve first in a new game, and either player on the receiving team can receive first.

Changing Ends

Players change ends at the end of each game and in the middle of the third game. This occurs when the leading scorer reaches 6 points in an 11-point game, or 8 points in a 15-point game. If players forget to change ends, they will do so as soon as the mistake is discovered, but all points will remain.

Faults and Lets

Service faults were covered in "Serving." Faults also occur in play, when the shuttle

- hits outside the court;
- passes through or under the net;
- does not pass the net;
- touches the roof, ceiling, or any side walls;
- touches a player or a player's clothing;
- touches any person or object out of bounds;
- is caught, held, and slung on the racket;
- is hit twice in a row by the same player on the same play; and when

- both partners hit the shuttle before it is returned to the other side.

A player also commits a fault when the shuttle is in play and he

- hits a shuttle when it is on the opponent's side of the net;
- touches the net or posts with his racket, clothing, or any part of his body;
- has his racket or any part of his body over or under the net (exception: a racket can cross the net, without touching it, on a follow-through, so long as the shuttle contact was on the hitter's side of the net); or when he
- obstructs an opponent's stroke (e.g., obstructing a follow-through as described in the above situation).

A *let* is a situation that calls for a halt in play. Lets occur when

- a shuttle remains suspended on top of the net, or passes the net and then becomes caught on the other side of the net (except on a serve; this is a fault on a serve);
- the server and receiver commit faults at the same time;
- the server serves before the receiver is ready; and when
- the shuttle comes apart.

When a let is called, no score counts for that play, and the server who began the play serves again.

TERMS

A **fault** occurs in a number of situations (see "Faults and Lets"). A fault committed by the serving side gives the serve to the opponents; a fault by the receiving side gives a point to the serving side.

A **let** occurs when a point must be replayed. See "Faults and Lets" for such situations.

The **serve** is the hit that begins each play.

The **shuttlecock**, also called the shuttle or the birdie, is the feathered object the players hit with their rackets.

COURT

The court is 17 by 44 feet for singles matches and 20 by 44 feet for doubles (see figure 5.1). The *short service line* is 6.5 feet from the net. The *long service line* for doubles is 12.75 feet behind the short service line. The long service line for singles is 2.4 feet behind the long service line for doubles. This is also the back boundary line. The *singles sideline* is 1.4 feet inside the sideline for doubles play. The cord net stretches across the center of the court, 5 feet high at center court and 5.08 feet high at the posts. The net is 2.5 feet in depth.

PLAYERS

A singles match consists of one player on each side; a doubles match is contested by two teams of two players each. Players may not have play

suspended to catch their breath or recover from an injury, nor may they receive coaching or instruction from anyone else during a game (except during the five-minute break between games two and three).

EQUIPMENT

The *shuttlecock* contains either 16 feathers or is made of a synthetic mesh. It has a cork base covered by a thin layer of leather; the base is 1 to 1.13 inches in diameter. If feathers are used, they can be from 2.5 to 2.75 inches long (the same length must be used in any one shuttle). The shuttle weighs from .17 to .19 ounce.

The racket frame may not be longer than 27.2 inches or wider than 9.2 inches. The stringed portion may not be over 11.2 inches long and 8.8 inches wide.

COURT

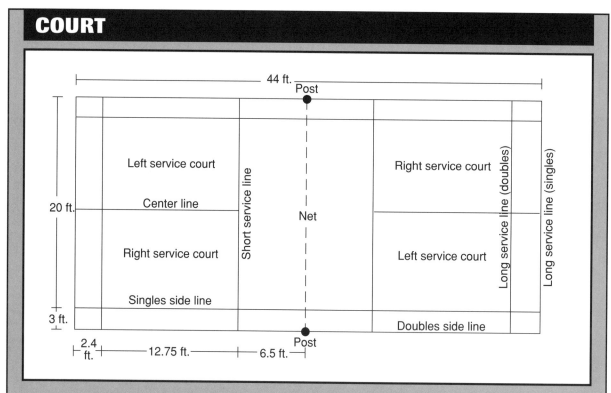

Figure 5.1. A badminton court with its dimensions and features.
Adapted from White 1990.

OFFICIALS

An *umpire* is in charge of the match. Other officials may include a *service judge* to call service faults and a *line judge* to indicate whether a shuttle is in or out of bounds.

ORGANIZATION

United States Badminton Association
One Olympic Plaza
Colorado Springs, CO 80909
719-578-4808

Baseball

© Photophile/Matt Lindasay

In 1886, a Baltimore Orioles pitcher named Matt Kilroy struck out an all-time record of 513 batters. Unbelievable? Almost . . . until you realize that pitchers that year could take a running start before throwing home. And home plate was only 50 feet from the pitcher's rubber, not the 60.5 feet it is today.

The following year, the rulesmakers allowed batters four strikes instead of three and permitted pitchers only one step toward home before releasing the ball. So what happened? For one, Kilroy struck out nearly 300 *fewer* batters in 1887.

Baseball's rulesmakers have been busy through the years. The sport has undergone many changes in field dimensions, equipment, and rules. The pitcher's mound has been raised, then lowered, and then raised again. Glove sizes and construction have evolved to make fielding both a more sure and less painful experience. The designated hitter rule has changed the flavor and strategy of the game.

Changes in the game have not been restricted to the professional level. Leagues for players of all ages and abilities have modified rules for the varying skills and safety of their players. We present rules modifications at the end of this chapter. Major League Baseball rules are the focus of this chapter.

PROCEDURES

A game is made up of the components shown in table 6.1.

Table 6.1: Components in a Baseball Game			
Teams	Players per team	Innings	Outs per inning
2	9	9	3

Before the game, managers of both teams present their starting lineup cards to the home plate umpire. These cards contain the batting orders of their players. The home team takes the field and warms up. The visiting team bats first in the top half of the *inning;* the home team bats in the bottom half of the inning.

The pitcher attempts to get the batter out, preventing him from reaching base; the batter's object is to reach base and eventually score. A runner advances at his own risk around the bases. A team scores a run when a player safely touches first, second, third, and home before three outs are made.

Winning Ways

The team that scores the most runs at the end of a regulation game wins. That win may be recorded in a variety of ways:

- *Nine-inning win for the visitors.* If the visitors are ahead after nine complete innings, the game is over.
- *Nine-inning win for the home team.* If the home team is ahead after the visitors bat in the top half of the ninth, the game is over. Or if the home team scores the winning run in the bottom of the ninth, the game is over when the winning play is completed (e.g., on a game-winning base hit, the game is over when the runner scores and when the batter touches first base safely).
- *Extra-inning victory.* If the game is tied at the end of nine innings, it goes into *extra innings* and is played until one team has scored more than the other at the end of a complete inning, or until the home team scores the winning run.

- *Weather-shortened game.* A game stopped for rain or other reasons is considered complete if after five innings one team has more runs than the other team. The game is considered complete if after four and a half innings the home team has scored more than the visitors.
- *Forfeit.* A forfeit may be called by the umpire-in-chief for many reasons, including failure to appear for the beginning of a game on time, failure to remove an expelled player from a game, and failure to provide sufficient police protection to preserve order. A forfeit is recorded as a 9-0 win.

TERMS

An **assist** is credited to a fielder when his throw leads to the **putout** of a runner. Two or more fielders can receive an assist on the same play.

A **balk** is an illegal move (usually toward home plate) by the pitcher with a runner or runners on base. All runners automatically advance one base when a balk is called.

The **ball** is cork or rubber wrapped in yarn and covered by cowhide or horsehide. It weighs 5 ounces to 5.25 ounces and is 9 inches to 9.25 inches in circumference. *Also:* A pitch that the batter doesn't swing at and that is outside of the **strike zone** is called a ball.

A batter is credited with a **base hit** when he reaches base safely on a hit, without aid of an **error.**

A batter receives a **base on balls** (is awarded first base) when he takes four balls during a time at-bat. This is also called a *walk.*

The **base line** extends three feet on either side of a direct line between bases. A runner is out when he runs outside the base line, except to avoid interfering with a fielder fielding a batted ball.

First, second, and third **base** are made of white canvas, 15 inches square, between 3 inches and 5 inches thick, and secured in the ground. Home plate is five-sided, 17 inches wide, 8.5 inches long on three sides, and 12 inches long on the sides that meet to form the point at the rear of the plate.

The **bat** is a smooth, round stick not more than 2.75 inches in diameter at its thickest, and no

Does the Run Count?

A runner slides but misses home plate. The catcher misses tagging the runner. The runner goes to the dugout, making no attempt to touch the plate. The catcher, holding the ball, touches the plate and appeals to the umpire for a decision. Is the runner out or safe?

A runner is out when, in running or sliding for home base, he fails to touch home base and makes no attempt to return to the base while a fielder holding the ball in his hand, touches home base and appeals to the umpire for the decision.

longer than 42 inches. The bat handle can be treated with a sticky substance to improve the batter's grip, but this substance may not extend beyond 18 inches from the bottom of the bat.

Batter's boxes are four feet by six feet on either side of home plate.

Batter's circles, or on-deck circles, are in foul territory between home plate and each team's bench.

The **battery** refers to the pitcher and the catcher.

Batters must wear **batting helmets** with at least one ear flap (facing the pitcher as the batter is in his stance).

A batter **bunts** the ball by letting the ball meet the bat to drop a soft ground ball on the infield. A bunt can be an attempt to beat out a base hit or a **sacrifice** to move a runner or runners up a base.

A **catch** means a fielder has secured the ball in his hand or glove. A fly ball is not caught if the fielder simultaneously falls or collides with the fence or another player and the ball is dislodged. A fly ball that is dropped may still be ruled a catch if the fielder had control of the ball long enough before he dropped it.

A **catcher's box**, 43 inches wide and eight feet long, is directly behind home plate.

Catcher's interference occurs when the catcher hinders the batter from hitting the ball.

Coaches' boxes are set near first and third base, in foul territory, for the offensive team.

A pitcher is credited with a **complete game** when he starts and finishes a regulation game.

A **cutoff** throw is one that is received by a fielder who is not the final target of the throw. For example, a right fielder may throw to the second baseman, who then relays the throw to the third baseman in an attempt to put out a runner.

A **designated hitter** takes the place of the pitcher in the batting order but does not play defense.

A **double play** is recorded by the defense when two outs are made on the same play.

A **double** is a hit in which the batter safely reaches second base.

An **earned run** is charged against a pitcher every time a run scores on a hit, **sacrifice, bunt, sacrifice fly, wild pitch, stolen base, putout, fielder's choice, base on balls,** batter **hit by pitch,** or **balk.** A run is unearned if that runner scores by benefit of an **error,** a **passed ball,** or defensive interference or **obstruction.** A **relief pitcher** who enters a game is not charged with any run, either earned or unearned, scored by any runners already on base.

An **error** is charged to a fielder who misplays a ball (e.g., a dropped fly ball or throw, or a fumbled ground ball) that prolongs an at-bat for a batter or the life of a base runner or that permits a runner to advance one or more bases. An error can be charged even if the fielder does not touch the ball (e.g., a ground ball that goes through the legs).

A game goes into **extra innings** when it is tied at the end of nine innings.

Fair territory and **foul territory** are marked by two foul lines. Each line extends from home plate. One line creates a third base line and left field line, stopping at the left field fence; the other creates a first base line and right field line, stopping at the right field fence. Anything on or in between the foul lines is considered fair territory. Foul poles rise above the fence in left field and right field. A ball striking a foul pole is a **home run.**

A **fielder's choice** occurs when an infielder fields a ground ball and elects to throw to another base, rather than to first base to put out the batter-runner.

A **fly ball** is a ball batted high in the air.

A **fly-out** is a fly ball caught before it touches ground or the fence.

A **force play** occurs when a runner is forced to advance to the next base because the batter becomes a runner. When a batter hits a ground ball with a runner on first, the runner is forced to run to second. If a fielder touches second base with the ball in his possession before the runner reaches second, the runner is "forced out" at second. If a runner is on second when a ground ball is hit, he is not forced to advance, because first base is unoccupied.

A **foul ball** is any ball hit into foul territory.

Foul territory is all territory outside the foul lines. A ball striking a foul line is a fair ball.

A **ground out** refers to a batter being thrown out at first base after hitting a ground ball.

A **ground rule double** is awarded a batter when his fair ball bounces into the stands, passes through or under the fence, or is caught in vines or shrubbery in the fence.

When a batter is **hit by a pitch** that is not in the **strike zone** and that he attempts to elude, he is awarded first base.

Fan Interference—Or Foul Ball?

The first baseman reaches near the stands to catch a foul fly ball. A fan reaches onto the playing field and jars the ball loose just as the first baseman is catching it. The ball falls to the ground. Is the batter out, or is the play ruled simply a foul ball?

If spectator interference clearly prevents a fielder from catching a fly ball, the umpire shall declare the batter out. However, no interference shall be allowed when a fielder reaches over a fence, railing, rope, or into a stand to catch a ball. He does so at his own risk. In this case, because the fan reached onto the playing field and interfered with the play, the batter is out.

A **home run** is recorded when a batter hits a fair ball over the fence, or circles the bases on an inside-the-park hit without being thrown out.

The **infield** refers to the portion of the field that contains the four bases. In terms of players, the infield is made up of the first, second, and third basemen, and the shortstop. The pitcher and the catcher are also positioned in the infield.

The **infield fly rule** prohibits an infielder from intentionally dropping a fair fly ball that can be caught with normal effort. This rule is in effect with first and second, or first, second, and third bases occupied before two are out. When an umpire calls an infield fly rule, the batter is automatically out and runners may advance at their own risk.

The **losing pitcher** is the pitcher charged with the runs that give the opposing team a lead that is not relinquished.

A **no-hitter** is credited to a pitcher who pitches a **complete game** and allows no hits.

A fielder can be called for **obstruction** if he impedes the progress of a runner if the fielder does not have the ball or is not fielding the ball.

An **out** can be recorded in a variety of ways, including **strikeout, force-out, tag-out,** and **fly-out.**

The **outfield** is that portion of fair territory between the infield and the fence. In terms of players, the outfield consists of the left fielder, the center fielder, and the right fielder.

A **passed ball** is charged to the catcher when he fails to control a catchable pitch and allows a runner or runners to advance.

A **perfect game** occurs when a pitcher pitches a **no-hitter** and allows no base runners at all (e.g., by walks, hit batters, or errors).

A **pinch hitter** is a player who bats for another player. The player replaced cannot return to the game.

A **pinch runner** is a player who runs for another player. The player replaced cannot return to the game.

The **pitcher's mound** is a circular mound of dirt 18 feet in diameter and 59 feet from its center to the back of home plate. The mound has a rectangular rubber plate, called the pitcher's rubber, set perpendicular to home plate. The pitcher's rubber is set in the ground, and its front edge is 60.5 feet from the back of home plate. The rubber is 6 inches by 24 inches and is set 10 inches higher than home plate.

A **putout** occurs when a batter-runner or baserunner is called out (e.g., force out, tag out, caught stealing, etc.).

A **relief pitcher** is any pitcher who enters a game after the **starting pitcher** has thrown at least one pitch.

A batter is credited with the appropriate number of **runs batted in** (RBIs) when his hit is responsible for one or more runners scoring. RBIs are not tallied for runs scored as a result of **errors,** or if a run scores as the batter grounds into a **double play.**

A **sacrifice bunt** is placed by a batter to advance a runner or runners. A successful sacrifice bunt does not count as a time at bat; an unsuccessful attempt does.

A **sacrifice fly** is credited to a batter whose caught fly ball results in a runner on third base **tagging up** and scoring. A sacrifice fly does not count as a time at bat. A run must score for a sacrifice fly to be recorded.

A pitcher may be credited with a **save** when he finishes a game his team wins and he is not the winning pitcher—if he meets one of these criteria:

- He enters the game with a lead of no more than three runs and pitches for at least one inning.
- He enters the game, regardless of the count, with the potential tying run either on base, or at bat, or on deck.
- He pitches effectively for at least three innings.

The **set position** is one of two positions from which a pitcher can deliver a pitch. In the set position, a pitcher *comes set*—or halts his motion just before pitching. This is also known as the *stretch position*.

A **shutout** occurs when a team is held scoreless. A pitcher must pitch a **complete game** to receive credit for a shutout.

A **single** is a one-base hit credited to the batter.

The **starting pitcher** is the pitcher who begins the game for his team.

A runner is credited with a **stolen base** when he advances one base without aid of a hit, **putout, error,** force-out, **fielder's choice, passed ball, wild pitch,** or **balk.**

The batter's **strike zone** is over home plate, between the top of the knees and the midpoint between the top of the shoulders and the top of the pants (see figure 6.1).

A **strike** is a pitch that the batter takes (doesn't swing at) in the strike zone; that the batter swings at and misses; or that the batter hits into foul territory.

A **strikeout** is recorded after a batter has three strikes. Exceptions to this are if the third strike is a foul ball that is not caught in the air, or a strike that the catcher does not catch. In the latter case, if first base is unoccupied, or if it is occupied with two out, the defensive team must put out the batter by either throwing the ball to first base before the batter reaches first, or by tagging him with the ball before he reaches first. Batters attempting to bunt on the third strike are out if the ball is picked up in foul territory. This play is considered a strikeout.

Figure 6.1.   A batter takes a swing at the ball. The strike zone for batters is between the top of their knees and their chest.

Substitutions can be made when play is dead. Once a player leaves the game he cannot return.

A **suspended game** is one that is halted, to be completed at a later date. The game is resumed at the exact point of suspension, with the same lineups intact.

A **tag out** is one way a fielder can record a putout. When a force play is not in order, such as with a runner on second, the runner must be tagged out (touched with the ball, which can be in a fielder's glove or bare hand) when the runner is not touching a base.

On a caught fly ball, a runner must **tag up** (be in contact with his base) after the catch before advancing.

A **three-foot line** to guide the runners, is parallel to the first base line, beginning halfway between home plate and first base and ending beyond first base.

A **triple play** occurs when the defense records three outs on the same play.

A batter is credited with a **triple** when he reaches third base on his hit.

The outfield has a dirt **warning track** that alerts outfielders that they are approaching the fence.

A **wild pitch** occurs when a pitch eludes the catcher, allowing one or more runners to advance one base. A wild pitch is judged to be the pitcher's fault, not the catcher's. A ball that bounces in the dirt and allows any base runners to advance is automatically a wild pitch.

The **windup position** is one of two positions from which a pitcher can deliver a pitch. The windup is normally used with no runners on base.

The **winning pitcher** is the **starting pitcher** if he pitches five or more innings, leaves the game with the lead, and the lead is never relinquished. If a pitcher leaves a game with the lead, but the game is later tied or the opponent takes the lead with runs not charged to that pitcher, that pitcher cannot be either the winner or loser. In most cases, if the winning pitcher is a **relief pitcher,** he is the pitcher of record when his team has taken a lead that it does not relinquish.

FIELD

Figure 6.2 shows player positions and dimensions of a major league field. Distance to outfield fences vary, but distances of 320 feet or more down the lines, and 400 feet or more to center field, are preferable. The figure also shows player positions.

EQUIPMENT

Balls, bats, bases, and batter's helmets were described under "Terms." The *catcher's glove*, or mitt, may not be more than 38 inches in circumference and not more than 15.5 inches from top to bottom. The *first baseman's glove* may be a maximum of 12 inches from top to bottom and 8 inches across the palm. All other fielders' gloves may measure up to 12 inches from top to bottom and 7.75 inches across the palm. In addition to gloves, catchers wear other protective gear: *helmet, face mask, chest* and *throat protectors*, and *shin guards*. Players may not wear pointed spikes on their shoes.

PITCHING

Following are specific pitching rules that have not been previously stated.

1. Once a pitcher begins his motion to home, he must throw home or be called for a balk (see figure 6.3).

2. With the bases empty, a pitcher has 20 seconds to pitch, or the umpire will automatically call a ball.

3. A pitcher may not bring his pitching hand into contact with his mouth or lips while on the mound, although exceptions can be made in cold weather if both managers agree. Penalty: automatic ball called.

4. Other reasons for an automatic ball being called include

   • applying a foreign substance to the ball;

   • spitting on the ball, on either hand, or on the glove;

   • rubbing the ball on the glove, body, or clothing;

   • defacing the ball; and

FIELD AND PLAYER POSITIONS

8

7   Second base   9

4

90 ft.

6

Foul line   Foul line

Pitcher's
plate

5   127.25 ft.   3

Third   1   First
base   base

60.5 ft.

4 ft.

Batter's   6 ft.
box

2
Catcher's
box

43 in.

1   Pitcher
2   Catcher
3   First baseman
4   Second baseman
5   Third baseman
6   Shortstop
7   Left fielder
8   Center fielder
9   Right fielder

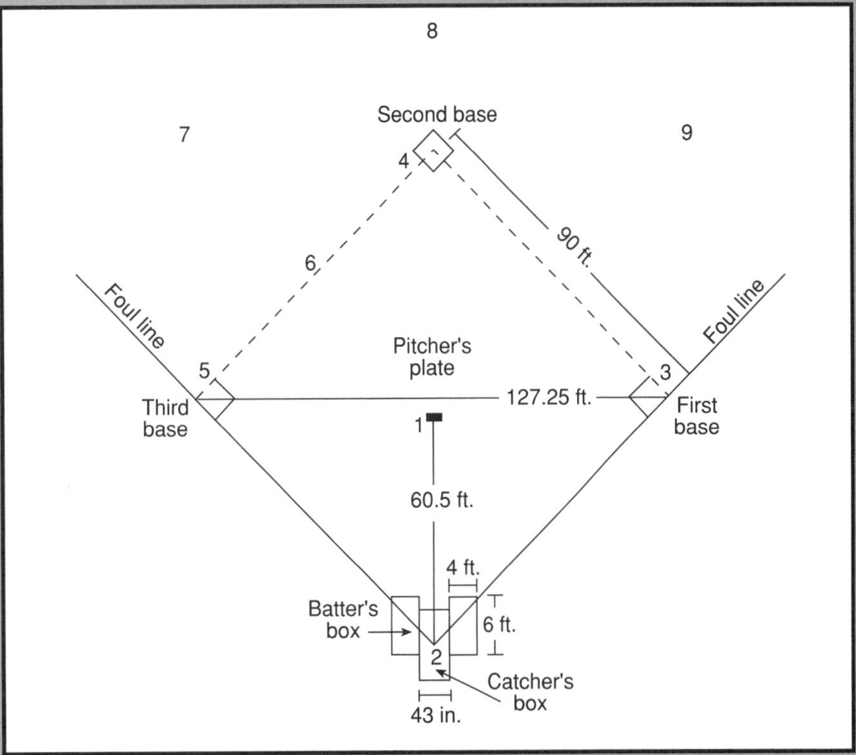

Figure 6.2. A baseball field and its dimensions, features, and player positions.
Adapted from White 1990.

© Claus Andersen

Figure 6.3.   A pitcher must continue to throw home once he has started his pitch.

- pitching a "shine" ball, spitball, mudball, or "emery" ball.

5. The pitcher may rub the ball in his bare hands.

6. Pitchers cannot intentionally throw at a batter. An umpire can expel a pitcher and his manager for this, or warn the pitcher and managers of both teams.

7. A manager or coach can make two trips to the mound during an inning to talk to a pitcher. On the second trip, the pitcher must be removed.

BATTING

Batting rules that have not been previously stated include the following.

1. Players must hit in the batting order decided by the manager.

2. A batter cannot leave the batter's box once the pitcher comes set or begins his windup.

3. Both feet must be in the batter's box (the lines are part of the box). If the batter hits the ball—either fair or foul—with one or both feet on the ground entirely outside of the box, the batter is automatically out.

4. A batter may request time, but the umpire does not have to grant this request. If a batter refuses to take his position in the batter's box, the umpire will order the pitcher to pitch and call each pitch a strike, no matter the location.

5. A batter makes an out when
   - his fair or foul fly ball is caught by a fielder;
   - a third strike is caught by the catcher;
   - a third strike is not caught by the catcher when first base is occupied before two are out;
   - he bunts foul on the third strike;
   - an infield fly rule is called (see page 28);
   - his fair ball touches him before touching a fielder (such as on a bunt);
   - after hitting a ball in fair territory, his bat hits the ball a second time (unless the umpire judges there was no intent on the batter's part to interfere with the ball);
   - after a third strike or after he hits a fair ball, he or first base is tagged before he touches first base;
   - he runs outside the three-foot line toward first base, interfering with the first baseman taking the throw, or with a fielder fielding the ball;
   - a runner on first intentionally interferes with the second baseman or shortstop on a double play opportunity (if the runner leaves the base line to try to "take out" the pivot man, both the runner and the batter are automatically out);
   - he interferes with the catcher's fielding or throwing; and when
   - he uses a bat tampered with to increase hitting distance (bats that are filled, hollowed, grooved, or covered with paraffin or wax, etc.).

BASE RUNNING

The following are base-running rules that have not been previously covered.

1. A runner is entitled to an unoccupied base when he touches it before he is put out.

2. The base line belongs to the runner. A fielder not in the act of fielding the ball cannot block the path of a runner between any base. In such a case the ball is dead and the runner is awarded the base he would have reached, in the umpire's judgment, had he not been obstructed.

3. A runner is out when
   - he is tagged by a fielder with the ball while not on a base (however, a runner can run or slide past first base without risking being tagged out if he returns immediately to first base without stepping or turning to second);
   - he fails to reach the next base before a fielder tags him or the base (the latter case being when the runner is forced to advance because the batter has become a runner);
   - he runs out of the base line (more than three feet or away from a direct line between the bases, unless he is doing so to avoid interfering with a fielder fielding a batted ball);
   - he intentionally interferes with a thrown ball, or hinders a fielder making a play on a batted ball;
   - two runners occupy the same base and one runner is tagged with the ball;
   - he is hit by a batted ball in fair territory before it touches a fielder or an umpire (unless he is on a base and an infield fly rule has been called);
   - he passes a runner on the base paths;
   - he misses a base in advancing to the next base and a fielder appeals before the next pitch by touching the base with the ball in his possession;
   - he fails to touch each base in order; and when
   - he intentionally interferes with a fielder or the ball in trying to break up a double play. In this case both the runner and the batter are out.

UMPIRES

The *umpire-in-chief* (home plate umpire) is in full charge of the game. Any umpire may disqualify any player, coach, or manager for objecting to decisions or for unsportsmanlike conduct or language. The umpire's decision on any judgment call is final and may not be appealed. A manager may, however, appeal any call that he believes goes against the rules.

For common umpire signals, see figure 6.4.

MODIFICATIONS

Major modifications for various levels of play follow. Note that these modifications are general; local leagues may follow different rules. For more complete information, contact the organizations listed at the end of this chapter.

Field Dimensions

For general field dimensions, see table 6.2.

Figure 6.4.   Common umpire signals in baseball.

Other Modifications

The following modifications are recommended by many youth leagues for pitching, game length, batting, base running, and defense.

Pitching

For players eight years of age and under, a batting tee, a pitching machine, or an adult pitcher is recommended. Safety balls, which are more pliable, are recommended for eight-and-under leagues. Limits are placed on the number of innings a youngster may pitch per game and per week. For sample limits for both game lengths and an individual pitcher's innings, see table 6.3.

Batting

Some leagues allow a team's complete roster to bat each inning. If batting from a tee, a batter may receive six swings to hit the ball in fair territory. If receiving pitches from a machine or an adult, a batter gets up to six pitches to hit fairly.

Some leagues limit the number of runs a team may score in an inning. For instance, if a team scores five runs in one inning, their half-inning is over, regardless of the number of outs made. Some leagues use a 10-run rule, in which a game of regulation length (e.g., four innings of a six-inning game) ends when a team is ahead by 10 runs.

Base Running

Younger divisions of youth leagues typically have "no lead-off" and "no-stealing" rules. Older divisions (often beginning with 9- and 10-year-olds) may lead-off and steal.

Table 6.2:	Field Dimensions			
Age	Bases (ft)	Pitching distance (ft)	Fence, down the lines (ft)	Fence, center field (ft)
5 to 6	50	38	125	200
7 to 8	50	38	150	200
9 to 10	60	44	175	225
11 to 12	70	48	225	275
13 to 14	80	54	265	315
15 to 16	90	60.5	300	350
17 to 18	90	60.5	300	350

Adapted from PONY Baseball and Softball 1995.

Table 6.3:	Game Length and Pitching Restrictions		
Age	Innings per game	Maximum innings for one pitcher per game	Maximum innings for one pitcher per week
7 to 8	5 (or 1.5 hr)	2	4
9 to 10	6	3	6
11 to 12	6	7	10
13 to 14	7	7	10
15 to 16	7	7	10
17 to 18	7	9	—

Defense

Younger divisions often allow up to 12 players on defense, and have no infield fly rule.

T-Ball

T-ball, where players hit a ball placed on a T, is played at younger levels, usually between the ages of five and nine. Rules for T-ball include the following:

- All players on the roster bat.
- An inning is over when nine players have hit or three outs are made, whichever occurs first. The ninth batter must attempt to score; his scoring or his being put out will end the inning, if three outs are not already made.
- No bunting is allowed. The ball must travel at least 25 feet in fair territory; a 25-foot arc is drawn from foul line to foul line.
- Balls not hit beyond the 25-foot arc are foul balls.
- A "pitcher" on the mound must be in contact with the pitching rubber and make a pitching motion before the batter swings.
- Three misses is a strikeout.
- No stealing or leading off.
- Nine players are on defense.
- Each player must play at least two innings in the field.
- The coach of the defensive team may stand beyond the infielders and instruct her players.
- A regulation game is six innings; a game is complete if three and a half or four innings are played.

ORGANIZATIONS

All-American Amateur Baseball Association
340 Walker Drive
Zanesville, OH 43701
614-453-7349

American Amateur Baseball Congress
118-19 Redfield Plaza
Marshall, MI 49068
616-781-2002

American Legion Baseball
P.O. Box 1055
Indianapolis, IN 46206
317-630-1213

Babe Ruth Baseball
1770 Brunswick Pike
Trenton, NJ 08638
609-695-1434

George Khoury Association of Baseball Leagues
5400 Meramec Bottom Road
St. Louis, MO 63128
314-849-8900

Little League Baseball
P.O. Box 3485
Williamsport, PA 17701
717-326-1921

National Amateur Baseball Federation
P.O. Box 705
Bowie, MD 20718
301-262-5005

National Baseball Congress
Box 1420
Wichita, KS 67201
316-267-3372

National Federation of State High School Associations
11724 NW Plaza Circle, Box 20626
Kansas City, MO 64195-0626
816-464-5400

National Semi-Professional Baseball Association
P.O. Box 29965
Atlanta, GA 30359
404-908-3339

Pony Baseball
P.O. Box 225
Washington, PA 15301
412-225-1060

USA Baseball
2160 Greenwood Ave.
Trenton, NJ 08609
609-586-2381

7

Basketball

© Mary Langenfeld

Basketball began with 13 fundamental rules that have been added to and amended greatly over the years since the game's beginnings in 1891. Invented by James Naismith, basketball first featured nine players per team because Naismith had 18 students in his YMCA Training School. In a few years that number was changed to five per side, a metal ring with a net replaced the original peach baskets that players shot at, and running with the ball was eliminated. The objective, however, has remained constant throughout the years: accumulate more points than the opponent.

Basketball is a widely enjoyed participant sport, with leagues for all ages and abilities. The rules in this chapter are general basketball rules, with specific references to college, professional, and international play. We note important modifications throughout, and at the end of the chapter we list organizations you can contact for specific basketball rules books.

PROCEDURES

A game, and any overtime period, begins with a *jump ball* in the center circle. In the National Basketball Association (NBA), the team that wins the opening tip is also awarded the ball to begin the fourth period; the ball is awarded to the opposing team to begin the second and third periods. In college and high school, the *alternating possession rule* determines which team initiates play for any period after the opening period.

A team advances the ball by dribbling and passing, and attempts to score. A shot that does not go into the basket is usually *rebounded* by a player. If that player is on offense, he can either shoot or set up another scoring opportunity. If the player who rebounds is on defense, he and his team advance the ball down court and try to set up their own scoring opportunity.

After a successful *field goal* (two- or three-point basket) or *free throw* (one-point basket), the opposing team throws the ball inbounds. On the *throw-in*, the thrower cannot step on or over the line while still possessing the ball. Defensive players cannot cross over the line or touch the ball before it is inbounds.

After a made basket, the player throwing the ball in may run the length of the baseline with the ball. On any inbounds play other than a made basket, the thrower-in must establish, and may not move, a *pivot foot* before releasing the ball. The thrower-in has five seconds to release the ball, or it is turned over to the other team.

Scoring

When the ball enters the basket from above, and remains in or passes through the net, a goal is scored. If that goal is scored with at least one of the shooter's feet on or inside the three-point line, a *two-point field goal* is scored. If neither of the shooter's feet is on or inside the three-point line, a *three-point field goal* is scored. After releasing the ball, the shooter may touch the three-point line or land inside the line and still be awarded three points on a successful shot. If a goal is mistakenly scored in the opponent's basket by a defender, two points are awarded to the nearest offensive player.

A successful *free-throw* attempt counts as one point. If the free throw is not made but the rebound is tapped in, the player who tapped it in is awarded two points. Free throws must be attempted within 10 seconds (college, professional, high school) or five seconds (international).

Defensive players and offensive players alternate positions along the free-throw lane, with the defensive team getting the positions closest to the basket. The shooter must remain behind the free-throw line until the ball touches the basket. The players in the lane must remain in their positions on the free-throw lane until the ball leaves the shooter's hands.

A player who is fouled while attempting a two-point field goal gets two free throws; a player gets three free throws if fouled during a three-point field goal attempt. One free throw is awarded a player who was fouled while making a field goal. After a certain number of fouls are committed in a quarter or a half, a team may be in the *bonus* situation, where the next player fouled (not in the act of shooting or as the result of taking a charge from an offensive player) receives a chance to make a free throw. If the first free throw is successful, that player receives a bonus of one more free-throw attempt. Bonus free throws are awarded as follows:

- College—The one-and-one bonus is awarded beginning with the 10th foul in a half.
- Professional—Two free throws are granted for each foul after four fouls in a quarter (or three in overtime).
- International—Two free throws are awarded after eight fouls in a half.

The penalty for most technical fouls is two free throws and the ball out of bounds to the team attempting the free throws. Any player on the floor may be named by the coach to attempt free throws awarded from a technical foul.

Time

Game length and other time factors differ according to the level of play; see table 7.1.

The *shot clock* governs the time a team is allowed to be on offense before attempting a shot. If the ball does not leave the shooter's hand before the clock expires, and the shot does not touch the rim

Table 7.1:	Game Length and Time Factors			
Level	Length	Overtime	Shot clock	Time-outs
High school	Four 8-min quarters	3 min	none	Four per game
College	Two 20-min halves	5 min	30 sec for women; 35 sec for men	Four per regulation (three per televised game); one per overtime
Professional	Four 12-min quarters	5 min	24 sec	Seven per regulation plus one 20-second timeout per half; three per overtime
International	Two 20-min halves	5 min	30 sec	Two per half

or go into the basket, a shot clock violation is called and the ball is given to the other team. The clock is stopped at the end of each period and when an official blows a whistle for

- a violation,
- a foul,
- a held or jump ball,
- a ball that goes out of bounds,
- suspension of play because of an injury to a player,
- suspension of play for any other reason,
- when the shot clock sounds (if the shot is in the air when the clock sounds and the shot hits the rim, the clock is ignored and play continues without time stopping), and
- timeouts.

Defense

Guarding a player with the ball. When a defender is guarding a player with the ball, the maximum distance between the two players is 6 feet. (No minimum distance is required.) To establish legal position, the defender must have both feet on the floor, with the torso facing the opponent. If the opponent is airborne, the defender must have established a legal position before the other player left the floor and must maintain that position.

Guarding a player without the ball. The defender must give the opponent time and up to two steps to avoid contact. If the opponent is airborne, the defender must have established a legal position before the other player left the floor and maintain that position.

Legal use of hands and arms. A defender may vertically extend hands and arms, reach to block or slap the ball away, and hit the hand of the opponent when the ball is in contact with the opponent's hands. If the extension is not vertical and any contact hinders the offensive player, this movement by the defender is not legal.

Defenders may use their hands to protect their faces or bodies in absorbing a charge from an opponent, but they can't use their hands to push the offensive player away. Defenders cannot use any part of their bodies to force their way through screens or to hold a screener and then push that player away.

In professional basketball a team cannot play a *zone defense,* in which each defender is assigned a certain portion of the court, rather than an individual player. In college and high school, zone defenses are allowed, as are *man-to-man* defenses, in which each player defends a specific opponent.

TERMS

These terms are not described elsewhere in this chapter.

A **dribble** is bouncing the ball on the floor, using one hand at a time. (Dribbling with both hands at once is "double dribbling," a violation that results in a turnover.) Players may move on the court or be stationary when they dribble. The dribble ends when the ball is caught by the dribbler, who cannot dribble again until another player touches the ball.

A team's **frontcourt** is that half of the court that includes its basket. The **backcourt** is the half of the court that includes the other team's basket. No part of the end line or the center line is considered part of the frontcourt.

A **held ball** occurs when two players from opposite teams each has a firm grasp on the ball and when an opposing player places a hand on the ball to prevent an airborne player from attempting a pass or shot. The team with the possession indicator in its favor is awarded the ball out of bounds.

Incidental contact occurs when opponents are in equally favorable positions to perform normal defensive or offensive movements, and contact (even severe contact) is made, such as in going for a loose ball. No foul is called. Similarly, a blind screen may be ruled incidental contact, regardless of the violence of the collision.

A **pass** is the movement of the ball by a player who throws, bats, or rolls the ball to another player.

A **pivot** occurs when a player holding the ball pivots with one foot kept in its point of contact with the floor while stepping in any direction. Picking up the pivot foot before dribbling or getting rid of the ball is a traveling violation.

A **rebound** is when a player controls possession of a missed shot, either by a teammate (offensive rebound) or an opponent (defensive rebound).

A **screen** is when an offensive player reaches a desired position first, causing a defensive player to go around him and delaying the progress of the defender. The offensive player must have feet planted and remain stationary.

Substitutes are alternative players who may enter a game by reporting to the scorer and being beckoned by an official. Substitutes may enter during a dead ball and when time is out (except in college, where a substitute may enter after a successful field goal in the last minute of a game and overtime). A substitute may not enter a game for a player shooting a free throw unless that player is injured.

Verticality applies to ascertaining who has legal position. A defender who has already established position and who raises hands and arms within his or her vertical plane is in legal position and shouldn't be charged with a foul if an offensive player causes contact. The defender can leave his or her feet within this plane, but cannot "belly up" or use the lower part of the body to contact the offensive player outside the vertical plane.

COURT

Court sizes vary according to the level of play; see table 7.2.

At least three feet of unobstructed space should lie beyond the *sidelines* and *endlines* (or *baselines*) that mark the boundaries of the court. The court is split in half by a *center line*, around which are two *center circles*. Each end of the court has a *free-throw line*. A *free-throw lane* borders each free-

Table 7.2: Court Size				
	Size	Free throw line	Free throw lane	3-point arc
High school	50 × 84 ft	15 ft	12 ft	19 ft, 9 in
College	50 × 94 ft	15 ft	12 × 19 ft	19 ft, 9 in
Professional	50 × 94 ft	15 ft	16 × 19 ft	21 ft, 9 in
International	49 ft, 2 in × 91 ft, 10 in	15 ft	12 ft at free throw lane, widening to 19 ft at baseline	22 ft

throw line. This lane has a semicircle with a six-foot radius from the center of the free-throw line.

Two *coaching boxes* are behind the sidelines, 28 feet long and extending toward center court from each endline. See figure 7.1 for standard court attributes.

PLAYERS

A team consists of five players. Typically a team will play two guards (a *point guard,* considered the team's playmaker and an *off guard* or *shooting guard*), a *small forward,* a *power forward,* and a *center* or *post* player. These are loosely defined roles; players may be defined differently in different systems. Players are sometimes referred to by position numbers (which have nothing to do with their uniform numbers):

1. Point guard
2. Off guard or shooting guard
3. Small forward
4. Power forward
5. Center or post

EQUIPMENT

The *ball* is round, with a circumference of 29.25 to 30 inches for men and 28.5 to 29 inches for women. A men's ball weighs 20 to 22 ounces; a women's ball weighs 18 to 20 ounces. Youth league balls can be smaller and vary in size.

The ball has a leather cover with eight panels joined by rubber ribs. (Balls with synthetic covering may be used if both teams agree.)

The *backboard,* which supports the *basket,* can be either 6 by 4 feet or 6 by 3.5 feet for college and high school play; professional basketball uses only the smaller size. In high school play, a fan-shaped backboard may be used. A 24- by 18-inch rectangle is centered on the backboard, behind

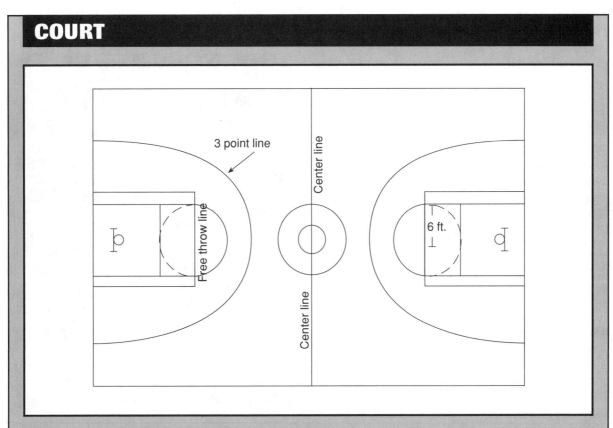

COURT

3 point line

Center line

Free throw line

Center line

6 ft.

Center line

Figure 7.1. Dimensions for basketball courts vary according to the level of play, but many of the same features are included on all basketball courts.
Adapted from White 1990.

and above the basket. The bottom and sides of the backboard are padded, as is the backboard *support*.

The basket is an orange metal ring, 18 inches in inside diameter, with a white cord net hanging from the basket, 15 to 18 inches in length. The upper edge of the basket is 10 feet above and parallel to the floor. The nearest point of the basket is 6 inches from the backboard.

Other equipment includes

- a *scoreboard*,
- *game clock*, and a
- *possession indicator* (that indicates which team will get possession of the ball in the next held ball or double-foul situation).

FOULS

A foul occurs when a player or coach breaks a rule in any of a variety of ways. A player is disqualified and removed from a game after being assessed five fouls (high school, college, and international) or six fouls (professional). Specific fouls include these:

Away from the ball. This is a foul committed by a player in a play not involving the player with the ball.

Blocking and charging. Blocking is illegal contact by a defender, impeding the progress of an offensive player. Charging is illegal contact by an offensive player by pushing or moving into the defender's torso.

Delay of game. This is called when a player prevents the ball from being promptly put into play, such as after a made basket or such as batting the ball away from an opponent before the player can throw the ball inbounds.

Double personal. A double personal occurs when two opposing players commit personal fouls at about the same time. No free throws are awarded; in professional ball, the team in possession of the ball at the time of the fouls retains possession; if neither team was in possession, a jump ball is used to put the ball into play. In college, the alternating-possession arrow determines the team that gets possession.

Double technical. A double technical is called when two opposing players commit technical fouls at about the same time. In college, each team receives two free throws (see figure 7.2), and the alternating-possession arrow determines which team gets possession. In professional ball, this penalty is handled the same way as a double personal foul.

Elbow. In professional ball, two free-throw attempts are awarded for an elbow foul. If the contact is made above shoulder level, the player throwing the elbow may be ejected. In college and in high school play, excessive swinging of elbows—even without making contact—may result in a foul called.

Excessive timeout. A team calling a timeout when it has no timeouts left is assessed a technical foul. The timeout is granted, but two free throws and the ball out of bounds are awarded to the opposing team.

Face guarding. A defender cannot place a hand in the face or eyes of the opponent he or she is guarding from the rear if the opponent does not have the ball. Such a play results in a technical foul.

Figure 7.2. A free throw awarded to the opposing team is often the punishment for violations in basketball.

Fighting and flagrant fouls. In the NBA, fighting results in technical fouls assessed against those involved and automatic ejection. No free throws are awarded. In both college and the pros, a flagrant foul results in two free throws awarded to the offended team and possession of the ball. Any player committing a flagrant foul is automatically ejected in college; a professional player may be ejected at the discretion of the official.

Hand checking. Defenders cannot use their hands to check the progress of offensive players when those players are in front of them.

Hanging on the rim. If either an offensive or a defensive player hangs on the rim, a technical foul is assessed. The only exception is if a player hangs on the rim to protect himself or other players from injury.

Intentional. In college, an intentional foul occurs when a player commits a personal foul without attempting to directly play the opposing player or the ball. It does not depend on the severity of the foul; it depends on whether the official judges the foul to be intentional. Holding or pushing a player in full view of an official, in order to stop play, and shoving a player in the back as he or she is attempting a lay-up that cannot be defended, are examples of intentional fouls. The penalty for such fouls is two free throws and the ball out of bounds.

Offensive. Any player can commit a foul on offense. If a defender has established legal position in a dribbler's path, the dribbler cannot make contact with the opponent. A screener cannot move into an opponent after setting a legal screen. A shooter cannot charge into a defender who has established legal position and who maintains that position.

Personal. The term "personal foul" covers a wide variety of contact fouls that players can commit, including holding, pushing, charging, tripping, and illegally interfering with a player's progress.

Player-control. "Player-control foul" is another term for charging—when the dribbler commits an offensive foul by charging into a defender who has established legal position. Free throws are not awarded, but the opposing team gets the ball.

Punching. In professional ball, a punching foul results in one free throw being awarded, and the ball out of bounds. The player throwing the punch—whether it connects or not—is automatically ejected. (In college this foul would be handled the same as a flagrant foul.)

Technical. A technical foul is a foul committed by anyone—players on the court or bench, coaches, other team officials—that does not involve contact with the opponent while the ball is alive. Examples of technical fouls include use of profanity, delay of game, excessive timeouts, unsportsmanlike conduct, and hanging on the rim (except to prevent injury). Two free throws and the ball are awarded the offended team when a player commits a technical foul. If a coach, substitute, or other team personnel commits a technical foul, two free throws are awarded (and in college, the offended team would retain possession of the ball). If a player commits two technical fouls, he or she is removed from the game. If a coach commits two technical fouls, he or she is removed from the competition area.

Throwing the ball at an official. Throwing the ball, or any object, at an official is a technical foul and cause for possible ejection.

Unsportsmanlike conduct. Unsportsmanlike conduct is a technical foul resulting from any of numerous unsportsmanlike actions, including disrespectfully addressing an official, trying to influence an official's decision, arguing with an official, taunting an opponent, inciting undesirable crowd reactions, throwing items on the court, and so on. The penalty is two free throws and the ball out to the opposing team.

VIOLATIONS

Violations occur when players break the rules in a way that does not involve contact. Violations include the following:

Backcourt. If a team is in possession of the ball in its frontcourt and the ball goes into the backcourt (last touched by an offensive player), an offensive player cannot touch the ball before a defensive player does. If this happens, the ball goes over to the defensive team automatically. If, however, the ball was deflected into the backcourt by a defender, an offensive player may retrieve the ball in the backcourt.

Basket interference and goaltending. A player cannot touch the ball or the basket when the ball is on or within the basket. A player cannot touch the ball when it is in the cylinder (the basket extended upward), or touch the ball if it is in flight downward toward the basket and has a possibility of entering the basket. Defensive basket interference and goaltending result in two points for the offense; offensive basket interference results in no points and the ball out of bounds to the defense.

Double dribble. A player may not stop his or her dribble and then resume it. A player can resume a dribble, however, if the ball has been batted out of his or her hands, or a pass or fumble has been touched by another player.

Faking a free throw. A player cannot fake (intentionally miss) a free throw. The penalty is the awarding of the ball out of bounds to the opposing team.

Kicking or hitting the ball. A player cannot intentionally kick the ball or strike it with his or her fist. Doing so results in the ball being given out of bounds to the other team.

Out of bounds. Any ball that goes out of bounds is awarded to the team opposing the player who last touched the ball.

Shot clock. Any shot that does not beat the shot clock results in the ball being turned over to the other team. If the ball is released before the clock expires, and hits the rim after the buzzer goes off, no violation has occurred.

Traveling. A player cannot advance with the ball without dribbling it.

Throw-in. A player throwing the ball inbounds may not

- carry the ball onto the court,
- hold the ball longer than five seconds,
- touch the ball on the court before another player has touched it,
- leave the designated throw-in spot (except after a made basket), or
- step over the boundary line while still touching the ball.

OFFICIALS

A *referee* and one or two *umpires*, depending on the level of play, call fouls, violations, and make all on-court calls. A *scorekeeper* operates the scoreboard and records the play; a *timekeeper* operates the game clock; a *shot clock operator* is in charge of the shot clock.

For common officials' signals, see figure 7.3.

MODIFICATIONS

Youth leagues vary in how they modify rules. Smaller balls are used; older divisions may elect to use a shot clock. Younger divisions play 6- or 7-minute quarters; older divisions play 18- or 20-minute halves.

ORGANIZATIONS

Amateur Athletic Union
3400 W. 86th St.
P.O. Box 68207
Indianapolis, IN 46268
317-872-2900

Continental Basketball Association
701 Market St., Ste. 140
St. Louis, MO 63101-1824
303-331-0404

Fédération Internationale de Basketball Amateur
Kistlerhofstrasse 168
P.O. Box 700607
München 70, Germany W-8000
Fax: 49 89 785 3596

National Amateur Basketball Association
6832 W. North Ave., Ste. 4A
Chicago, IL 60635
312-637-0811

National Association of Basketball Coaches of the United States
9300 W. 110th St., Ste. 640
Overland Park, KS 66210-1486
913-469-1001

Figure 7.3. Common official signals for basketball.

(continued)

Three-point field goal attempt

Intentional foul

Traveling

Illegal dribble

Three-second violation

Player control foul

Figure 7.3. *(continued)*

National Basketball Association
645 Fifth Ave., 10th Fl.
New York, NY 10022
212-826-7000

National Collegiate Athletic Association
6201 College Blvd.
Overland Park, KS 66211-2422
913-339-1906

National Federation of State High School Associations
11724 Plaza Circle

P.O. Box 20626
Kansas City, MO 64195
816-464-5400

USA Basketball
5465 Mark Dabling Blvd.
Colorado Springs, CO 80918-3842
719-590-4800

Youth Basketball of America
P.O. Box 3067
Orlando, FL 32802-3067
407-363-0599

8

Biathlon

© Claus Andersen

Biathlon is a winter sport that combines cross-country skiing and smallbore rifle shooting. Men, women, and juniors compete in various biathlon competitions, including individual, sprint, relay, and team competitions. Biathletes ski a certain distance first, then stop for a shooting bout at the first of several target areas, and then ski the final few kilometers to the finish. Both ski time and shooting accuracy figure into a final score for each competitor or team. One- or two-minute penalties can be imposed on competitors. One such penalty is imposed when a biathlete does not hit all his or her targets and does not ski the required penalty loop. Biathlon is an Olympic sport, governed by the International Biathlon Union, which is the source of rules for this chapter.

PROCEDURES

A competition has four main components: the start, the skiing, the shooting, and the finish. Biathletes or teams are randomly assigned start numbers before the competition. In relay competition, each team's start number also signifies its start track number and shooting lane number.

Individual competition starts are made with 30-second intervals (or sometimes one-minute intervals) between each start. For *sprint competitions,* the start can be either an individual or group start. *Relay competitions* hold a mass start for the first competitors of each team. In *team competitions,* each team starts together, with one-minute intervals between starts.

In the first 100 meters of relay mass or group starts, biathletes cannot use a skating technique (one or both legs going sideways). The starter's assistant will stop a biathlete or team that false starts. Competitors who false start are required to return behind the start line and start again. The time lost in doing so counts against them. If the air temperature is below minus 20 degrees Celsius (minus 4 degrees Fahrenheit) or the wind chill is severe, a competition will not be started.

Skiing

Biathletes must follow the marked course precisely, using skis and poles and any skiing technique they choose. They carry their rifles on their backs, barrel pointing up; they also must carry their ammunition. If a rifle is damaged so that the biathlete cannot carry it on her back, she may carry it in her hands.

In team competition, a team must ski the entire distance in closed formation, and cross the entrance line to the shooting range with no more than 15 seconds between the first and last team member. The two nonshooting members stop in a waiting area while the two shooting members shoot. A biathlete who takes a wrong trail must return to the point where he went off course before resuming.

A competitor who wants to pass another competitor must yell "Track!" The person being passed must clear the track or trail except in the final 100 meters before a handover zone or finish line.

A biathlete must ski a 150-meter *penalty loop* for each shot that misses a target. In team competition, both shooters must ski a penalty loop for each missed shot either of them make.

A biathlete may be disqualified for intentionally or unintentionally obstructing another competitor. This especially pertains to the final 100 meters and during the approach and exchange in the handover zone.

A competitor may exchange one ski if it is broken or damaged. Biathletes may exchange broken poles and straps as often as necessary. In a team competition, team members may exchange skis among themselves. Competitors may receive wax and wax their skis during competition.

Shooting

Biathletes shoot at targets on a shooting range after completing each required course section on their skis. See table 8.1 for shooting specifications.

Competitors may choose their *shooting lanes* in individual, sprint, and team competitions. In team competitions, teammates must shoot from adjoining lanes.

In *relay competitions,* lanes are assigned to each team. Each competitor fires the first five rounds; if targets remain standing, he must use the three *spare rounds* that are available at the site. A biathlete shoots until all five targets are down or all eight rounds are spent.

In *team competitions,* all four team members must cross the line at the end of the shooting range with no more than 15 seconds passing between the first and the last. Two members shoot from adjoining lanes; neither can fire a shot until both are in their lanes.

Competitors shoot in two positions: prone and standing. In the *prone position,* the rifle may touch the hands, shoulder, and cheek. The wrist of the arm supporting the rifle must be noticeably above the ground. The other arm may touch the ground up to 10 centimeters past the elbow. In the *standing position,* the hands, shoulder, cheek, and chest may touch the rifle; the arm supporting the rifle may be held against the chest or rest on the hip.

Class	Competition	Shooting bouts and positions	Number of shots per bout	Shot penalty[1]
Men	20-km individual	P, S, P, S[2]	5	1 min
	10-km sprint	P, S	5	150-m penalty loop
	4 × 7.5-km relay	Each member P, S	5 + 3 spares	150-m penalty loop
	10-km team	First 2 shooters P; second 2 shooters S	5 per shooter	150-m penalty loop
Women	15-km individual	P, S, P, S	5	1 min
	7.5-km sprint	P, S	5	150-m penalty loop
	4 × 7.5-km relay	Each member P, S	5 + 3 spares	150-m penalty loop
	7.5-km team	First 2 shooters P; second 2 shooters S	5 per shooter	150-m penalty loop
Junior men	15-km individual	P, S, P	5	1 min
	10-km sprint	P, S	5	150-m penalty loop
	4 × 7.5-km relay	Each member P, S	5 + 3 spares	150-m penalty loop
	10-km team	First 2 shooters P; second 2 shooters S	5 per shooter	150-m penalty loop
Junior women	10-km individual	P, S, P	5	1 min
	7.5-km sprint	P, S	5	150-m penalty loop
	3 × 7.5-km relay	Each member P, S	5 + 3 spares	150-m penalty loop
	7.5-km team	First 2 shooters P; second 2 shooters S	5 per shooter	150-m penalty loop

Table 8.1: Shooting Specifications

[1]Imposed for each target left standing [2]P = prone; S = standing
Adapted from Union Internationale de Pentathlon Moderne et Biathlon 1994.

A shooter may not remove either ski or place anything beneath the skis. She may use a sling in either the prone or standing position. To ensure *safety*, biathletes must

- be behind the shooting line when the range is open for shooting,

- load and unload their rifles with the barrel pointing toward the targets,
- make sure that no live ammunition is left in the chamber after each shooting,
- place their unloaded rifles on their backs before moving on to the next firing point,

- aim and fire only at the targets,
- not remove a strap of their rifle-carrying harness before they reach their firing lanes and place their ski poles on the ground, and
- have their rifles checked at the finish.

A competitor may replace *lost or misfired rounds* if she is carrying spare rounds or gets them from the range official. If a rifle is damaged and cannot be repaired, the competitor may use the team's *reserve rifle*, which is kept on a designated rack on the range.

If a competitor shoots at another biathlete's target and that biathlete is also shooting at it, officials must immediately stop the competitor who is firing at the wrong target and reset any targets that she hit. If the competitor whose target is being shot at is not shooting at it, the biathlete who is crossfiring at the target will not be stopped, but the only hits counted will be those made on her own target. If a competitor loses time because another biathlete has shot at her target, necessitating it to be reset, officials will make an appropriate time adjustment for the competitor whose target was fired on in error. Each rifle is checked at the finish to make sure it contains no live ammunition.

The competition organizers put in place a scoring system for the shooting. Each shot is observed by three independent people or methods.

Finish

A biathlete finishes when he breaks the electric eye beam at the finish line, or, for manual timing, when one or both feet cross the finish line. In team competitions, a team is finished when the last team member crosses the line. Time is recorded to one-tenth of a second. If two competitors or two teams tie, the score is recorded as a tie.

Penalties

Biathletes may incur penalties for incorrect, unfair, or unsafe behavior. Penalties can come in the form of a *reprimand*, a *start prohibition*, a *one-minute* or *two-minute penalty*, or a *disqualification*.

A *one-minute penalty* is assessed for

- crossing the range line or finish line with more than 15 seconds between the first and last team members,

- one or both of the nonshooting members crossing the waiting enclosure boundary before the shooting members are past the enclosure,
- not allowing a competitor to pass,
- not placing the three spare rounds in the cup or on the shooting ramp before firing them,
- team members not shooting from adjoining lanes,
- one team member shooting before the other shooting member reaches his shooting lane, and
- a very minor violation of sportsmanship and fair play.

A *two-minute penalty* may be assessed for

- a penalty loop not completed immediately when it is required;
- using a sideways skating technique in the first 100 meters in the relay mass start or in a group start;
- every round not fired if the biathlete begins to ski before firing all five shots (individual, sprint, or team competition), or all eight shots (relay competition, if all targets haven't been hit); and
- a minor violation of sportsmanship and fair play.

A competitor may be *disqualified* for competing in a competition for which he is not eligible, for being doped or evading doping control, for receiving prohibited assistance, and for using nonregulation equipment. A biathlete may also be disqualified for deviating from the marked course and gaining a time advantage, for not carrying his rifle while skiing, for obstructing another biathlete, and for firing more than the allowed rounds.

TERMS

The **course** is the network of ski trails that competitors must follow.

Prone is one of two shooting positions. In the prone position, a competitor lies on the snow and mat.

A **shot-penalty** is one incurred because a competitor missed a target. The penalty is one minute added to the finish time in individual competitions, and a 150-meter penalty loop in sprint, relay, and team competitions.

Standing is one of two shooting positions.

A **track** is the parallel grooves along a trail that fit the skis.

A **trail** is a single ski loop, marked by a color.

Zeroing is the act of sighting in a rifle by shooting several rounds to test it.

COURSE AND RANGE

Competitions take place in a stadium area and a range. The stadium area contains the start and finish area, shooting range, penalty loop, and relay handover zone. The start area must be level and its snow groomed and packed. For relay and group start areas, at least eight tracks, 1.5 to 2 meters apart, are set 100 meters from the start line. After the first 100 meters of track, there are another 50 to 100 meters of level, groomed, trackless snow that begin to converge with the competition trail.

Course

The course is the network of ski trails that the competitors must traverse. It has flat areas, downhills, and climbs. A course must have at least two separate trail loops.

A course may not be higher than 1,800 meters above sea level. For major competitions, trails must have at least 5 meters, width of groomed snow. The length of the course may vary by 5 percent of its specified distance for the competition. See table 8.2 for course specifications.

Trails must be groomed, packed, and as level as possible; they cannot be artificially frozen. Downhill turns must be banked as needed.

The course must be clearly marked so that competitors know which trails to follow. Trails may be used up to three times in a competition if they are at least 5 meters wide. They are marked on the right side, using boards, with Trail 1 being red, Trail 2 green, Trail 3 yellow, Trail 4 blue, and Trail 5 brown.

A *handover zone* for relay competitions is 30 meters long and 6 to 8 meters wide. Handover zones are at the end of a straight section of trail, marked at the beginning and end with red lines.

A *penalty loop,* 150 meters long by 5 meters wide, is set up immediately after the shooting range for sprint, relay, and team competitions.

Range

The shooting range is located in the central area of the stadium. The range must be level and surrounded by adequate safety berms behind and to the sides of the targets. The distance between the front edge of the shooting mat and the target should be 50 meters, plus or minus 1 meter.

The *shooting ramp* and the target should each be at least 30 centimeters above the ground. The ramp should be covered with groomed, solid, level snow. The ramp has *shooting lanes,* each between 2.5 and 3 meters wide. Each lane has a *shooting mat,* 1.6 meters square and 1 to 2 centimeters thick.

The *targets* are set up in a level, straight line, parallel to the front edge of the shooting ramp. The center of the target is in the middle of the width of the shooting lane. A target and its corresponding firing point have the same number. *Wind flags* are set up at the side of every third shooting lane.

Finish Area

The finish area begins 10 meters before the finish line and ends at the finish control point, which is at least 35 meters after the finish line. Only officials and competitors are allowed in the finish area.

COMPETITORS

On November 1 of the year they turn 20, competitors are eligible to compete in the men's or women's class. Before that, they are eligible to compete in the junior men's or junior women's class.

The types of competitions are as follows:

Men—20-kilometer individual; 10-kilometer sprint; 4 × 7.5-kilometer relay; 10-kilometer team (four members)

			Table 8.2:	Course Specifications		
Class	Competition	Shooting bouts (km)	Maximum distance between bouts (km)	Maximum height difference (m)	Maximum climb (m)	Total climb (m)
Men	20-km individual	Between 3 and 17.5	3	200	75	600 to 750
	10-km sprint and 10-km team	Between 2.5 and 7.5	3	200	75	300 to 450
	4 × 7.5-km relay	At 2.5 and 5	—	100	75	200 to 300
Women	15-km individual	Between 3 and 12	2.5	150	75	400 to 500
	7.5-km sprint and 7.5-km team	At 2.5 and 5	—	100	75	200 to 300
	4 × 7.5-km relay	At 2.5 and 5	—	100	75	200 to 300
Junior men	15-km individual	Between 3 and 12.5	3	150	75	400 to 500
	10-km sprint and 10-km team	Between 2.5 and 7.5	—	100	75	300 to 450
	4 × 7.5-km relay	At 2.5 and 5	—	100	75	200 to 300
Junior women	10-km individual	Between 2 and 8	2	150	75	200 to 350
	7.5-km sprint and 7.5-km team	At 2.5 and 5	—	100	75	200 to 300
	3 × 7.5-km relay	At 2.5 and 5	—	100	75	200 to 300

Adapted from Union Internationale de Pentathlon Moderne et Biathlon 1994.

Women—15-kilometer individual; 7.5-kilometer sprint, 4 × 7.5-kilometer relay; 7.5-kilometer team (four members)

Junior Men—15-kilometer individual; 10-kilometer sprint; 4 × 7.5-kilometer relay; 10-kilometer team (four members)

Junior Women—10-kilometer individual; 7.5-kilometer sprint; 3 × 7.5-kilometer relay; 7.5-kilometer team (four members)

EQUIPMENT

Targets are usually either metal or paper. A target has a white face and black scoring plates.

The diameters of these scoring plates are 115 millimeters for metal and 110 millimeters for paper. This applies to areas for aiming and scoring while standing, and aiming while prone. The diameter for scoring while prone is 45 millimeters for metal and 40 millimeters for paper.

Skis must be at least as long as the competitor is tall, minus 4 centimeters; there is no maximum length. They must be between 43 and 47 millimeters wide at the ski waist, and at least 30 millimeters wide at the tip. They must weigh at least 750 grams. The gliding surface may be smooth or slightly grooved; scales to help climbing are okay.

A competitor uses two *ski poles* of fixed, equal length, not longer than the competitor's body. There is no weight limit for the poles. *Rifles* may not be automatic or semiautomatic; loading and unloading must be fully executed by the competitor. No sighting device that magnifies is allowed. A sling and a carrying harness are permitted. Including all the accessories (except ammunition and magazines), a rifle must weigh at least 3.5 kilograms. Magazines capable of carrying more than five rounds are not permitted. Spare rounds may be carried in a separate magazine. Competitors use long rifle rimfire ammunition.

OFFICIALS

Referees officiate biathlon events. They monitor the action at the start and finish area, on the shooting range, and on the course. They are also in charge of equipment and material control.

ORGANIZATIONS

U.S. Biathlon Association
421 Old Military Road
Lake Placid, NY 12946
518-523-3836

9

Bowling

© Mary Langenfeld

Bowling was introduced in North America in the 1600s. Tenpin bowling, which is currently played, is believed to have sprung up when nine-pin bowling was declared illegal in Connecticut in the 1840s.

The American Bowling Congress and the Women's International Bowling Congress, the sources of the rules for this chapter, standardized rules and equipment around the turn of this century. One of bowling's attractions is it can be played by young and old, large and small, male and female.

The object is to score the most points by knocking down pins with a ball rolled down a lane. The game can be played either between individuals or between teams, with up to five players on a team.

PROCEDURES

Tenpin bowling consists of 10 *frames*. A player delivers two balls in each of the first nine frames, unless she scores a *strike* on the first ball by knocking down all the pins. In the 10th frame, the player delivers either two or three balls. If she scores a strike, she rolls two more balls. If she scores a *spare* (by knocking down all the pins in two attempts), she rolls one more ball.

Players take turns, rolling one frame at a time. In team play, players must bowl in the order they have designated and switch lanes after every frame, bowling five frames on their own lane and five on their opponent's.

Scoring

Except when a strike is scored, the number of pins knocked down by the player's first delivery is marked next to the small square in the upper right corner of that frame (see figure 9.1). The number of pins the player knocks down on the second delivery is marked down inside the small square. If none of the pins is knocked down by the second delivery, the player marks the scoresheet with a minus sign.

When a player scores a strike, he marks an "x" in the small square in the upper right-hand corner of that frame. His final score for that frame will be 10 (for the strike) plus however many pins he knocks down in his next two deliveries. For example, if he rolls three consecutive strikes, his score for that first frame is 30 points. The score for a perfect game—12 strikes—is 300.

Fouls

A *foul* occurs when any part of the player touches any part of the lane or the foul line during or after a delivery. On a foul, the delivery counts, but any pins knocked down are not recorded. Except in the case of a deliberate foul, the player who fouls on her first delivery still would be allowed her second delivery, but any pins knocked down on the first delivery would first be respotted.

Pins

Pinfalls are *legal* when pins are knocked down by the ball or another pin, including a pin that rebounds from a side panel, rear cushion, or sweep bar when the bar is at rest on the pin deck. A pin that leans and touches the kickback or side partition is also considered to have legally fallen. These pins are called "dead wood" and must be removed before the next delivery.

Pinfalls are not legal when

- a ball leaves the lane before reaching the pins,
- a ball rebounds from the rear cushion and knocks down any pins,
- a pin is touched by the mechanical pinsetting equipment,
- a pin is knocked down while dead wood is being removed,
- a pin is knocked down by a human pinsetter, and when
- the bowler fouls.

Any pins that have illegally fallen on a player's first delivery must be respotted before the second delivery. A pin that rebounds onto the lane

1	2	3	4	5	6	7	8	9	10
☒	☒	☒	7 ꞁ 2	⑧ ◹	F ꞁ 9	☒	7 ◹	9 ꞁ —	☒ ☒ ꞁ 8
30	57	76	85	95	104	124	143	152	180

Figure 9.1. This scorecard shows strikes were bowled in frames 1-3. The bowler knocked down seven pins on the first ball in frame 4 and two pins on the second ball. Frame 10 shows two strikes and two pins left standing.

Courtesy of American Bowling Congress/Women's International Bowling Congress/Young American Bowling Congress 1995-96 Playing Rules Book.

and remains standing is not considered to have been knocked down.

If the pins are improperly set and the player delivers a ball, the delivery and pinfall count. Once a delivery has been made, the pin position cannot be changed, unless the pinsetter moved or misplaced a pin.

Dead Ball

When a dead ball is called, the delivery does not count. Any pins knocked down with a dead ball must be respotted, and the player receives a new delivery. A dead ball occurs in the following cases:

- After a delivery, a player immediately reports that one or more pins were missing from the setup.
- A human pinsetter interferes with any standing pin before the ball reaches the pins.
- A human pinsetter interferes with a downed pin before it stops rolling.
- A player bowls out of turn or on the wrong lane.
- A player is interfered with during delivery. (The player can choose to accept the resulting pinfall.)
- Any pin is knocked down as a player delivers the ball but before the ball reaches the pins.
- The ball contacts a foreign obstacle on the playing surface.

Provisional Ball

When a protest involving a foul, legal pinfall, or dead ball is made and is not immediately resolved, a *provisional ball* can be rolled. A record of both scores (with and without the provisional ball) for the frame is kept, and the protest is referred to the league board or tournament director for a decision.

The procedures for rolling a provisional ball vary according to the situation:

<u>First ball of a frame or second ball in the 10th frame if the first ball was a strike</u>

Foul The player completes the frame and then bowls one provisional ball at a full setup of pins.

Illegal pinfall The player completes the frame and bowls one provisional ball at the same setup that would have occurred had the disputed pin or pins not fallen.

Dead ball The player completes the ball and bowls a complete provisional frame.

<u>Spare attempt or third ball of the 10th frame</u>

Foul and illegal pinfall No provisional ball is necessary.

Dead ball The player bowls a provisional ball at the same setup that was standing when the disputed ball was bowled.

TERMS

A **double** means a player has rolled two consecutive strikes.

An **error** is made by a player who leaves any pins standing in a frame, unless the remaining pins left standing after the first delivery constitute a split.

A **frame** consists of two deliveries by a player (unless the first delivery is a strike, in which case the frame is over).

A **spare** is scored by a player who knocks down any remaining pins on the second delivery of the frame. The player scores 10 points plus the number of pins he knocks down on his next delivery.

A **split** refers to a setup of pins left standing after the first delivery, when the head pin is down and the remaining pins are far apart.

A **strike** is recorded by a player who knocks down all the pins on her first delivery. A strike cannot occur on the second delivery, even if no pins were knocked down on the first delivery. A strike counts 10 points plus the number of pins the player knocks down on her next two deliveries.

A **triple** or **turkey** refers to three successive strikes by one player.

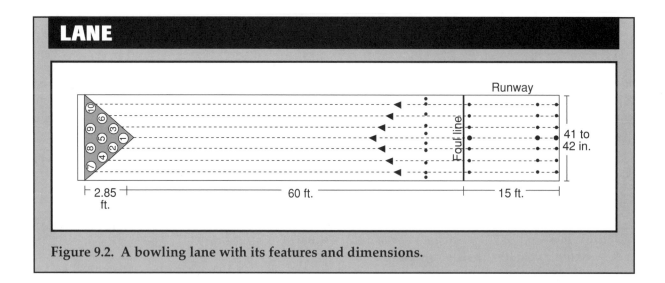

Figure 9.2. A bowling lane with its features and dimensions.

LANE

The *lane,* or alley, measures 60 feet from the *foul line* to the center of the head (first) pin (see figure 9.2). The total length of the lane, to the back of the *pin deck,* where the pins stand, is 62.85 feet. A lane's width is 41 to 42 inches.

The *pins* are wood or plastic-coated wood or synthetic material. Each pin is 15 inches tall and weighs between 3 pounds, 6 ounces and 3 pounds, 10 ounces. Pins are set 12 inches apart from each other in a triangular pattern on the pin deck.

The approach, or *runway,* which ends at the foul line, is a minimum of 15 feet. Grooved *gutters* (channels) are on either side of the lane to catch errant balls.

EQUIPMENT

A *ball* is made of a nonmetallic composition (usually a plastic or urethane compound) with a circumference no greater than 27 inches and a weight of no more than 16 pounds. It can have up to five holes for finger grips.

OFFICIALS

Officials can be used for both scoring and judging fouls, but automatic scoring and foul-detection devices are typically used.

ORGANIZATIONS

American Bowling Congress
5301 S. 76th St.
Greendale, WI 53129-1127
414-421-6400

Ladies Pro Bowlers Tour
7171 Cherryvale Blvd.
Rockford, IL 61112
815-332-5756

The National Bowling Association
377 Park Avenue South, 7th Fl.
New York, NY 10016
212-689-8308

Professional Bowlers Association
1720 Merriman Rd.
P.O. Box 5118
Akron, OH 44334-0118
216-836-5568

USA Bowling
5301 S. 76th St.
Greendale, WI 53129
414-423-3295

Women's International Bowling Congress
5301 S. 76th St.
Greendale, WI 53129
414-421-9000

Young American Bowling Alliance
5301 S. 76th St.
Greendale, WI 53129
414-421-4700

10

Boxing

© Claus Andersen

Boxing dates back more than 5,000 years. It became a more formally organized sport in 18th-century England; bare-knuckle contests were the norm until the 1870s, when padded gloves were introduced.

The sport is contested at both the amateur and professional levels; boxers that become professional cannot return to amateur status. Amateur boxing begins at age eight and continues through several age divisions and weight categories. The length and number of rounds depend on the division.

The object of amateur boxing is to score points by landing scoring blows on the opponent. The boxer with the most points wins. A boxer may also win in other ways (see "Decisions," page 61). The source of rules for this chapter is USA Boxing, the national governing body for the sport.

PROCEDURES

Boxers weigh in on the day of their competition. A boxer must weigh more than the maximum for the weight class below, and no more than the maximum for the weight class he desires to box in.

Boxers draw numbers to determine the bouts in which they will compete. The length and number of rounds are shown in table 10.1.

Table 10.1: Number and Length of Rounds		
Division (ages)	Rounds	Length (min)
Bantam (8 to 10)	3	1
Junior (11 to 12)	3	1
Intermediate (13 to 14)	3	1.5
Senior (15 to 16)	3	2
Novice and subnovice	3	2
Masters (34+)	3	2
Open, feature bout (17 to 33)	5	2
Open (17 to 33)	3	3

Note: A novice is a boxer who has competed in 10 or less sanctioned USA Boxing matches; a subnovice is one who has competed in no sanctioned matches.
Adapted from United States Amateur Boxing, Inc. 1995.

Before a bout begins, boxers touch gloves in the center of the ring.

Count

If a boxer is knocked down during a round (see "Down but Not Out"), the referee begins to count to 10, with one second between numbers, indicating each second with his hand. The count begins one second after the boxer is down. The opponent must go to a neutral corner; the referee will not start, or continue, the count until the opponent does so.

The bout shall not continue before the count of eight, even if the downed boxer rises and is ready to continue before then. If the boxer is unable to continue at the end of the count, the bout is over and the opponent wins.

Down but Not Out

A boxer is considered down if he

- touches the floor with any part of his body other than his feet, as a result of being hit;
- hangs helplessly on the ropes or is outside or partially outside the ropes because of being hit; or if he
- is standing but is semiconscious and the referee feels the boxer cannot continue.

If a boxer is down at the end of a round, the referee will count as normal. If a boxer is ready to continue before the count of eight but then falls before being hit again, the referee resumes counting from the count of eight.

If both boxers are down at the same time, counting continues as long as one remains down. If both remain down past the count of 10, the bout is stopped and the boxer who has the most points wins. If a boxer has three counts in one round, or four counts in a bout, the bout is stopped and the opponent wins.

Fouls

A referee may caution, warn, or disqualify a boxer who commits a foul. A referee may caution a boxer without stopping the bout; he must stop the bout to issue a warning. If a referee warns a boxer about a particular foul, he may not later issue a caution for the same foul. Three cautions for the same foul require a warning. A boxer will be disqualified if he receives three warnings in one bout.

Examples of fouls include

- hitting below the belt, holding, tripping, kicking, butting;
- head butts or blows, hitting with the shoulder, forearm, elbow;
- pushing and shoving;
- pressing an arm or elbow in the opponent's face;

- pressing the opponent's head back over the ropes;
- hitting the opponent's back, neck, kidneys, or back of head;
- hitting with an open glove;
- hitting while holding the ropes;
- hitting an opponent who is down or who is rising;
- holding and hitting;
- locking the opponent's arm or head;
- not stepping back when ordered to break;
- aggressive or offensive language; and
- spitting out the mouthpiece.

Points

A boxer's score is affected by the number of *scoring blows* he lands each round. A scoring blow is one that lands directly with the knuckle part of the closed glove on any part of the front or sides of the head or body above the belt. In case of a flurry of blows from both boxers, the boxer who has had the better exchange in the rally is credited according to the degree of his superiority.

At the end of each round, the more skillful boxer for that round is awarded 20 points and the other boxer proportionately fewer. If boxers are judged equal for that round, they both receive 20 points. No extra points are awarded for a knockdown.

If the winner of a round committed a foul, his opponent receives one point. (If the score was 20-19, it becomes 20-20.) If the loser of a round committed a foul, he loses one point. (If he lost the round, 20-19, the score becomes 20-18.) If the round is tied, the boxer who committed a foul has one point subtracted.

Electronic scoring was introduced in the 1992 Olympics. Five judges record scoring blows on keypads linked to a mainframe computer; in order for a blow to be recorded by the computer, three of five judges must record the blow within a one-second interval. Scores are reported in terms of number of blows recognized by a majority of judges over the course of the bout. For example, a 29-25 win for the Red corner indicates that Red was credited with 29 blows, while Blue was credited with 25.

Decisions

Types of decisions are as follows:

- *Win by points.* The boxer with the most points wins.
- *Win by retirement.* If a boxer quits a bout because of injury or fails to resume after a round break, the opponent wins.
- *Win by referee stopping contest.* A referee may stop a bout if a boxer is being outclassed, injured, or if he has reached the compulsory count limit. A referee may stop a bout for excessive body injury (RSC) or as a result of head blows (RSCH).
- *Win by disqualification.* If a boxer is disqualified, the opponent wins.
- *Win by walkover.* If a boxer fails to appear within three minutes of the bell, the opponent wins.

Stopping a Bout for Injury

If the referee believes a boxer is unable to continue because of injury, he may stop the bout and declare the opponent the winner. This decision is the referee's, although he may consult with a doctor. The ringside physician also has the right to terminate a bout for medical reasons. If the referee consults a doctor, he must abide by the doctor's recommendation.

TERMS

A referee may **caution** a boxer for a foul. The action does not stop for a caution.

A referee begins a **count** one second after a boxer is down. If a boxer is not ready to resume the bout by the count of 10, the bout is over.

A boxer may be **disqualified** for fouls that have resulted in three warnings.

A boxer is **down** when a part of his body other than his feet touch the floor, when he is hanging on the ropes, or when he is standing but semi-conscious and not fit to continue.

A **low blow** is a hit delivered below the beltline. This is a foul.

A boxer receives a **mandatory eight count** after he has been down. If he is ready to go after a count of eight, the bout resumes. Even if he is ready to go before eight, the referee will count to eight before allowing the bout to resume.

A **round** is a determined length of time, depending on the division, in which the boxers compete before breaking. The number of rounds varies depending on the competition.

RSC refers to body injuries to one boxer that are severe or excessive enough to cause the referee to stop the bout and declare the opponent the winner.

RSCH refers to head blows sustained by a boxer sufficient enough to cause the referee to stop the bout and declare the opponent the winner.

A referee may issue a **warning** to a boxer for a foul.

RING

The *ring* is a square, 16 feet to 20 feet long on each side, measured from inside the *ropes* (see figure 10.1). The ring is bordered by at least four ropes, made of manila rope, synthetic, or plastic rope, and not less than one inch in diameter. The apron of the ring extends at least 2 feet beyond the ropes.

The floor of the ring is not more than 4 feet above ground.

BOXERS

Weight classes are as shown in table 10.2. Women may compete against other women, although various medical restrictions apply (e.g., pregnant women may not compete).

Boxers must be clean-shaven, with no beard or goatee, to protect against coarse facial hair cutting the eye or face. (A thin-line mustache is okay.) They may not wear any grease or vaseline. They may wear soft contact lenses.

They must wear a sleeveless *singlet* or *jersey*, and loose-fitting *trunks* that reach not lower than the knees. The beltline of the trunks should not be above the waistline. They must wear *shoes* of soft material, with no spikes or heels.

Approved *headgear* and custom-made or individually fitted *mouthpieces* must be worn. *Gloves* are 10 ounces for weight classes up to 156 pounds, and 12 ounces for heavier weight classes, except for masters competitors, who wear 12-ounce gloves, regardless of weight.

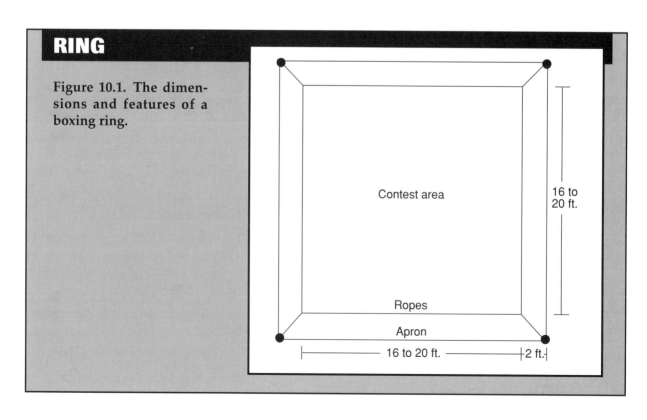

RING

Figure 10.1. The dimensions and features of a boxing ring.

Contest area

16 to 20 ft.

Ropes

Apron

16 to 20 ft.   2 ft.

Table 10.2:	Weight Classes	
Class	Pounds	Kilograms
Light flyweight	106	48
Flyweight	112	51
Bantamweight	119	54
Featherweight	125	57
Lightweight	132	60
Light welterweight	139	63.5
Welterweight	147	67
Light middleweight	156	71
Middleweight	165	75
Light heavyweight	178	81
Heavyweight	201	91
Super heavyweight	over 201	over 91

Adapted from United States Amateur Boxing, Inc. 1995.

OFFICIALS

The *referee* controls the bout. He uses three basic commands: "Stop," "Box," and "Break" (the latter in breaking a clinch). The referee may terminate a match at any time if it is too one-sided or a boxer is endangered. He also issues cautions, warnings, and may disqualify a boxer for fouls.

The *judges* independently judge the merits of the boxers and determine the winner. Either five or three judges are present. A *timekeeper* keeps time for each round and between rounds. During championship events, a three- or five-panel *jury* checks the scorecards of the judges to ensure points and penalties are correctly recorded.

ORGANIZATIONS

International Boxing Federation
134 Evergreen Pl., 9th Fl.
East Orange, NJ 07018
201-414-0300

International Veteran Boxers Association
35 Brady Ave.
New Rochelle, NY 10805
914-235-6820

USA Boxing
1 Olympic Plaza
Colorado Springs, CO 80909
719-578-4506

11

Canoeing & Kayaking

© Claus Andersen

Canoeing and kayaking offer several forms of competition, including flatwater, slalom, and wildwater racing. This chapter will focus on those three types of competitions, using rules from the International Canoe Federation to delineate the regulations for each event.

Flatwater competition takes place on an unobstructed course; the fastest time wins. In *slalom racing*, competitors negotiate a rapid river course defined by gates. The object is to record the fastest time and not accrue any penalties in negotiating the course. The time of the run, in seconds, plus the penalty points, determines a competitor's final score; low score wins. Competitors in *wildwater racing* (known as "downriver racing" in Europe) attempt to demonstrate mastery of their boat while running a prescribed whitewater course in the shortest time possible.

PROCEDURES

Procedures for flatwater competition are as follows. Procedural differences for slalom and wildwater racing are noted immediately after the flatwater procedures.

Flatwater

Men's flatwater events include 200-meter, 500-meter, 1,000-meter, and 5,000-meter; women's races include 200-meter, 500-meter, and 5,000-meter. A race involves at least three kayaks or canoes; if heats are necessary, lots are drawn to place competitors into the heats. However, heats are not used for 5,000-meter races. Lots are also used to determine the starting position.

To start a race, the bows of the boats must be on the starting line and stationary. An official uses a starter's pistol to begin the race. The starter may recall the race to realign the boats. If a racer makes two false starts, she is disqualified. If a racer breaks a paddle within the first 25 meters, the starter will recall the race.

During the Race

A competitor may not take pace or receive assistance from boats not in the race. Such boats may not proceed on the course, even outside the boundary buoys. In races up to 1,000 meters, competitors must stay in their marked lanes. In 5,000-meter races, they may go outside their lane, as long as they do not obstruct other competitors.

In races with turns, competitors must make the turns counterclockwise. If two competitors are approaching a turn together, the competitor on the outside must leave room for the competitor on the inside if the inside competitor's bow is even with the front edge of the cockpit of the outside boat. A competitor may touch a turning buoy as long as he doesn't gain an advantage from the touch.

A craft that is being passed by a kayak or canoe cannot obstruct the craft overtaking it. The craft that is passing must, however, keep clear of the boat it is overtaking. A competitor who causes a collision can be disqualified.

Finish

A competitor finishes a race when her craft's bow crosses the finish line with all the crew members in the boat. In case of a tie for a position that determines which boat will advance to the next level of competition, and not enough lanes are available to accommodate both boats, the two boats race again. This race takes place one hour after the last race of the day. If the two tie again, lots are drawn to determine who advances.

Slalom

In individual competition, each craft is allowed two runs, the best of which counts. In team competition, either one or two runs can be allowed. Team members may be substituted for between runs.

Competitors may make standing starts only. Starts may be directly upstream or downstream; starts angled into or against the current are not allowed. Boats are held in position by the starter's assistant until the start. In team events, the second and third boats must be stationary until the first boat begins. Start intervals are 45 seconds or greater.

Negotiating Gates

Competitors negotiate gates according to the established direction. A gate consists of two suspended poles painted with five green and five white rings for downstream gates and five red and five white rings for upstream gates. The poles are between 1.2 and 3.5 meters apart. They are 3.5 to 5 centimeters in diameter. The lower end of the pole should be about 15 centimeters above the water.

The gates are numbered, and competitors must negotiate them in numerical order. Negotiation begins when a competitor crosses the line between the two poles or when a competitor's boat, body, or paddle touches a pole. Negotiation of a gate ends when a competitor begins to negotiate the next gate, or when he finishes the race.

To correctly negotiate a gate, a competitor must

- maneuver his boat and body between the poles on the correct side of the gate;
- cross his boat between the poles at the same time as his body crosses between;

- pass at least his entire head between the poles, and in the proper direction; and
- not touch a pole with his body, paddle, or boat for a faultless negotiation.

Penalties

Competitors are penalized for incorrect gate negotiations and other acts as follows.

5 points—touching one or both poles while correctly negotiating the gate. Repeated touching of the same pole or poles is penalized only once.

50 points—touching one or both poles while incorrectly negotiating the gate. Intentionally pushing a gate to facilitate negotiation, crossing a gate line while the body is upside down, and negotiating the gate in the wrong direction are each a 50-point penalty. Missing a gate and failing to cross the finish line within 15 seconds of teammates are also 50-point penalties.

A competitor is not penalized for undercutting a gate or for making repeated attempts at a gate, as long as she does not touch the poles or pass her body across the line between the poles. A competitor cannot be penalized more than 50 points at any one gate.

On the Course

A competitor that is being overtaken must give way if the section judge whistles for him to do so. However, the competitor who is passing must be attempting to properly negotiate the course. If he is passing because the competitor ahead has missed a gate, he cannot hinder the competitor as he approaches. Any competitor who is hindered may repeat the run if authorized to do so by the chief judge.

A craft is considered capsized when it has turned upside down and the competitor has left the boat. After a capsize, a competitor may not negotiate any further gates. An Eskimo roll is not a capsize.

Finish and Point Calculations

A competitor finishes when her body crosses the finish line (in team competition, when the first body in the boat crosses the line). In team events, all three craft must finish within 15 seconds of each other. The time for team events begins when the first boat starts and ends when the last boat finishes.

A competitor's or team's point total is figured by adding the time of the run, in seconds, plus penalty points. For example, a running time of 135.8 seconds plus 55 penalty points equals a final score of 190.8. If two competitors are tied, the one with the better non-counting run is placed ahead of the other competitor. A competitor who accepts outside assistance or leaves her boat is disqualified.

Wildwater

The start is directly upstream or downstream; no angled starts are allowed. Boats are held in the starting position until the start; competitors may use only standing starts. Individual starts are separated by at least 30 seconds; team starts have intervals of at least one minute.

A craft being overtaken by another craft must allow passage if the competitor on the overtaking craft shouts, "Free!" If a competitor sees another in real danger, he must help him, or risk disqualification for life. A competitor may resume competition after capsizing. If two or more competitors record the same score, the tie stands.

TERMS

A **brace** is a defensive maneuver in which a kayaker uses a paddle blade and hip action to keep upright.

A boat is **broached** when it is pinned to a rock.

Class I to VI is the whitewater river rating system, from easiest to most difficult.

The **deck** is the top of the boat that keeps the water out.

An **eddy** is a calm spot in whitewater, just downstrean of a rock.

Flotation bags, filled with air, are fitted on either side of a kayak's walls to provide buoyancy in case of a capsize.

A **J lean** is named for the shape of a competitor's spine when she leans into a boat tilt with her body weight centered over the boat.

Kayak paddle blades are **offset**, which means the blades face in different directions. The difference in blade direction is usually around 70 degrees.

A **spray skirt** fits around the rim of the boat and around the competitor's waist to keep water out.

A **sweep** is the primary stroke used to turn a boat.

COURSE

Following are course descriptions for Flatwater, Slalom, and Wildwater racing.

Flatwater

The start and finish are at right angles to the course and are marked by red flags. The 25-meter distance, from which competitors can be recalled for a fresh start, is marked by yellow flags. Each boat has an individual course at least 5 meters wide at the beginning.

For races up to 1,000 meters, the course is straight and in one direction. For races beyond 1,000 meters, turning points are permitted. Turning points are marked by at least six diagonally divided flags, with one half in red and one half in yellow.

Slalom

The course must be entirely negotiable and provide the same conditions for right-handed and left-handed paddlers. Ideally, the course should require reverse maneuvers and consist of natural and artificial obstacles (see figure 11.1). The course must be at least 300 meters wide and 600 meters long, with 20 to 25 gates. The last gate must be at least 25 meters before the finish.

The current velocity must not be less than 2 meters per second. Competitors are allowed a training run on the course before the race.

Wildwater

The course must be at least 3 kilometers long, and part of it must be Class III difficulty. As an alternative to a single run, competitors may be required to make two runs of 500 to 1,000 meters each, with the results being an aggregate of both runs. This latter event is called a Wildwater Sprint event. A boat must be able to navigate the complete course without touching bottom. Dangerous passes may be marked with gates to indicate the correct channel. Competitors may take a training run a day before the competition.

Figure 11.1.   Ideally, both natural and artificial obstacles should be used in a slalom course.

COMPETITORS

In slalom and wildwater racing, competitors must wear safety helmets and buoyancy jackets. Competitors must be able to free themselves immediately from their boats at all times. Competitions are held in the following classifications.

Flatwater:

Men—K1, K2, K4, C1, C2, C4

Women—K1, K2, K4

Slalom:

Individual men—K1, C1, C2

Individual women—K1

Team men—3 × K1, 3 × C1, 3 × C2

Team women—3 × K1

EQUIPMENT

Craft specifications for flatwater, slalom, and wildwater racing are shown in tables 11.1, 11.2, and 11.3.

Flatwater Boats. Canoes and kayaks may be constructed of any material; electric or electronic devices, such as pumps, are not allowed. Kayaks may have one steering rudder and may be propelled only with double-blade paddles. Canoes

Table 11.1: Flatwater Boat Specifications

Boat	Maximum length (cm)	Minimum beam (cm)	Minimum weight (kg)
K1	520	51	12
K2	650	55	18
K4	1,100	60	30
C1	520	75	16
C2	650	75	20
C4	900	75	30

Adapted from International Canoe Federation 1993.

Table 11.2: Slalom Boat Specifications

Boat	Maximum length (m)	Minimum beam (m)	Minimum weight (kg)
K1	4.00	.60	9
C1	4.00	.70	10
C2	4.58	.80	15

Table 11.3: Wildwater Boat Specifications

Boat	Maximum length (m)	Minimum beam (m)	Minimum weight (kg)
K1	4.50	.60	10
C1	4.30	.70	11
C2	5.00	.70	18

may not have a steering rudder or any guiding apparatus; Canadian canoes may be propelled only with single-blade paddles. The paddles may not be fixed to the boat.

Slalom Boats. The boats must have a handle attached no more than 30 centimeters from the bow and the stern. Handles may be an integral part of the boat construction, or loops of rope. A competitor cannot tape the handles. If a competitor breaks or loses a paddle, he may use an extra paddle that he carries on the boat.

Wildwater Boats. Wildwater boats must be rudderless. As with flatwater boats, kayaks are propelled only with a double-blade paddle and Canadian canoes only with a single-blade paddle.

OFFICIALS

Officials who supervise competitions include *chief officials, starters, aligners, 25-meter judges* for flatwater racing, *course* and *turning point judges, finishing line judges, timekeepers,* and *boat controllers.*

ORGANIZATIONS

American Canoe Association
7432 Alban Station Road, #B226
Springfield, VA 22150
703-451-0141

American Whitewater Affiliation
Box 85
Phoenicia, NY 12464
914-688-5569

International Canoe Federation
Dozsa Gyorgy UT 1-3
1143 Budapest
Hungary
36-1-163-4832

U.S. Canoe & Kayak Team
201 S. Capitol Ave., #470
Indianapolis, IN 46225
317-237-5690

12

Cricket

Courtesy of the C.C. Morris Cricket Library Association

At a glance—but only at a glance—cricket may seem a bit like baseball. It is played on a grassy field and has, after all, bowlers (who act much as pitchers do in baseball) and batsmen. Cricket, like baseball, is played in innings, and the team in the field tries to get the batsmen out and stop them from scoring runs; the team with the most runs wins.

But when you notice rules governing play with leads of 200 runs or more, and notes for test matches extending up to five days, and you further note that all this takes place in a game lasting only one or two innings (with, of course, necessary meal intervals), you begin to appreciate that cricket is indeed quite distinct from baseball.

Cricket, in fact, is the older of the two sports, with records of games being played in London in the early 1700s. The Marylebone Cricket Club (MCC), formed in 1787 in London, drew up the code by which the game is played and has continued as the governing body for the sport ever since. The first official cricket club in America was formed at Haverford College near Philadelphia in 1833, but the sport has never caught on in the states as it has in other countries. The rules drawn up by the MCC are the source for this chapter's rules.

PROCEDURES

Each team officially has *11 players*. Teams play either one or two *innings*; an inning is finished when all 11 batters on the batting team have come to bat and 10 have been put out, one after the other (the last batter does not have to be put out; more on that later). The team in the field then bats in the same way.

Two *wickets* are set up 22 feet from each other; between the wickets is a stretch of turf called the *pitch*. A *batsman* stands at each wicket; the *bowler* for the team in the field, much like a baseball pitcher, delivers a ball to the batsman standing near the opposite wicket. The bowler must deliver the ball with a straight, locked arm; he may deliver it either in the air or on a bounce.

The batsman may swing and miss any number of times; he cannot "strike out," as in baseball. He also cannot hit a "foul ball," because all territory is "fair"—even if he hits the ball to the side or behind him. Batsmen do not have to run after hitting the ball, but if they choose to, they *score a run* each time they cross their opposite *popping creases* (see figure 12.1, page 76). For every time they both make it safely from one wicket to the other while the ball is in play, their team scores a run.

While the batsmen have to carry their bats with them when they run, this can be an advantage, because the bat is considered an extension of their arm, and they can reach over with their bats to touch the popping crease to score a run. Each time a batsman hits a fly ball over the *boundary line* (similar to a "home run" in baseball), his team gets six runs; each time a ground ball goes over the boundary line, his team scores four runs. This is true whether or not a *fieldsman* has touched the ball or is in possession of it when it crosses the boundary line.

A batsman continues to hit until the fielding team can get him out. One way to get a batsman out is for the bowler to sneak a delivery by him, knocking at least one *bail* off his wicket. (Bails are cylindrical pieces of wood set in grooves on the tops of the wickets.) Other ways to get a batsman out are detailed in "Outs" on page 75.

Because a batsman is at each wicket, the direction of bowling is reversed every six deliveries.

Scoring Plays

A team scores one or more runs in these situations:

Lost ball. When the fielding team claims "lost ball," the batting team gets six runs—or the number that it had already scored on the play, if that's more than six.

Penalty runs. A team scores one run when the opposing bowler delivers a *wide ball* (out of reach of the batsman) or a *no ball* (illegal delivery); a team adds five runs to what it has already scored on the play when a fieldsman illegally stops the ball.

Bye. Any number of runs may score when a fair delivery does not touch the batsman or his bat and gets by the wicket-keeper. (This is similar to a "passed ball" in baseball.)

Leg-bye. Similar to a bye, except in this case the batsman is hit by the delivery. He must make an attempt to get out of the way, or to hit the ball with his bat.

A bowler throws six fair deliveries toward one wicket, and then another fielder becomes the bowler and throws six fair deliveries toward the opposite wicket. This change of direction is called an *over*, and this pattern continues throughout the match. The fielding team may change bowlers for every over, and a bowler may throw multiple overs, but he may not throw two overs in a row.

A *wicket-keeper* acts something like a baseball catcher; he is the only player with gloves (he has, in fact, one on each hand). He shuttles from wicket to wicket after every over; he is always behind the wicket opposite the bowler.

Batsmen always bat in pairs, one at each wicket; therefore the last (11th) batsman does not have to be put out, because he cannot bat alone. Once the 10th is retired, the inning is over. Even so, a normal two-inning match can go on for days. At the end of the match, the team with the most runs (quite often a team will score more than 200 runs) wins. If the team batting second needs 200 runs to win, and scores 200 when, say, its seventh batsman is hitting, then the contest is over and its win is scored "200 for 7," signifying it scored the winning run on its seventh wicket, or batsman. The teams draw, regardless of the score, if it is not possible to finish the match. If the match is finished with the score even, it is a tie.

"Limited overs" cricket, typically played in one day, is becoming more popular. The length of the game is controlled by the number of overs each team is allowed. A "40-over" match is one in which each team bats for 40 overs (that is, each team gets 240 deliveries). Typically, not all batsmen get to bat in limited overs.

TERMS

A **back-up** is the non-striker's, or non-batsman's, "lead-off" of his popping crease when he expects to run. As the bowler releases his delivery, the non-striker goes over his popping crease, taking a few steps towards the opposite wicket.

A **beamer** is a fast, head-high delivery.

A **bouncer** is a "brushback pitch" delivered short and fast so it will bounce up at the batsman's head.

A **boundary** is a "four" (ground ball hit over the boundary line) or a "six" (fly ball over the boundary line).

A batsman is **bowled** when the delivery gets by him and knocks a bail off his wicket. This is similar to a baseball strikeout.

The **center** (or middle) **stump** is the center pole of the wicket.

A batsman makes a **century** when he scores 100 runs in a single at-bat (roughly equivalent to rushing for 100 yards in American football).

A **cutter** is a medium-paced delivery spinning or bouncing into or away from the batsman.

A **dead pitch** is one that bounces low and straight—an easy pitch to hit.

A **declaration** is a strategy in which the team batting may stop before all of its batsmen are out; this is usually done to allow enough time to get the opponents out.

A **duck** signifies an at-bat in which the batsman doesn't score any runs.

Fall of wicket refers to an out; "the sixth wicket fell" means the batting team has made its sixth out.

Follow on is a strategy in a two-innings match that allows the team that bats first, if ahead by a certain number of runs, to reverse the second-inning batting sequence.

A **four** is a ground ball that goes beyond the boundary line; this automatically scores four runs.

A **grubber** is a delivery that's rolled on the ground.

A **hat trick** occurs when a bowler takes three wickets on three successive deliveries.

A **leg-bye** is a run scored from a delivery that hits the batsman's body.

The **leg stump** is the pole of the wicket closest to the batsman.

A **maiden** is an over in which no runs are scored off the bat.

No ball signifies an illegal delivery; the batting team gets an automatic run.

Off side is the half of the playing area that the batsman is facing.

The **off stump** is the pole of the wicket farthest from the batsman.

On side is the half of the playing area behind the batsman.

An **over** is a set of six, fairly delivered balls to one wicket. The direction of the deliveries switches to the opposite wicket at the end of each over.

The **pitch** is the area between the two wickets.

A **quick single** is a run scored on a shallow hit, similar to a baseball bunt.

A **shooter** is a fast delivery that stays low.

A **short run,** which does not count as a run, occurs when a batsman fails to touch part of his body or his bat behind the popping crease when running.

A **six** is six runs automatically scored when a fly ball goes beyond a boundary line.

A **sticky wicket** is a damp delivery that's drying out. It bounces erratically and is difficult to hit.

Stone-walling is batting with the intention of not getting out, rather than trying to score runs.

A **strike rate** is the average number of runs a batter makes per 100 deliveries.

A **stump** is the name for a wicket's three individual poles. A wicket is often referred to as "the stumps."

BOWLERS

Rules applied to bowlers, and strategies applied by them, that were not already stated in the "Procedures" section, include the following:

The bowler may take a runup before delivering, but he must have at least part of his front foot behind the popping crease, and part of his back foot inside the return creases, when he releases the ball. Failure to do so results in the umpire calling a *no ball*, which gives the opponents a penalty run. He will also be called for a no ball if he fails to deliver the ball with a straight, locked arm. A no-ball does not count as part of the over.

The bowler must deliver the ball within reach of the batsman. Failure to do so will result in the umpiring calling a *wide*, which also results in a penalty run for the opponents. A wide does not count as part of the over.

However, the bowler most often will try to "attack the off stump" (keep the ball outside) and bounce the ball at the wicket, not *too* close to the

Dead Ball

A ball is ruled dead when

- it settles in the hands of the wicket-keeper or the bowler;
- it goes over the boundary;
- a batsman is out;
- it lodges in the equipment or clothing of a batsman or umpire;
- it lodges in a protective helmet of a fieldsman;
- the ball is lost; and when
- the umpire calls "over" or "time."

batter. Most bowlers don't want to bowl short; when it bounces far from the batter, a high, easily hit long hop results. They also usually stay away from *full tosses*, which are deliveries that reach the batsman in the air; these are easiest of all to hit. Bowlers often try to vary the angle of their deliveries, sometimes bowling *over the wicket* (e.g., on the right side of the wicket, if the batsman is left-handed), and sometimes *around the wicket* (on the left side, using the same example).

BATSMEN

Following is a brief glimpse at the strategies a batsman employs.

A skilled batsman doesn't just swing indiscriminately "for the fences," as many American baseball players do (which is good, because there typically *are* no fences in cricket!). Rather, he may start out swinging with a high-percentage, vertical stroke, deflecting or spoiling a bowler's good deliveries, and using various strokes for various deliveries, including baseball-like "cross-bat" strokes, "sweep or reverse-sweep" strokes to sweep the ball to his left or right; he may even go over the popping crease to meet the ball and drive it straight over the bowler's head.

Regardless of the stroke or situation, the batsman doesn't want to give the fieldsmen a chance to catch a ball in the air. The skilled batsman may score a century (100 runs) during an at-bat; he may also be able to "carry his bat" (outlast all his teammates until he's the last "not-out" batsman).

FIELDSMEN

The wicket-keeper is the only player who wears gloves; he wears one on each hand and acts much as a baseball catcher. He positions himself opposite the bowler and behind the batsman who is batting. The other nine fieldsmen vary their positions, according to the skills of the bowler and the batsman, but in loose terms they fit into these positions:

Slips. One or more slips play behind the wicket-keeper, and to the off side of the field (the right side, from the striking batsman's point of view). The faster the bowler is, the more slips might be employed, expecting the batsmen to hit, in baseball terminology, "foul balls."

Gullys. A gully stands behind the slip for deeper-hit balls.

Points, covers, and mid-offs. A point, cover, and mid-off fieldsman stand on the off side, beginning with the point about 15 yards from the batsman; these fieldsmen are 5 to 10 yards apart from each other. They attempt to stop balls from getting past their side of the field.

Mid-ons, mid-wickets, square legs, and fine legs. These positions are on the on side, or leg-side, of the field. Mid-on plays farthest from the striking batsman; square legs and fine legs play closest. A fine leg plays behind the batsman, while a square leg plays in front.

A team may shift to play a batsman *finer* (more parallel to the line of the pitch), or *squarer* (at more of a right angle to the line of the pitch).

Other rules regarding fieldsmen include the following:

- No more than two *on-side fieldsmen* may be behind the popping crease when the bowler delivers the ball. The umpire will call "no ball" if more than two are on side behind the popping crease.
- Until the batsman makes contact with the ball, or the ball strikes the batsman or goes past him, no fieldsman besides the bowler may be on the pitch. Penalty: A "no ball" call.
- When fieldsmen's protective helmets are not in use, they are placed behind the wicket-keeper. If a ball in play strikes a helmet, the batting team is awarded five penalty runs.

OUTS

A batsman is out when he

- allows a delivery to knock a bail off his wicket ("out, bowled");
- hits a ball caught in the air by a fieldsman ("out, caught");
- hits his own wicket and knocks off a bail ("out, hit wicket");
- uses his body to block a delivery from hitting his wicket, even if unintentional ("out, leg before wicket");
- is not over the popping crease when a fieldsman throws a ball and knocks the bail off the wicket toward which the batsman is approaching, or when a fieldsman holds the ball and knocks the bail off by hitting it ("run out");
- crosses the popping crease while trying to hit the ball and the wicket-keeper grabs the ball and knocks the bail off his wicket before the batsman can return ("out, stumped");
- touches a ball in play ("out, handled the ball");
- hits a ball twice ("out, hit the ball twice");
- intentionally interferes with a fielder ("out, obstructing the field"); or when he
- breaks his wicket while receiving, or preparing to receive, a delivery ("out, hit wicket").

FAIR PLAY

The following rules fall under the category of fair play:

Changing the ball's condition. No player may rub the ball on the ground, rub artificial substance on the ball, or take any other action to alter the condition of the ball, except to dry a wet ball or remove mud from a ball.

Obstructing batsman in running. If a fieldsman intentionally obstructs a batsman in running, the umpire will signal "dead ball" and allow any completed runs, plus the run in progress, to score.

Bowling fast, short-pitched balls. This is not fair if it is intended to, or likely to, injure the batsman. The umpire may call a "no ball" and caution the bowler.

Bowling fast, high, full pitches. This is a delivery that passes, on the fly, above waist height of a batsman. The umpire will call "no ball" and caution the bowler.

Wasting time. This is unfair and results in a caution.

Players damaging the pitch. Any player damaging the pitch to assist a bowler will be cautioned by the umpire.

Batsman unfairly stealing a run. Unless the bowler makes a play on him, the non-striker may not attempt to steal a run during the bowler's runup. The umpire will signal "dead ball" and order the batsmen to return to their original wickets.

FIELD

The field is an open, circular expanse of closely cropped turf divided into two equal halves by an imaginary line running down the middle of the *pitch* (see figure 12.1). From a right-handed striking batsman's point of view as he faces the bowler, the right side of the ground is the *off side*; the left side is the *on* (or *leg*) *side*. The field is encircled by a roped or chalked *boundary line*. There is no official size for the field, but most high-level contests are played on fields with diameters of 150 to 200 yards or more.

Wickets are placed opposite each other, 22 yards apart. Each wicket is made of three poles, or *stumps*. The stump closest to the batsman is the *leg stump*; the stump in the middle is the *center stump*; and the stump farthest from the batsman is the *off stump*. The wickets are 28 inches high and 9 inches wide; set in grooves on the tops of the stumps are two *bails*. These bails are 4.38 inches.

Running 4 feet in front of, and parallel to, each wicket is a 12-foot chalk line: the *popping crease*. Any time a batsman is away from his wicket and beyond his popping crease, he may be put out. If any part of his body or his bat is behind the line, he may not be put out. Intersecting the popping crease are two lines, 8 feet, 8 inches apart, running back toward the wicket. These are the *return creases*. These creases mark the area in which the bowler may operate.

The *bowling crease* runs parallel to, and 4 feet behind, the popping crease. The wickets are set on this crease. The *pitch* is the stretch of turf between the two wickets; it's usually the width of the area between the two return creases. The grass on the pitch is very short and smooth; in many instances the pitch is artificial turf.

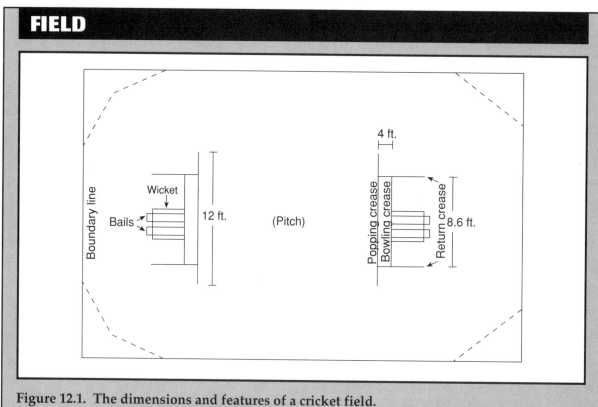

FIELD

Figure 12.1. The dimensions and features of a cricket field.
Adapted from Bowling Green State University 1993.

PLAYERS

Officially there are 11 players per side. The lineup is set before each inning and may not be changed without the consent of the opposing captain. If both sides agree, more or less than 11 may play, but no more than 11 may field. The traditional cricket uniform is *white* or *cream pants, shirts, sweaters,* and *shoes.* Club insignias are on players' *caps.*

A *substitute* may field for a teammate only if the teammate is injured or ill. If a fieldsman has to leave for another legitimate reason, and the opposing captain consents, a team may substitute for the fieldsman. However, no substitute may play for the wicket-keeper, or be allowed to bat or bowl.

A player who was substituted for may return to bat, bowl, or field. However, if he was gone longer than 15 minutes, he must be on the field for the length of time he was gone before he may bowl. A *runner* may run for a batsman who is ill or injured. He must wear the same protective equipment that the batsman wears. An injured batsman is out when his runner is put out.

EQUIPMENT

The *ball* is a hard ball, weighing between 5.5 and 5.75 ounces and measuring between 8.8 and 9 inches in circumference; see figure 12.2. It is red, with a single-stitched seam down the middle, made of cork and wool and bound in leather.

The *bat* is paddle-shaped. It is made of willow and may be of any weight. Its maximum length is 38 inches and maximum width is 4.25 inches.

The batsman wears *protective gear:* padded leg guards, padded gloves, and a helmet with a face guard. It is not illegal to hit a batsman with a delivery. The wicket-keeper wears two flat, long-cuffed leather *gloves.* (He is not required to throw, but he is required to scoop deliveries from the bowler.) He also wears *leg guards.*

OFFICIALS

Two *umpires* officiate a match; one umpire stands near each wicket.

ORGANIZATIONS

Association of Cricket Umpires and Scorers
5 The Glade
Enfield
Middlesex, Greater London EN2 7QH, England
44 181 363 9397

Marylebone Cricket Club
Lord's Cricket Ground
London NW8 8QN, England
44 071 289 5686

World Cricket League
301 W. 57th St., Ste. 5-D
New York, NY 10019
212-582-8556

13

Cross-Country Skiing

© Cheyenne Rouse

A petroglyph on a rock wall in Norway depicts a skier on long skis. Dating to 2000 B.C., this petroglyph attests to the longevity of Nordic, or cross-country, skiing. Skiing has long been used as transportation in snow, both in flatlands and mountainous regions. Modern cross-country ski techniques are, in fact, borrowed from ancient, functional methods of skiing.

Scandinavian immigrants sparked interest in cross-country skiing in the United States in the 19th century. Advances in equipment helped to create two distinct forms of skiing: downhill (Alpine) and cross-country. The latter experienced a boom in the United States in the 1970s, and in the 1980s two forms of cross-country skiing evolved: classical (traditional) skiing in tracks and freestyle (skating) out of tracks, on groomed trails. Nordic downhill, which combines both Alpine and Nordic elements, has also emerged as a type of skiing.

Competitions include individual, relay, and pursuit events, as well as combination events, which take place over two days and include both classical and freestyle forms of skiing. Regardless of the competition, the object is to record the fastest time over the course. The rules source for this chapter is the United States Ski Association, the national governing body for the sport.

PROCEDURES

This section includes procedures for the start, the race itself, and the finish. Depending on the type of start employed, a draw is held to determine starting order.

Starting

The starter calls "Attention" 10 seconds before the start, then counts down beginning at 5. The competitor's feet must be stationary and behind the start line; the poles should be over the start line and stationary. If electric timing is used, the competitor may take off anywhere from 3 seconds before to 3 seconds after the command to go. If he starts more than 3 seconds before, he must go behind an extension of the start line outside the start gate.

The following starts are used in competitions.

Single or double start. One or two skiers begin, and after a specified interval—either 30 or 60 seconds—another skier or pair of skiers starts.

Group or mass start. Competitors are divided into groups. Individual starting places are at least 1.5 meters apart. The start line is an arc of a circle, with a radius of 100 meters. For the *classical technique,* the first 100 to 200 meters is marked with parallel tracks that the competitors must follow. The number of tracks are cut in half over the next 100 meters and converge into two or three tracks shortly after that. For the *freestyle technique,* competitors ski in 100 to 200 meters of parallel tracks; they cannot use skating techniques in the tracks. The course then opens up into at least 100 meters without tracks.

Pursuit start. The winner of the first combined competition starts first; the second-place finisher starts second; and so on. The start intervals are the same as the differences between the competitors' times from the first day's results. The first 200 meters must be prepared at least 6 meters wide. A *modified pursuit start* may be used when time differences are substantial. The bottom half of the field may use a mass start one minute after the last person from the top half of the field has started.

Reverse finish order start. The slowest competitor from the first day begins first; then the next slow-est; and so on. They start in intervals of 10, 15, or 30 seconds. A modified version of this is to have the bottom half of the field begin in a mass start, and then after two minutes pass, the first skier from the top half begins, followed in intervals by the rest.

Racing

Competitors use one of two skiing techniques: classical or freestyle. *Classical skiing* includes what most people associate with traditional cross-country skiing: using a diagonal stride, double-poling, and using a herringbone technique with-out a gliding phase. Skiers cannot skate in a classical race. For individual competitions, ski-ers follow a single track. *Freestyle skiing* employs skating methods, including marathon and no-pole skating. This is normally a faster method than classical skiing.

Competitors must follow the marked course from start to finish, using their marked skis and their own means of propulsion. They cannot be paced or pushed. In individual competitions, a competi-tor may exchange poles, but not skis. During re-lays and combined competitions, a competitor may exchange one ski if it is broken or damaged.

A competitor may not wax, scrape, or clean her skis during competition, with one exception: In classical skiing, a competitor may scrape her skis to remove snow and ice and add wax if neces-sary. She must do this on her own, outside the track.

A competitor who is being overtaken must give way on the first demand, unless he is in the final 200 meters of the course. This is true in classical competitions even if two tracks are in use.

Finishing

The final 200 meters should be as straight as pos-sible. For classical competitions, the final 200 meters is set with three tracks; for freestyle com-petitions, the final 200 meters is prepared at least 9 meters wide.

A competitor finishes when he contacts the elec-tric beam in electric timing, or, in hand timing, when his first foot crosses the finish line. Times are recorded to one-tenth of a second.

TERMS

A **christie** is a skidded turn in which both skis skid on the same edges.

Cross-country downhill skiing is a combination of Alpine and Nordic skiing also known as "telemarking."

A **diagonal stride** is the most common cross-country maneuver for gliding across flat terrain and up hills. It employs arm and leg actions similar to walking.

A **diagonal V** is a skating maneuver in which the skier glides aggressively uphill with the skis in a V-shaped position.

Double poling is a manuever in which a competitor uses both arms to push simultaneously on the poles to provide momentum.

A **gliding herringbone** is a maneuver used to slide uphill with skis in a V shape.

A **herringbone** is a maneuver used to step uphill with skis in a V shape.

A **kick double pole** refers to pushing off with both poles while also pushing off from the leg to provide more power. This is also known as single-step double pole.

A **marathon skate** is a technique that combines double poling with an extra push from an angled or skating ski. Skiers use this to gain extra power in tracks.

Poling refers to a skier planting the poles to increase momentum or to guide through a turn.

The **power side** is the side on which poling occurs during skating moves.

Sideslipping refers to skidding on the skis to the side and forward down a hill.

Sidestepping refers to lifting one ski at a time across the snow to move sideways.

A **skate turn** is a technique used to accelerate around turns, using the skis in a V shape. The competitor steps off one ski and onto the other, bringing the first ski parallel.

Skating with no poles occurs when the skier steps off one ski, glides onto the other, and then glides back to the first ski.

A **snowplow** is a downhill maneuver a skier uses to control speed by angling the skis in an A shape and pressing them into the snow.

A **telemark turn** occurs when the skier sinks into a curtsy and the skis form one long curve.

V1 is a skating maneuver that combines skating with double poling. The skier poles once for every two steps. This maneuver is done on groomed snow with no tracks.

V2 is a fast skating technique that combines double poling with skating. The skier poles twice for every two steps. As with V1, this maneuver is done on groomed, trackless snow.

A **wedge turn** is a turn made with the skis in an A-shape.

COURSE

Cross-country courses range from 5 to 50 kilometers; they are marked with various colored boards, arrows, and ribbons, depending on the competition. A course must be at least three to four meters wide and prepared so that skiers can safely compete. An individual's two ski tracks are set 17 centimeters to 30 centimeters apart, measured from the middle of each track. The tracks are 2 centimeters to 5 centimeters deep.

A typical course consists of

- one-third uphills, with climbs between 9 and 18 percent, plus some steeper, short climbs;
- one-third rolling terrain, with short climbs and downhills and height differences of 1 to 9 meters ; and
- one-third varied downhills.

Table 13.1 shows rules for height differences, maximum climbs, and total climbs.

COMPETITORS

Events include the following:

Men—10-kilometer, 15-kilometer, 30-kilometer, 50-kilometer, 70-kilometer; 4 × 10-kilometer relay; pursuit races; and overall

Distance (km)	Maximum height differential (m)	Maximum single climb (m)	Maximum total climb (m)
5	100	50	150 to 225
10	150	80	250 to 450
15	200	100	400 to 650
30	200	100	800 to 1,200
50 and longer	200	100	140 to 1,800

Table 13.1: Height and Climb Regulations

Adapted from United States Ski and Snowboard Association 1993.

Women—5-kilometer, 10-kilometer, 15-kilometer, 20-kilometer, 50-kilometer; 4 × 5-kilometer relay; pursuit races; and overall

Disabled men—5-kilometer, 10-kilometer, 10-kilometer pursuit, 20-kilometer, 30-kilometer; 3 × 5-kilometer relay; and overall

Disabled women—5-kilometer, 7.5-kilometer pursuit, 10-kilometer, 20-kilometer; 3 × 5-kilometer; and overall

Competition is categorized in junior, senior, and masters divisions. *Junior classifications* include the following:

Junior 5	9 to 10 years old
Junior 4	11 to 12 years old
Junior 3	13 to 14 years old
Junior 2	15 to 16 years old
Junior 1	17 to 18 years old
Older Junior	19 to 20 years old

Seniors are at least 21 years old during the competition year. *Masters* are 30 or older. Masters divisions are split into five-year categories (30-to-34, 35-to-39, and so on).

EQUIPMENT

Skis may be made of any material. They must be at least as long as the height of the skier, minus 10 centimeters; they cannot be longer than 230 centimeters. The middle of the ski must be be-tween 43 and 47 millimeters wide. The *tips* must be curved at least 5 centimeters for classical skis or 3 centimeters for freestyle skis. The *tail* must not rise more than 3 centimeters. Skis must weigh at least 750 grams per pair.

Both skis must be constructed in the same way and be of the same length. Edges may not face upward. The *running surface* can be smooth or slightly grooved. Scale patterns, to aid climbing, are allowed. There are no limitations for *boots* and *bindings*.

A skier's *poles* must be of equal length; they may not be longer than the competitor's height, nor shorter than hip-to-ski. The poles' length must be constant; they may not have telescopic quali-ties. They also may not have any springs or me-chanical devices to assist in pushing off. Poles have no weight restrictions.

Poles may be constructed with differences be-tween them. A grip must attach to the shaft, but there are no limits on the grip's material or de-sign nor on the shaft's material.

OFFICIALS

A competition committee is responsible for conducting the technical aspects of the com-petition. The committee includes a *chief of com-petition*, a *competition secretary*, and *chiefs of course, timekeeping, stadium*, and, at large com-petitions, *security*.

ORGANIZATIONS

American Ski Association
P.O. Box 480067
910 15th St., Ste. 500
Denver, CO 80202
303-629-7669

U.S. Skiing
P.O. Box 100
Park City, UT 84060
801-649-9090

14

Curling

© Mary Langenfeld

Curling dates back to 16th-century Scotland; originally it was played on frozen ponds, and players used stones of varying shapes, which often curved, or curled—hence, the name "curling"—as they slid down the ice. Players used brooms to clear the snow in the stone's path.

The game was introduced by immigrants to North America in the 18th century. By the 1850s, curling clubs had sprung up in various Canadian and northern U.S. cities. In the 20th century the game moved indoors and equipment was standardized. Today there are more than one million curlers in Canada and curling has spread to 31 countries.

The object of the game is to score points by getting your stones closer to the tee than those of your opponents within the 12-foot circle called the "house." The team with the most points wins. The rules for this chapter came from the United States Curling Association.

PROCEDURES

Two teams of four players each compete against each other. Before the game the opposing Player 3s draw lots to determine which team goes first in the opening *end*, or inning; games last 8 or 10 ends. After that, the team that scores in an end goes first in the next end.

Player 1 from Team A delivers a stone, followed by Player 1 from Team B. Each player shoots two stones (or "rocks") per end. The score is determined after each end of 16 stones is completed. A stone that is within a six-foot radius of the *tee*, and that is closer to the tee than any opponent's stone, scores a point. The area within the six-foot radius is called the *house*; the tee is in the center of the house.

While one player shoots, two teammates *sweep* the ice, if necessary, to help the stone travel farther. The *skip*, or team captain, determines the strategy for his or her team. Some rocks may not be scoring rocks but may be placed to block or guard other rocks that are in scoring position.

When it is the skip's turn to shoot, the *acting skip* may take charge of the house. The acting skip is the only player other than the skip allowed in the house when the opponents are shooting. The skip of the shooting team chooses where to stand within the house; the other skip may not interfere with her position. The other players stand along the side of the rink between the *hog lines* (see figure 14.1). The only exception to this is when they are sweeping or delivering a stone.

Stones

A stone is removed from play when it

- rolls over or comes to rest on its side or top,
- does not clear the far hog line and has not struck another stone in play,
- comes to rest beyond the back line, or
- hits a sideboard or touches a side line.

A stone's position is not measured until the last stone of the end is delivered unless it is so requested by a skip to determine whether the stone is in play. All 16 stones are delivered in an end unless the players in charge of the house agree on a score for that end or one of the teams concedes the game.

If a running stone is touched by either a player or equipment of the playing team, the stone is removed from play. The opposing skip may choose, however, to place the stone where she thinks it would have ended up if not touched, if she believes it is to her opponents' advantage to have the stone removed. She may also reposition any stone inside the hog line at the playing end that would have been displaced, had the running stone not been touched.

If a running stone is touched by an opponent or opponent's equipment, the skip of the playing team may place the stone where he believes it would have come to rest, had it not been touched.

If a stone is moved by a touched stone, the skip of the team not at fault may either restore any stone to its position before it was moved by the touched stone or leave the stones as they are.

If a stone that would have altered the course of a running stone is displaced by the playing team, the running stone is allowed to come to rest and may either remain in its position or be removed at the discretion of the opposing skip. If the running stone is removed, then all displaced stones are placed where the opposing skip believes they originally lay.

A stationary stone that is displaced and has no effect on the outcome of the running stone shall be replaced by the opposing skip where it originally lay. If a stone is broken in play (extremely rare), it is replaced where the largest fragment comes to rest. If the handle of a stone completely separates from the stone during the delivery, the delivering team has the option to shoot that stone again.

Delivery

Right-handed players deliver stones from the hack (a rubber foothold) on the left side of the center line; left-handers play from the hack on the right side of the center line. A stone is removed from play for a violation of this rule.

The player must release the stone before the stone reaches the nearer hog line. Otherwise, the stone is removed from play. Any displaced stone hit by a stone released in violation of this rule will be replaced in its original position to the satisfaction of the opposing skip.

If a player does not release a stone before the stone reaches the nearer tee line, the player may redeliver the stone. If a player delivers an opponents' stone, a stone of his own will be put in its place. If a player delivers a stone out of the proper delivery rotation, that stone is removed from play. If the mistake is not discovered until after the stone has struck other stones or come to rest, however, the stone is not removed and the play stands as is.

If one team delivers two stones in succession in the same end, the opposing skip will remove the second stone, replace any stones displaced by the second stone, and the end will continue. The player who delivered the second stone does not lose her turn; she will redeliver the stone as the last stone for her team in that end. If the mistake is not discovered until other rocks have been delivered, the end is replayed. If a player delivers three stones in one end, play continues as if no mistake has been made and the fourth player of the offending team delivers only one stone in that end.

Sweeping

Players may sweep between the tee lines for their teammates' delivered or struck stones. They cannot sweep for their opponents' stones between the tee lines.

Behind the tee line, only one player from each team—the skip or acting skip—may sweep at any one time. A player may not begin sweeping an opponents' stone until it reaches the tee line. If the delivering team's choice is not to sweep behind the tee line, that team may not prevent the opposing team from sweeping the stone.

The sweeping motion is from side to side and shall leave no debris in front of the stone. Neither the sweeper nor his equipment may touch the stone at any time.

TERMS

A **bonspiel** is a tournament.

A **cashspiel** is a tournament with cash prizes.

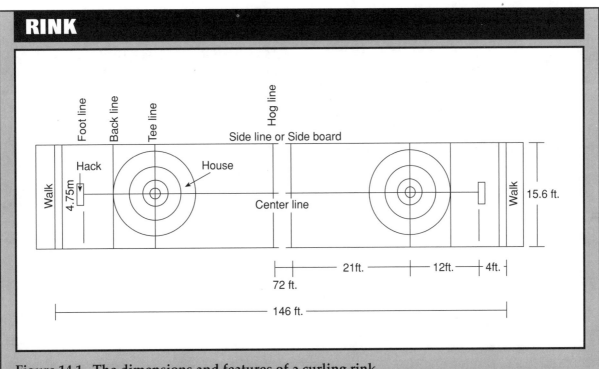

RINK

Figure 14.1. The dimensions and features of a curling rink.
Courtesy of USA Curling TM 1995.

An **end,** also referred to as an inning, is a portion of the game where all eight players (four on a team) have delivered two stones each. Scoring is determined at the completion of each end; a game lasts 8 or 10 ends.

The **house** is the scoring area of the rink, with a 12-foot diameter and a tee at the center.

A **match** is a contest between two or more teams on each side; the winner is determined by the total number of points or by games won.

A **skip** is the team captain. Only the skip or the acting skip can be in the house when the opposition is throwing.

PLAYERS

Four players are on a team: lead, second, third (or vice-skip), and skip. Each player delivers two stones each end, delivering alternately with her opponent. The established rotation for delivery must be maintained throughout the game.

When a player is unable to start or continue play, his skip may finish the game with the first two players delivering three stones each or substitute for the player at the beginning of the next end.

If a player is late, the skip may begin the game with three players and add the late player when she arrives.

A team may not substitute for more than one of the original players in a competition (or one male and one female in mixed competition). However, any number of substitutions are allowed for that one player (or couple, in mixed competition).

EQUIPMENT

Stones are circular and weigh no more than 44 pounds, with a circumference no greater than 36 inches. Stones must be at least 4.5 inches in height.

Brooms or *brushes* are used for sweeping. Players may not wear shoes that damage or mark the ice; shoes should be flat-soled and grip the ice well for walking.

OFFICIALS

An *umpire* supervises the game and settles any disputes between opposing skips.

ORGANIZATIONS

United States Curling Association
100 CenterPoint Drive
Box 866
Stevens Point, WI 54481
715-344-1199

Canadian Curling Association
1600 James Naismith Drive, Ste. 803
Gloucester, ON, Canada K1B 5N4
613-748-5628

World Curling Federation
81 Great King St.
Edinburgh EH3 6RN, Scotland
131 5564884

15

Cycling

© Claus Andersen

Bicycle races take many shapes and forms within the three main types of racing: track racing, road racing, and off-road racing. Road racing is the most popular brand of cycling, with the annual Tour de France, covering 3,900 kilometers in approximately 24 days, well-known to even the most casual of fans. Off-road racing has evolved from recreational off-road bicycling and is a fast-growing sport in itself.

Races are held for individuals and for teams, over one or more events. Depending on the event, the object of cycling is to finish first, to finish with the overall best time, or to score the most performance points. The rules for this chapter come from the U.S. Cycling Federation and the National Off-Road Bicycle Association.

PROCEDURES

Cyclists begin a race in one of three ways: all with holders; all with one foot on the ground; or all with a rolling start. Holders cannot step over the starting line. When a rolling start is used on a track, at least one neutral lap is taken to ensure a fair start. A race is begun with a signal—usually a gun or a whistle.

Any rider who appears to present a danger to the other competitors may be disqualified. Pushing or pulling among riders is prohibited in all races except the *madison* (see page 91); no rider may hold back or pull an opponent. A cyclist can make no progress unaccompanied by a bicycle. A cyclist who crashes can run with his bike.

The last lap is indicated by the ringing of a bell. A cyclist finishes a race when her front tire first penetrates the finish line.

Should two or more track riders tie for a place in which there is a prize, they may ride either the full distance or a shorter distance, as determined by the chief referee, to determine their places. In road races, a tie for first place is broken by reriding the final 1,000 meters. Other ties are not broken in road races; the prizes for places are equally divided or duplicated.

TERMS

A **criterium** is a circuit road race held on a course closed off to traffic. Primes (sprints) are held within the race.

A **cyclocross** is a race held on rough terrain, about 75 percent of which is traversable on bike.

A **handicap start** is one in which the faster riders either ride longer or start later.

A **keirin** is a paced sprint, held on a velodrome, in which a motorized bike leads a pack of riders, accelerating until the next-to-last lap, upon which the pacer drops out and the riders sprint for the finish.

A **mass start** is a race where all riders begin on the same line.

In a **miss-and-out** race, the last rider on designated laps is forced to withdraw from the race.

In a **pursuit race,** riders begin at equal intervals around the track. The race is run until one rider catches the others, or until a certain distance is covered, as specified in advance.

A **stage race** is a series of road races for individuals and teams.

In a **time trial,** riders compete one at a time over a fixed distance.

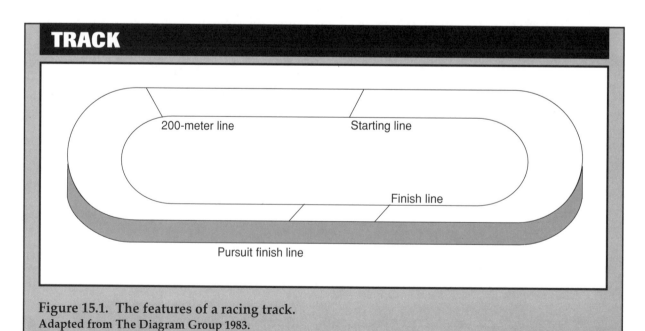

TRACK

200-meter line

Starting line

Finish line

Pursuit finish line

Figure 15.1. The features of a racing track.
Adapted from The Diagram Group 1983.

TRACK RACING

Track races are held on an oval track, usually .16 to .54 kilometer in length (see figure 15.1). The track is usually slightly banked on the straightaways and more so on the turns. Marked lines include the *starting line* (if it doesn't coincide with another line), the *200-meter line* (placed 200 meters before the finish line), two *pursuit finish lines* (in the middle of the two straightaways), and a *finish line*.

Track races include the following:

Mass Start. All riders start from the same point at the same time. The race is run over a specified number of laps; lapped riders are normally removed from the race.

Handicap. The faster riders must travel farther or must start later than the other cyclists.

Miss-and-Out. This is a mass-start race in which the last rider over the line on designated laps is eliminated. This may occur on every lap, every other lap, or on some other announced schedule. The winner is either the last rider left, or the race may be run until a specified number of riders remains, at which point a free lap may be followed by a sprint lap to determine the finish.

Sprint. Track sprints involve a series of short races with a small number of competitors. The rounds may be preceded by a flying start 200-meter time trial to seed or select riders. Round-robin sprints, held with a small number of riders, pit each competitor in an individual race against every other competitor. In championship formats, riders are advanced through qualifying sprints to the finals.

Riders may not stand still for more than three minutes during a race. A rider must always leave room on his right for others to pass but does not have to leave room on his left.

Tandem Sprint. These races are run over the integral number of laps nearest to 1,500 meters for the particular track. No more than four tandems are raced together (no more than three on tracks smaller than 333 meters).

Keirin. Up to nine riders compete in a paced event for five laps on tracks of 333 meters or less, or for four laps on longer tracks. A pacer rides a motorized bike. Sprint rules apply; during the first lap, the speed is about 45 kilometers per hour to 50

kilometers per hour. On the next-to-last lap, the pacer gradually accelerates and then moves off the track.

Time Trial. Riders compete one at a time over a fixed distance. In a kilometer time trial, two riders start at the same time, on opposite sides of the track.

Individual Pursuit. Racers start at equal intervals around a track. The race is run until one rider catches all the other riders; any rider passed by another must withdraw from the race.

Team Pursuit. Various team pursuit races involve two or more riders per team.

Points Race. Riders begin in a mass rolling start; sprints for points are held on designated laps. On these laps, the first four riders are awarded points (5, 3, 2, and 1). The number of points is doubled on the sprint nearest the midpoint of the race and on the final sprint.

Madison. Teams of two or three riders each compete in a relay points race. No more than two members of a team may ride at the same time. Sprints for points are conducted the same as in a points race. In case of a mishap, a teammate may take over until the injured rider returns. If a bicycle is judged to be damaged, then the team involved is not penalized any laps while its rider is off the track.

Omnium. Riders compete for points in a set of races; final places are determined by total points for all the events, with points being awarded in each event on a 7-5-3-2-1 basis for first place through fifth. A tie is broken by the rider who has the most first-place finishes; if still tied, the rider who has the most second-place finishes wins, and so on. If still tied, the rider who placed highest in the final event wins.

These rules apply to mass-start, handicap, miss-and-out, madison, and point races:

- Leaders must occupy the sprinters' lane unless they are able to do otherwise without interfering with other riders.

- A rider must pass on the outside unless the rider ahead is riding above the sprinters' line.

- In the homestretch on the last lap, a rider must ride a straight line parallel to the edge of the track.

- Riders may not ride on the blue band below the track surface.
- If a crash causes a hazard to other riders, the race may be "neutralized"—the riders ride slowly around the top of the track, maintaining their positions, until the race may be safely resumed.
- Riders who crash may receive assistance in restarting.

ROAD RACING

A road course may be out-and-back, around a circuit, from place to place, or any combination of these. However, the course may not cross itself, forcing riders to cut through other riders.

A marker denotes the final 1,000 meters. A white flag indicates the final 200 meters, which should be a straightaway.

If the road is open to traffic, riders must keep to the right of the center line. A rider may pass on either side of another rider. If the lead riders are stopped by a temporary road closure (such as at a train crossing), the race is neutralized and all riders begin at the same time intervals as their arrival at the closure. If the lead rider or riders make it through and others are stopped, this is an unforeseeable incident, and no compensation is allowed.

Riders may exchange food and drink among themselves. Tires, tools, and other equipment can only be exchanged among team members. A rider who suffers a mishap may be helped back on her bike and may be pushed for 10 meters.

Road races fall into the following categories:

Individual road races include mass-start races and handicap races. Lapped riders may be called off the course. Riders on different laps may not pace one another.

A *criterium* is a circuit race held on an 800-meter to 5-kilometer course that is closed to traffic. Riders on different laps may work with each other, but no rider can drop back to assist a rider who has broken away from the pack (see figure 15.2). Primes, or sprints within the race, are held either at preassigned times or are designated by a bell preceding the lap that will be-

Figure 15.2. Cyclists cut wind resistance, a major factor in road racing, by staying in packs.

gin the prime. Lapped riders are not eligible for primes.

An *individual time trial* may be out-and-back, circuitous, or point-to-point. Riders start at intervals (typically one minute apart). No rider may match pace (draft) with another rider closer than 25 meters ahead or 2 meters to the side. Time penalties are given for such violations.

In a *team time trial,* two or more riders make up one team. The starting interval between teams is typically two minutes. Teammates on different laps may not work together; the team is disqualified for this violation. Teammates may exchange food, drink, and repair tools.

Cyclocross takes place on rough terrain, no more than half of which is paved. About 75 percent of a cyclocross course can be covered on a bicycle. The lap is at least 1 kilometer long; no jumps (such as ditches or streams) should be longer than 1 meter, and no artificial barriers should be higher than 40 centimeters. Bicycles may be exchanged in case of mechanical failure.

A *cross-country time trial* may be an individual or team event. A rider who takes pace from another rider closer than 25 meters ahead or 2 meters to the side will receive a time penalty.

A *stage race* is a series of road races for individual riders and teams. The maximum duration is 10 days of racing, except that national tours may have up to 20 days of racing. Rest days are not included in this count; at least one rest day must be given for an event 10 days or longer. Up to two stages may be held in one day. Riders are not compensated for time loss if they take a wrong turn. A rider in an accident within a kilometer of the finish receives the same time as the last riders of any group he was riding with. Riders receive points for individual finish placings and hill climbing. Riders also receive time bonuses for finish order (e.g., 30 seconds off for first place, 20 seconds off for second, and so on).

RIDERS

Riders compete in both individual and team competitions, which may be further classified according to gender and age. Age groups normally are in five-year groupings (30-34, 35-39, and so on). Junior age groups are 10-12, 13-14, 15-16, and 17-18.

EQUIPMENT

Bicycles may be no more than 2 meters long and 75 centimeters wide; tandem bicycles may be up to 3 meters long. Bicycles may be propelled only by the riders' legs. They may have no protective shield to reduce wind resistance.

Wheels may be either spoked or of solid construction. Handlebars should be solidly plugged; ends that point up or forward or provide support for the rider's forearms are allowed only in time trials and pursuits.

For track races, only a bicycle with a single-cog fixed wheel (one gear on the rear wheel) and without derailleurs may be used. For road races, only a bicycle with a freewheel (multiple gears on the rear wheel) and one working brake on each wheel

shall be used. Riders must wear a protective *helmet* and a jersey that covers the shoulders.

OFFICIALS

Races are officiated by a *head referee, assistants, starters, timers,* and *judges.*

MODIFICATIONS

Off-road racing has grown in recent years, drawing on the enthusiasm of off-road recreational cyclists. The brief overview of this sport's rules comes from the National Off-Road Bicycle Association.

Off-Road Competitions

Off-road competitions include the following:

- *Cross-country.* Held on a circuit course of forest and field roads and trails as well as paved and unpaved gravel roads.
- *Point-to-point.* Same as cross-country but on a point-to-point course.
- *Hill climb.* A mass start or a time trial of sustained climbing in which the finish is higher than the start.
- *Downhill.* A time trial in which the finish is lower than the start. Competitors typically start in 30-second intervals.
- *Dual slalom.* Two riders race head-to-head down two parallel slalom courses.
- *Stage races.* This is a series of different events leading to an overall score or time. These races may be held over one or several days.
- *Observed trials.* In a race over an obstacle course, riders attempt to manuever the course without putting down a foot (dab). Each dab adds a point to the rider's score. Low score wins.
- *Ultra endurance.* This is an event in excess of 75 miles.

Equipment

All riders must wear a protective *helmet.* The bicycle must have two working *brakes; footgear* must be fully enclosed. Riders must wear appropriate attire, including shirts. Eye protection is recommended, as is additional helmet padding for downhill and dual slalom events.

Regulations

Following is a very truncated version of the regulations for the general sport of off-road racing, and for its specific races.

Racers must begin and complete the event on the same bicycle. Any repairs must be made by the racer; no outside support is permitted. Spare parts and tools must be carried by the racer. A rider will be disqualified for short-cutting or cutting trail switchbacks.

Cross-country. Water and food are available only in designated zones. Riders have the right-of-way over racers pushing bicycles. Lapped riders must yield to other riders. A rider cannot bodily interfere with another rider's progress.

Dual slalom. Each rider gets at least one qualifying run. The fastest qualifier is seeded against the slowest, and so on. The winner of each head-to-head competition moves on to the next heat. A rider who gets a jump start is penalized 1.5 seconds. Riders must ride around gates; a missed gate costs 1.5 seconds. Other 1.5-second penalties include changing from one course to another, not passing both wheels around a gate, interfer-

ing with the other rider, and not finishing in possession of the bike. Ties are broken by comparing the overall times on the course that both riders completed.

Observed trials. Low score wins. The first dab (hand or foot touching ground) costs one point; the second dab, two points; the third and fourth, three points each; and the fifth and subsequent dabs, five points each. Two or more dabs at the same time costs five points. Other penalties include riding outside the limits with either tire, five points; breaking the ribbon, or knocking down a marker, five points; sliding one foot on the ground, three points; gate foul, five points; exceeding the event time limit, five points; preriding the course, 100 points.

Ultra endurance. No mechanical support other than wheel changes in designated areas is permitted.

ORGANIZATIONS

National Off-Road Bicycle Association
One Olympic Plaza
Colorado Springs, CO 80909
719-578-4717

United States Cycling Federation
One Olympic Plaza
Colorado Springs, CO 80909
719-578-4581

16

Diving

© Claus Andersen

Diving became an Olympic sport for men in 1904 and for women in 1912. Competitions are conducted from 1-meter and 3-meter springboards, as well as from 5-meter, 7.5-meter, and 10-meter platforms.

Several components of the dive are judged. Each dive has a degree of difficulty rating, which is multiplied by the judges' scores to obtain a total point award for the dive. Divers perform a series of dives in various body positions, with different degrees of difficulty, depending on the level of competition. The rules for this chapter come from U.S. Diving, the sport's national governing body.

PROCEDURES

Divers submit, within a designated deadline, a diving score sheet listing the dives to be performed. The meet secretary checks each sheet for correctness and conformity to the rules.

The order of diving is decided by random draw. The diver's name, dive, and its degree of difficulty are announced before each dive. The judges' scores and all computations are performed by the scoring table and checked for accuracy before the results of the contest are announced.

After each dive, on a signal from the referee, each of the judges, without communicating with any other judge, immediately and simultaneously flashes his or her award.

A diver may not

- perform a dive other than that announced (doing so will result in a failed dive, with no score awarded) or
- repeat the same dive, even in a different body position.

In competitions other than national championships, a diver may elect not to perform a dive and take no points. This is to ensure the safety of the participants.

Dives

There are six types of dives that may be performed:

Forward. Diver begins facing forward toward the water and rotates toward the water.

Backward. Diver begins standing backward on the end of the springboard or platform and rotates toward the water.

Reverse. Diver begins facing forward toward the water and rotates toward the springboard or platform.

Inward. Diver begins standing backward on the end of the springboard or platform and rotates toward the springboard or platform.

Armstand. Diver begins from a handstand on the end of the platform; this dive is performed only in platform diving.

Twisting. Diver includes a twist in any of the above five groups of dives; this is the largest group of dives.

Divers may execute dives in four body positions:

Straight—no bending at the knees or hips; feet together and toes pointed

Pike—bent at the hips with legs straight; feet together and toes pointed

Tuck—bent at the hips and knees; feet and knees together and toes pointed

Free—any combination of the other three positions when executing a twisting dive

Three categories of dives may be performed, and the requirements for each are specified by the level of competition:

Required. A specific dive and/or body position is designated. All divers in the contest must perform a required dive.

Voluntary with limit. Divers perform a number of dives from different groups. The dive choice is up to the diver, but the total degree of difficulty of all dives cannot exceed a predetermined limit.

Voluntary without limit. The diver performs a number of dives from different groups; there is no limit on the total degree of difficulty. These dives are commonly referred to as "optional" dives.

Scoring

A dive is judged on five parts:

Approach—the walk or run to the end of the springboard or platform; this begins forward, reverse, and some twisting dives

Takeoff—springing and jumping from the end of the springboard or platform to begin a dive

Elevation—the amount of height in the air achieved after takeoff

Execution—the technique and grace in the air

Entry—the angle of entry, which should be vertical; the straightness of the body; and the amount of splash

Judges award points in half-point increments based on the following scale:

- Very good—8 1/2 to 10 points
- Good—6 1/2 to 8 points
- Satisfactory—5 to 6 points
- Deficient—2 1/2 to 4 1/2 points
- Unsatisfactory—1/2 to 2 points
- Completely failed—0 points

When nine judges are on hand, the two highest and two lowest scores are thrown out. When seven judges are used, the high and low scores are thrown out. In either case, the sum of the remaining scores is multiplied by the degree of difficulty and then by .6 to obtain the equivalent of a three-judge score. When five judges are used, the high and low scores are eliminated and the sum of the remaining three scores is multiplied by the dive's degree of difficulty.

Judging Dives

The starting position for dives with an approach is assumed when the diver is ready to take the first step. For standing dives, the starting position is assumed when the diver stands still on the front end of the springboard with head erect and body and arms straight.

If the diver begins her approach or press and stops, she has committed a *balk.* She may move her arms preparatory to her approach or press without a balk being called. The first balk results in two points being deducted from each judge's score. A second balk on the same dive results in a failed dive. Any action before the diver takes the starting position does not count.

The *forward approach* should be smooth, straight, and graceful, and take not less than three steps and a hurdle.

The *takeoff* for the "hurdle"—the jump to the end of the springboard—must be from one foot only.

In *running dives,* the takeoff from the springboard must be from both feet simultaneously.

Springboard dives with a forward takeoff may be performed either standing or with an approach.

In *running platform dives,* the diver must take at least three steps and a hop for a two-foot takeoff, and at least four steps for a one-foot takeoff. Two

points will be deducted from each judge's score for violations here.

On a *backward* or *standing front dive,* the diver must not bounce on the board or rock it excessively before takeoff. Doing so will result in a deduction of not more than two points from each judge, at the individual judge's discretion.

Touching the end of the board or diving to the side during the execution of the dive will result in a deduction of points, up to the discretion of each judge. While the diver is in the air, the judges look for the following:

Straight position. Points are deducted if the knees or hips are bent.

Pike position. The pike should be as compact as possible; the legs must be straight (see figure 16.1).

Tuck position. The tuck should be as compact as possible. One to two points will be deducted for opening the knees.

Figure 16.1.   With legs straight, a diver performs a pike.

Free position. Any combination of the three other positions must conform to the criteria of those positions.

A *twist dive* is considered failed if the twist is greater or less than 90 degrees of the announced twist.

As described earlier, the *entry into the water* for all dives must be vertical, with the body straight and the toes pointed. On *head-first entries,* the arms should be stretched beyond the head in a line with the body, with the hands close together. If any part of the body below the waist enters the water before the hands, the dive is considered failed. On *feet-first entries,* the arms should be held close to the body, without bending at the elbows. (Novice divers performing certain dives are allowed to hold their arms straight overhead.)

TERMS

A **diving list** contains the dives to be performed by the diver in a competition.

A **draw** is performed by judges to select the order of the divers.

Preliminaries are the first round or series of dives in a contest. Some divers advance from preliminaries and some do not.

Quarterfinals are sometimes used after a preliminary round to advance divers to a semifinal round.

A diver **scratches** from the competition when he withdraws.

Semifinals are the portion of the contest between preliminaries and finals. Only a certain number of divers advance through the semifinal round to the finals.

POOL

The competition *springboard* is made of flexible material and a nonskid surface. It is 20 inches wide and 16 feet long, and set at either 1 or 3 meters above the water's surface. Three-meter springboards should have guard rails extending to at least the pool's edge; boards should project

at least 1.5 meters, and preferably 1.8 meters, beyond the pool's edge and over the water.

The *platform* is solid and nonflexible and has a nonslip surface. It is at least 20 feet long and 6.5 feet wide. The platform height is 10 meters; intermediate platforms can be set from 5 to 7.5 meters.

For synchronized diving events, the 10-meter-high platform should be at least 8 feet wide, and preferably 10 feet. The water depth varies, depending on the height of the platform.

DIVERS

Divers compete in these classifications:

Senior—open, except to Junior Olympic Intermediate, Novice, and Limited Athletes

Junior Olympic—19 years old and younger

Masters—21 years old and older

Seniors Competition

Divers may compete in the 1-meter springboard, 3-meter springboard, and 10-meter platform in national and international competitions. These competitions consist of preliminaries, semifinals, and finals.

Preliminaries consist of five (women) or six (men) voluntary dives with no limit on degree of difficulty. The total points for all dives are determined to select the top 18 divers to advance to the semifinals.

Semifinals consist of four (platform) or five (springboard) dives for men and women, with total degree of difficulty limits of 7.6 and 9.5, respectively. The total score from the semifinals is added to that from the preliminaries to select the top 12 divers who advance to the finals.

In the finals, the total points obtained in the semifinals are carried forward. Points from the preliminaries are eliminated. The finals consist of five (women) or six (men) voluntary dives without any limit on the degree of difficulty. These may or may not be the same dives performed in the preliminary contest. The total points scored in the semifinal and final contests are added to determine place finish.

Junior Olympic Competition

Junior Olympic competitions are held in age brackets, beginning with 9-and-under and going to 18- and 19-year-olds. Divisions have varying requirements for required and voluntary dives.

OFFICIALS

A *referee* is in charge of the competition and oversees the *judges* (typically three for dual meets and five for regional meets). A *secretary* oversees the scoring table and verifies the results. The scoring table may consist of three or more *recorders*.

ORGANIZATIONS

United States Diving
Pan American Plaza
201 S. Capitol Avenue, Ste. 430
Indianapolis, IN 46225
317-237-5252

17

Equestrian

© Claus Andersen

Horsemanship has been around for thousands of years; the sport of equestrian evolves from these roots. American Horse Shows Association (AHSA), the national governing body for the sport, today regulates the competitions for 24 *breeds* and *disciplines* of show horses. A "breed" signifies the type of horse, such as Saddlebred, Arabian, and Connemara; "discipline" refers to the type of riding.

While there are many disciplines, this chapter will concentrate on the three Olympic disciplines: *dressage, show jumping,* and *three-day eventing.* The breed of horse in the discipline is not relevant, although certain breeds lend themselves better to the demands of certain disciplines.

For more in-depth rules on these disciplines or on other disciplines, contact the source of information for this chapter, the AHSA.

PROCEDURES

The sport of dressage displays and tests the complete training of the horse as demonstrated through the walk, trot, and canter. Although dressage is a very popular competitive sport, it is also the training system employed in the training and development of young horses. In dressage, a horse and rider perform a prescribed test in an enclosed, flat arena. The requisite movements, such as transitions among the gates, circles, or lead changes, must come at markers on the borders of the arena. Dressage competition is divided into nine levels of competition, with the last four being at the international, or Fédération Equestre Internationale (FEI) level. Each test reviews the basics of training, as demonstrated through the collection or extension of stride and lateral movements. The horse and rider are judged according to numerous criteria; the highest mark wins.

In show jumping, the horse and rider jump a course of 16 to 20 obstacles, trying to jump "clean" (not knocking down the obstacle), and within the time allowed. The team of horse and rider that covers the course in the shortest time with the fewest jumping faults wins.

The three-day event, also known as "combined training," is the all-around test of the horse, based on the military uses of the animal. It is very similar to pure dressage but performed at less demanding levels. The event consists of dressage, endurance, and stadium jumping. It begins with the dressage phase, which tests the animal the same as it is tested in pure dressage. The endurance phase begins with trotting and cantering (roads and tracks) for a few miles and moves on to four-part steeplechase, which is a high-speed gallop over a course of obstacles. The endurance phase continues with a second set of roads and tracks, before concluding with a cross-country race, where horse and rider negotiate solid jumps, ditches, banks, and streams. The final phase, stadium jumping, requires the horse and rider to compete on a modified show jumping course. The team of horse and rider completing the three days of competition with the fewest penalties is the winner.

TERMS

A **canter** is a three-beat gait, similar to a gallop.

A **clean round** signifies a jumper has completed a course within the allotted time and without incurring any jumping faults.

A **combination** is two or three jumps taken in quick succession, separated by only a stride or two. If a horse stops or runs out at any part of the combination, it must rejump the entire series.

A **curb** is a bit with leverage action that works on the top of the horse's head, the chin, and the mouth.

A **gait** is a pace: a walk, trot, canter, and gallop, and varying speeds of each, as well as the rack and slow gait of the American Saddlebred horse, and variations of each.

A **hand** is a unit of measurement equaling 4 inches. A horse is measured from the ground to the top of its shoulder.

A **knockdown** occurs when a horse or rider lowers an element of a jump that establishes the height of an obstacle.

A **snaffle** is a bit that works directly on the corners of the horse's mouth.

A **trot** is a two-beat gait, faster than a walk and slower than a canter.

DRESSAGE

In dressage (French for "training"), the horse and rider attempt to attain harmony; the horse should be calm, supple, and loose, as well as confident and attentive. The horse must be on the bit at all times, with the neck raised and arched. It must submit to the bridle with no resistance. Following are brief descriptions of the main elements of dressage.

The Walk

The horse's walk should be regular, free, and unconstrained. There are four types of walks—*collected, medium, extended,* and *free*—that should demonstrate the proper training of the horse.

The Trot

The horse's trot should be free, supple, regular, active, and sustained. The pace is "two-time" on alternate, diagonal legs, separated by a moment of suspension. The trot is judged by its general impression, the elasticity and regularity of the steps, and the rhythm and balance. The *collected*, *working*, *medium*, and *extended* trots should demonstrate the training of the horse.

The Canter

The horse's canter should be united, light, and cadenced. The pace is "three-time"; there is a moment of suspension when all four feet are in the air before each stride begins. The canter is judged on general impression, the regularity and lightness of the pace, and the rhythm. The proper training of the horse is demonstrated through four canters: the *collected*, *working*, *medium*, and *extended* canters.

Performance and Judging

During a test, the horse and rider may perform the following figures and movements:

- *Volte*—a circle with a diameter of 6 meters, 8 meters, or 10 meters.
- *Serpentine*—S-pattern movements demonstrating changes of direction
- *Figure eight*—two voltes or circles of equal size, joined at the center
- *Rein back*—backing up in a two-beat rhythm

The following factors are judged: collection and balance, correct outline of the horse and impulsion, and the position of the rider. A judge may warn a competitor of an error in the test, such as a wrong turn or incorrect movement, by ringing a bell. Subsequent errors are penalized by two points, then by four, then eight, and then by disqualification. Riders perform their tests from memory, although at the lower levels, the tests may be read to them.

Judges rate performances on a scale of 0 to 10, with 0 being "not executed" and 10 being "excellent." Judges award collective marks for gaits, impulsion, submission, and rider's position and seat.

SHOW JUMPING

Jumpers are scored on faults incurred while on the course, including disobediences, falls, knockdowns, touches, and time penalties. In combinations, each obstacle is scored separately. If a horse refuses to jump or runs out at one element, it must repeat the entire combination. Events that are tied are decided by a jump-off.

Course

Horse and rider must enter the starting timers within one minute of being called to start. The course must include at least one *change of direction* and one *combination*. It must have at least eight *obstacles*; each obstacle of a combination counts as an individual obstacle. At least three of the first eight obstacles must be spread obstacles. (Note: Certain categories of competitions have variances to these course rules.) The height of *obstacle rails* ranges from 3 feet, 6 inches to 6 feet.

Water obstacles must be at least 16 feet wide at the face and have at least an 8-foot spread of water; they may be up to 15 feet long. For every foot in length, they may have 2 inches in depth of water. They may have an obstacle no higher than 2.5 feet on the take-off side. Knocking down or displacing such an obstacle is not a penalty.

Penalties

Horse and rider may be penalized for disobediences, knockdowns and touches, falls, and time penalties. For every quarter-second over the time allowed, one fault is assessed. Following are examples of *disobediences*:

- Refusal to jump (stopping in front of the obstacle, and then backing up or circling to make the jump)
- Run-out (evading or passing the obstacle)
- Loss of forward movement (when the horse comes to a standstill before attempting the obstacle)
- Circling

The first disobedience costs three faults; the second, six faults; the third, elimination.

A *knockdown* occurs when a horse or rider lowers any part of an obstacle that establishes the obstacle's height. A knockdown is also charged if any part of the obstacle that establishes the height is moved so that it rests on anything other than its original support. A knockdown costs four faults. A *touch* of the obstacle, flags, or timing equipment may cost a horse and rider either one-half or one fault. A *fall* of the horse or rider results in elimination.

THREE-DAY EVENTING

The three-day event consists of dressage, endurance, and stadium jumping; each event takes place on a separate day. The endurance test itself has four phases: road and tracks (phases A and C); steeplechase (phase B); and cross-country (phase D). Cross-country is considered the heart of the sport.

International three-day events are held in accord with FEI regulations; horses and riders compete in one-star, two-star, three-star, or four-star events, with one-star being introductory level and four-star being experienced international level.

Two- and three-star competitors have some international experience.

Dressage rules have previously been outlined. For the endurance test specifications for heights and spreads, see table 17.1; for endurance test speeds, times, and distances, see table 17.2. For similar information for the jumping test, see tables 17.3 and 17.4.

OFFICIALS

A *ground jury* is responsible for adjudicating and judging the event, although additional judges may be appointed for dressage and jumping events. An *appeals committee* addresses any protests or charges.

ORGANIZATIONS

**The American Horse Shows Association
(The National Equestrian Federation)**
220 E. 42nd St.
New York, NY 10017-5876
212-983-7286

Table 17.1: Endurance Test: Heights, Spreads, Drops				
Obstacles	One-star (m)	Two-star (m)	Three-star (m)	Four-star (m)
Heights				
Steeplechase, fixed	1.00	1.00	1.00	1.00
Steeplechase, brush	1.40	1.40	1.40	1.40
Cross country, fixed	1.10	1.15	1.20	1.20
Cross country, brush	1.40	1.40	1.40	1.40
Spreads				
Steeplechase and cross country				
Highest point	1.40	1.60	1.80	2.00
Base	2.10	2.40	2.70	3.00
Without height	2.80	3.20	3.60	4.00
Drops				
Cross country	1.60	1.80	2.00	2.00

Adapted from American Horse Shows Association 1996.

Table 17.2:	**Endurance Test: Speeds, Times, Distances**			
	One-star	Two-star	Three-star	Four-star
A and C phase				
Speeds (mpm)	220	220	220	220
Times (min)	40 to 55	50 to 65	60 to 75	70 to 85
Distances (m)	8,800 to 12,100	11,000 to 14,300	13,200 to 16,500	15,400 to 18,700
B phase				
Speeds (mpm)	640	660	690	690
Times (min)	3.5	3.5 or 4	4 or 4.5	4.5 or 5
Distances (m)	2,240	2,310 or 2,640	2,760 or 3,105	3,105 or 3,450
Maximum jumping efforts	6 to 8	6 to 8	6 to 8	8 to 10
D phase				
Speeds (mpm)	520	550	570	570
Times (min)	7.5 to 9.5	9 to 11	10 to 12	12 to 14
Distances (m)	3,900 to 4,940	4,950 to 6,050	5,700 to 6,840	6,840 to 7,980
Maximum jumping efforts	30	35	40	45

Adapted from American Horse Shows Association 1996.

Table 17.3:	**Jumping Test: Heights and Spreads**			
Obstacles	One-star (m)	Two-star (m)	Three-star (m)	Four-star (m)
Heights	1.10	1.15	1.20	1.20
Spreads				
Highest point	1.40	1.60	1.80	1.80
Base or triple bar	1.90	2.10	2.30	2.30
Water	2.50	3.00	3.50	3.50

Adapted from American Horse Shows Association 1996.

Table 17.4:	**Jumping Test: Speeds, Times, Distances**			
	One-star	Two-star	Three-star	Four-star
Speeds (mpm)	350	375	400	400
Times (sec)	102 to 120	104 to 120	105 to 120	113 to 128
Distances (m)	600 to 700	650 to 750	700 to 800	750 to 850

Adapted from American Horse Shows Association 1996.

18

Fencing

© Claus Andersen

Fencing involves the attack and defense of two opponents who are using one of three weapons: the *foil,* the *épée,* or the *sabre.* A *bout* is a scored competition (the French refer to a bout as a "match"). A *match,* in English terms, is the aggregate of bouts between fencers of two different teams. A *competition* is the aggregate of bouts or matches between two teams.

The object is to score touches by touching the opponent's target area with the point of the weapon (for foil and épée) or with the edges (sabre). The object of the game is to touch and not be touched; the winner is the fencer who accumulates the appointed number of touches first. Each bout is timed, and if no fencer has reached the appointed number of touches within that time, various rules apply to determine the winner. See "Scoring."

The rules in this chapter provide an overview of general fencing competition, including specific rules for the foil, the épée, and the sabre. The source of information for this chapter is the United States Fencing Association, the country's national governing body for the sport.

PROCEDURES

When the command "Fence" is given, the bout begins. A fencer attempts to score touches by touching his target on his opponent's body with the point of his weapon. The weapon must be held and used with one hand only; a fencer may not change hands during a bout unless permitted to do so because of injury.

In foil and sabre, the fencer may not place his non-weapon arm forward of the shoulder of the weapon. He also may not cover the valid target surface with his unarmed hand or arm or any unvalid surface, or take hold of any part of his electrical equipment.

The durations for bouts are shown in table 18.1.

Table 18.1:	Durations for Fencing Bouts	
Weapon	Touches	Minutes
Epée	1	5
All weapons	4	5
All weapons	5	6
All weapons	8	8
All weapons	10	10

The bout may be halted if the fencing is dangerous or contrary to the rules, or if one of the fencers is disarmed or leaves the competition strip. After each valid touch, the fencers return to the on-guard lines.

The competitors in épée change position after each encounter, or after one of them has scored one more than half the maximum number of touches he may score. However, competitors wearing electrical scoring apparatus do not change ends.

When two fencers are in contact, the bout is stopped. In foil and sabre all contact is prohibited. In épée, no intentional contact is allowed. Warnings and penalties are issued for such contact. A fencer may duck, move her target, and touch her unarmed hand to the ground, but she may not turn her back to her opponent.

If a fencer passes his opponent during a bout, the bout is halted and both fencers move back to their previous positions. A touch made in the course of passing is valid; a touch made after passing, by the fencer who makes the passing movement, is not valid. However, a touch made by the fencer who has been passed is valid.

When a bout is temporarily halted, it is resumed at the spot where it was halted until a touch is made. When a fencer leaves the strip, the bout is halted. A fencer who steps beyond the rear boundary of the strip receives a penalty touch. When a fencer crosses a lateral boundary, the bout is halted and the opponent is allowed to advance one meter from the position he occupied when the crossing occurred. A fencer is not penalized for accidentally leaving the strip (e.g., in being jostled).

Scoring

Fencers score by making legal touches on valid targets. Each competition is set for a maximum number of touches, with a time limit. Following is an overview for scoring in foil, épée, and sabre competitions.

Foil

To score a touch, the point must touch the target, which is the trunk of the opponent. The limits of the target are the collar (6 centimeters above the collarbone), the seams of the sleeves, and the tops of the hipbones (see figure 18.1).

Bouts are for five touches in six minutes. If time expires before either fencer has reached five touches, but one fencer has more touches than the other, the final score is determined by adding the number of touches to the leader's score to reach five and adding the same number of touches to the other fencer's total. If the two fencers are tied, the score is set at 4-4 and they fence for the final touch without any time limit.

Epée

The touch must be made on the target, with the point. The target is the whole of the fencer's body, including clothing and equipment. Nonviolent contact is allowed, although a fencer who intentionally jostles his opponent will be penalized.

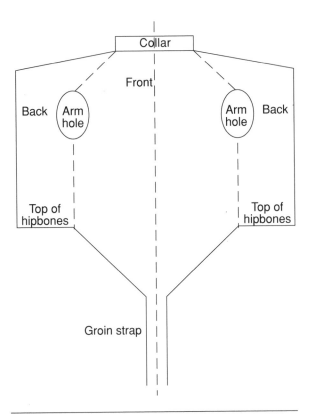

Figure 18.1.   A point is scored when the foil point touches the target. The boundaries of the target are the collar, seams of sleeves, and the tops of the hipbones.
Adapted from United States Fencing Association 1994.

Bouts are for five touches, with a six-minute limit. If both fencers score a fifth touch on a double touch, they continue for one or more touches, until the time limit expires.

When time expires before the bout is completed in épée for one touch, a defeat is scored against each fencer. In épée for multiple touches, the final score is determined by adding the number of touches to the leader's score to reach five and adding the same number of touches to the other fencer's total. If the two fencers are tied, a defeat is counted against both. The exception here is in direct elimination matches, where the tie is broken without any limit of time, and a winner is declared.

Sabre

Touches made with the cutting edge, the side edge, or the back edge of the blade are valid. Hit-

ting with the guard of the weapon is not valid and is penalized. Touches with the point that graze the target or cuts that slip along the opponent's body are not valid.

The target comprises the entire body above a horizontal line between the top of the folds formed by the thighs and the trunk when in the on-guard position. Body contact results in a penalty. The action is stopped, and any touch made during the body contact is not counted.

Bouts are for five touches with a six-minute limit. When time expires before a fencer reaches five touches, the final score is arrived at by adding the number of touches to the leader's score to reach five and adding the same number of touches to the other fencer's total. If the two fencers are tied, the time limit is off, the score is set at 4-4, and the next touch wins.

TERMS

The **attack** is the initial offensive action made by extending the arm and continuously threatening the opponent's target. A **direct attack** is one made in the same line. An **indirect attack** is one that changes lines on the way in. A **compound attack** is one made in more than one movement.

A **bout** is a timed, scored match in a competition.

A **competition** is the aggregate of bouts or matches that determine a winner. Competitions are distinguished by weapon. They can also be categorized by gender, age, or other classification, and by individual or team events.

A **counterattack** is an offensive or an offensive-defensive action made during the opponent's offensive action.

A **counter-riposte** is an offensive action of a fencer who has parried the riposte.

A **parry** is a defensive action made to prevent the attack from arriving.

Redoublement describes a new action against an opponent who has parried without riposting or who has retreated from or evaded the action.

A **remise** is a simple and immediate offensive action that follows an attack, without withdrawing the arm, after the opponent has parried or retreated.

A **reprise** is a new attack performed immediately after a return to the "on-guard" position.

A **riposte** is an offensive action that may be immediate or delayed, depending on the speed and execution of the action.

FIELD

The field of play is a strip of even surface of wood, linoleum, cork, rubber, or other material (see figure 18.2). The strip is 1.5 to 2 meters wide and 17 to 18 meters long, 14 meters of which is in bounds. If the strip is mounted on a platform, the height of the platform can be no higher than .5 meter.

If the competition is judged with electrical apparatus, the strip must be covered by metal or a metallic mesh to neutralize touches made on the ground. The strip has seven lines:

- A center line
- Two on-guard lines, located 2 meters on either side of the center line
- Two warning lines, located 5 meters on either side of the center line
- Two rear limit lines, located 7 meters from either side of the center line

FENCERS

Fencers compete in individual or team competitions, and in various age divisions, including open, under 20, and under 17.

EQUIPMENT

All weapons are composed of a *flexible steel blade* that comes to a tip; a *grip,* which may include a

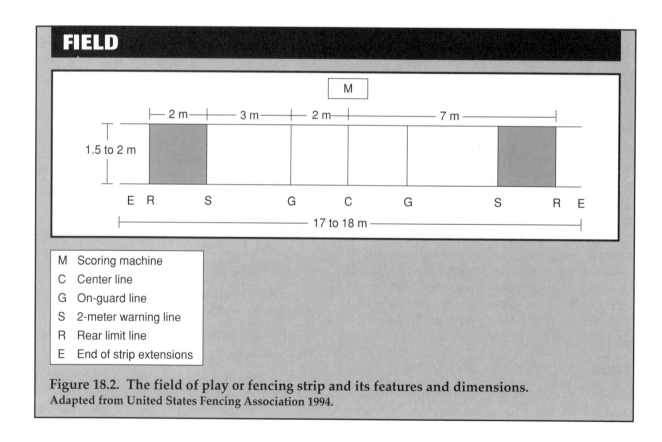

FIELD

M	Scoring machine
C	Center line
G	On-guard line
S	2-meter warning line
R	Rear limit line
E	End of strip extensions

Figure 18.2. The field of play or fencing strip and its features and dimensions.
Adapted from United States Fencing Association 1994.

handle and a pommel (which locks the handle onto the tang of the blade); and a *metal guard* between the blade and the hilt, to protect the hand. The guard can be padded; for electrical weapons, it contains the connector to which the body cord is attached.

General specifications for the weapons are as follows:

Table 18.2:	General Specifications for Fencing Weapons	
	Weight (g)	Maximum length (cm)
Foil	<500	110
Epée	<770	110
Sabre	<500	105

A *fencer's outfit* must be white or a light color on the torso. The rest of the clothing may be of a different, singular color. The *glove's cuff* must cover about half of the forearm of the sword arm. The *mask* is made of mesh.

OFFICIALS

Fencing bouts are directed by a *referee*, who may be assisted by *judges*. Judges are required when there is no metallic strip and in the final bout of a competition. *Scorers* and *timekeepers* are also used. When a judge sees a touch arrive, he raises his hand to advise the referee. The judges and the referee vote on the "materiality of the touch" to decide whether to award a touch to the fencer. Each judge's opinion counts as one vote; the referee's opinion counts as a vote and a half.

In bouts judged with a scoring machine, the referee places himself in view of the machine, and the materiality of the touch is indicated by the machine. Only touches that are registered by the machine are counted as such.

ORGANIZATIONS

United States Fencing Association
1 Olympic Plaza
Colorado Springs, CO 80909-5744
719-578-4511

19

Field Hockey

© Claus Andersen

Modern field hockey dates back to Princeton in the late 1700s. The sport was introduced to Harvard in 1901 and soon caught on at many women's colleges in the eastern United States. The game is played by both females and males at high school, college, and club levels. The object of the game is to score more goals than the opponents. The rules for this chapter were provided by the International Hockey Federation.

PROCEDURES

Each team is allowed 11 players, including the goalkeeper, on the field. A game consists of two 35-minute halves, and begins with a *center pass*, in which a member of the attacking team hits the ball from the center line (see figure 19.1 on page 116) to a teammate. A game is also restarted with a center pass after a goal is scored; the opponents scored upon put the ball into play.

During a pass back, opponents must be at least 5 yards from the ball. The player passing back must move the ball at least 1 yard and may not play the ball again until another player has played it.

A field player may only *play the ball* with the flat side of the stick. A goalkeeper may use any part of her body to stop the ball within the shooting circle so long as she has a stick in her hands.

A *goal is scored* when an attacking team member plays the ball within the shooting circle and it completely passes the goal line between the goal posts. The ball may be deflected by a defender and still count as a goal, but it may not go outside the shooting circle.

A *bully* is a play used to restart a game when each team commits a simultaneous foul, when the ball lodges in the goalkeeper's pads, and when time is stopped for an injury or for any other reason. Two opposing players face each other where the stoppage happened, with the ball between them and all other players at least 5 yards away. (If the occurrence happened inside the shooting circle, the ball is placed 16 yards from the goal line, even with the edge of the circle.) The two players tap their sticks on the ground, on their side of the ball, and then tap the flat face of the opponent's stick three times, over the ball. At this point the players may attempt to put the ball into play.

When a ball goes *out of bounds* it is put back into play according to where and how it went out.

When the ball goes out *over a sideline*, play is restarted by a member of the opposing team. The restart occurs where the ball went out, but the player does not have to be wholly in or out of bounds.

When the ball goes out *over a back line*, play restarts in one of three ways:

When the attack knocks the ball out of play, a defender puts the ball back into play up to 16 yards from, and opposite, where it crossed the back line, parallel with the sideline.

When the defense unintentionally knocks the ball out of play over a back line, an attacker restarts play on the sideline 5 yards from the corner flag nearest where the ball went out.

When the defense intentionally knocks the ball out of play over a back line, the attacking team is awarded a *penalty corner* on the back line, 10 yards from the closer goal post (see "Penalties"). A player may be in this position as long as she is not passed the ball.

Rules of Conduct

Players may not

- intentionally play the ball with the rounded side of the stick;
- participate in a play without a stick in hand;
- play the ball above shoulder height with the stick;
- lift their sticks over the heads of players;
- use their sticks dangerously, or play the ball in a way that is likely to lead to dangerous play;
- hit, hook, hold, or strike another player's stick or uniform;
- catch or stop the ball with the hands (except in protection);
- use their bodies to propel the ball;
- use their feet or legs to support the stick in a tackle;
- intentionally raise the ball from a hit, except for a shot at goal;
- intentionally raise the ball over a long distance so that it lands in the shooting circle;
- approach within five yards of a player receiving a pass in the air (the ball must be played and on the ground); and
- use their bodies or sticks to shield the ball from an opponent (obstruction).

TERMS

A **bully** is a play that restarts action by employing a face-off between two opponents who tap each other's sticks three times and then attempt to play the ball.

A **center pass** is used to begin play and to resume play after a goal has been scored. It takes place at the center line and involves a member of the attacking team passing the ball back to a teammate.

Dangerous play is any action that endangers any player, including a raised ball, tackling from the wrong position, and playing the ball while lying on the ground.

A **flick** occurs when a player pushes the ball and raises it off the ground.

A **free hit** is given for a foul committed outside the shooting circle.

A **penalty corner** results from a foul committed inside the circle; an attacker hits the ball from a point on the goal line at least 10 yards away from a goal post.

A **penalty stroke** occurs from a foul committed inside the circle if the defenders have intentionally fouled. An attacker shoots at goal from 7 yards away, in a one-on-one confrontation with the goalkeeper.

PENALTIES

Penalties are awarded for fouls that clearly disadvantage the player or team fouled. (For fouls, see sidebar "Rules of Conduct.") An umpire may award a free hit, a penalty corner, or a penalty stroke.

Free Hit

A free hit is awarded for a foul by an attacker or for an unintentional foul by a defender outside the shooting circle. The hit takes place at or near where the foul occurred.

Penalty Corner

A penalty corner is awarded when the defense commits an intentional foul, when the defense intentionally plays the ball out of bounds over their back line, and when the defense unintentionally fouls an attacker within the circle who does not have the ball. An attacker takes a penalty corner from a spot on the back line 10 yards from a goal post. At least one of the attacker's feet must be out of bounds; no other player may be within 5 yards. The other attackers must be outside the circle. Not more than five defenders, including the goalkeeper, may be behind the back line; the remaining defenders must be beyond the center line.

An attacker may not attempt a shot at goal until the ball has come to a complete rest outside the circle. If the first shot at goal is a drive, the ball must cross the goal line no higher than the backboard for a goal to be scored, unless it touches a defender or a defender's stick while in flight. The attacker putting the ball into play may not score directly.

Penalty Stroke

A penalty stroke is awarded when the defense commits an intentional foul in the circle to prevent a goal from being scored, or when the defense unintentionally fouls in the circle, thereby preventing a probable score. A penalty stroke is also awarded when the defense persists in breaking the back line at penalty corners.

Time stops when a penalty stroke is taken. The player taking the stroke stands behind the ball, which is placed 7 yards from the goal. All other players, other than the goalkeeper, must stand beyond the 25-yard line. The goalkeeper may not move until the attacker plays the ball. The attacker may push, scoop, or flick the ball from the penalty spot, raising the ball to any height. She may touch the ball only once, and she may not feint before she touches it.

If the player scores a goal, the game restarts with a pass back. If the player doesn't score, the game restarts with a defender playing the ball 16 yards in front of the center of the goal line.

FIELD

The field is 100 yards long and 60 yards wide (see figure 19.1). It has a *center line* marking and two

25-yard markings. The *shooting circles* are 16-yard semicircles in front of the goal. *Penalty spots* for penalty strokes are marked 7 yards in front of each goal. The *goals* are 4 yards wide, 7 feet high, and at least 4 feet deep. Each goal has a *backboard* 18 inches high spanning the width and sides of the goal. Goals are netted loosely to prevent the ball from rebounding onto the field.

PLAYERS

A team has 16 players in international matches, 11 of which may be on the field at one time. Players wear uniforms and may wear guards for shins, ankles, and mouths. Goalkeepers may wear upper body protectors and must wear a different colored shirt from that of either team. Goalkeepers also wear protective helmets and may wear protective padding on their legs and elbows.

A team captain wears a distinctive armband. Time is not stopped for a substitution, except when a goalkeeper is replaced; the substitute may enter the field only after the player coming out is off the field. Players coming in and out may do so only at the center line or some other designated area.

EQUIPMENT

The *ball* is spherical, weighing 5.5 to 5.75 ounces, with a circumference of 8.8 to 9.25 inches. Its surface is smooth.

The *stick* has a flat side and a rounded side. The maximum length of the curved head, measured from the lowest part of the flat face, is 4 inches. The stick must weigh between 12 ounces and 28 ounces. The diameter of the shaft must not exceed 2 inches.

OFFICIALS

Two *umpires* control the game. Each umpire is primarily responsible for play on his half of the field, diagonally from the near left corner to the far right corner as he faces the field.

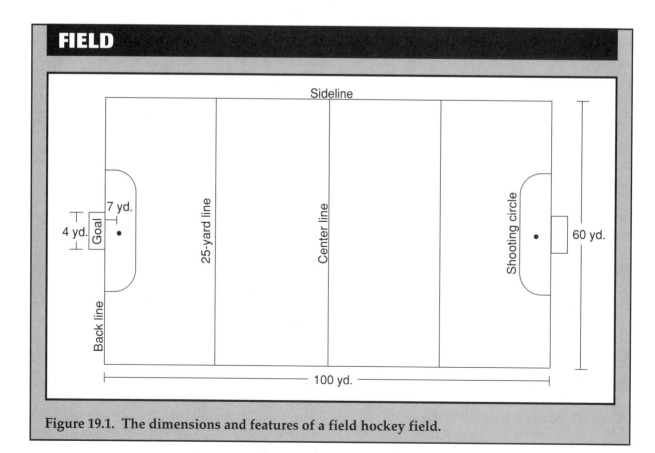

FIELD

Sideline

7 yd.

4 yd. Goal

25-yard line

Center line

Shooting circle

60 yd.

Back line

100 yd.

Figure 19.1. The dimensions and features of a field hockey field.

ORGANIZATIONS

Fédération Internationale de Hockey
Avenue des Arts
Bte. 5 - 1210 Bruxelles
Brussels, Belgium
2 219 45 37

U.S. Field Hockey Association
1 Olympic Plaza
Colorado Springs, CO 80909
719-578-4567

20

Figure Skating

© Claus Andersen

In the early 20th century, figure skating competitions and tests became established in the United States and in Canada; figure skating was an Olympic sport in 1908 and was reintroduced to the Winter Games in the first Winter Olympics in 1924. In 1976 ice dancing was added as an Olympic sport. Competitions are held in various events, including *singles skating*, *pairs skating*, *fours*, *ice dancing*, and *precision skating*. The grace, strength, and athleticism of figure skating has made the sport popular among athletes and spectators.

The basic object of the sport is for individuals, pairs, and teams to score points for technical merit and for presentation. The United States Figure Skating Association, the sport's national governing body, is the source for this chapter's rules.

PROCEDURES

The order of skating is based on an officials' draw. Competitors must begin their program within two minutes of being called to perform. Lengths of skating programs in senior level competitions, at national championships, and at international competitions, such as the World Championships and the Olympics, are as follows:

- *Short program (singles)*—not to exceed 2 minutes, 40 seconds; may be shorter if all the required elements are completed
- *Free skating (singles)*—ladies, 4 minutes; men, 4.5 minutes
- *Short program (pairs)*—not to exceed 2 minutes, 40 seconds; may be shorter if all the required elements are completed
- *Free skating (pairs)*—4.5 minutes
- *Compulsory dance*—length varies with type and tempo specified in the description and diagram of the dance
- *Original dance*—no set time
- *Free dance*—4 minutes
- *Precision skating (short program)*—not to exceed 2 minutes, 40 seconds; may be shorter if all the required elements are completed
- *Precision skating (long program)*—4.5 minutes
- *Free skating fours*—4 minutes

Competitors may finish within 10 seconds of their allotted time. For every 10 seconds they go beyond that, .1 is deducted from their marks. They receive no marks if they skate 30 seconds or more beyond their allotted time plus the 10-second allowance.

Except for compulsory dances, competitors choose their own music. For free skating and short programs, vocals are not allowed. Competitors may receive coaching during warm-ups but not during the actual performance.

TERMS

A **crossover** is the most efficient way to gain speed on a curve and can be done skating forward or backward.

Death spirals are pair moves where the man performs a back pivot and the lady circles around the man on one foot with her body bent backward and her head toward the ice.

A **double jump** is a jump with two complete revolutions and allowable further rotation of less than 360 degrees.

Edges are sustained one-foot glides on a curve with the body of the skater leaning into the center of the curve.

A **flying spin** is a spin that begins with a jump in which the position of the spin is evident during the jump.

Footwork includes steps, turns, and edge and directional changes that are performed by the skater in a deliberate way and in time to the music to connect other moves.

A **half-revolution jump** is a jump of one-half revolution (180 degrees) in the air.

A **lift** is when one partner (usually the man) assists the jumping partner in a continuously ascending and descending movement, limited to three revolutions of the lifting partner.

A **Mohawk turn** is a turn from forward to backward, or vice versa, from one foot to the other in which the curve of the exit edge continues the curve of the entry edge. There are many variations of Mohawk turns.

A **pattern** of a dance is the dance's design. A pattern can be *set*, in which the steps are prescribed; *optional*, which allows for more than a set pattern; and *border*, in which the pattern is laid out progressively around the rink, never repeating at the same place in the rink.

A **single jump** is a jump of one complete revolution and allowable further rotation of less than 360 degrees.

A **spin** is a move in which the skater continuously rotates around himself in small circles. Spins can be rotated forward and backward in a variety of positions.

A **spiral** is a move in which the upper body bends forward at the hip, the back arches, and the head and the free leg are up, with the free leg past the horizontal level.

A **throw** is a combination of a lift and jump in which the man assists the lady on the take-off by lifting and "throwing" her. The lady continues the rotation and landing of the jump alone.

A **twist** is a pairs move in which the man lifts and throws the lady in the air, where she completes a set amount of positions and rotations before being caught by the man and lowered to the ice.

SHORT PROGRAM FOR SINGLES

The short program consists of eight required elements with connecting steps. The following features are common to short programs:

- *Jumps*—jumps and jump combinations
- *Spins*—spins, spin combinations, and flying spins
- *Step sequences*—step sequences, spiral step sequences, straight-line step sequences, circular-step sequences, and serpentine-step sequences

Judges award two marks on a scale of zero to six: the first mark is for required elements; the second is for presentation. The six mark levels and what they represent are

- 0—not skated,
- 1.0—very poor,
- 2.0—poor,
- 3.0—mediocre,
- 4.0—good,
- 5.0—very good, and
- 6.0—perfect and faultless.

Judges consider the following in marking for the required elements:

- Jumps—height, length, technique, and clean starting and landing of required jumps
- Spins—strong, controlled rotation of spins; number of revolutions and speed of rotation; height (for flying spins)
- Step sequences—difficulty of steps; swing, carriage, and flow

Judges consider the following in marking the presentation:

- Harmonious composition
- Difficulty of steps
- Speed
- Utilization of the ice surface
- Easy movement and sureness in time to the music
- Carriage and style
- Originality
- Expression of the character of the music

FREE SKATING SINGLES (LONG PROGRAM)

Free skating consists of a program including jumps, spins, steps, and other linking movements executed with a minimum of two-footed skating in harmony with nonvocal music. The skater may choose the elements of the program. Special attention is given to choreography, expression, interpretation of the music, and intricacy of footwork. The skater must use the full ice surface. A well-balanced senior singles program must contain:

- Jumps—an unlimited number of double and triple jumps; however, only two different triple jumps of the skater's choice may be repeated in combinations or jump sequences
- Jump combination—At least one jump combination or sequence of jumps (the number of jumps is unlimited)
- Spins—A minimum of four spins of different natures, including a spin combination and a flying spin
- Steps—Men must perform two step sequences of different natures (e.g., straight line, circular, or serpentine), fully utilizing the ice surface. Ladies must perform one step sequence and one sequence of spirals or of free skating movements, such as turns, arabesques, and spread eagles, fully utilizing the ice surface.

Judges award two marks on a scale of zero to six; the first mark is for technical merit, the second for presentation. For technical merit, the factors considered are

- performance difficulty,
- variety, and
- cleanness and sureness.

For presentation, factors considered include

- harmonious composition,
- speed,
- utilization of the ice surface,
- easy movement and sureness in time to the music,
- carriage and style,
- originality, and
- expression of the character of the music.

PAIRS SKATING

Pairs skating is performed by two skaters (a woman and a man) skating in unison and harmony to nonvocal music (see figure 20.1). Skaters perform moves of single skating either symmetrically (mirror skating) or in parallel fashion (shadow skating), executing spins, lifts, partner-assisted jumps, and similar moves, linking their moves with harmonious steps. Judges give special attention to the selection of an appropriate partner; a serious imbalance in physical characteristics that impairs the skaters' unison will be reflected in their marks for technical merit and presentation.

In a *short program for pairs*, skaters must perform eight required elements with connection steps. These elements include

- one overhead lift (minimum of two revolutions of the lady),
- one twist lift (double),
- one solo jump (double or triple),
- one solo spin (with one change of foot and minimum of two positions),
- one combination pairs spin (one change of foot and minimum two positions),
- one death spiral,
- one spiral-step sequence, and
- one step sequence (circular, straight line, or serpentine).

Judges award two marks from zero to six, one for the required elements and one for presentation. Judges give special attention to choreography, unison, expression, interpretation of the music, and intricacy of the footwork. Partners may separate, but they must always give the impression of unison and harmony. They must keep movements on two feet to a minimum.

A *senior pairs program (long program)* must contain

- three to five different lifts (one of which must be a twist lift, but not more than two);
- one throw jump;
- two different solo jumps;
- one jump sequence;

Figure 20.1. Pairs skaters perform during a figure skating competition.

© Claus Andersen

- one pairs spin combination;
- one solo spin;
- one death spiral;
- a pairs spin or a second death spiral, different from the first one;
- a step sequence using the full ice surface; and
- a sequence of spirals or arabesques, turns, pivots, or spread eagles, using the full ice surface.

ICE DANCING

A dance couple is composed of a woman and a man. Ice dancing includes compulsory dances, an original dance, and free dancing. Theatrical poses are forbidden.

Compulsory Dances. Compulsory dances consist of set pattern dances and optional pattern dances set to music. Judges watch for accuracy of positions, steps, and movements; placement of steps and use of the ice surface; upright carriage and flowing motion; close and effortless unison; timing to the music; and expression of the character of the music. Judges give couples two marks on a scale of zero to six, one for technique and one for timing and expression.

Original Dance. Couples dance to music with a prescribed tempo; only music with constant and regular tempo may be used. The dance may not be a free dance. Lifts are not allowed. The skaters may separate for one measure of music only to change dance holds. Judges award two marks on a scale of zero to six, one for composition and one for presentation.

Free Dancing. Free dancing is performed by a couple who may express the character of their chosen music without performing any prescribed steps. The dance must contain combinations of new or known dance movements with technical aspects that show the athleticism of dancing. Dancers may perform all steps and turns; they may perform free skating movements that are appropriate to the music's character. They may separate to execute intricate footwork and to change holds and positions, provided the separation does not exceed 5 meters or 10 seconds. At least one skate of each partner must be on the ice at all times, except during jumps and lifts. Judges award two marks on a scale of zero to

six, one for technical merit and one for artistic impression.

FOURS

Fours are composed of two ladies and two men; the required elements include

- three or four different lifts,
- pairs throw jump (not more than two),
- one double jump performed in unison by all skaters,
- one pairs spin combination or one solo spin performed in unison by all four, and
- sequences that incorporate the skating and ice coverage of all four skaters.

One creative lift involving all four members is optional. Marking is the same as for pairs skating.

PRECISION SKATING

In precision skating, eight or more skaters perform various maneuvers and formations to music. Men and ladies may skate on the same team. Maneuvers include circles, lines, blocks, and wheels, linked with harmonious transitions. Judges watch for unison and synchronization among the skaters and accuracy of formations. No lifts are allowed; only jumps of one revolution or less are permitted. Intersections incorporating back spirals are not permitted. Judges award two marks on a scale of zero to six, one for technical merit and one for presentation.

The *precision short program* consists of five required maneuvers: a circle, a line, a block, a wheel, and an intersection. Skaters may perform them in any order. Judges award two marks on a scale of zero to six, one for the required elements and one for presentation.

RINK

The rink consists of a smooth ice surface, typically 100 feet by 200 feet (minimum size is 85 feet by 185 feet). It has rounded corners and a low wall.

SKATERS

Skaters must wear modest, dignified clothing, not garish or theatrical. They may choose clothing that reflects the character of the music, but they will be marked off for clothing considered inappropriate. Men must wear *full-length trousers,* not tights. Clothing must have sleeves. Ladies must wear *skirts* or *pants* that cover the posterior and the hips. Unitards and bare midriffs are not allowed, and clothing must not have excessive decoration.

EQUIPMENT

Blades must be standard stock blades that are generally available to figure skaters. The cross section of the blades may be slightly tapered.

OFFICIALS

Officials for skating competitions include a *referee, assistant referees,* and an odd number of *judges* (three to nine). The referee is in overall charge of the event and decides on any disputes not specifically covered in the rules.

ORGANIZATIONS

United States Figure Skating Association
20 First St.
Colorado Springs, CO 80906
719-635-5200

21

Football

© Mary Langenfeld

American football evolved from rugby, which was a spin-off from soccer. Early roots of the modern game can be traced to a college game played in 1869 between Princeton and Rutgers universities. Each team had 25 men on the field; the game more resembled soccer than football, as running with the ball, passing, and tackling were not allowed. Harvard and McGill universities played a game in 1874 that combined elements of rugby and soccer; this game caught on in Eastern U.S. schools and developed into the beginnings of modern football.

Early rules included playing with a round ball and needing to make 5 yards in three downs. Rules have continually evolved to make the game fair, exciting, and less violent. From its beginnings in America on college campuses, it has grown into a widely popular sport played in youth leagues, high schools, and professionally.

The rules in this chapter are general football rules, with specific references to both National Collegiate Athletic Association (NCAA) rules and National Football League (NFL) rules. Important modifications for other levels and variations of the sport are addressed near the end of the chapter.

The object is simple: Two teams of 11 players each attempt to score points against each other by advancing the football across the goal line or kicking it through goal posts. The team with the most points wins.

PROCEDURES

Before the game, the winner of a coin toss chooses to receive the kickoff, or which goal his team will defend. At the end of the first and third periods, the teams change goals. To start the second half, the team that lost the pregame coin toss chooses between the same two privileges.

The game begins with a *kickoff* at the kicking team's 30-yard line in the NFL, 35-yard line in college, or 40-yard line in high school play. All players on the kicking team must be behind the yard line from which the ball is kicked, and all players on the receiving team must be no closer than 10 yards away from the kickoff line.

If the kickoff goes out of bounds without being touched by a receiver, the receiving team may elect to take the ball where it went out of bounds, or 30 yards beyond the kickoff line. If the kick touches a receiver and then goes out of bounds, the receiving team puts the ball into play at the yard line where the ball went out of bounds.

Each team normally *huddles* before a play, to call the play and coverage. (Sometimes an of-

fensive team will go without a huddle and go directly to the line of scrimmage, where the quarterback will call the play through coded signals.) They line up on the *line of scrimmage* before the snap of the ball. The offensive team must have at least seven players on its line at the snap. Offensive players not on the line must be at least 1 yard behind it.

After the ball is snapped, the offensive team may advance the ball by *running* with or *passing* it (see figure 21.1). While a team may only attempt one *forward pass* during a down, it may attempt multiple *backward passes* or *laterals*. Backward passes may be advanced even if the ball touches the ground before a receiver secures possession.

An NFL receiver must have *both feet in bounds* (on the ground in the playing field) while in possession of the ball in order to record a legal reception. At other levels, *only one foot needs to be in bounds*. In the NFL and in high school, if a receiver is pushed out of bounds but would have landed inbounds otherwise, the catch is allowed.

In the NFL, a ball carrier may fall and get back up and continue running if he is not tackled or

Figure 21.1.   A football player runs up the field after receiving the ball from the quarterback.

touched by a defender while on the ground. In amateur play, once a runner touches any part of his body to the ground, except for his hands and feet, he is considered down.

During each play, offensive players attempt to *block* defenders to protect the passer and ball carrier. The defense attempts to *tackle* or knock the ball carrier out of bounds, or *intercept* or *knock down* a pass. A defender records a *sack* when he tackles the quarterback during a pass attempt.

The offensive team has four *downs,* or plays, to make 10 yards from the line of scrimmage at the *first down.* A team may, in certain instances, be awarded a *first down* (a new set of four downs) on a defensive penalty, even if the necessary 10 yards are not made.

In many cases if a team has not made a first down in three plays, it will *punt* (kick) the ball on fourth down to the opponents. The player receiving the punt may attempt to catch and advance the ball, let it roll dead (it may not be recovered by the kicking team if it does not touch a player on the receiving team), or call for a *fair catch* by waving a hand above his helmet. The kicking team may not touch a player who has signaled for a fair catch, unless the player fumbles.

A *change of possession* occurs when the defense *recovers a fumble, intercepts a pass, stops the offense* from making 10 yards in four downs, or *maintains control of a punt or kickoff.*

Time

Game length and other time factors differ according to the level of play (see table 21.1).

The *clock starts* when

- a player kicks off (except in the last two minutes of a half, when the clock doesn't start

until a player receiving the kick has touched the ball);
- the ball is snapped after a timeout;
- the ball is placed ready to play after a penalty; and when
- an official spots the ball at the inbounds mark following an out-of-bounds play, and the referee gives the ready signal (except in the last two minutes of the first half and last five minutes of the game, when the clock doesn't start again until the next snap).

Note: In NCAA play, the clock doesn't start on any kickoff until a player on the receiving team touches the ball.

The *clock stops* when

- the ball is out of bounds;
- a pass drops incomplete;
- a play is completed during which a foul occurs;
- two minutes remain in a half (NFL only);
- a period expires;
- a field goal, safety, or touchdown is scored;
- an official signals timeout; and when
- a down involving a change of possession is completed.

If *time expires as a play is in progress,* time is not called until the play is completed. If the defense commits a foul on the last play of a half, the offense may run another play. If the offense commits a foul on the last play of a half, the half is over.

Scoring

Players may score

- a touchdown—six points,
- a field goal—three points,

Table 21.1: Time Factors			
Level	Length	Overtime	Timeouts
High school	Four 12-min quarters	Yes	3 per half
College	Four 15-min quarters	Yes	3 per half
NFL	Four 15-min quarters	First team to score; maximum overtime is 15 min	3 per half

- a safety—two points, and
- a conversion—one or two points.

A player scores a *touchdown* (six points) when he possesses the ball and the ball touches the plane of, or crosses over, the opponent's goal line. A touchdown can be made by running the ball, catching a pass, or by recovering a fumble on or over the opponent's goal line. The defense may intercept a pass or recover a fumble or blocked punt and return it for a touchdown.

After a touchdown is scored, a team has the choice of attempting a *one-point* or *two-point try* or *conversion*. In the NFL, the ball is placed at the 2-yard line for a conversion attempt; in amateur football, the ball is placed at the 3-yard line. A *one-point conversion* is scored by kicking the ball through the uprights. A *two-point conversion* is scored by an offensive player possessing the ball on or over the goal line (in what normally would be considered a touchdown).

A *field goal* (three points) is scored by place-kicking or drop-kicking the ball through the opponent's goal post uprights (though drop-kicking is rare in modern football). If the kick is no good and the ball is beyond the opponent's 20-yard line, the ball is given to the opponents at the line of scrimmage. If the unsuccessful kick was attempted from on or inside the 20-yard line, the ball will be given to the opponents at the 20-yard line. If, however, the kick is blocked and recovered by the opponents, the ball will go to the opponents at the spot where the ball is downed, regardless of the yard line.

A *safety* (two points) is scored when the defense tackles or otherwise downs the ball on or behind the opponent's own goal line. A safety is also scored if the offense maintains possession of the ball out of bounds on or behind its own goal line. Examples of safeties are a runner or quarterback being tackled in his own end zone or a punt being blocked and going out of bounds beyond the goal line. Following a safety, the team that was just scored upon kicks off from its own 20-yard line.

TERMS

Following are brief explanations for terms that are not described elsewhere in this chapter.

A **dead ball** is when the ball is dead and the play is over, when a ball carrier is downed or out of bounds, when a quarterback drops to his knee, when a ball carrier slides feet first, when a ball carrier is held or otherwise restrained so that his forward progress is stopped, when a pass drops incomplete, when a kick receiver does not attempt to run out a kick from the end zone, when a fair catch is caught, when a field goal attempt passes the crossbar, and when an official sounds his whistle.

A **free kick** happens when a kick is "free" (undefended) during a kickoff and after a safety. A team may also choose to free kick immediately following a fair catch of a punt. A free kick may be a drop kick, place kick, or punt.

A **fumble** occurs when a player loses possession of the ball while the play is still in progress.

During a kickoff, the kicking team may put on a play—an **onside kick**—to retain possession of the ball. The kick must travel 10 yards or first touch a player on the receiving team before the kicking team can recover the ball.

A player or a ball is **out of bounds** when either has touched a boundary line (or touched ground beyond the boundary line).

Special teams is a term used for the units on the field during kickoffs, placekicks, and punts.

A **touchback** occurs when a ball is dead on or behind a team's own goal line, provided the ball's impetus came from an opponent and it is not a touchdown.

FIELD

The *playing field* is 53.33 yards wide by 120 yards long (see figure 21.2). The length of the field is marked by boundary lines called *sidelines*. The end zones, located at both ends of the field, are 10 yards deep, bordered by a goal line in front and an end line in back. The two goal lines are 100 yards apart. Any part of the goal line is considered part of the end zone; any part of the end line and the sideline that borders the end zone is considered out of bounds.

The front and back corners of the end zones are marked with pylons. These pylons are in bounds.

FIELD

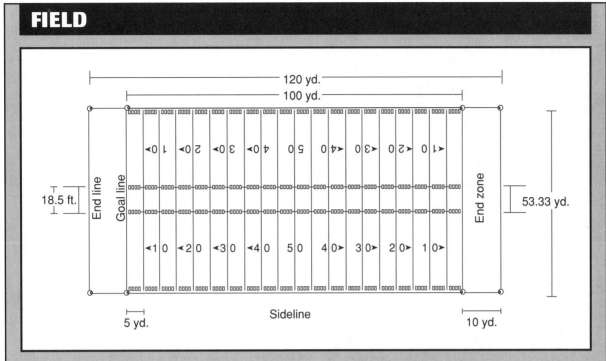

Figure 21.2. The dimensions and features of a football field.
Adapted from National Football League 1994.

The field is lined, width-wise, at intervals of 5 yards; along the sidelines each yard is marked. Yard lines are numbered every 10 yards in multiples of 10; these numbers are 2 yards long. Inbounds lines, or *hash marks*, run parallel to the yard lines. Hash marks are set 70.75 feet from each sideline in professional football and 53.25 feet from each sideline in college football.

Goal posts are at the back of each end zone, with a horizontal crossbar 18.5 feet in length and 10 feet above the ground. The crossbar is directly above the end line. Two vertical posts extend 30 feet above the crossbar and are topped by ribbon 4 inches by 42 inches.

PLAYERS

Offensive and defensive units have 11 players each. Player positions are designated depending on the system and terminology employed by the coach. Generally speaking, positions are identified as follows:

- Offense—quarterback, running back, wide receiver, tight end, center, tackle, guard, punter, and placekicker
- Defense—end, tackle, linebacker, cornerback, and safety

Substitutes may enter a game during a dead ball (when play is out). A player is not limited to a certain number of times he may enter a game, but neither team may have more than 11 players on the field at the snap of the ball.

EQUIPMENT

The *ball* is oval-shaped, leather-bound, inflated to a pressure 12.5 to 13.5 pounds per square inch, and weighing 14 to 15 ounces. It is 11 to 11.5 inches long and 28 to 28.5 inches at its largest circumference. (Youth league footballs are smaller.)

Players wear *helmets, face masks, pads,* and other protective equipment (see figure 21.3). This gear includes shoulder, chest, rib, hip, thigh, knee, shin, elbow, wrist, and forearm pads. *Jerseys* must

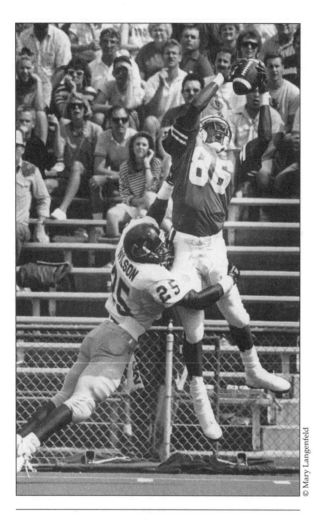

© Mary Langenfeld

Figure 21.3. The high-impact nature of football makes protective equipment an essential ingredient.

cover all pads on the torso and upper body. *Pants* must cover the knee, and *stockings* must cover the lower legs from the feet to the bottom of the pants. *Metal and aluminum cleats* are prohibited. Conical cleats with tips measuring less than .375-inch in diameter are also prohibited. *Nylon cleats* with flat steel tips are permitted.

A crew of three operates *yardage chains* on the sidelines. The chains are 10 yards long and are attached to two sticks 5 feet in height. The *down marker* has four flip-over numbers (1, 2, 3, and 4) on a stick 4 feet in height. These numbers denote what down is coming up (see page 127), and the marker is placed at the nose of the ball.

A *play clock* is used between plays. Various levels have rules denoting how much time can run off

a play clock (which begins at the end of one play and ends with the snap of the ball beginning the next play) before a team is penalized for *delay of game.* In the NFL, it's 40 seconds between plays; in the NCAA, 25 seconds are allowed from the time the ball is ready to be put into play to the snap.

FOULS AND PENALTIES

On the following pages are brief explanations of common violations, listed in alphabetical order, that result in penalties. The length of the penalty appears at the end of each listing. Note that many penalties are listed under one infraction called "Personal Foul."

Batting, punching, or kicking the ball. A player cannot bat or punch a ball toward the opponent's end zone, or bat or punch a ball in any direction in the end zone. Although *stripping the ball* (raking the ball from the player's grasp) is legal, attempting to bat or punch the ball in a player's possession is not legal. Neither is kicking any loose ball or ball in a player's possession.   *10 yards*

Delay of game. When a team does not put the ball into play in the allotted time (40 seconds from the end of the previous play, or 25 seconds after a timeout, measurement, injury, or other delay).   *5 yards*

Double (offsetting) foul. When fouls are committed by both teams, the penalties offset each other, and the down is replayed at the previous spot. Exception: if one penalty is a 15-yarder and the other is a 5-yarder, the 15-yard penalty is marked off from the previous spot.

Encroachment. When any part of a player's body is in the *neutral zone* and contact occurs before the ball is snapped. The neutral zone is a space the length of the ball between the offense's and defense's scrimmage lines.   *5 yards*

Fair catch interference. A player signaling for a fair catch of a punt must be given the opportunity to make the catch before the ball hits the ground. No contact may be made by a defender unless the ball has touched the receiver and the ground.   *15 yards*

False start. This occurs when an offensive player, once in the set position, moves in such a way as to signify the snap of the ball.   *5 yards*

Helping a runner. No offensive player can assist a runner (other than blocking for the runner) or use *interlocking interference* to aid a runner. Helping a runner includes pushing him or lifting him. *10 yards in NFL play; 5 yards in NCAA play*

Offensive holding. No offensive player, in attempting to block, can use his hands to grab or obstruct a defender, except to initially contact the defender. The hands cannot be used to hang onto, encircle, or restrict the opponent's movement. *10 yards*

Defensive holding. No defensive player can tackle or hold an opponent other than the ball carrier. *5 yards and automatic first down*

Illegal contact. A defender may make contact with an offensive receiver who is in front of him and within 5 yards of the line of scrimmage, but beyond 5 yards (or if the receiver has moved beyond the defender), the defender may not make contact that impedes or restricts the receiver. Incidental contact is legal, as long as it does not significantly impede the progress of the receiver or create a distinct advantage for the defender. *5 yards and automatic first down*

Illegal forward pass. A team may make one forward pass from behind the line of scrimmage (a player with the ball may not cross the line of scrimmage and then retreat behind it and throw a pass). Any other forward pass is illegal with penalties as follows: for passing from a point beyond the line of scrimmage—*5 yards from the spot of the pass and loss of down;* for a second forward pass thrown, or for a pass thrown after the ball was returned behind the line of scrimmage—*loss of down from the previous spot;* for a forward pass not from scrimmage—*loss of 5 yards from the spot of the pass.*

Illegal motion. Only one offensive player—a backfield player—may be in motion before the snap. The motion can be parallel to, or backward from, the line of scrimmage. Any other motion by other players—including movement of head, arms, and feet, and swaying of body—is illegal. *5 yards*

Ineligible player downfield. Before a pass is thrown, an offensive lineman (unless he is designated as an eligible receiver) may not lose contact with an opponent and advance beyond the line of scrimmage. *5 yards*

Intentional grounding. A passer may not throw an incomplete pass without a realistic chance of completing it in order to avoid being tackled. (However, a quarterback may stop the clock by receiving a snap and immediately throwing the ball to the ground in front of him.) *loss of down and 10 yards from the previous spot. If the foul occurs more than 10 yards from the line of scrimmage, loss of down at the spot the foul occurs*

Offside. A player is offside when any part of him is beyond the line of scrimmage when the ball is put into play. *5 yards*

Pass interference. Once a ball is thrown, no player may hinder the progress of an opponent who has a chance to catch the pass. Incidental contact that does not impede a player or affect his chance to catch the ball is legal. Restrictions on pass interference end once the pass is touched. *10 yards for offensive pass interference; first down at the point the foul occurred for defensive pass interference*

Personal Fouls

The following fouls result in penalties.

Blocking below the waist. Players on the receiving team on a kickoff or punt cannot block below the waist. After a change of possession, neither team may block below the waist. *15 yards*

Chop block. No offensive player may block a defensive player at the thigh level or below while the defender is being blocked by another offensive player. *15 yards*

Clip. Except for close-in line blocking, no player may clip an opponent below the waist from behind. *15 yards*

Crackback block. An offensive player aligned 2 yards or more from an offensive tackle may not clip or contact a defender below the waist while he is within 5 yards either way of the line of scrimmage. *15 yards*

Grabbing the face mask. No player may grasp the face mask of an opponent. *5 yards for incidental grasping and 15 yards for twisting, turning, or pulling the mask*

Head slap. A defensive player may not contact an opponent's head with his palms except to ward him off the line. This exception may not be a repeated act during a single play. *15 yards*

Piling on. Players may not pile on a runner after the ball is dead or intentionally fall upon any prostrate player. *15 yards*

Roughing the passer. After the passer has released the ball, the rusher may make direct contact only up through the rusher's first step. After the first step, the rusher must attempt to avoid contact and not "drive through" the rush. Even if the timing of the contact is legal, a rusher may not be unnecessarily rough, club the passer's arm, or hit the knee or below if the rusher has a direct route to the passer.　*15 yards*

Roughing or running into the kicker. No defensive player may run into or rough a kicker unless the defender has touched the ball or the kicker initiates the contact. There is no penalty if a defender is blocked into the kicker.　*5 yards for running into the kicker and 15 yards for roughing the kicker*

Striking, kicking, or clubbing. No player may strike with his fists, club, kick, or knee another player in the head, neck, or face.　*15 yards*

Tripping. No player may intentionally trip an opponent.　*10 yards*

Too many players on the field. A team may not have more than 11 players on the field at the snap of the ball. (There is no penalty for having fewer than 11.)　*5 yards*

Unnecessary roughness. This call covers a variety of illegal actions, including spearing with the helmet, tackling out of bounds, throwing the runner to the ground after the ball is dead, running or diving into a player who is obviously out of the play, and kicking an opponent above the knee.　*15 yards*

Unsportsmanlike conduct. This call is used for any act that is unsportsmanlike, including baiting, taunting, or using abusive or threatening language; unnecessary physical contact with an official; and jumping or standing on another player in an attempt to block a kick.　*15 yards*

Enforcing Penalties

In general, a penalty is enforced from the *spot of the foul* unless otherwise governed by a specific rule. Most fouls on forward passes and kicks are enforced from the *previous spot;* most fouls on runs and between downs are enforced from the *succeeding spot.*

The offended team may choose to *decline a penalty,* in which case the play continues as though no foul were committed. A team may also accept a penalty but decline the yardage normally assessed with the penalty. Unless a *loss of down* is included as part of the penalty, the yardage is assessed and the down remains the same.

MODIFICATIONS

Football can be played in various forms, including flag, touch, and Canadian. Different professional leagues have also been formed; some of these leagues, such as the Arena Football League and the World Football League, play using rules that vary from those listed in this chapter. Youth leagues also have rule variations, to enhance players' safety.

Flag and Touch Football

Flag and touch football have several variations. For general game guidelines for flag and touch football see table 21.2.

Contact blocking allows for contact between the opponent's waist and shoulders. Blockers must be on their feet before, during, and after the block; no cross-body blocks or rolling blocks are allowed. An open-hand, straight-arm block is permitted; the blocker may not lock his hands together.

Table 21.2:　Flag and Touch Football			
Game	Players per team	Blocking	Field
Flag	8	Contact	53 1/3 yd × 100 yd
Touch	7	Contact	53 1/3 yd × 100 yd
Screen flag	7	Screen	53 1/3 yd × 100 yd
Ineligible linemen flag	9	Contact	53 1/3 yd × 100 yd
4 on 4	4	Screen	25 yd × 40 yd

Screen blocking allows for no contact with the opponent's body. Blockers must be on their feet before, during, and after the block.

A game lasts *48 minutes* (two 24-minute halves). The clock runs continuously for the first 22 minutes of a half; it stops as with regular football rules during the last two minutes of a half. Teams get three *timeouts* per half, lasting one minute each. A team may take no more than two timeouts in the last two minutes of a half. In regular season *overtime* games, Team A starts with a first-and-goal on the opponents' 20-yard line. Team B then gets a chance to score in the same situation. The game is continued in this fashion until the tie is broken. Team B always gets a chance to tie or win. In championship games, overtime is decided by sudden death—the first team to score wins.

In flag football, when a flag is removed from the ball carrier, the play is over (see figure 21.4). In touch football, the play is dead when the ball carrier is legally touched. A new set of downs is awarded each time a team advances to the next zone (a regulation field is divided into five zones of 20 yards each).

Figure 21.4. A flag football player runs up the field. The play is over when a player's flag has been pulled off by a defensive player.

In *4 on 4* play, there are *no run* zones from each 5-yard line to the goal line, and from 15-yard line to 15-yard line (i.e., 10 yards across midfield).

Points are awarded as follows:

- Touchdown = six points
- Touchdown (made by female in co-ed play) = nine points
- Extra point (from the 3-yard line) = one point
- Extra point (from the 10-yard line) = two points
- Return of extra point by defense = two points

A team may choose to attempt the extra point from either the 3-yard line or the 10-yard line.

Canadian Football

Canadian football is similar to American football. The following list includes some of the significant differences:

- The playing field is 65 yards by 165 yards; goal lines are 110 yards apart.
- The goal posts are on the goal line.
- The end zone is 25 yards deep.
- Teams play with 12 players each.
- Teams have three downs to gain 10 yards.
- Fair catches on punts are not permitted.
- A punt that is not returned from the end zone results in one point awarded to the kicking team.
- Each team gets one timeout per half, to be used only during the last three minutes of a half.
- There is no sudden death; overtime games have two five-minute periods.
- The ball is placed on the 5-yard line for extra-point conversions; one point is awarded for kicking an extra point; two are awarded for running or passing the ball over the goal line.

Youth Football

Many leagues have both age and weight classifications. Some have a mandatory play rule, with players required to play a minimum of plays per game, depending on the number of players on the team. Leagues for younger players (11-and-under) often choose to use an 80-yard field. The smaller field is also used for six-man and eight-man leagues. Periods last 10 to 12 minutes, with two-minute breaks between the first and second periods and between the third and fourth periods, as well as a 15-minute halftime.

Six-Man Football

A few of the differences in the six-man game follow:

- The offense must advance the ball 15 yards in four downs.
- At least three offensive players must be on the line of scrimmage at the snap.
- The ball may not be run directly across the line of scrimmage; it may, however, be advanced by passing, kicking, or by lateralling behind the line of scrimmage (the player receiving a lateral may then run across the line).
- Kickoffs are made from the 30-yard line.
- On a touchback, the ball is brought out to the 15-yard line (on an 80-yard field).

Eight-Man Football

A few of the differences in the eight-man game follow:

- At least five offensive players must be on the line of scrimmage at the snap.
- Backs and the right and left ends are eligible to receive passes.
- Direct running across the line of scrimmage is allowed.

OFFICIALS

Any official may rule on any foul; there is no territorial division in this regard. While each official has many duties, the main duties for each include the following.

The *referee* has general control; he has the final say in any disagreement, including score and number of downs. He starts and stops play, spots the ball after each play, signals coaches for the two-minute warning (in NFL play) and when they have used their timeouts, and announces penalties.

The *umpire* watches for equipment scrimmage line violations. He records timeouts, watches for line violations on short passes, and assists the referee in ball possession decisions close to the line.

The *linesman* watches primarily for offside, encroachment, illegal motion, and other violations occurring on the line before or at the snap. He is in charge of the chain crew. He works on one side of the field in the first half and the other side in the second half.

The *line judge* operates on the opposite side of the field from the linesman. He is responsible for timing the game and for spotting violations, including illegal motion and illegal shift, on his side of the field. He advises the referee when two minutes are left in a half and when time has expired in a quarter. He assists on calls of holding, encroaching, offside, forward laterals, and false starts, and he marks the out-of-bounds spot of all plays on his side.

The *back judge* operates on the same side of the field as the line judge, 20 yards deep. He counts the number of defensive players and watches the eligible receivers on his side of the field, concentrating on action in the area between the field judge and the umpire. He signals when time is out and when the ball is dead, and assists in calls regarding legal catches. He also judges whether field goals are good.

The *side judge* operates on the same side as the head linesman, 20 yards deep. He counts the number of defenders and watches the eligible receivers on his side. He watches the action between the umpire and the field judge and assists on calls regarding legal catches, fumble recoveries, and out-of-bounds plays.

The *field judge* is primarily responsible for covering kicks and forward passes that cross the goal line. He times the halftime and timeouts and the time between plays. He also assists on calls regarding legal catches, fumble recoveries, and out-of-bounds plays.

Official Signals

For common officials' signals, see figure 21.5.

ORGANIZATIONS

National Football League
410 Park Ave.
New York, NY 10022
212-758-1500

National Touch Football Leagues
1039 Coffey Ct.
Crestwood, MO 63126
314-621-0777

Pop Warner Football
920 Town Center Drive, Ste. I-25
Langhorne, PA 19047
215-752-2691

United States Flag Football League
5834 Pine Tree Drive
Sanibel, FL 33957
813-472-0544

U.S. Flag and Touch Football League
7709 Ohio St.
Mentor, OH 44060
216-974-8735

Time out   Touchdown   Personal foul

Illegal use of   Illegal contact   Offside
hands

(continued)

Figure 21.5.   Common football official's signals.

Delay of game   Holding   Illegal motion

First down   Pass interference   Roughing kicker

Missed kick, penalty refused,
or incomplete pass

Figure 21.5. *(continued)*

22

Golf

© Photophile/J.R. & E.C. Stangler

Golf is believed to have had its beginnings in 15th-century Scotland, where players first used wooden balls and then leather balls stuffed with feathers. Golf was introduced in the United States in the late 1700s and has grown in popularity with the advent of improved equipment, professional tours, and television coverage.

The object of golf is to use as few strokes as possible to hit the ball into a series of holes arranged on a course. There are two main playing formats: stroke play and match play. In stroke play, the side (individual player or partners) that has the lowest total score wins.

In match play, the winner is the side that wins the most holes. The match is over when one side leads by a number of holes that is greater than the number of holes left. For instance, if after 15 holes, Player A has won four more holes than Player B, the match is over, because even if Player B wins the remaining 3 holes, he cannot beat Player A. In such a case, Player A wins four and three, meaning he or she is four holes up with three holes remaining. The rules in this chapter are from the United States Golf Association.

PROCEDURES

Sides determine the order of play by a draw. Partners may decide their own playing order. The side that wins the hole "takes the honor" by going first at the next tee. If each side scores the same on a hole, the side that teed first at that hole retains the honor.

In match play, if the sides are tied at the end of regulation, play continues until one side wins a hole, which ends the match. In stroke play, also known as medal play, if sides are tied at the end of a match, they play until one side has a lower score on a hole. This is a sudden-death playoff. In tournaments, ties are sometimes broken by an 18-hole playoff, after which sudden-death applies.

TERMS

A player is said to **address the ball** when he takes his stance and grounds the club in preparing to strike the ball.

An **approach shot** is a shot that is made to hit the ball onto the green.

A **birdie** is one stroke under **par**.

A **bogey** is one stroke over **par**. A **double-bogey** is two strokes over.

A **bunker** is an area of the course usually filled with sand. It is also called a sand trap and is considered a hazard.

A **caddie** carries a player's clubs and offers advice on how to play holes.

Casual water is a temporary accumulation of water.

A **chip** shot is a low approach shot from a position close to the green.

A **divot** is a piece of turf dug from the ground by the clubhead.

A **draw** is a controlled right-to-left shot (as opposed to a hook, which curves sharply to the left).

A player **drives** the ball when she strikes it from the tee on a par 4 or 5.

An **eagle** is two strokes under **par**.

A **fade** is a controlled left-to-right shot (as opposed to a slice, which curves sharply to the right).

A **halved hole** occurs when each side scores the same on a hole.

A **hazard** is any bunker or water hazard.

A **hook** is a shot that curves sharply to the left (or to the right, for a left-handed player).

Loose impediments are natural objects on the course, such as pebbles or leaves, that are not permanently attached to the ground.

Obstructions are any artificial objects except for out-of-bounds markers or objects that are an integral part of the course.

Out describes the first nine holes; **in** signifies the second, or back, nine holes.

Boundary markers denote all areas that are **out of bounds**; play is not allowed out of bounds.

Par is the number of strokes that an expert player is expected to take to hole out. The yardage guidance for par is shown in table 22.1.

Table 22.1:	Yardage Guidance for Par	
Par	Men	Women
3	Up to 250	Up to 210
4	251 to 470	211 to 400
5	471 and over	401 to 575
6	—	576 and over

Adapted from United States Golf Association and the Royal and Ancient Golf Club of St. Andrews, Scotland 1994.

A **pitch** is a high shot near the green that is intended to roll minimally after landing.

A group may **play through** when the group ahead of them is slowing them down.

"Rub of the green" is the term used when a ball is deflected or stopped by something or someone other than the player, the player's partner or caddie, or an official.

A **shank** is a shot that goes off to the right (or the left, for a left-hander).

A player's **"short game"** refers to her pitching, chipping, and putting.

A **slice** is a shot that curves sharply to the right (to the left for a left-hander).

Winter rules allow for improving the lie of the ball on the fairway (but not closer to the hole); check local rules.

COURSE

While courses vary in hole lengths, design, and playing characteristics, they share common components (see figure 22.1).

A standard course contains 18 *holes* usually between 100 and 600 yards long; each hole is on a putting green and is 4.25 inches in diameter and at least 4 inches deep.

Each hole has a *teeing ground* from which play for that hole begins. The most forward point from which the ball may be played is designated by *tee markers;* the farthest point back from which a ball may be teed is two club lengths behind these markers.

The *fairway* lies between the teeing ground and the *putting green,* which is the short-cropped surface around the hole. The *apron* (short collar) around the green is not considered part of the green.

Hazards—both bunkers and water hazards—lie between and around the teeing ground and the green. The *rough* is the longer grass and rough terrain bordering the fairway and green.

The *flagstick,* or *pin,* is a movable pole about 8 feet long that is placed in the hole to show the position of the hole on the putting green.

EQUIPMENT

A maximum of 14 *clubs* are allowed. They are carried in a golf bag; players may carry the bag

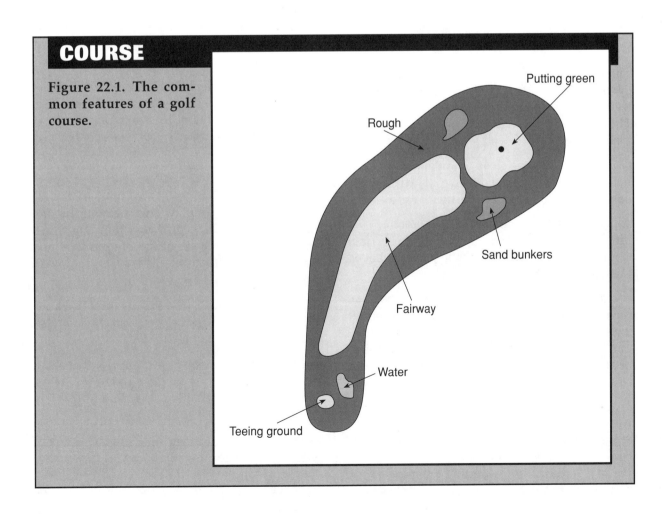

COURSE

Figure 22.1. The common features of a golf course.

Putting green

Rough

Sand bunkers

Fairway

Water

Teeing ground

or transport it in a hand- or motorized cart. The three types of clubs include the following:

- *Woods.* The clubhead is wood (modern woods also have metal, carbon, and titanium heads); these clubs are used for longer shots. Woods are numbered 1 through 10; the most commonly used are 1, 3, and 5.
- *Irons.* The clubhead is usually steel, and the club has a shorter shaft than a wood. Irons are used for shorter shots and are numbered 1 through 10, plus the wedges.
- *Putters.* There are many styles of clubheads; putters are usually all metal and are used on the putting green.

The *ball* is dimpled and has a synthetic shell. It weighs not more than 1.62 ounces and is not less than 1.68 inches in diameter. On a teeing ground the ball is placed on a *tee*, which is a peg about 2 inches long. The tee allows the player to drive the ball.

THROUGH THE GREEN

The following rules apply to play "through the green," which is the entire course except for the teeing ground, the putting green, and hazards. The rules are in alphabetical order according to the key term.

No player may give *advice* to anyone other than her partner. A player may receive advice from her partner or from her or her partner's caddie.

A player will be penalized for *discontinuing play* unless the committee has discontinued play or is ruling on a disputed play, or the player believes there is danger from lightning.

In stroke play, when there is *doubt about procedure,* the player may play another ball after announcing this to her fellow competitor. The player reports the facts to the committee before signing her card; if the rules allow for play of the second ball, the player's score for the hole is what it was with the second ball.

A player *dropping a ball* should hold the ball at arm's length to the side and drop it. A ball may be redropped, without penalty, if it rolls into or out of a hazard, onto a putting green or out of bounds, if it rolls to an immovable obstruction,

or rolls more than two club lengths away from or closer to the green.

A ball *embedded* in a closely mown area may be lifted, cleaned, and dropped as close as possible to the spot but not closer to the hole.

When a ball is in a *hazard*—either a bunker or a water hazard—a player may not test the condition of the hazard, touch the ground or water of the hazard, or touch or move loose impediments in the hazard. If the ball is in a water hazard, a player may take a one-stroke penalty and either (a) play a ball from the spot it was last played, or (b) drop a ball behind the hazard. The player may also play the ball from the water, if possible.

To *identify a ball* (except in a hazard), a player may lift a ball she believes to be her own and clean it as necessary for identification. She must then return it to the same spot.

A ball *in motion* touched by an outside agency is played where it lies. In stroke play, if it is touched by the player, his partner, caddie, or any of his own equipment, he incurs a two-stroke penalty and plays the ball where it lies; in match play, he loses the hole.

A player may lift her ball if it is *interfering* with or assisting play. This may not be done while another ball is in motion. In stroke play, a player requested to lift her ball may choose to play first rather than lift.

A player must play the ball as it *lies.* He may not improve the position of his ball, the area of his swing, or his line of play. This includes moving or bending anything growing, tamping down grass, replacing old divots before the shot, and so on. Loose impediments may be removed, however.

When *lifting a ball,* a player must first mark the position of the ball. If the position is not marked, the player incurs a one-stroke penalty.

The *line of play* may be indicated by anyone, but no one may stand on or close to the line while the stroke is played. (See also "line of play" in "On the Green.")

If there is reason to believe a ball is *lost* out of bounds or outside a water hazard, a player may take a one-stroke penalty and play a provisional ball as close as possible to the spot the original ball was played. A ball is defined as "lost" if the player has searched for five minutes, or if the player has put another ball into play. If the original ball is found within five minutes, it must be played, even if it is in an unplayable lie or water hazard.

If a ball is *moved* by the player, partner, caddie, or equipment, the ball is replaced and a one-stroke penalty is incurred. If the ball is moved by the opponent in match play (except during a search), the opponent is assessed a one-stroke penalty. In stroke play, no penalty is assessed a fellow competitor for moving a ball. A ball moved by another ball is set back in place.

If a ball is played from *outside the tee area* in match play, the opponent may ask for the shot to be replayed (no penalty). In stroke play, there is a two-stroke penalty, and the ball must be replayed.

A player may not play a *practice stroke* except when between two holes. Then she may practice putting or chipping on or near the teeing ground of the next hole, provided the practice does not unduly delay play. Note that a practice *swing* is not a practice *stroke*.

A player is not necessarily entitled to *see his ball* when playing a stroke.

In *striking the ball*, the player must fairly strike at the ball and not push or scoop it. If the player strikes the ball twice on the same stroke, he receives a one-penalty stroke (two strokes total).

If a ball falls off a *tee* while a player is addressing it, he may replace it with no penalty. But if the player swings at the ball, whether the ball is moving or not, the stroke counts.

A player may declare her ball *unplayable* anywhere, unless it lies in or is touching a water hazard. She may take a one-stroke penalty and play a ball as near as possible to the spot where the last shot was played. Or she may drop a ball within two club lengths of where the unplayable ball lies (but not nearer to the hole) and add a penalty stroke. A third option is to take a penalty stroke and drop a ball behind the unplayable lie, keeping that spot between the hole and the drop area. There is no limit to how far back a player may drop the ball.

When a player plays a *wrong ball* (any ball other than the ball in play or a provisional ball) while in match play, he loses the hole. The only exception is if the ball is played from a hazard; in this case, no penalty is incurred, the stroke does not count, and the player places another ball in the spot from which the wrong ball was played. In stroke play, playing a wrong ball brings a two-stroke penalty.

ON THE GREEN

The following rules apply to play "on the green." The rules are in alphabetical order according to the key term.

A player may *clean* a ball when she lifts it. She must mark and replace the ball where she lifted it.

The *flagstick* may remain in place, be removed, or held up to indicate position. The flagstick may not be moved once a ball is in motion, except for putts. If a ball rests against a flagstick and falls in the hole when the flagstick is picked up, the ball is considered holed on the previous stroke.

A *line of play* for putting may be pointed out before the stroke, but the putting green may not be touched and no mark may be laid on it to indicate the putting line. In match play, breaking this rule results in loss of the hole; in stroke play, the player incurs a two-stroke penalty.

If a ball from off the green strikes and *moves* a ball on the green, there is no penalty and the ball moved is returned to its original position. If a player on the green strokes a ball that hits another player's ball, there is a two-stroke penalty in stroke play. There is no penalty in match play for this.

A player cannot take a *practice stroke* on the green.

SCORING

Players are responsible for their own scores. In stroke play, players add each stroke and penalty stroke to arrive at their total score. At the end of a round, each player should review and sign his scorecard before turning it in. If a player signs for a lower score for a hole than he shot, he is disqualified. If he records a higher score for a hole, that score stands. No changes on the scorecard may be made once it is turned in to the committee.

Handicaps allow players of varying abilities to compete fairly against each other. Handicaps are determined by a player's recent play. A player with a 10 handicap who shoots an actual 100 would finish with a score of 90.

ETIQUETTE

The following rules are matters of courtesy and safety:

- Before swinging, the player should make sure that no one is in a position to be hit with the club or ball.
- The player who has the honor should be allowed to play before the next player tees off.
- While a player is addressing or stroking the ball, no one should talk, move, or stand directly behind the ball or the hole (see figure 22.2).
- Players should play without delay.
- Players searching for a ball should signal the players behind them to pass when it becomes apparent that the ball will not be found quickly. In most cases they should not complete the five-minute search time before letting players behind them play through.
- When players complete a hole, they should immediately leave the green and record their scores elsewhere.
- Among players with similar abilities, two-ball matches have precedence over three-ball and four-ball matches. Players in the latter two matches should invite two-ball matches to pass through.
- A single player should give way to a match of any kind.
- Any match playing a whole round is entitled to pass a match playing a shorter round.
- A player should smooth over any holes and footprints she makes before leaving a bunker.
- A player should replace any turf he cuts through the green and repair any damage on the green made by the ball. Damage to the green made by golf spikes should be repaired after the hole is completed. All divots should be replaced and tamped down.
- Players should not damage the green by leaning on their putters.

© Photophile/Tom Tracy

Figure 22.2.   Silence is the rule while a player is addressing the ball.

- The player farthest from the hole plays first.
- A player should call "fore" if she thinks her ball may hit another person.
- A player should not take his golf bag, cart, extra clubs, or any other equipment onto the green or tee.
- A player holding the flagstick should take care that her shadow does not fall across the line of the putt.
- Players should place an identification mark on their golf balls.

Sides and Games

Variations of games are as follows:

A *match* pits one player or side against another. In a *threesome,* one player plays against two, and each side plays one ball. In a *foursome,* two players play against two others, with each side playing one ball and teammates alternating shots.

Three-ball has three players, each playing against one another. In *best-ball,* one player plays against the better ball of two others or best ball of three others. In *four-ball,* two players play against two others in match-play format, with only the best ball (best score) of each team counting.

In *four-ball stroke play,* two competitors team up, each playing her own ball; the lower score of the two balls for each hole is counted. In *bogey* and *par* competitions, players play against a fixed score at each hole. For example, par on a hole is the "opponent"; the winner is the golfer who is furthest ahead of par.

In *Stableford* competition, points are awarded in relation to a fixed score at each hole. For example, a birdie is worth three points, a double bogey or worse scores zero points. The person scoring the most points wins in Stableford competition. Table 22.2 shows how points are awarded in Stableford play.

Table 22.2: How Points Are Awarded in Stableford Play	
Hole played in . . .	Points
More than one over fixed score	0
One over fixed score	1
Fixed score	2
One under fixed score	3
Two under fixed score	4
Three under fixed score	5
Four under fixed score	6

Adapted from United States Golf Association and the Royal and Ancient Golf Club of St. Andrews, Scotland 1994.

ORGANIZATIONS

United States Golf Association
Golf House
Far Hills, NJ 07931
908-234-2300

23

Gymnastics

© Claus Andersen

The roots of gymnastics can be found in ancient Greece, but the modern development of the sport began in 19th-century Germany, where much of the sport's apparatus—the rings, the horse, and the bars—were developed. Immigrants brought the sport to the United States. Men competed in gymnastics in the first modern Olympics in 1896; women began Olympic competition in 1936.

Male and female gymnasts compete in various events, attempting to score the highest number of points possible through their performances. High score wins. Women compete in four artistic events (horse vault, uneven bars, balance beam, and floor exercise). Men compete in six artistic events (floor exercise, pommel horse, rings, vault, parallel bars, and horizontal bar). Women also compete in rhythmic gymnastics, which is a separate Olympic sport; we'll include a brief section on rhythmic gymnastics near the end of this chapter.

The source for rules for this chapter is the International Gymnastics Federation.

PROCEDURES

Gymnasts present themselves to a judge prior to (and after) their event. They begin their exercise when a green light is lit or when the judge signals for them to begin. If they fall during an exercise, they have 30 seconds to remount and continue.

Exercise Evaluation

Compulsory exercises are set routines that every gymnast must complete. (Beginning in 1997, compulsories were eliminated from international competition.) Each competitor begins compulsories with 10 points.

Women competing in *optional* exercises begin with 9.40 points; they may earn .60 bonus points for performing extremely difficult skills or combinations, to reach a maximum of 10 points. Men competing in optional exercises begin with 9 points, and they may earn a maximum of 1 bonus point, for a maximum total score of 10. Each exercise has specific requirements and deductions, the latter based on types of errors made.

In competitions with six judges, the high and low scores are thrown out; the remaining four scores are added and then divided by four to arrive at an average score. The allowable difference between the two middle scores decreases as the scores increase.

Scoring is further affected by five *difficulty values*, ranging from easy (A) to high difficulty (E). Also, different events have different requirements; if these requirements are not successfully completed, points are deducted.

Gymnasts can earn *bonus points* for extremely difficult skills and combinations.

Gymnasts have points deducted for *faults*. For women, point deductions range from .05 to .20 point for a small fault, to .25 to .40 point for a medium fault, to .45 point or more for a major fault. For men, small faults result in a deduction of .10 point; medium faults, .20 to .30 point; and major faults, .40 to .50 point. Examples of faults include

- breaking form;
- touching the apparatus or floor for balance;
- incorrectly positioning hands or legs;
- interrupting an upward movement;
- losing balance during, or not completing, a dismount;
- bending arms in handstand, or falling out of the handstand;
- stepping outside the floor area during a floor exercise;
- falling off an apparatus; and
- failing to start on time.

TERMS

An **acrobatic element** is a salto (somersault) or handspring executed from a stand or a run.

The **difficulty** of an element is categorized into one of five value groups (A, B, C, D, or E), based on the strength and physical requirements of the movement.

An **element** is the smallest independently executed movement in gymnastics, with definite starting and ending points.

An **element of flexibility** shows an extreme range of motion in one or more joints (e.g., shoulders, hips, or spine).

An **element of flight** is a movement involving releasing a grip, a distinct flight phase, and regripping the apparatus.

An **element of strength** is a movement where gravity is conquered slowly or where a gymnast achieves balance through static force.

An **element of swing** is a dynamic movement executed with great amplitude and without stopping or visibly showing strength.

An **exercise** is the complete presentation of all the elements. **Compulsory exercises** contain specific criteria that the gymnast must meet; **optional exercises** have specific requirements but also allow for the gymnast's preferences.

A **gymnastic element** is a nonacrobatic move, such as a body wave, separating the legs, rolling, or jumping.

A **hold part** refers to the gymnast's holding his position for two seconds in a prescribed position.

WOMEN'S ARTISTIC EVENTS

Women compete in the following events: the horse vault, uneven bars, balance beam, and floor exercise (see figure 23.1).

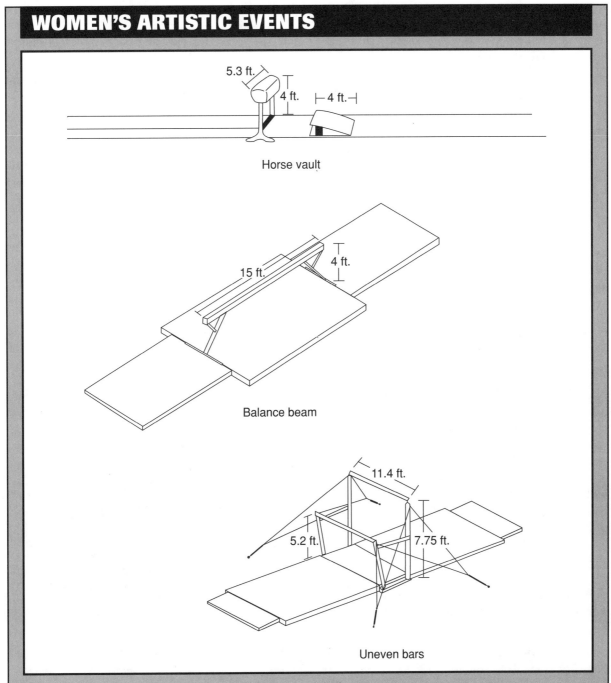

WOMEN'S ARTISTIC EVENTS

5.3 ft.

4 ft.

⊢ 4 ft. ⊣

Horse vault

15 ft.

4 ft.

Balance beam

11.4 ft.

5.2 ft.

7.75 ft.

Uneven bars

Figure 23.1. The equipment used in women's artistic events.
Adapted from American Coaching Effectiveness Program in cooperation with the United States Gymnastics Federation 1992.

Horse Vault

The vaulting horse is 5.3 feet long, 4 feet high, and 14 inches wide. It is made of wood on a metal frame and has a thin layer of padding covered with leather or vinyl.

In compulsories, women get one attempt; in optionals, they get two. In individual finals, both optional vaults are scored and averaged. In apparatus finals the two vaults must be different.

The vaulter runs down a runway, springs off a springboard, and vaults crosswise over the horse. She is judged on four portions of the vault, including

- the first flight phase (from the springboard to the horse),
- the support phase (pushing off the horse),
- the second flight phase (from the horse to the dismount), and
- the landing.

Uneven Bars

The upper bar is 7.75 feet high; the lower bar is 5.2 feet high. The bars are 11.4 feet long. They are made of wood or fiberglass, with a metal support.

The evaluation begins with the gymnast's take-off from the board or floor. The exercise must include at least 10 elements. The exercise must contain at least one directional change (a 180-degree pirouette, for example) and at least two flight elements of at least a "B" value. The exercise must include at least three bar changes. Elements must be performed without pause and without an intermediate swing.

Balance Beam

The balance beam is 15 feet long, 4 feet high, and 4 inches wide. The beam is wood padded with foam rubber and covered with vinyl or leather.

The evaluation begins with the take-off from the board or floor. The exercise must last from 70 to 90 seconds. A gymnast may use two static holds on the beam; additional pauses result in deductions. The routine must include both acrobatic and gymnastic elements. Acrobatic elements include forward, backward, or sideways flight;

gymnastic elements include leaps, turns, hops, step combinations, balance elements, and body waves. The gymnast must execute at least

- one 360-degree turn,
- one acrobatic series of two or more flight elements,
- one gymnastic series of two or more elements,
- one mixed series of two or more elements (gymnastic/acrobatic), and
- one element or connection close to the beam (i.e., not standing).

Floor Exercise

The floor exercise lasts between 70 and 90 seconds. The exercise is done to music and begins with the first gymnastic or acrobatic movement. Stepping outside of the floor area (a square measuring 12 meters on each side) results in a deduction of one-tenth point. The exercise should consist of both acrobatic elements and gymnastic elements (turns, leaps, jumps, balance elements in various positions, and body waves). It should include dynamic change between slow and fast movements and must be done in harmony with the music. The gymnast must perform

- one gymnastic series with three elements;
- one mixed series with three elements; and
- two acrobatic series, one with two saltos and one with one salto; all three saltos must be different.

MEN'S ARTISTIC EVENTS

Men compete in the following events: the floor exercise, pommel horse, rings, vault, parallel bars, and horizontal bar (see figure 23.2).

Floor Exercise

The floor exercise lasts 50 to 70 seconds. The gymnast must use the entire floor area—a square measuring 12 meters on each side. He may step on, but not over, any boundary line. He also may not pause for more than one second in his routine, unless he is holding a static element.

MEN'S ARTISTIC EVENTS

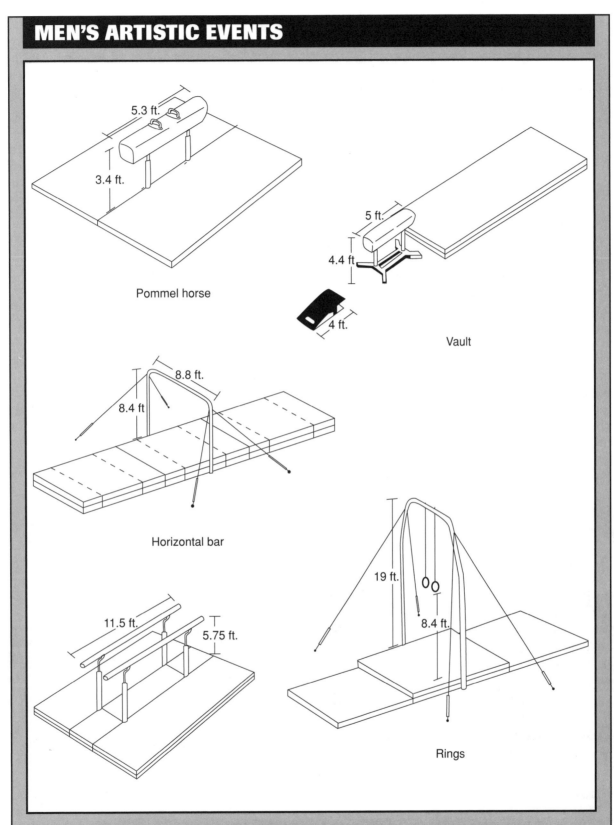

5.3 ft.

3.4 ft.

Pommel horse

5 ft.

4.4 ft

4 ft.

Vault

8.8 ft.

8.4 ft

Horizontal bar

11.5 ft.

5.75 ft.

19 ft.

8.4 ft.

Rings

Figure 23.2. The equipment used in men's artistic events.
Adapted from American Coaching Effectiveness Program in cooperation with the United States Gymnastics Federation 1992.

The exercise should consist of acrobatic jumps and include acrobatic and gymnastic elements of flexibility and balance. Examples of errors, for which points are deducted, include taking more than three running steps before a jump, attaining a low height during a jump, not having the knees and shoulders in a straight line during a standing scale, and stepping outside the floor area.

Pommel Horse

The pommel horse is 3.4 feet high and 5.3 feet long. The gymnast performs circular and pendulum swings on the horse, using various positions of support, and utilizing all three parts of the horse. The gymnast must execute leg circles with the legs together; he must perform two scissors (open-legged swings) in an optional connection. He must perform at least one "B" value element on one pommel with three hand placements. He may not pause during the routine. Errors, for which points are deducted, include not using all three parts of the horse equally, not executing a scissor, and performing more than 40 percent of the exercise with the legs straddled.

Rings

The rings are 8.4 feet above the mat. The gymnast must perform swing, strength, and hold parts, in about equal proportions. The gymnast executes these parts in a hang position, to or through a support position, and into a handstand position, with straight arms. The gymnast should not let the ropes swing; points are deducted for this. He must perform at least two handstands, one from swing, one from strength, and one static strength part.

Types of errors for which a gymnast is penalized include touching the ropes with his feet or any part of his body, using too many strength elements, and not holding strength elements level or for two seconds.

Vault

The vault is 4.4 feet high and 5 feet long. A gymnast runs up, jumps onto a springboard, and ex-executes simple or multiple turns around the axis of the vault. The gymnast must use the entire length of the horse. The vault is judged on its starting value, on the flight from the springboard to the horse, on the body position during execution, and on the pushoff from the horse to a landing position.

Male gymnasts perform only one vault except during apparatus finals, when they complete two different vaults and have their scores averaged.

Errors resulting in penalties include opening of or straddling of the legs while going from the board to the horse or while on the horse, insufficient vault height, deviation from the axis of the horse during the vault or during the landing, and insufficient distance during landing.

Parallel Bars

The parallel bars are 5.75 feet high and 11.5 feet long. The gymnast performs elements of swing and flight both above and below the bars. He can execute elements in a side position and elements of strength. He must perform at least one swinging part and one element from a hang or through a hang while releasing both hands. He may not perform more than three hold parts, or unnecessarily straddle his legs. Other errors that may result in penalties include walking during a handstand, touching the bars or floor with any part of his body other than his hands on the bars, and not holding strength parts for the required two seconds.

Horizontal Bar

The horizontal bar is 8.4 feet high and 8.8 feet long. The gymnast performs elements of uninterrupted swing, including giant swings (360-degree rotations), turns, and flight elements. He may perform a one-arm swing. The routine must include at least one release-and-regrasp of the bar that slows flight. He will be penalized for errors, including stopping in a handstand or any other position, executing swing elements with strength, deviating from the direction of the movement, bending his arms during a circular swing, and failing to regrasp the bar following a flight element.

WOMEN'S RHYTHMIC EVENTS

Rhythmic gymnastics involves body movements and dance, set to music and performed while handling small equipment: rope, hoop, ball, clubs, and ribbon. An individual exercise lasts for 60 to 90 seconds; a group exercise lasts for two to two and a half minutes. Gymnasts may perform three pre-acrobatic elements, such as rolls, but no handsprings or aerials are allowed. Each routine must contain at least four elements of "B" difficulty and four of "A" difficulty; in finals competitions, a "C" and "D" element are also required. The routine must cover the entire floor and include leaps, pivots, balances, and flexibility movements.

The base score for an individual is 9.60; a senior gymnast may earn up to .40 bonus points for a maximum of 10.00. A junior gymnast may earn up to .20 bonus points for a maximum of 9.80. A group begins with a base score of 19.20 and may earn a maximum of .80 bonus points for a possible 20.00 score.

During an exercise, the *ball* may be thrown, caught, rolled, and bounced. The *rope* may be thrown, caught, swung, and twirled. The *hoop* may be thrown, caught, swung, and passed through. The *clubs* may be thrown, caught, and swung. The *ribbon* may be thrown in loops, circles, and spirals.

GYMNASTS

Gymnasts must wear proper attire *(leotards)*. They may wear bandages and slippers or socks. Gymnasts must begin their exercise within 30 seconds once they are given the signal. On the horizontal bar and rings, a coach or another gymnast may assist a gymnast into a hanging position.

OFFICIALS

Up to seven judges evaluate each routine.

ORGANIZATIONS

International Gymnastics Federation (FIG)
Rue des Oecuches 10
Case Postale 333
Moutier CH-2740
Switzerland
41 321 936 666

National Gymnastics Judges Association
44 Lawrence Lane
Bay Shore, NY 11706
516-665-2103

USA Gymnastics
201 S. Capitol, Ste. 300
Indianapolis, IN 46225
317-237-5050

24

Handball

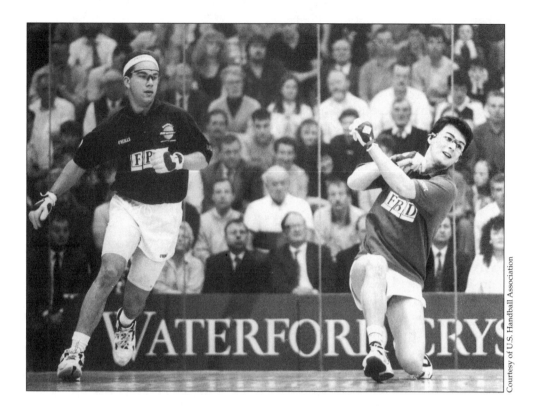

Courtesy of U.S. Handball Association

Handball's origins date back to ancient Rome. It was played on dirt floors in Ireland in the Middle Ages and brought to the United States by 19th-century Irish immigrants. Litte about the sport has changed since its introduction into America, with the exception of a smaller, harder ball and a smaller court.

Handball may be played on a four-walled, three-walled, or one-walled court. The rules for the main body of this chapter are for four-walled handball. The "Modifications" section addresses three-wall and one-wall rule differences.

The objective of the game is to win rallies and score points by serving or returning the ball so that the opponent cannot keep the ball in play. A rally is won when one player cannot return the ball before it hits the floor twice, or when a player returns a ball that hits the floor before it hits the front wall.

The source of rules for this chapter is the United States Handball Association.

PROCEDURES

A handball match is the best two-of-three games between two players (singles) or four players (doubles); a game is played to 21 points. If each player or side wins one game, the third game is a *tiebreaker,* played to 11 points. Points may be scored by the serving team only.

The winner of a coin toss chooses to serve or receive to begin the game. The other player or side chooses for the second game. To begin a tiebreaker, the player or team with the most points in the first two games chooses. If both sides have scored the same number of points, another coin toss is used to begin the tiebreaker.

Serving

The server serves from anywhere in the *service zone* (see figure 24.1 on page 157). A *foot fault* will be called if any part of either foot is beyond the outer edge of either service zone line. The server must remain in the service zone until the ball passes the *short line.*

The server must come to a complete stop before beginning a serve by bouncing the ball. She may bounce and catch the ball several times before beginning her serve, but when she begins her serve she must bounce the ball once and hit it. More than one bounce is a fault; bouncing the ball outside the service zone is also a fault. The serve must strike the front wall first, and it must hit beyond the short line. It can touch one of the side walls.

As soon as a rally ends, the referee calls either "point" or "sideout," and the receiver has 10 seconds to get into position. When the receiver is in position, or when 10 seconds elapse, whichever comes first, the referee announces the score and the server has 10 seconds to serve.

A server may commit one service fault. If he commits two faults on the same serve, he loses his serve. In doubles, the first serving team gets only one serving turn—when the receiving team wins the rally, it wins the serve. After that, both players on a team get a serving turn each time they gain the serve. The serving order of the partners is kept throughout the game. Each player continues his serve until the opponents score a *sideout.*

It is not necessary for partners on the receiving team to alternate receiving serve. The server's partner must stand within the service box until the ball passes the short line. A violation is a foot fault. Other faults include

- short serve—one whose first bounce hits before or on the short line;
- three-wall serve—a serve that hits the front wall and two other walls before hitting the floor;
- ceiling serve—a serve that hits the ceiling before hitting the floor;
- long serve—a serve that hits the back wall before hitting the floor;
- out-of-court serve—one that hits the front wall and then goes out of the court without touching the floor; and
- two consecutive screen serves—serves that pass too close to the server or the server's partner, obstructing the receiver's view.

The first screen serve is called a "defective serve" and is not penalized; the server serves again. Other defective serves that are replayed with no penalty include

- serves that hit the server's partner in the air (on the bounce results in a fault),
- straddle balls—serves that travel between the server's legs,
- court hinder—a serve that bounces erratically because of a court obstruction or wetness, and
- a ball that breaks on the serve.

The server loses her turn when she

- misses the ball while attempting to serve,
- serves so that the ball strikes anything other than the front wall first,
- serves so that the ball strikes her,
- strikes her partner with the serve when her partner's foot is outside the service box,
- commits two consecutive service faults,
- hits a crotch serve—a serve that hits the crotch in the front wall (if the serve hits a crotch in the back wall or side wall, after legally hit-

ting the front wall first and going beyond the short line, it is legal),

- serves out of order, or when she
- goes beyond her allotted 10 seconds in serving.

Returning Serve

The receiver must stand at least 5 feet behind the short line until the serve is struck. Not doing so will result in a point for the server.

No part of the receiver may extend on or over the plane of the short line when contacting the ball. A violation results in a point for the server. The receiver may go beyond the short line, however, after hitting the ball.

The receiver must return the ball before it strikes the floor twice. A serve can be returned before it strikes the floor. A return of serve can hit the back wall, one or both side walls, and the ceiling before it touches the front wall, but it must touch the front wall before it strikes the floor.

Rallies

A rally is played out until one side cannot legally return the ball. Teams alternate hits—Team A is obligated to return Team B's hit, and vice versa—but partners on a team do not have to alternate hits. In doubles play, both partners may swing at a ball, but only one player can touch it.

The front or back of the hand may be used to hit a ball; the wrist or any other part of the body may not be used.

If a rally needs to be replayed for any reason, any previous fault against the server is voided. A player loses a rally if she intentionally hinders her opponent from returning the ball. A rally is replayed for *dead-ball hinders,* such as unavoidable interference or contact.

Avoidable Hinders

An avoidable hinder results in an out if the offending player was serving, or a point if the player was receiving. A player commits an avoidable hinder when he

- doesn't move out of the way to allow his opponent a shot;

- moves into a position that blocks his opponent as he is about to return the ball;
- moves into the path of the ball just struck by his opponent;
- pushes his opponent;
- obstructs his opponent's view just before his opponent is about to strike the ball; or when he
- interferes in any way with the opponent's stroke, including restricting the opponent's follow-through.

Technicals

An offender loses one point for a technical, which may be assessed for frequent complaints, profanity, arguing, threats made to the opponent or the referee, excessive kicking or throwing the ball between rallies, failure to properly wear eye protection, and for any unsportsmanlike behavior. A technical does not result in a sideout or affect the serve order.

If a technical occurs between games, the offending player begins the next game with a negative score. Three technicals in a match result in a forfeit. A warning, with no point deduction, may be given instead of a technical. This is at the discretion of the referee. A player can be assessed a technical without first receiving a warning.

Timeouts

A timeout may be requested before the referee announces the score after a rally or calls "second serve." Each side receives three one-minute timeouts in games that go to 21; in 11-point games, each side receives two one-minute timeouts. Timeouts may be called consecutively.

Equipment timeouts—which may last up to two minutes—may be called at the referee's discretion for either side. These timeouts are not charged to either side. Such timeouts are taken for lost shoes, broken laces, wet gloves, and so on.

An injured player is not assessed a timeout. The player has 15 minutes to resume play. This injury time is cumulative; if a player uses seven minutes for an injury, he has eight minutes of injury timeout remaining in the match. Timeout between games is five minutes.

TERMS

An **ace** is a legal serve that eludes the receiver.

An **avoidable hinder** is interference that the offending player could have avoided; penalty is loss of serve or a point for the opponent.

A **back wall shot** is one that is made from a rebound off the back wall.

A **ceiling shot** is one that is hit directly to the ceiling.

A **court hinder** occurs when an erratic bounce is caused by an obstacle, construction abnormality, or wetness on the court.

A **crotch ball** is one that hits the juncture of any two walls, any wall with the floor, or any wall with the ceiling.

A **defensive shot** is one that is made to get the opponent out of an offensive position but is not made with the intent of winning the rally.

A **dig** is made by a player who retrieves a low shot.

A **fault** is an illegally served ball.

A **fly shot** is one that is played before it bounces.

A **foot fault** occurs when a portion of the server's foot is outside the service zone before the served ball passes the short line.

A **hinder** occurs when a player accidentally hinders an opponent from making a shot, or hinders the flight of the ball. A hinder is not penalized but is replayed.

A **hop serve** is a serve that has spin on it causing it to hop to the right or the left.

A **kill shot** is one that hits the front wall so low the opponent has no chance to return it.

A **lob** is a soft shot high on the front wall.

An **offensive shot** is one intended to win a rally.

A **passing shot** is one that is driven past an opponent's reach on either side.

A **point** can be scored only by the server or serving team.

The **service line** is the line parallel to and 5 feet in front of the short line.

The **service zone** is the area of the court between, and including, the short line and the service line.

The **short line** is the line halfway between, and parallel to, the front and back walls.

A **sideout** occurs when the receiving player or team wins a rally and gains the serve.

COURT

A standard four-wall court is 20 feet wide, 20 feet high, and 40 feet long (see figure 24.1). The recommended minimum height for the back wall is 14 feet.

The short line is parallel to the front and back walls; its outside edge is 20 feet from the front wall. The service line is parallel to the short line and its outside edge is 5 feet in front of the short line.

The service zone is the area between the outer edges of the short line and the service line. The service boxes are located at each side of the service zone. Each service box is marked by a line parallel to the side wall, 18 inches from the wall.

The receiver's restraining lines are 5 feet behind the short line. They are parallel to the short line and extend 6 inches from each side wall.

PLAYERS

Two, three, or four players can play handball. Games played by three players are called *cut-throat*. The player serving plays against the other two; the serve rotates. The rules for singles apply to the server; the rules for doubles apply to the two other players.

EQUIPMENT

The *ball* is rubber or synthetic, with a 1.9-inch diameter, with a variation of .03 inch. It weighs 2.3 ounces, with a variation of .2 ounce.

Players must wear *gloves* that are light in color and made of soft material or leather. The fingers may not be webbed, connected, or removed, and the gloves may not have holes that expose skin.

COURT

Figure 24.1. The dimensions and features of a handball court.
Adapted from U.S. Handball Association 1991.

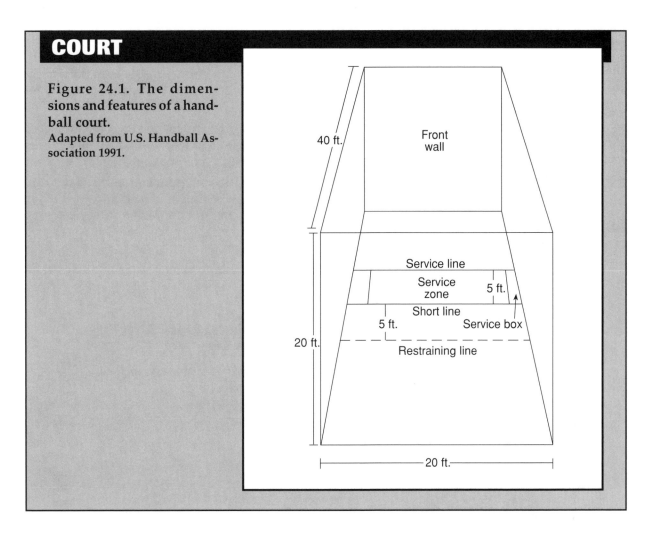

Players may not use foreign substance, tape, or rubber bands on the fingers or palms outside the gloves. They may wear metal or hard substances underneath if, in the referee's opinion, this does not create an advantage for the player wearing them. Players must change gloves when they become wet enough to dampen the ball.

Customary handball attire includes *full-length shirts;* players may not wear shirts cut off at the torso. Their *shoes* must have soles that do not mark or damage the floor. Players must wear *protective eyewear* at all times during play.

OFFICIALS

The *referee* is in charge of the match and makes all decisions regarding points, equipment, protests, and hinders. A *linesman* and a *scorer* are used for larger events.

MODIFICATIONS

Three-wall handball is played on a court that is 20 feet wide and 40 feet long. The three-wall game abides by four-wall rules, except for the following:

- Recommended length for side walls is 44 feet extending 4 feet beyond the long line, which runs parallel to the front wall and whose outer edge is 40 feet from the front wall.

- Shirts are not required for outdoor play unless requested by an opponent.

- A *long serve* is one that hits the front wall and rebounds past the long line before touching the floor.

- During tournament play, a referee will award the server a point when the receiver catches a serve the receiver assumes to be long.

- A *long ball* is one that hits the front wall and doesn't bounce until it is past the long line.

One-wall handball is played on a court measuring 20 feet wide and 34 feet. One-wall play abides by four-wall rules, except for the following:

- The wall is 16 feet high.
- A long line, parallel to the wall, is marked 34 feet from the wall.
- A minimum of 6 feet of floor, and ideally 20 feet, should extend beyond each side line; 16 feet should extend beyond the long line.
- The short line runs parallel to the wall, 16 feet from the wall.
- Two service markers, at least 6 inches long, extend from the sidelines, parallel with the short and long lines and halfway between them. The imaginary extension of these lines indicates the service line.
- The serving zone is the floor between the short line, the sidelines, and the service line.
- The receiving zone is the floor beyond the short line, inside and including the sidelines and long line.

- Shirts are not required in outdoor play unless requested by an opponent.
- The server's partner must stand outside the sidelines, straddling the extended service line until the served ball passes him.
- If a player attempting to play a ball is blocked by an opponent who has stood still after hitting her shot, no hinder is called.
- If a ball hits an opponent on the way to the wall, this is always a hinder, regardless of whether the referee believes the ball had a chance to hit the wall on the fly.
- During a rally, if a player on the serving side hinders an opponent, the serving side begins the next serve with a fault.

ORGANIZATIONS

United States Handball Association
2333 N. Tucson Blvd.
Tucson, AZ 85716
602-795-0434

25

Ice Hockey

© Claus Andersen

Hockey began as an outdoor sport in early 19th-century Novia Scotia. It spread throughout Canada and began its move indoors with a game played in 1875 in Montreal. Seven players per side were permitted on the ice; as leagues were formed, rules were developed and refined. Interest in the sport in the United States developed first on college campuses; the National Hockey League was formed in 1917.

Today, hockey is a fast-moving and exciting sport played by professionals and amateurs alike. The object is to score a goal by shooting a puck into the opponents' goal; the team that scores the most goals wins. The National Hockey League supplied the rules featured in this chapter.

PROCEDURES

A game consists of the components shown in table 25.1.

Table 25.1:	Components in Hockey Game		
Teams	Players	Time	Timeouts
2	6 per team	Three 20-min periods	1 per team

The home team chooses the goal it wants to defend at the start of the game. A game begins with a *face-off* (see page 163) at the center of the rink, where an official drops the puck between two opposing players. Face-offs are also used to begin each period and to resume play after a penalty or other stop in action.

Players advance the puck toward the opponents' goal by skating with the puck or passing it. The puck must be in motion at all times. A player may take the puck behind his own goal one time; otherwise, the team possessing the puck must advance it toward the opponents' goal.

A *goal* (one point) is scored when the puck crosses the goal line between the goal posts and under the crossbar. If a defender accidently knocks the puck into his own goal, the opponents are awarded a goal. The attacking player who last touched the puck is awarded the goal. The same is true if a puck deflects off an attacker and into the goal—that player is awarded the goal.

A goal does not count if an attacking player is in the *goal crease* (a marked area in front of the goal) when the puck crosses the goal line, or if an attacking player bats or kicks the puck across the goal line. If a puck deflects off an official and across the goal line, the goal does not count.

Each team receives one 30-second timeout, which must be taken during normal stoppage of play. If the score is tied at the end of regulation, a five-minute overtime is played. The first team to score wins. If the score is still tied at the end of overtime, the game is a tie. In team competition, a victory is worth two points, while a tie is worth one.

Player Interference: Goal or Not?

Team A has removed its goalkeeper. A player from Team B is racing toward Team A's goal with the puck in a *breakaway* situation; no players from Team A are in position to defend. A player from Team A's bench reaches out with a stick and interferes with the player's shot; the interference causes the shot to go wide of the net. What's the call?

Score this a goal for Team B. According to prevailing rules, if the opposing goalkeeper has been removed and the attacking player in possession of the puck has no player of the defending team to pass, then a goal is awarded to Team B if a stick or any other object should be thrown or shot by an opposing player. The same would be true if the player were to be fouled from behind, thereby being prevented from having a clear shot on an open goal.

TERMS

Following are terms that are not described elsewhere in this chapter.

A player receives an **assist** when his pass leads to the scoring of a teammate's goal. No more than two assists are allowed on any one goal. An assist counts for one point in the player's record.

A **body check** is the use of the body to block a player's progress.

A **breakaway** occurs when a player in control of the puck has no defenders between him and the opponents' goal.

Butt-ending is using the end of the stick in a jabbing motion.

Charging is called when a player jumps into or uses more than two steps to skate into another player.

A team **clears a puck** when it gets the puck away from the front of its goal.

Cross-checking occurs when a player holds his stick above the ice in both hands and impedes an opponent's progress with it.

Delayed offside is called when an attacking player precedes the puck across the attacking blue line, but the defending team possesses the puck and is in position to bring it out of its defending zone without any delay or contact with an attacking player. If the defending team advances the puck out of its defending zone, no offside is called.

A **drop pass** is one that is left behind for a teammate.

A **flat pass** is one that doesn't leave the surface of the ice.

A **flip pass** is one that travels through the air.

A player **freezes** the puck in an attempt to stop play.

A **hat trick** is accomplished by a player who scores three goals in one game.

High sticks means carrying or using the stick above shoulder height.

A **hip check** occurs when a player uses his hip to knock an opponent in possession of the puck off balance.

Hooking is called when a player uses his blade to interfere with an opponent's progress.

When a player goes **intentionally offside** to try to gain a stoppage in play, the puck is faced off at the end face-off spot in the defending zone of the offending team.

Possession of the puck is determined by the last player touching it (including deflections).

Control of the puck is determined by the last player to propel the puck in a desired direction.

A team is in a **power play** when it has more players on the ice than its opponent.

A **rebound** is a puck that bounces off the goalkeeper or the goal post.

A **save** is recorded by a goalkeeper who prevents a goal from being scored.

A team is **short-handed** when they have fewer players on the ice than their opponents. This occurs because of penalties. When a goal is scored against a short-handed team, the minor or bench minor penalty that caused the team to be short-handed is ended and the penalized player can return to action.

A **slap shot** is a shot taken by a player lifting his stick in a backswing before hitting the puck.

Slashing is called when a player hits, or tries to hit, an opponent with his stick.

A **slow whistle** refers to a play in which an official raises his arm in preparation for blowing his whistle for an infraction, depending on how the play turns out. For example, a delayed offside situation results in a slow whistle. The whistle will be blown in this case if the defending team does not advance the puck out of its defending zone and an attacker is offside.

Spearing occurs when a player uses his stick blade to stab an opponent.

A **wrist shot** is taken by a player who does not lift his stick off the ice before hitting the puck.

RINK

The rink has an ice surface; its components are shown in figure 25.1. The rink is divided into thirds by two *blue lines*, each of which is 60 feet from the nearest goal. The blue lines separate the rink into three zones: The *defending zone*, where the goal is defended; the *neutral zone*, or central portion; and the *attacking zone*, where the goal is attacked.

The *center spot*, 12 inches in diameter, is inside the *center circle*, which has a 15-foot radius. Two *face-off spots* are 5 feet from each blue line, and 44 feet apart, in the neutral zone. The *end zone face-off spots* are 20 feet from each goal line and 44 feet apart. These spots are in *end zone face-off circles* with a 15-foot radius.

The *goal cages* are 6 feet long by 4 feet high, centered on the *goal lines*, which run the width of the rink, 11 feet from the end of each rink. The *goal crease* is 4 feet by 8 feet, centered on each goal line. It has a semicircle with a radius of 6 feet.

The *referee's crease* is a semicircle with a 10-foot radius at the center of one side.

The *boards* around the rink are white wood or fiberglass, 40 inches to 48 inches high. Safety glass, 40 inches to 48 inches high, rises above the boards.

Players' benches are on one side of the rink, opposite the *penalty box*.

PLAYERS

Each team has 6 players on the ice: a *goalkeeper,* 2 *defensemen*, and 3 *forwards*. (Actually, all 6 players are defensemen when the other team has possession of the puck.) In most leagues, a team can dress 20 players, including two goalies. The team *captain* is the only player who can discuss calls with the referee.

Players may be changed at any time, but the player or players leaving the ice must be within five feet of the bench, and out of play, before the change is made. For minor injuries, play is not stopped. For injuries in which the player may not leave the ice, play is continued until the injured player's team has possession of the puck and is not in scoring position. At the officials' discretion, play may be stopped immediately for any severe injury, no matter who has possession of the puck.

EQUIPMENT

The *puck* is hard rubber, 1 inch thick and 3 inches in diameter. It weighs between 5.5 and 6 ounces.

The *stick* is wood or another approved material; its maximum length is 60 inches from the heel to the top of the shaft. Its blade can be no longer than 12.5 inches and no more than 3 inches and no less than 2 inches wide. Tape can be used to reinforce the stick.

The blade of the *goalkeeper's stick* may be up to 15.5 inches long. Its maximum width is 3.5 inches, except at the heel, where it may be 4.5 inches. The shaft extending up from the heel, for up to 26 inches, is 3.5 inches wide. Goalkeepers wear *leg guards, chest protectors, gloves* (one to block shots, the other to catch shots), *helmets,* and *full face masks* (see figure 25.2).

All protective equipment—*padded pants* and *pads for shins, hips, shoulders,* and *elbows*—must be

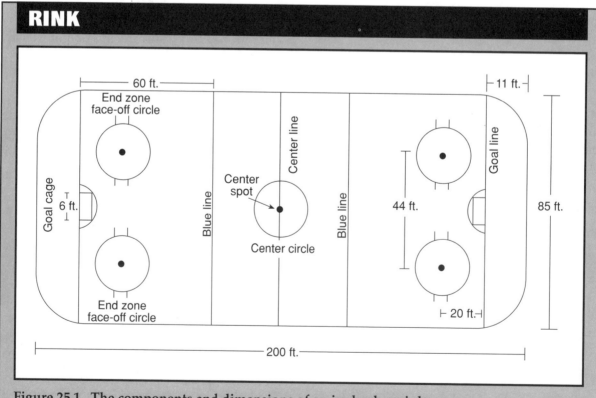

Figure 25.1. The components and dimensions of an ice hockey rink.
Adapted from White 1990.

Figure 25.2. The goalkeeper is fully protected from the puck which can travel up to speeds of 100 miles per hour.

worn under the uniform. All players must wear a *helmet* with a chin strap. Behind each goal, a *red light* is turned on when a goal is scored.

GENERAL RULES

Following are rules pertaining to face-offs, passes, offside, and the puck.

Face-Offs

A referee or linesman drops the puck between two opposing players whose stick blades are on the ice. The players face their opponents' end of the rink and try to hit the puck to a teammate. No other players may be in the face-off circle or within 15 feet of the players facing off. Players must stand on side during the face-off, and no substitutes may enter the game until the face-off is complete.

Face-offs may not take place within 15 feet of the goal or side boards. If an attacker in his team's attacking zone causes play to stop, the face-off occurs at the nearest face-off spot in the neutral zone.

If a defender in his team's defensive zone causes play to stop, the face-off occurs at the point of stoppage. Any stoppage of play in the neutral zone results in a face-off at the point of stoppage. If play is stopped between the end of the rink and the end face-off spots, the face-off occurs at the nearest end face-off spot.

Passes

A player in one zone may not pass forward to a teammate in another zone. A player in the defending zone may pass to a teammate to the center line, but the puck must pass the center line before the receiver does. The position of the puck, and not the players, determines from which zone the pass was made and received.

Once a player leaves the defending zone, he may not pass back to that zone unless his team is playing short-handed. If a player from the neutral zone enters the attacking zone after the puck has been passed into that zone, he is eligible to play the puck. The same is true for any player entering a new zone after the puck has entered that zone. If an attacking player passes the puck back toward his own goal while in the attacking zone, an opponent may play the puck anywhere regardless of whether he was in the same zone when the puck was passed.

Offside

An attacking player is offside if he is in the attacking zone before he receives the puck. Similarly, an attacking player already beyond the center line is offside if he receives the puck from a teammate in the defense zone. Both skates must be past the line when the puck enters the zone for a player to be offside. An offside call results in a face-off.

If a defender reaches the puck and passes or skates with it into the neutral zone, an attacking player is not offside. Similarly, if a player moves across the line before the puck but is in control and moving the puck forward, he is not offside.

The Puck

Puck out of bounds or unplayable. When the puck goes outside the playing area, it is faced off from where it was shot or deflected. When the puck becomes lodged in the netting outside the goal, or becomes "frozen" between opposing players, the puck is faced off at the nearest face-off spot—unless the referee believes an attacking player caused the stoppage, in which case the face-off takes place in the neutral zone.

Puck out of sight. Should a scramble take place and a player accidentally falls on the puck, play is stopped and a face-off occurs.

Puck striking official. Play is not stopped when a puck strikes an official. If a puck strikes an official and deflects into the goal, however, the goal does not count.

Preceding the puck into the attacking zone. Players on the attacking team may not enter the attacking zone before the puck does. Such a violation results in a face-off in the neutral zone.

Kicking the puck. Players may kick the puck in any zone, but a goal may not be scored by kicking the puck, whether or not the kick was intentional.

Icing the puck. If a player on a team that is not short-handed shoots a puck across the center line and past the opponents' goal line, play is stopped, and a face-off occurs at the end face-off spot of the offending team. If, however, a goal is scored on the shot, the goal counts.

PENALTIES

When a player whose team is in possession of the puck violates a rule, the referee blows his whistle and immediately imposes the appropriate penalty. The game is resumed with a face-off. If the player who commits the penalty is on the team that is not in possession of the puck, the referee blows his whistle and imposes the penalty after the play is completed (see figure 25.3). The kinds of penalties ae discussed next.

Minor Penalty

Any player, other than the goalkeeper, sits in the penalty box for two minutes; no substitutes are

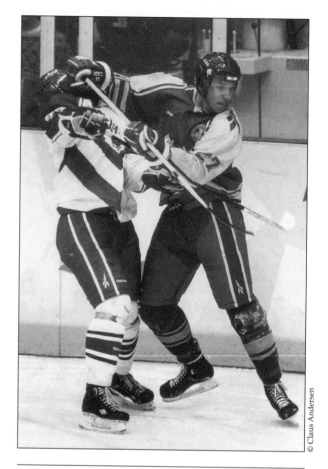

Figure 25.3. High-sticking can be either a double minor or major penalty.

allowed. The goalkeeper's penalty may be taken by a teammate.

A sampling of minor penalties includes

- delay of game,
- dislodging the net from its moorings,
- falling on the puck,
- handling the puck,
- holding an opponent,
- hooking,
- interfering with an opponent who is not in possession of the puck,
- interfering with the goalkeeper,
- playing with a broken stick, and
- tripping.

The following penalties depend on the severity of the offense:

- Board checking or checking from behind (minor or major)
- Charging (minor or major)
- Cross-checking (minor or major)
- Elbowing, kneeing, or head-butting (minor or major)
- High sticks (double minor or major)
- Slashing (minor or major)
- Roughing (Minor or double minor)

Bench Minor Penalty

A coach may remove any one of his players from the ice, except the goalkeeper, to serve this two-minute penalty. If a team is short-handed by one or more minor or bench minor penalties, and the opposing team scores, the first penalty assessed is terminated.

Major Penalty

Any player, except for the goalkeeper, who commits a major offense serves a five-minute penalty. No substitution is allowed. If a player commits three major penalties in a game, he is ejected from the game. Major penalties may be assessed for

- elbowing or kneeing an opponent and causing injury,
- fighting,
- grabbing or holding an opponent's face mask,
- hooking or cross-checking and causing injury,
- slashing and injuring an opponent, and
- spearing or butt-ending with the stick.

Misconduct Penalties

Players may incur misconduct penalties, game misconduct penalties, and gross misconduct penalties. Team personnel may also incur gross misconduct penalties. Any player, except the goalkeeper, who commits a *misconduct penalty* must sit for 10 minutes. This player may be replaced immediately. A player whose misconduct penalty has expired must remain in the penalty box until a stoppage in play.

When a player commits a misconduct penalty and either a major or a minor penalty at the same time, his team must put a substitute player in the penalty box to serve the major or minor penalty. For a *game misconduct penalty,* a player is suspended for the duration of the game, but a substitute is allowed. If a player accumulates three game misconducts during the season, he is suspended for one game. For each subsequent game misconduct, that player's suspension would increase by one game.

A *gross misconduct penalty* may be levied against any player or team personnel. It results in suspension for the rest of the game. Acts resulting in misconduct or game misconduct penalties, depending on the severity of the violation, include:

- abusing officials;
- continuing to dispute after receiving a penalty;
- continuing to fight after being ordered to stop;
- entering the referee's crease while officials are in it consulting;
- first player to intervene in an altercation;
- leaving the players' bench or penalty bench to enter an altercation;
- using obscene, profane, or abusive language or gestures;
- physically abusing officials;
- shooting a puck out of reach of an official who is retrieving it;
- spearing an opponent;
- throwing the puck or any equipment out of the playing area;
- touching or holding an official in any way; and
- using threatening or abusive language to incite an opponent.

Match Penalty

The player is replaced for the rest of the game and ordered to the locker room. A substitute may replace this player after five minutes of playing time have elapsed.

Match penalties are assessed for

- attempting to injure an opponent,
- deliberately injuring an opponent, and for
- kicking or attempting to kick another player.

Goalkeeper's Penalty

A teammate may serve a goalkeeper's minor or major penalty. If a goalkeeper incurs three major penalties in one game, he is ruled off the ice and a substitute goalkeeper may take his place. A goalkeeper must serve his own misconduct or match penalty, but his place on the ice may be taken by a substitute.

Delayed Penalty

If a third player of a team is penalized while two teammates are serving penalties, the penalty time of the third player doesn't begin until the first teammate's penalty time elapses. However, the third player must go to the bench immediately and be replaced by a substitute who can play until the third player's penalty time officially begins.

Penalty Shot

A penalty shot may be awarded for numerous reasons; the following list includes some of the common violations that result in a penalty shot:

- Falling on the puck, holding the puck, or gathering the puck into the body when the puck is within the goal crease (goalkeeper exempted)

- Interfering with an opponent in possession of the puck and with no defender between him and the goalkeeper

- Throwing a stick or any object at the puck in the offending player's defending zone (if a goal is scored on the play, no penalty shot is given)

The referee places the puck on the center face-off spot, and the player taking the penalty shot attempts to score on the goalkeeper. The player may take the puck anywhere in the neutral zone or in his own defending zone, but once the puck crosses the blue line into the attacking zone, it must be kept in forward motion, and once it is shot, the play is complete. No goal may be scored on a rebound. While the penalty shot is being taken, all other players except the two involved withdraw to the sides of the rink on the attacker's side of the center line.

If a goal is scored on a penalty shot, play resumes with a face-off at center ice. If the goal is not scored, play resumes with a face-off at one of the end face-off spots in the zone in which the penalty shot was attempted.

MODIFICATIONS

Age classifications for USA Hockey, the sport's national governing body, are shown in table 25.2.

All players at Junior level or younger must wear facemasks. Players at the Pee Wee level or younger must wear mouthpieces. For differences between NHL and play in leagues for youth or seniors, see table 25.3.

Table 25.2: Age Classifications		
Classification	Males	Females
Mites	8 or under	—
Squirts	10 or under	8 to 12
Pee Wees	12 or under	13 to 15
Bantams	14 or under	—
Midgets	17 or under	16 to 19
Juniors	19 or under	—
Seniors	20+	Any age

Adapted from USA Hockey 1993.

OFFICIALS

The *referee* is in charge of the game and of the other officials, who include

- two *linesmen*, who watch for rules violations;

- two *goal judges*, who are stationed behind the goals and determine whether a goal has been scored;

- a *penalty timekeeper*, who records all the penalties and keeps the time for the players in the penalty box;

- an *official scorer*, who records all game data; and

- a *game timekeeper*, who runs the game clock.

See figure 25.4 for officials' signals.

Table 25.3: Differences Between NHL and USA Hockey Play				
	Rink (ft)	Goal posts (ft from end)	Length of timeouts (sec)	Overtime (min)
USA Hockey	Not less than 185 × 85	12 to 15	60	10
NHL	200 × 85	11	30	5

ORGANIZATIONS

National Hockey League
1800 McGill College Ave., Ste. 2600
Montreal, PQ, Canada H3A 3J6
212-789-2000

USA Hockey
4965 N. 30th St.
Colorado Springs, CO 80919
719-599-5500

Holding

Cross checking

Tripping

Charging

Hooking

Boarding

(continued)

Figure 25.4.   Common official's signals for ice hockey.

Icing

Misconduct

Interference

Slashing

High-sticking

Spearing

Kneeing

Elbowing

Unsportsmanlike
conduct

Figure 25.4.   *(continued)*

Judo

Judo is a martial art that was developed from jujutsu (also called jujitsu) by Professor Jigoro Kano in Japan in 1882. *Ju* means gentleness; *do* means way. While judo is concerned with attacks and defenses against an opponent, it also develops physical conditioning and total health. More than 4 million worldwide participate in judo; about 400,000 in the United States take part.

As in other martial arts, competitors are grouped into various skill levels. Judo skills involve a combination of knowledge, speed, timing, balance, and coordination of mind and body. Judo is a form of wrestling that emphasizes throws, pins, hold-downs, chokes, and arm locks. Competitions are often highlighted by spectacular throws. Timing and technique are the keys to a competitor's success. The object is not to match strength against strength but rather to defeat one's opponent by using his own force. Points are scored with various throws and techniques; the competitor with the most points wins. The source for this chapter's rules is the International Judo Federation.

PROCEDURES

A contest lasts five minutes for men, four minutes for women, and three minutes for juniors (real contest times). To begin a contest, the competitors stand facing each other, bow, and take one step forward. The referee then calls out "hajime" to begin the competition.

Competitors attempt to score points by using various techniques to throw, pin, or hold down their opponents (see "Scoring"). The referee may temporarily halt a match, during which the competition clock stops, when

- one or both competitors go outside the competition area,
- a competitor performs a prohibited act (see "Prohibited Acts"),
- a competitor is injured or ill, and
- the competitors are entangled on the ground and not making progress.

A contest ends when

- a competitor scores *ippon* (one point) or two *waza-ari* (which equal one point; see "Scoring");
- a competitor is awarded *sogo-gachi* (compound win);
- a competitor wins due to default, disqualification, or injury; or
- contest time expires.

TERMS

Hantei is a call by the referee for a judge's decision.

A **hike-wake** is called when the match is a draw.

Ippon is one point; **waza-ari** is a half-point; **yuko** is a score less than a waza-ari; and a **koka** is a score less than a yuko.

A **shiai** is a judo contest, which is fought on a mat called a **tatami**.

In a judo competition, the attacker is called a **tori**.

In judo, technique is called **waza**.

A **yusei gachi** is a win by the judges' decision.

SCORING

A competitor scores an ippon, worth one point and a victory, when he

- throws his opponent largely on his back with considerable force and speed,
- pins his opponent's back and at least one shoulder to the mat (*osaekomi*) and the opponent is unable to get away from this hold within 30 seconds,
- causes his opponent to give up because of the hold he is using, or
- employs a strangle technique or arm lock from which his opponent cannot escape.

If a competitor is penalized *hansoku make* (see "Prohibited Acts"), his opponent is awarded ippon and the match. Waza-ari is worth one-half point. A competitor scores waza-ari when he throws his opponent, but the technique is not deserving of ippon (e.g., the throw was not executed as well). A contestant also scores waza-ari when he holds his opponent's back and at least one shoulder to the mat and the hold lasts 25 seconds or more, but less than 30 seconds. If a competitor is penalized *keikoku* (see "Prohibited Acts"), his opponent is awarded waza-ari. If a competitor scores two waza-ari, which equal an ippon, he wins the match.

A yuko is awarded when a competitor throws his opponent but his technique is lacking in two of the other three elements necessary for ippon. For example, the opponent thrown may not be largely on his back, or the throw itself may have been lacking in speed or force. If a contestant is penalized *chui* (see "Prohibited Acts"), his opponent receives a yuko.

A koka is awarded when a competitor throws her opponent onto the front of her body, knees, hands, or elbows. An osaekomi that goes beyond nine seconds is worth a koka. A referee will call sogo-gachi (compound win) when a contestant already has waza-ari and his opponent is penalized keikoku.

PROHIBITED ACTS

There are four types of prohibited acts for which a contestant may be penalized.

- A *shido* is a minor infringement.
- A *chui* is a serious infringement; two shidos equal one chui.
- A *keikoku* is a grave infringement; a chui and one more infringement of any kind equal keikoku.
- A *hansoku-make* is a very grave infringement; a keikoku and one more infringement of any kind equal hansoku-make.

A few examples of each type of infringement follow.

A shido can be called for stalling or preventing action, adopting an excessively defensive posture, or failure to attack. A chui may be called for applying leg scissors to the opponent's trunk, neck, or head; kicking the opponent's hand or arm to be freed from his grip; or bending back the opponent's fingers to break his grip.

Keikoku may be called by a referee for attempting to throw an opponent by winding a leg around his leg while facing in the same direction and falling backward onto him, locking joints (except for the elbow joints), acting in a way that could injure the opponent's neck or spinal cord, lifting an opponent off the mat while the opponent is lying on it, and slamming him back onto the mat, or applying techniques outside of the contest area.

The gravest infringement, hansoku-make, may be called for diving head first onto the mat while performing, or attempting to perform, various techniques or intentionally falling backward when an opponent is clinging to one's back.

COMPETITION AREA

The competition area is a mat that is at least 14 by 14 meters and no more than 16 by 16 meters (see figure 26.1). The mat is made of pressed straw or foam. It is divided into two zones in which competition may take place: a *danger zone*, in red, and the *contest area*, generally in green. The danger zone is usually 1 meter wide, on the outside of the contest area, which is at least 8 by 8 meters, and no more than 10 by 10 meters. The area outside the danger zone is called the *safety area*; it is 3 meters wide.

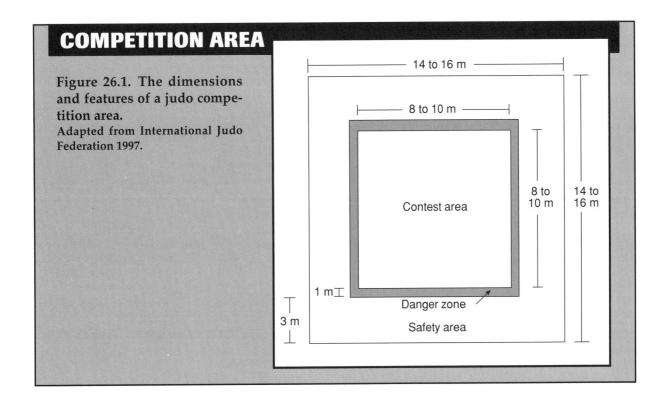

COMPETITION AREA

Figure 26.1. The dimensions and features of a judo competition area.
Adapted from International Judo Federation 1997.

14 to 16 m

8 to 10 m

Contest area

8 to 10 m

14 to 16 m

1 m

Danger zone

3 m

Safety area

COMPETITORS

Contestants wear a white or off-white *judogi* (uniform). The judogi jacket must be long enough to cover the thighs, and the arms of the jacket must reach the wrist joints when the arms are extended down. The trousers must reach to the ankle joints. Contestants wear a belt, with the color corresponding to grade level, over their jackets. Each contestant wears a red or white sash over the grade belt. Fingernails and toenails must be cut short.

The United States Judo Association has 12 degrees for junior competitors (16 years old and younger). They range from Junior First Degree through Junior Twelfth Degree. Senior ranks, for those 17 years old and older, are split into two categories:

- Beginner (six ranks, with sixth-class rank being lowest and first-class rank being highest)
- Black belt ranks (ranging from lowest rank at 1st degree to highest rank at 10th degree)

EQUIPMENT

Judges use *chairs*, placed on either end of the safety area and diagonally opposite each other.

A *red flag* and a *white flag* are affixed to each chair. A *scoreboard* is used to show points and penalty points for each contestant. *Clocks* are used to time the match and to time the length of each osaekomi.

OFFICIALS

One *referee* and two *judges* conduct the match. They are assisted by *contest recorders* and *time-keepers*.

ORGANIZATIONS

United States Judo Association
19 N. Union Blvd.
Colorado Springs, CO 80909
719-633-7750

United States Judo Federation
P.O. Box 338
Ontario, OR 97914
541-889-8753

United States Judo, Inc.
P.O. Box 10013
El Paso, TX 79991
915-565-8754

27

Karate

© Photophile/Glasheen Graphics

People as young as 6 years old can compete in karate in various age, weight, and experience level groups. The sport includes competition in *Kumite* (free-fighting), *Kata* (forms), and *Weapons Kata* (forms with weapons). Both team and individual competitions are held.

The object is to score *ippons* or *waza-ari* by performing techniques according to specific criteria. The contestant with the highest score wins. The international organization for the sport is the World Karate Federation; the national governing body is the USA Karate Federation, which is the source for rules in this chapter.

PROCEDURES

A tournament may consist of Kumite, Kata, or both. Individual matches are divided by weight classifications; in team Kumite matches, each team must have an odd number of participants. A Kata team consists of three people.

The coach determines his team's fighting order (from one to five) before the match begins. A contestant or the coach presents this order to the officials before the first match; it cannot be changed. Specific procedures vary for Kumite and Kata competition; see the following sections.

TERMS

A **hansoku** is a foul that results in a victory for the contestant fouled.

An **ippon** is a score awarded to a contestant who has performed according to these criteria: good form, correct attitude, vigorous application, proper timing, correct distance, and perfect finish.

A win by **kiken** is awarded a contestant if his opponent is absent, withdraws, or is withdrawn.

A **sanbon** has a value of three ippons. It may be reached by scoring three ippons or by scoring six waza-ari, or by scoring the appropriate combination of the two.

Shikkaku means "disqualification." A contestant is awarded the victory if his opponent commits an act leading to shikkaku.

A **waza-ari** is worth half an ippon. It is awarded for a technique almost comparable to that needed to score an ippon.

Yame is the command to "stop." Yame can be called in the middle of a bout as well as at the end.

KUMITE

The referee, judges, and contestants take their positions, exchange bows in the prescribed manner, and the match begins. When a referee sees a scoring technique or a penalty, he will stop the match, award an ippon, waza-ari, or penalty, and order the contestants to take their original positions to restart the bout.

When a contestant scores a sanbon (any combination that totals three ippons), the referee stops the bout and declares him the winner. Whether or not a contestant has scored a sanbon, each bout between adult males is finished after three minutes; women's and junior bouts are limited to two minutes. If the score is tied at the end, a majority vote among the referee and judges determines the winner. If the referee and judges believe neither contestant exhibited superiority, an overtime period begins. The first contestant to score wins.

A contestant wins a match by scoring either three ippons, six waza-ari, or a combination that equals three ippons. In addition to the criteria listed under "Terms," an ippon may be awarded for

- deflecting an attack and scoring to the opponent's unguarded back;
- sweeping or throwing, followed by a scoring technique;
- delivering a combination technique (each part is scored in its own right);
- scoring to the head with a kick; and
- scoring as the opponent attacks.

A waza-ari is awarded for a technique almost equal to that needed to score an ippon. No technique will score if a contestant delivers it outside the competition area. Similarly, effective scoring techniques delivered simultaneously by both contestants cancel each other out. A referee will temporarily stop a bout when

- there is a penalty or a score;
- either or both of the contestants are out of the competition area;
- a contestant needs to adjust his uniform;
- a contestant breaks, or is about to break, a rule;
- a contestant grabs his opponent but does not immediately execute an effective technique;
- a contestant falls or is thrown and no effective techniques occur; or
- a contestant is injured and cannot continue.

Legal and Illegal Acts

A contestant may attack an opponent in the head, face, neck, abdomen, chest, back (excluding shoulders), and side. The following acts are illegal:

- Contact to the throat
- Excessive contact to the head, face, or neck; attacks to these (and all) areas must be controlled
- Attacks to the groin, joints, or instep
- Open-hand attacks to the face
- Dangerous throws
- Direct attacks to the arms and legs
- Repeated exits from the competition area
- Wrestling, pushing, or grabbing without immediately executing a technique
- Reckless actions
- Faking injury to gain an advantage

Such acts are penalized on the following scale:

- *Atenai yori* is a warning called for minor infractions.
- A *keikoku* may be imposed for minor infractions for which a contestant has been previously warned. A waza-ari is added to the opponent's score.
- A *hansoku-chui* is usually imposed for a major infraction or for an infraction in which a keikoku has been previously issued. An ippon is added to the opponent's score.
- A *hansoku* is a very serious infraction that raises the opponent's score to sanbon (victory). Hansoku may be imposed for an infraction for which a hansoku-chui has previously been imposed.
- A *shikkaku* is a disqualification from the match, with the victory going to the opponent. Shikkaku may be called when a contestant takes an action that harms the honor and prestige of karate.

Note: The referee can award any of these penalties for the first penalty. Each succeeding penalty must be awarded at a higher level, even if it is a less serious infraction.

KATA

When the competitor's name is called, she stands on the designated line, bows to the panel of judges, and announces the name of the Kata that she will perform. (The four major styles of karate recognized by the World Karate Federation are Goju-Ryu, Shito-Ryu, Shoto-Kan, and Wado-Ryu. Within these four styles, there are 22 approved Katas.) She then performs the Kata. At the end of the Kata she returns to the line and awaits her score.

In the first round, the competitor performs a Kata from the approved list. In the second round, she performs a different Kata from the list, and in the third round, she may perform any Kata from the list not previously performed.

After the first round, 16 competitors remain; after the second round, eight remain. The third round determines the winner and final placings. Scores from each round are not carried over; each round starts fresh.

In Kata, contestants receive scores according to how well they demonstrate

- competence and a clear understanding of the principles involved in the chosen Kata;
- correct focus, use of power, balance, and proper breathing; and
- other points within the Kata.

In team Kata, movements are synchronized, but the Kata should not alter in rhythm or timing for the sake of synchronization. In either individual or team Kata, if a contestant interrupts or varies a Kata, the contestant (or team) is disqualified.

In team competitions, the three team members performing face the chief judge. Movements must begin and end in unison; otherwise points are deducted. Points are also deducted for momentary imbalances and brief pauses. If a contestant completely loses balance, falls, or comes to a distinct halt, she is disqualified.

WEAPONS KATA

Weapons Kata is judged using the same criteria as open-hand Kata, with the additional criterion of demonstrating the characteristics of the weapon used. A contestant must perform a Kata that does not endanger people or property; loss of control of the weapon results in disqualification. Weapons are inspected before the competition to ensure they are in good shape and are of authentic design and proper weight. Weapons include the following:

- *Bo*—a hardwood staff, either the height of the contestant or 6 feet.
- *Sai*—a metal club with blunt edges and a sharp point; two hooks face outward from the grip. While held hooked between the thumb and forefinger, this piece should extend beyond the tip of the elbow one to two inches.
- *Tonfa*—two hardwood sticks, round or square, with a handle off one side about 6 inches from the end.
- *Nunchaku*—two hardwood sticks held together by a cord the length of the competitor's wrist.
- *Kama*—bladed weapon, like a scythe; the blade is at least 6 inches long. The handle may not have a rope or cord attached to it.
- *Ieku*—an oar, about 5.5 feet long with a handle about 3.25 inches long and a blade about 2.25 feet long.
- *Nunti*—a 6-foot Bo with a Manji Sai attached to one end.
- *Kuwa*—a garden hoe with a round or oval-shaped 4-foot-long handle with a 4- by 10-inch rectangular curved blade at one end.

COMPETITION AREA

The Kumite competition area is a matted square, 8 meters on each side (see figure 27.1). The area may be elevated up to 1 meter above the floor. If it is elevated, it should measure 10 meters on each side, with the outer 2 meters being a safety area. Two parallel lines, each 1 meter long, are 1.5 meters from the center of the competition area. The contestants are positioned on these lines. A line .5 meter long and perpendicular to the contestants' lines is 2 meters from the center of the competition area. This is the referee's line. A warning line is drawn 1 meter inside the edges of the mat on all four sides.

CONTESTANTS

Competitions can be held according to age group, experience level, and weight.

Age Group

Junior—6-17 years old

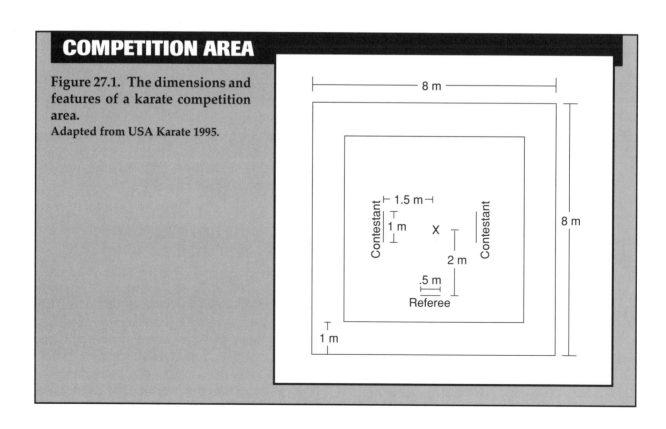

COMPETITION AREA

Figure 27.1. The dimensions and features of a karate competition area.
Adapted from USA Karate 1995.

Adult—18 and over

Senior—35 and over

Senior advanced, male and female—ages 35-44, ages 45 and over

In Weapons Kata, age groups may be combined. Males and females may not compete against each other.

Experience Level

Beginner—Not more than one year of experience; 7th-10th *kyu* or equivalent

Novice—one to two years of experience or green belt or 4th-6th kyu or equivalent

Intermediate—two to three years of experience or brown belt or 1st-3rd kyu or equivalent

Advanced—three or more years of experience or black belt

Weight Divisions

Junior age group—may be divided into divisions at the discretion of the tournament director

Adult, advanced male—under 132 pounds (60 kilograms); 132 pounds (60 kilograms) to 143 pounds (65 kilograms); 143 pounds (65 kilograms) to 154 pounds (70 kilograms); 154 pounds (70 kilograms) to 165 pounds (75 kilograms); 165 pounds (75 kilograms) to 176 pounds (80 kilograms); and 176 pounds (80 kilograms) and over

Adult beginner, novice, and intermediate; male—under 154 pounds (70 kilograms); over 154 pounds (70 kilograms)

Adult, advanced; female—under 117 pounds (53 kilograms), 117 pounds (53 kilograms) to 132 pounds (60 kilograms); 132 pounds (60 kilograms) and over; open weight (no limitation)

Adult beginner, novice, and intermediate; female—under 132 pounds (60 kilograms); 132 pounds (60 kilograms) and over

Contestants wear a white, unmarked karate *gi*. The back of the gi may be numbered. Their *jackets* must cover their hips but hang no lower than mid-thigh. The jacket sleeves may not reach less than halfway down the forearm but must not extend beyond the wrists. The *pants* must cover at least two-thirds of the shins. Men wear *groin cups*. *Mitts* and *mouthguards* are mandatory in Kumite; *soft shin pads* are allowed.

OFFICIALS

Matches are officiated by a *referee, judges*, and a *scorekeeper*.

ORGANIZATIONS

American Amateur Karate Federation
1930 Wilshire Blvd., Ste. 1208
Los Angeles, CA
213-483-8261

U.S.A. Karate Federation
1300 Kenmore Blvd.
Akron, OH 44314
216-753-3114

U.S.A.-Korean Karate Association
P.O. Box 1401
Great Falls, MT 59403
406-452-5675

28

Lacrosse

© Photophile/Matt Lindasay

Lacrosse originated in North America, where it was played by Native Americans in what is now Canada and New York. French missionaries playing the game thought the sticks they used resembled the bishop's staff, or *crozier*; thus they called it "la crosse." Certainly the biggest rule change from its early days centers on the length of the game and field: When Native Americans played the sport, a game stretched on for days and the goals could be 15 miles apart!

Rules in place by 1860 remain pretty much the standard for the game as it is played today. The object of the game, both then and now, is to score more goals than one's opponents. Players use long-handled sticks to try to throw a ball into the opponents' goal.

The rules in this chapter are divided into two segments: one for women and one for men. The women's rules were supplied by the United States Women's Lacrosse Association, while the men's rules came from the National Collegiate Athletic Association.

WOMEN'S LACROSSE

The maximum regulation playing time is 50 minutes (60 minutes in college play), split into halves, with up to a 10-minute halftime. The clock stops after a goal is scored and on every whistle in the last two minutes of each half. If a team is leading by 10 or more goals, the clock does not stop after a goal. In high school and college, each team may take one timeout per half.

PROCEDURES

A game starts with a *draw*—two opposing players toeing the center line, their crosses held in the air, parallel to the center line. The umpire places the ball between the players, calls "Ready," and blows the whistle. The players pull their sticks up and away, lifting the ball into the air. All other players must be outside of the center circle during the draw. The team that has the ball attempts to score a goal by advancing the ball down the field by carrying, throwing, rolling, or batting it.

If the ball goes out of bounds, it is given to the nearest player. If two players of opposing teams are an equal distance from the ball, the game is restarted with a *throw*. The players stand one meter apart; the umpire, standing four to eight meters away, throws the ball in the air so that the players take it as they move toward the field. No other players may be within four meters of the players taking the throw. A throw also is taken when the ball lodges in the clothing of a player or umpire or when two players commit offsetting fouls.

Only one player (the goalkeeper or her deputy) may be in the *goal circle* (see figure 28.1 on page 182). Within the goal circle, the goalkeeper must clear the ball within 10 seconds. She may use her hands and body to stop the ball, as well as using her crosse. She may also use her crosse to reach out and bring the ball into the goal circle, provided no part of her body is grounded outside the circle. When the goalkeeper leaves the goal circle she loses all goalkeeping privileges.

TERMS

Blocking occurs when one player moves into the path of an opponent with the ball without giving the opponent a chance to stop or change direction without contact.

Body checking occurs when a defender moves with an opponent without making body contact, but causing her to slow, change direction, or pass off.

The **critical scoring area** is at each end of the field, where the attacking team shoots for a goal. It runs from approximately 15 meters in front of the goal circle to 9 meters behind the goal circle, and 15 meters to either side of the goal circle. It is not marked on the field.

Cross-checking occurs when a defender tries to dislodge the ball from her opponent's crosse by tapping it with her own crosse.

A **deputy** is a player on the defensive goal-keeper's team who may enter the goal circle when her team is in possession of the ball and the goalkeeper is out of the goal circle.

The **8-meter arc** is the area in front of each goal circle, intersecting the circle and the goal line extended, and connected by an arc marked 8 meters from the goal circle.

Free space to goal describes the path to goal within the critical scoring area, defined by two imaginary lines extending from the ball to the outside of the goal circle.

Marking is the term used to describe guarding an opponent within a stick's length.

A **penalty lane** is the path to goal that is cleared when a free position is awarded to the attacking team within the critical scoring area in front of the goal line. All players must clear this lane.

A **pick** is a technique used by a player without the ball to force an opponent to take a different direction. The player must give the opponent time to see the pick and react to it.

Slashing is viciously or recklessly swinging a crosse at an opponent's crosse or body. Contact doesn't have to be made for the umpire to call a foul.

A **slow whistle** occurs when an attacking team is fouled on a scoring play within the critical scoring area; the play is finished and the umpire assesses a foul only if the attacking team does not score a goal.

The **12-meter fan** is a semicircle in front of each goal circle, bounded by an arc 12 meters from the goal circle.

SCORING

A team scores a goal when the ball passes completely over the goal line, between the posts, and under the cross bar of the opponents' goal. A goal counts if it bounces off a defender and goes into the goal.

However, if the ball is last touched by an attacking player, it must be propelled by the player's crosse; a goal does not count if the ball bounces off an attacking player and goes into the goal. A goal may also be disallowed when

- the ball enters the goal after the whistle has blown,
- the attacking player or her crosse breaks the plane of the goal circle,
- any other attacking player is in the goal circle,
- an attacking player interferes with the goalkeeper, or
- the umpire rules the shot or follow-through dangerous.

FOULS

Players may be called for major, minor, or goal circle fouls. *Major fouls* include

- rough or reckless checking or tackling;
- slashing;
- holding a crosse around the face or throat of an opponent;
- hooking an opponent's crosse;
- blocking;
- remaining in the 8-meter arc for more than three seconds, unless marking an opponent within a stick's length;

- setting picks, detaining or tripping opponents, charging or backing into an opponent; and
- shooting dangerously.

Minor fouls include

- guarding a ground ball with the player's foot or crosse,
- checking or tackling an opponent's crosse when the opponent is trying to gain possession of the ball,
- touching the ball by hand by anyone other than the goalkeeper,
- throwing one's crosse,
- drawing illegally,
- taking part in the game without holding one's stick,
- intentionally delaying the game, and
- deliberately causing the ball to go out of bounds.

Goal circle fouls may be called when

- a field player enters the goal circle or holds her crosse over the goal circle line,
- the goalkeeper allows the ball to remain within the circle for more than 10 seconds,
- the goalkeeper reaches beyond the circle to play the ball,
- the goalkeeper draws the ball into the circle while she is partially grounded outside the circle, or
- the goalkeeper steps back into the circle while she has the ball.

A player may be given a *misconduct* or *suspension* for playing in a rough, dangerous, or unsportsmanlike manner. The penalty for a misconduct or suspension violation is the same as for major fouls (see "Penalties").

PENALTIES

The penalty for major and minor fouls is a *free position*, awarded to the player who was fouled. The player with the free position may run with the ball or throw it with his crosse. All other players must be at least 4 meters away.

When a defender commits a major foul within the 8-meter arc, the free position is awarded at the spot of the foul. When a defender commits a minor foul within the 12-meter fan, the player fouled takes the free position at the nearest spot, with her defender at least 4 meters away. This is an *indirect free position,* and the player taking this position may not take a shot until another player has played the ball.

The penalty for a goal circle foul by the defense is an indirect free position taken 12 meters out to either side, level with the goal line. The exception here is for an illegal deputy; this is treated as a major foul.

A slow whistle occurs on a major foul; the referee throws a signal flag and allows the attacking players to continue a scoring play in the critical scoring area. If the attackers score a goal, the referee does not assess the foul; if the attackers don't score, the referee assesses the foul.

FIELD

The field has no set boundaries, but an area measuring 110 by 64 meters is desirable (See figure 28.1). The goals are 92 meters apart, with 9 meters of playing space behind each goal line, running the width of the field. Minimum width is 55 meters. The goal circles, 8-meter arcs, 12-meter fans, and center circle are as shown in figure 28.1.

WOMEN'S FIELD AND PLAYER POSITIONS

Figure 28.1. The dimensions, features, and player positions of a women's lacrosse field. Adapted from U.S. Women's Lacrosse Association 1996.

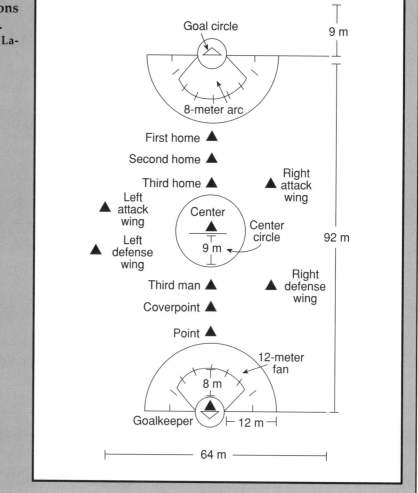

The *goals* are of wood or metal, 6 feet high and 6 feet wide. A goal line is marked between the two goal posts. Netting is attached to the posts and is firmly pegged to the ground 6 feet behind the center of the goal line.

PLAYERS

Twelve players for each team may be on the field at one time. See figure 28.1 for player positions.

Players wear composition or rubber-soled *shoes; spikes* are not allowed. Goalkeepers may wear *padding* on their hands, arms, legs, shoulders, and chest; they must wear a *helmet* with a *face mask*, a *throat protector*, and a *chest protector*. All players must wear *mouthguards*.

Substitutions are unlimited and may be made at any time the ball is not in play. Players may re-enter the game.

EQUIPMENT

The *ball* is rubber; it is solid yellow and not less than 20 centimeters or more than 20.3 centimeters in circumference. It weighs between 142 grams and 149 grams.

The *field crosse* is made of aluminum, fiberglass, gut, leather, nylon, plastic, rubber, or wood; the head of the crosse is triangular. The pocket is strung with four or five thongs, with 8 to 12 stitches of cross-lacing. The crosse is 36 to 44 inches long. The head is 7 to 9 inches wide and 10 to 12 inches long. Its pocket may have a maximum depth of 2.5 inches deep. Maximum overall weight is 20 ounces. The goalkeeper's crosse is 36 to 48 inches long and can weigh a maximum of 26 ounces.

OFFICIALS

An umpire, a scorer, and a timer officiate the game.

MEN'S LACROSSE

For the most part, this section contains only the men's collegiate rules that differ from women's rules. In places where it would be more confusing to leave a rule out, even if it's a rule already covered in the women's section, we will repeat the rule for clarity's sake.

A game lasts 60 minutes (four 15-minute quarters). Intervals of 2 minutes separate the second and third quarters and third and fourth quarters; halftime lasts 10 minutes. After each period in regulation time, the teams change goals. Each team gets three timeouts per game, with no more than two taken in one half. If the game is tied at the end of regulation, sudden-death overtime is played in 4-minute periods until a goal is scored. Teams get one timeout each per sudden-death period.

PROCEDURES

The ball is put into play to begin the game, and after each goal, with a face-off between two opposing players at the center of the field. The referee places the ball between the two players' crosses, blows a whistle to begin the action, and the two players attempt to take control of the ball.

After gaining possession of the ball in their *defensive area* (see figure 28.2 on page 185), a team must advance the ball past the defensive area line within 10 seconds, or turn the ball over to its opponents. The team clearing the ball may throw the ball back across the defensive area line one time on each restart.

After crossing the center line in possession of the ball, the attacking team must advance the ball into the attack area (see figure 28.2 on page 185) within 10 seconds. Once the ball is in the attack area, players may take it back outside that area, unless warned to "keep it in" (this warning occurs automatically in the final two minutes of regulation if the team in possession is winning). If a team takes the ball outside the attack area, a new 10-second count begins, and the attacking team must advance the ball inside the attack area before it expires, or lose possession of the ball.

A player may body-check an opponent who has the ball or who is within 5 yards of a loose ball. The check must be from the front or side, above the waist and below the neck.

When a player who has the ball steps on or over a boundary line, or his crosse touches on or beyond the boundary line, the ball is out of bounds and is awarded to the opponents. On a restart, no player may be within 5 yards of the player with the ball.

If the *ball becomes caught in a player's crosse,* the referee will count four seconds. If the player has not freed the ball by then, the ball is awarded to a team according to the *alternate-possession rule.* The team that wins the coin toss to begin the game gets first possession; possessions alternate after that for plays in which the official cannot determine which team should be awarded the ball.

If the *ball becomes caught in a player's uniform or equipment* other than his crosse, the ball is immediately awarded in accordance with the alternate-possession rule.

A team is *offside* when it has fewer than three men in its attack half of the field, or fewer than four men in its defensive half of the field. In such cases, a technical foul (see "Penalties") is called against the offending team.

Within the goal crease area, the goalkeeper may stop the ball with any part of his crosse or body, including batting it with his hands; however, he may not catch the ball. If the ball is outside the crease area, he may not touch the ball with his hands, even if *he* is within the crease area. No opponent may make contact with the goalkeeper while he is in the crease area, whether or not the goalkeeper has the ball. An attacking player may not be in the crease area at any time. A defending player with possession of the ball, including the goalkeeper, may not enter the crease area. If a defending player gains possession of the ball within the crease area, he must get rid of the ball or leave the crease area within four seconds.

SCORING

A team scores a goal when the ball passes from the front and completely through the imaginary plane formed by the rear edges of the opponents' goal line, the goal posts, and the crossbar.

A goal does not count when

- it passes the goal's plane after the period-ending horn or whistle,

- it passes the goal's plane while an attacking player is in the goal crease area,

- the attacking team has more than 10 men on the field (including the penalty area),

- the attacking team is offside as the goal is scored, and when

- an official has whistled the play dead for any reason.

FOULS

Players may be called for personal, technical, and expulsion fouls.

Personal fouls include illegal body-checking, slashing, cross-checking, tripping, unnecessary roughness, unsportsmanlike conduct, and using an illegal cross. A player committing a personal foul is suspended for one to three minutes, depending on the severity of the foul. The ball is given to the team fouled. A player who commits five personal fouls in a game is disqualified and may be replaced by a substitute when any penalty time for the fifth foul is over.

Technical fouls are less serious in nature than personal fouls. They include violations of rules that aren't covered under personal fouls and expulsion fouls. Examples of technical fouls include holding, pushing, offside, crease violations, illegal offensive screening, interference, and stalling. A player must serve a 30-second penalty if his opponents had possession of the ball at the time of his foul; if his team had possession of the ball, the ball is awarded to the opponents for a technical foul.

A player is assessed an *expulsion foul* for fighting. That player is suspended from the game and from the next game. He may be replaced after three minutes.

FIELD

The *field* is 110 yards long by 60 yards wide (see figure 28.2). A *center line* runs across midfield. While the field itself is 60 yards wide, its three major portions—the defensive area, the wing area, and the attack area—are 40 yards wide, with

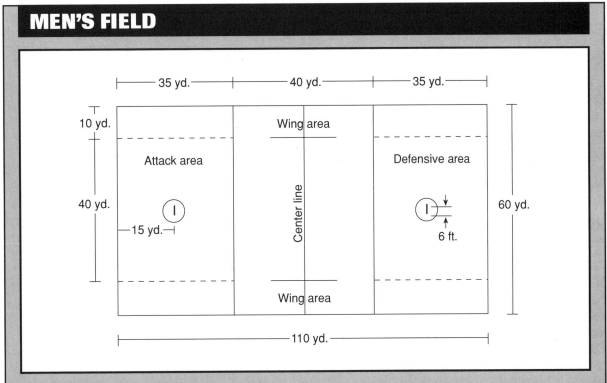

MEN'S FIELD

Figure 28.2. The features and dimensions of a men's lacrosse field.
Adapted from National Collegiate Athletic Association 1996.

10 yards on either side of these portions of the field extending to the sidelines. The defensive area begins at a team's own end line and measures 35 yards long; the wing area is 40 yards long, with its center being midfield; and the attack area is 35 yards long and ends at the opponents' end line.

The two *goals* have openings 6 feet wide and 6 feet high. Goal posts are made of metal pipe and joined by a crossbar. Each goal is centered between the sidelines and 15 yards from the nearest end line; the goals are 80 yards apart. Each goal has a mesh *net* fastened to the posts, crossbar, and ground 7 feet behind the center of the goal.

Each goal has a goal crease—a circle with a 9-foot radius—drawn around it. The center of the crease is the midpoint of the goal line.

The goal areas are marked at each end of the field by lines 40 yards long, centered on the goal and parallel to and 20 yards from the goal line at that end of the field.

PLAYERS

A team is made up of 10 players in the following designations: goalkeeper, defense, midfield, and attack. Four players at most, not counting the goalkeeper, may use long crosses 4.5 feet to 6 feet long.

A team may play with less than 10 players if they have injured or expelled players, as long as onside provisions are maintained. Substitutes may enter the game when officials have suspended play, or "on the fly," with one player entering the field from the table area after the player he is replacing has left the field by the table area.

EQUIPMENT

The *ball* is rubber, weighing between 5 and 5.25 ounces and having a circumference between 7.75 and 8 inches.

The crosse is made of wood or synthetic material. It is 40 to 42 inches long for a short crosse, or 52 to

72 inches long for a long crosse. The goalkeeper's crosse may be 72 inches or less. The circumference of the crosse handle may be no greater than 3.5 inches; the head at its widest point is between 6.5 and 10 inches; the head for the goalkeeper's crosse may range from 10 to 12 inches in width.

All players must wear *protective helmets* and *mouthpieces.* They must also wear *protective gloves, shoulder pads, shoes,* and *jerseys.* The goalkeeper must wear protective goalkeeper equipment.

OFFICIALS

A referee, umpire, and a field judge control the game. At least two officials must be used; a fourth may be used as a chief bench official.

ORGANIZATIONS

International Lacrosse Federation
P.O. Box 1373
Piscataway, NJ 08854
908-445-4211

United States Club Lacrosse Association
2600 Whitney Ave.
Baltimore, MD 21215
410-235-8532

United States Women's Lacrosse Association
P.O. Box 2178
Amherst, MA 01004
413-253-0328

29

Modern Pentathlon

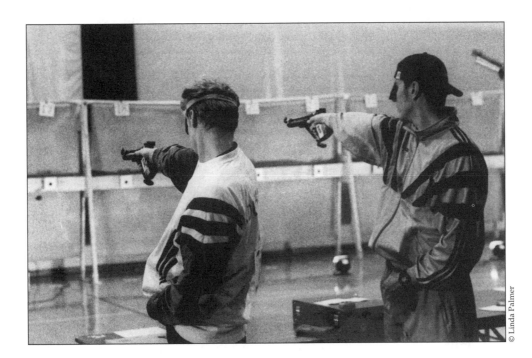

© Linda Palmer

The roots of modern pentathlon stretch back to 708 B.C., when the pentathlon—which then consisted of running the length of the stadium, broad jumping, throwing a spear and a discus, and wrestling—climaxed the 18th Olympiad. The pentathlon in ancient Greece was used to train Spartan soldiers. The disciplines for the modern pentathlon—which consists of *shooting, fencing, swimming, riding, and running*—also have military roots, springing from the concept of a liaison officer whose horse is brought down in enemy territory; the officer defends himself with pistol and sword, swims across a raging river, and delivers a message on foot.

The modern pentathlon was introduced to the modern Olympic Games in 1912; from 1912 to 1980, it was contested over a five-day period, with one event taking place each day. From 1984 to 1992, the competition was held over a four-day period; in 1996, it was held in one day. The goal is to score the most points; the point system for each event is based on a standard performance worth 1,000 points.

The modern pentathlon offers opportunities for individual and team competitions. There is some flexibility regarding the order of events, but running or riding is always the last event at official competitions sanctioned by the International Modern Pentathlon Union (UIPMB), which supplied the rules for this chapter.

PROCEDURES

The order of events for major competitions is usually shooting, fencing, swimming, riding, and running. Following are basic descriptions of each event, including scoring.

Shooting

In the individual event, competitors fire 20 shots, 1 per target, on a 10-meter shooting range with an air pistol. Each shooter has 40 seconds to shoot one shot. A target score of 172 out of 200 earns 1,000 points. A shooter has 12 points added or deducted for each target point above or below 172.

In the team event, three team members fire 10 shots each, 1 shot per target. A team scoring 258 target points earns 1,000 points; each target point above or below 258 is worth plus or minus 12 points.

Fencing

Fencers in individual competition use an épée, and scores are recorded with electronic apparatus; bouts are for one decisive hit. Bouts last one minute. The competitor who wins 70 percent of his bouts earns 1,000 points. Each victory differential adds or subtracts 30 points. In team competition, bouts are for three decisive hits in three separate minutes.

Swimming

Swimmers in individual competition compete in a free-style event against the clock: men race 300 meters; women race 200 meters. Men can earn 1,000 points for completing the swim in 3 minutes, 54 seconds; women can earn 1,000 points for a time of 2:54. Four points are added or deducted for each half-second faster or slower.

In the team event, three team members swim in a relay: men swim 200 meters each; women swim 100 meters each. Men earn 1,000 points for a time of 6:40; each half-second slower or faster deducts or adds 4 points. Women earn 1,000 points for a time of 3:30; each half-second slower or faster deducts or adds 4 points.

Riding

Riders in individual competition complete a 450-meter course with 12 obstacles. A clear round within the time limit is worth 1,100 points. Riders have points deducted for various penalties, including refusals, knockdowns, and for exceeding the time limit. In the team event, three team members ride over a 350-meter course with nine obstacles.

Running

Runners in individual competition compete over a cross-country course (4,000 meters for men; 2,000 meters for women). Runners begin according to handicap; the runner with the most points after four events has the advantage. A man earns 1,000 points for a time of 14:15; three points are added or deducted for each second faster or slower than that time. A woman earns 1,000 points for a time of 7:40; five points are added or deducted for each second faster or slower than that time.

In the team event, men race an aggregate of 6,000 meters, with each of three team members running 2,000 meters; women race a total of 3,000 meters, with each of three team members running 1,000 meters. A men's relay earns 1,000 points for a total time of 19:00; each second faster or slower adds or deducts 3 points. Women earn 1,000 points for a time of 10:30, and have .5 point added or deducted for every second faster or slower than that time.

TERMS

A **bout** is a fight between two fencers.

An **épée** is the weapon used by a fencer.

A **knockdown** occurs when a horse or rider causes an obstacle, or any integral part of its support, to fall.

A **match** is the aggregate of bouts fought between fencers of two teams.

A **piste** is the competition area for fencing, 1.5 to 2 meters by 14 meters.

A **refusal** occurs when a horse refuses to jump an obstacle. If the horse doesn't knock the obstacle down, doesn't back up, and does make a standing jump, the rider is not penalized.

A **run-out** occurs when a horse escapes the control of its rider and avoids an obstacle it is to jump. The rider is penalized for a run-out and is eliminated if the horse does not attempt the jump.

SHOOTING

The shooter stands without support and holds and fires the pistol with one hand. The shooter may not wear a bracelet, wristwatch, wrist band, or anything else that might provide support to the shooting hand and arm. Judges give competitors the following commands: "Load," "Start," "Stop," and "Change targets."

Shots are scored by two scoring officials. Shots are given the value of the highest scoring zone or ring they are in or touch. If a shooter's pistol does not discharge due to malfunction, the shooter may be awarded another chance at the shot if the malfunction was not due to the shooter's error. If two shooters are tied for first place, the shooter with the higher number of 10s wins. If they are still tied, the shooter with the higher number of 9s wins, then 8s, and so on.

FENCING

A fencer's target is the opponent's whole body, clothing, and equipment. The fencer may use only one hand in handling the épée and may not throw the épée . He may not change hands during the bout. He may not use his unarmed hand in any defensive or offensive action. Doing so results in a 10-point penalty after an initial warning. Double hits (simultaneous hits by both fencers) cancel each other, and the fencers resume the on-guard position they were in before the double hit occurred.

Competitors may fence at close quarters as long as they can wield their weapons correctly. However, they may not have contact. Moving, ducking, and turning are allowed, and the unarmed hand may come in contact with the piste (the competition strip), but a fencer may not turn his back on his opponent. Penalty is 10 points after a competitor has been warned once. When a fencer passes her opponent, any hits made immediately during the pass are valid, but no hits made after the pass are valid, and the fencers are returned to the positions they held before the pass.

Competitors may not leave the piste during the bout. A fencer who crosses a lateral boundary with both feet is penalized; when the fencers resume the on-guard position, the opponent steps forward one meter from her position at the time the penalty occurred. If the competitor crosses the lateral boundary to avoid a hit, she is warned and then penalized 10 points for a repeated infringement. If, however, a competitor crosses a boundary because of a collision or other accident, she is not penalized.

If a fencer crosses the rear boundary of the piste, he is penalized one hit. Competitors may not place the points of their weapons on the piste. After a warning, a second such offense results in a 10-point penalty. A hit that doesn't land before the bell (ending the bout) doesn't count. If time expires with neither fencer scoring a winning hit, both fencers are counted as being hit, and a defeat is scored against both of them.

SWIMMING

The free-style swim begins with a dive. A swimmer is allowed one false start; a second false start results in a five-second penalty. The swimmer must touch the end of the pool with some body part; failure to do so results in a 40-point penalty.

Any swimmer who impedes another swimmer will be eliminated. A swimmer who has been impeded may be allowed to swim again. Swimmers may not wear devices to aid buoyancy or speed. A swimmer using oil or grease will be penalized 40 points. Swimmers may stand on the bottom of the pool, but when they do so they may not advance.

RIDING

Competitors draw for starting order. They are given 20 minutes to walk the riding course before the competition, but they may not show their horses an obstacle, attempt a jump, or exercise their horses in the arena before the competition. Once the competition begins, a competitor who enters the arena on foot will be eliminated.

Competitors start an individual competition in 3-minute intervals. In team-relay competitions with three horses, competitors start in 7-minute intervals. The clock starts when the nose of the horse crosses the starting line and stops when the competitor crosses the finish line.

Competitors must ride at a speed of 350 meters per minute. The *time allowed* for individual competitions is between 1 minute and 1:17, depending on the distance. The *time limit* is twice the allowed time. Competitors or teams who exceed the limit are eliminated. In the team relay with three horses, the time allowed is 3:00 and the time limit is 6:00. In relays with one horse, the time allowed and time limit are 2:30 and 5:00, respectively.

The rider must pass between the flags on the course, keeping the red flags on her right and the white on her left. There is no penalty for knocking down a flag. Each rider must cover the whole course and make all the required jumps. A knockdown occurs when the rider or the horse causes an obstacle or its support to fall, either wholly or in part. Touching or displacing any part of an obstacle, while not in the act of jumping, does not count as a knockdown.

A *water-jump fault* is recorded when a horse puts one or more feet on the lath bounding the water jump, or in the water itself. It is also a fault if a horse jumps between the two red flags or between the two white flags at the water jump. (See table 29.1 for a listing of faults and penalties.)

A *disobedience* is recorded when a horse

- deviates from the course,
- refuses a jump,
- commits a run-out (escapes control of the rider and avoids an obstacle),
- resists to go on,
- circles, and
- crosses over the track between obstacles.

A competitor is considered to have *fallen* when he is separated from his horse and must use some

Table 29.1:   Riding Faults and Penalties

Fault	Penalty points
Exceeding the time allowed	3 per sec
Knocking down an obstacle while jumping	30
Horse placing foot in water at water jump	30
Falling (rider, horse, or both)	60
Committing a disobedience	40 per act
Jumping the same obstacle (after three jumps)	40 per attempt
Starting wrong (team relay)	40

Adapted from Union Internationale de Pentathlon Moderne et Biathlon 1996.

Eliminations

Following is a partial list of the acts for which a competitor may be eliminated.

- Jumping an obstacle
  a. before the start of a round
  b. that is not part of the course
  c. in the wrong order or in the wrong direction
  d. before correcting a course deviation
  e. for the fourth time
- Showing the horse an obstacle before the start or after a refusal
- Crossing the starting or finish line outside the flags
- Omitting an obstacle
- Failure to attempt a third jump at an obstacle before going on to the next one
- Not jumping all the elements of a combination again after a refusal, run-out, or fall
- Exceeding the time limit

form of assistance or support to get back in the saddle. A horse is considered to have fallen when its shoulder and quarters touch the ground. In a combination jump, the competitor must retake all the jumps if there is a refusal, run-out, or fall. If he does not, he is eliminated. If a horse has three refusals at an obstacle in the first round, the rider may request a change of horses.

RUNNING

The start is handicapped. The start may be conducted by brief time intervals between each start (one-third second for men and one-fifth second for women), or it may be conducted using different start lines. In this case, the competitor with the highest score starts at the first start line. Individual start lines are set consecutively 1.5 meters apart behind the first start line, and the other runners start from these lines, based on their standings.

In relay competitions, the team in first place will be given the advantage. In relays, team members much touch each other within the 20-meter start area as one runner ends and another begins. In a *pack start*, all runners start together, with the athlete or team in first place in the best starting position.

A false start in a handicap start costs a competitor 40 points. A false start in a pack start results in a recall; if there is a second false start, the competitor who made it is penalized 40 points. A runner who jostles or impedes another runner is subject to disqualification.

COMPETITION AREAS

Competition takes place in the following areas:

Shooting. Ranges have a line of targets and a firing line. Range officials have space behind the firing points to perform their duties. Each firing point has a table and a chair or stool for the competitor. The range has a large clock that can be seen clearly by competitors and officials alike.

Fencing. Competition takes place on a piste that is 1.5 to 2 meters wide by 14 meters long. Five lines are drawn across the width of the piste: a center line; two on-guard lines, both 2 meters away from the center line; and two rear limit lines, each 7 meters from the center line. The last 2 meters before these rear limit lines are also clearly marked, often by a change in color.

Swimming. For major competitions, pool dimensions are 50 meters in length, at least 21 meters in width, and 1.8 meters in depth. The minimum number of lanes is eight. A false-start rope is suspended across the pool at least 1.2 meters above the water.

Riding. The arena is enclosed. The starting line is between 6 and 25 meters from the first obstacle, and the finish line is between 15 and 25 meters from the last obstacle. The course is marked with red flags and white flags that indicate the start, the side limits of obstacles, compulsory turning points, and the finish. A continuous line or a series of arrows indicates the progression of the course.

Running. The course can be on any surface, in one or more laps, with each lap making up at least 20 percent of the course. The first and last 50 meters must be straight and at least 10 meters wide. The course is marked with flags to indicate direction. The maximum climb for men is 50 meters; for women, 30 meters. For relays, the hand-over zones are 20 meters long, marked by lines. Start and finish is in the same place.

COMPETITORS

Age groups for males and females include

- 14 years old and under (Youth C),
- 15 to 16 (Youth B),
- 17 to 18 (Youth A),
- 19 to 21 (Junior),
- 22 and over (Senior), and
- 40 and over (Masters).

EQUIPMENT

Competitors use the following equipment:

Shooting—Competitors may use a 4.5-mm *air pistol* of any caliber with a weight not to exceed 1,500 grams. Only open sights are allowed; optical, telescopic, or other sights are prohibited. A competitor must use the same pistol throughout the event. *Ammunition* is any caliber 4.5 mm. *Targets* are made of paper and have 10 scoring rings.

Fencing—Each fencer wears a *mask with a collar,* and a *glove with a gauntlet* that covers about half of the fencing forearm. The *épée* must weigh less than 770 grams and be no longer than 110 centimeters. The épée has a connection socket inside the guard and a special point for registering hits. Signal lamps on top of judging apparatus light up when a hit is registered.

Riding—Riders must wear *protective headgear* with a chinstrap. They may use spurs and whips that do not have cutting edges and that are not weighted. A *bell* signals when to start, when to stop, and when to continue after an interruption. *Obstacles* are numbered in the order they are to be jumped.

Running—Runners wear *running uniforms* and may choose to run with or without *shoes.*

OFFICIALS

Each event has its own set of officials governing the competition.

MODIFICATIONS

The International Modern Pentathlon Union's guidelines for shortened pentathlons for youth include

- swim, run (one day);
- swim, shoot, run (one day); and
- fence, swim, shoot, run (two days).

For recommended swimming and running distances for youth, see table 29.2.

Table 29.2: Youth Competitions		
Age	Swim (m)	Run (m)
14 and under	100	1,000
15 to 16	200	2,000
17 to 18	300	3,000

Adapted from Union Internationale de Pentathlon Moderne et Biathlon 1996.

ORGANIZATIONS

Union Internationale de Pentathlon Moderne et Biathlon (UIPMB)
Hotel Hillerod
Milversvej 41
DK - 3400 Hillerod
Denmark
45 4824 3911

30

Netball

© John Sherwell

Netball's origins stem from basketball, which was invented by Dr. James Naismith in the United States in 1891. In fact, in Australia and New Zealand, where netball is most popular, the game was first known as nine-a-side basketball. The first game was played in England in 1895, with wastepaper baskets hung on the walls for goals instead of peach baskets that Naismith had used for basketball. A few years later the first outdoor game was played, and rings were used instead of baskets. The court was also divided into three equal spaces.

Netball spread to other Commonwealth countries, each of which played its own variation of the game. In 1960 an international code of play was introduced, and in 1963 the first world championship was held in England, where Australia and New Zealand established themselves as dominant teams. Australia won that first title and has gone on to win all but two world championships.

While the game is much more popular among women, netball is growing in popularity with men. The object is to score more goals than the opponents. A goal may be scored by one of two scoring players on each side. The source for rules in this chapter is the International Federation of Netball Associations.

PROCEDURES

A game consists of four 15-minute quarters with 3-minute breaks between the first and second quarters and the third and fourth quarters, and a 5-minute halftime break. Each team has seven players on the court. Teams change ends at the end of each quarter. In hot climates or in tournaments where teams play more than one match a day, the teams may agree to play for less time, such as two 20-minute halves.

A coin toss determines which team may choose to either take the first center pass or defend the goal of its choice. To begin play, only the two teams' centers may be in the center third of the court (see figure 30.1, page 197). The game begins with one of the centers making a center pass from inside the center circle. The opposing team's center may not obstruct the throw. The center may pass to one of four teammates—the goal attack, the goal defense, the wing defense, or the wing attack. The player must catch the ball in the center third of the court, moving in any direction to do so. The team controlling the ball continues to pass, attempting to get the ball to one of its shooters (the goal shooter or goal attack). When the goal shooter or goal attack has the ball in the goal circle, she may shoot. She may also pass the ball if she's not in good position to shoot.

When a player catches a ball, she may take one step with it before passing. She may not bounce it or drop it and retrieve it. She may, however, bounce the ball or pass it in the air to a teammate, so long as the ball does not cross a whole third of the court (i.e., a player in the defensive goal third of the court may not throw a pass that crosses the center third and is caught by a teammate in the attack goal third of the court, or vice versa).

Players are restricted to certain portions of the court (see "Players," page 197). For example, a wing attack may be in the attack goal third and the center third of the court; if she enters the defensive goal third of the court, she is offside, and a free pass (see "Penalties," page 196) is awarded to the opponents.

When a player scores a goal, the ball is brought back out to the center circle, where a center pass is taken to restart the game. The center pass alternates between the two teams. Play may be stopped for injury or illness for up to two minutes; at this time the team must decide whether the player can continue, or substitute for her. Both teams may substitute and change their positions during this time. The ball is declared out of court when it touches outside the court or touches a person in contact with the ground outside the court. In such cases, a throw-in is awarded to the opposing team.

TERMS

A **center pass** is made by one of the team's centers to begin play and to restart play after a goal has been scored. Center passes alternate between the two teams.

A **free pass** is awarded for rule infringements other than obstruction, contact, simultaneous offenses by two opponents, and interference with the goalpost. See "Penalties," page 196.

Obstruction is called when a player makes any movements that interfere with an opponent's throwing or shooting action. A penalty pass or a penalty pass or shot results. For other plays that result in a call of obstruction, see "Obstruction," page 195.

A player is **offside** when she crosses into an area of the court that she is not allowed to enter. The opposing team receives a free pass.

A **penalty pass or penalty pass or shot** is awarded for calls of obstruction and contact. See "Penalties," page 196.

A **throw-in** is made by a team to put the ball into play after it has gone out of court. See "Penalties," page 196

A **toss-up** is taken between two opponents when they both have possession of the ball, when they both go offside at the same moment, or when the ball goes out of court and the umpire can't determine who touched it last. See "Penalties," page 196.

PLAYING THE BALL

A player who possesses the ball must pass or shoot it within three seconds. In playing the ball, a player may throw it in any direction and manner to another player, including bouncing it. A player may also

- catch the ball with one or both hands;
- bat or bounce the ball to another player without gaining possession of it;
- tip or bat the ball and then catch it or direct it to another player;
- bounce the ball once and then catch the ball or direct it to another player;
- roll the ball to herself to gain possession of it;
- fall while holding the ball, regain footing, and throw the ball within three seconds of receiving it;
- lean on the ball to stop from going offside or to gain balance; and
- jump from within the court and play the ball outside the court, so long as neither the player nor the ball touch out of court before the player plays the ball.

A player *may not*

- strike the ball with a fist;
- deliberately fall on the ball;
- attempt to gain possession of the ball or throw it, while lying, sitting, or kneeling on the ground;
- use the goal post as a support in trying to recover the ball or in regaining balance;
- deliberately kick the ball;
- roll the ball to another player;
- throw the ball and then touch it before it has been touched by another player;
- replay the ball after tossing it in the air, dropping the ball, or bouncing the ball; or
- replay the ball after an unsuccessful shot unless the ball has touched part of the goal post.

SCORING

Only two players on each team may shoot: the goal shooter and goal attack. They must be within the goal circle (see figure 30.1 on page 197) when they shoot. The goal circle includes the lines bounding it. When the goal shooter or goal at-

tack throws the ball through the ring from within the goal circle, a goal is scored.

If any other player throws the ball through the ring, no goal is scored and play continues unabated. If the ball deflects off a defender and goes through the ring, a goal is scored. If the umpire whistles for "time" before the ball goes completely through the ring, no goal is scored.

OBSTRUCTION

Obstruction is a fault that can be committed by either an attacking (offensive) player or a defensive player. A defensive player commits obstruction if she is within three feet of the player with the ball and she interferes with the throwing or shooting action. The defensive player may attempt to intercept or defend the ball by jumping toward the player with the ball, so long as she doesn't land within three feet of that player. The distance is measured from the nearest foot of the defender to the offensive player's landing, grounded, or pivoting foot.

It is not considered obstruction if a defending player is within three feet of an opponent who does not have the ball and the defender attempts to prevent the opponent from moving to a free space on the court or from catching a ball, so long as the defender does not use her arms away from her body except to maintain body balance. If she uses arm movements beyond those needed to balance her body, then she is obstructing the opponent.

A player may be within three feet of an opponent with the ball, so long as she makes no effort to defend. Obstruction is called when a player with or without the ball (including an attacking player) intimidates an opponent. The defending player is not penalized if the player with the ball lessens the distance between them to under the three-foot limit.

Players may use outstretched arms to catch, deflect, or intercept a pass, to signal for a pass, to feint a pass, and to rebound a missed shot. Players using their arms for these purposes will not be called for obstruction. The penalty for obstruction is a penalty pass or a penalty pass or shot, taken from where the fault occurred.

CONTACT

No player may contact another and interfere with her play, either accidentally or deliberately. Such contact includes pushing, bumping, holding, or tripping an opponent; using any part of the body to interfere with an opponent's play; and taking up a position so that contact with an opponent cannot be avoided.

A player holding the ball may not touch or push an opponent. A defender may not, accidentally or deliberately, place a hand on or remove a ball from an opponent's possession. The penalty for contact is a penalty pass or a penalty pass or shot from where the fault occurred.

PENALTIES

There are four types of penalties that can be awarded when a rule is broken: a *free pass*, a *penalty pass* or *penalty pass* or *shot*, a *throw-in*, and a *toss-up*. Except when a toss-up is warranted, a team may decide which player will take the penalty. The player taking the penalty has three seconds to throw the ball after taking her position.

Free Pass

A free pass is awarded for any rules infringement except obstruction, contact, simultaneous offenses by two opposing players, and interference with the goal post. A free pass may be called when

- a player is offside,
- a player receives a center pass in the wrong area of the court,
- a player commits a ballhandling or footwork fault, and
- a shooter shoots from outside the goal circle.

A free pass may be thrown by any member of the awarded team that is allowed in the area where the throw is taken.

Penalty Pass

A penalty pass is awarded for obstruction and contact faults. The player who committed the

fault must stand beside the opposing player making the pass and take no part in the game until the ball has been thrown. Other defenders may defend against the pass. Any player who is allowed in the area can make the pass, which is taken from where the player who committed the fault stood, unless this puts the offended team at a disadvantage. Where this may be the case, the player takes the pass from where she stood. If the offense is committed within the goal circle, the goal shooter or goal attack may take either a penalty pass or a penalty shot, without indicating which she will take.

Throw-In

A throw-in is awarded when the ball goes out of court. The ball is awarded to the opponents of the team that touched the ball last. The player throwing in must throw into the nearest third of the court; the ball may not pass completely over a third of a court. When the umpire gives the player the ball and calls "Play," the player has three seconds to throw the ball in.

Toss-Up

A toss-up is taken between two opposing players when

- opposing players gain possession of the ball simultaneously;
- opposing players knock the ball out of court at the same time;
- the umpire can't determine which player knocked the ball out of court;
- opposing players are simultaneously offside, with one in possession of, or touching, the ball; or
- opposing players make simultaneous contact, interfering with the play.

The players involved in the toss-up stand 3 feet apart, with their arms straight and their hands at their sides. Each player faces her attacking goal end. The umpire throws the ball up between the two players, who may attempt to catch the ball or bat it. Other players may stand or move anywhere in their playing areas, so long as they don't interfere with the toss-up.

COURT

The *court* is 100 feet long and 50 feet wide (see figure 30.1). It is divided into three equal parts: a *center third* and two *goal thirds*. Each goal third has a *goal circle,* which is a semicircle with a radius of 16 feet. A *center circle,* 3 feet in diameter, is in the center of the court.

The *goal posts* are 10 feet high. The *rings* are 15 inches in diameter and are projected horizontally 6 inches from the goal posts.

PLAYERS

A team consists of seven players who wear the initials of their positions on their uniforms and are restricted to certain areas of the court by their position. See table 30.1 for the positions, the areas the players in these positions may be in, and their main responsibilities.

Team captains may ask umpires for clarification of the rules during breaks in the game. A team captain also notifies the umpires and the opposing team captain when substitutions are made. Up to three substitutions may be made by each team in one game. No team may take the court with fewer than five players.

If a player arrives late, she may not take the place of the player who has taken her position, except in case of injury or during a break. A player who is replaced may later return to the game, but she is counted as one of the team's three allotted substitutions.

EQUIPMENT

The *ball* is between 27 inches and 28 inches in circumference and weighs between 14 ounces and 16 ounces. It is made of leather, rubber, or similar material. It is the same as a size 5 (English) football.

COURT

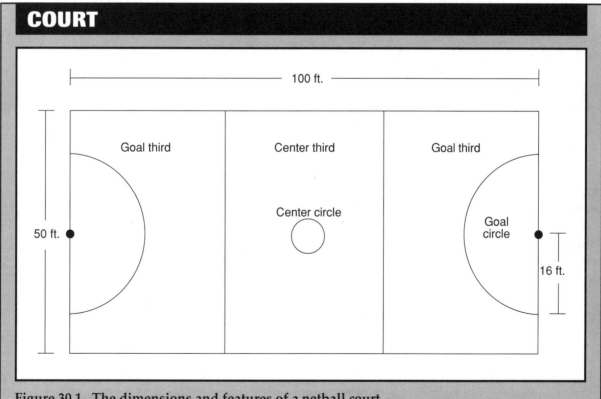

Figure 30.1. The dimensions and features of a netball court.
Adapted from Shakespear 1997.

	Table 30.1: Player Areas and Duties	
Player	Areas allowed in	Main responsibilities
Goal shooter (GS)	Goal circle, attack goal third	Scoring
Goal attack (GA)	Goal circle, attack goal third, center third	Scoring, contributing to the attack
Wing attack (WA)	Attack goal third, center third	Receiving the ball in the attack goal third and passing the ball into the circle
Center (C)	Both goal thirds and center third	Contributing to both the attack and the defense
Wing defense (WD)	Center third, defense goal third	Defending the opposing wing attack
Goal defense (GD)	Center third, defense goal third, goal circle	Defending the opposing goal attack and shots on goal
Goal keeper (GK)	Defense goal third, goal circle	Defending the opposing goal shooter and shots on goal, and rebounding

Adapted from Federation of Netball Associations, Magnay, and Thomas 1991, 1991, and 1994.

OFFICIALS

Two *umpires* control the game and give decisions. Each umpire has control over one half of the court, from one goal third to the center circle. Two *scorers* keep records of the score, the center pass, and unsuccessful shots. A *timekeeper* tracks time.

ORGANIZATIONS

All England Netball Association
Netball House
9 Paynes Park
Hitchin, Herts. SG5 1EH, England
161 442343

International Federation of Netball Associations
Birmingham Sports Centre
201 Balsall Heath Road
Highgate
Birmingham B12 9DL, England
121 4464659

Netball NZ
P.O. Box 99-170
Auckland, New Zealand
9 6233200

31

Orienteering

© Richard B. Levine

Orienteering is a sport in which participants use a detailed topographic map and a compass to reach a series of navigational checkpoints. The sport originated in Sweden in the early 1900s and was introduced in the United States in the 1940s. Orienteering appeals to a variety of people of all ages, including fitness enthusiasts, hikers, backpackers, and recreational athletes.

The object is to complete the course in the shortest time. Most courses are laid out in forested terrain; both physical fitness and navigational skills are tested. Types of orienteering events include individual, individual with team results, multi-day, relay, and group team. World championships and many national championships are based on one race; however, many other events incorporate two races on two separate days, with the fastest total time determining the winner. Most events have a variety of courses for competitors, ranging from novice to elite. The rules for this chapter were supplied by the United States Orienteering Federation.

PROCEDURES

The typical race is point-to-point. With compass and map in hand, a participant chooses any route he pleases, so long as he reaches each control point in sequence and punches his control card to indicate he reached each point. Each control point has a punch with a different pattern.

Individual starts are done in intervals, two or three minutes apart. The start is arranged so the competitor about to start doesn't know which way the previous orienteer went. *Mass starts* are used for score competitions in which orienteers can find the control points in any order.

Each competitor moves along as silently as possible, giving no indication of location to other competitors. Certain terrain is out of bounds, including yards and gardens, cropland, limited access highways, and so on; these areas are clearly marked on the map. Competitors must take care to cause no damage in any area through which they pass.

Orienteers may receive no outside assistance and may not check the course before the event. The finish line is bounded by tapes. After finishing, orienteers turn in their control cards to event officials. Finish times are recorded to the nearest full second. Ties between orienteers are not broken.

In a relay race, the position of the team is determined by its last runner. An orienteer will be disqualified for omitting a control mark, for marking at an incorrect control location, or for marking out of sequence if this can be proved. Some control points at large events may have officials present to determine if any particpant's controls have been taken out of order.

Each competitor has an equal amount of time to complete the course. For most events the time allowed is three hours, unless otherwise stated. An orienteer completing a course beyond the allotted time will not receive a time or place.

TERMS

A **control card** is carried by each orienteer; it has numbered boxes, which must be punched in proper order at the control sites throughout the course.

Control flags mark the spots circled on the map, indicating control sites. A flag is either hung from a branch at the site (North America) or stuck on a stake in the ground (Europe).

A **control site** is a checkpoint on the course at which each orienteer must stop to punch her control card.

COURSE

Courses have varying lengths and technical difficulties. See figure 31.1 for a sample orienteering course. Hazardous terrain is marked with blue and yellow streamers, and orienteers are routed around these areas with orange and white streamers. Special control locations are set by safe crossing points near deep waters or dangerous gorges. Courses are set so that swimming is neither necessary nor tempting as a route choice. Course length is measured as the shortest course a competitor could reasonably take. See table 31.1 for approximate lengths and winning times.

Control sites are marked by control flags, which are made of fabric and hung on a triangular wire frame. Each of the three cloth faces has a white upper triangle and an orange or red lower triangle. One or more *punches* are placed near the control flag. Each punch has a code on it to help orienteers confirm they are at the correct control site. The codes are listed in the description sheet that defines the course's controls. The orienteers punch their control cards in the correct boxes before continuing on their route.

COMPETITORS

Orienteers may compete in age and sex classifications; there may be both noncompetitive and competitive categories. Clothing is up to the individual, but usually orienteers wear long pants to protect their legs.

EQUIPMENT

An orienteer uses a *compass* to take bearings and to orient the *map* so it is aligned with the terrain. However, it is quite possible in most areas with some prominent features to navigate the course without a compass.

COURSE

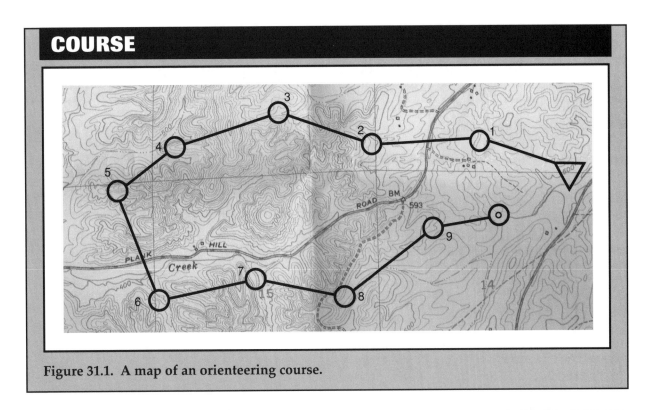

Figure 31.1. A map of an orienteering course.

Table 31.1: Course Lengths and Times		
Navigational difficulty	Approximate length (km)	Approximate winning time (min)
Beginner	3 or less	30
Advanced beginner	3.5 to 4.5	40
Intermediate	4 to 5	50
Short expert	4 to 6	50
Medium expert	6 to 8	60
Long expert	8 to 12	60 to 80

Adapted from White 1990.

Maps are similar to government issue maps, with the addition of north lines running from magnetic south to magnetic north, spaced 500 meters apart on the map. Most maps are scaled at 1:15,000; some are at 1:10,000. Events typically are on five-color maps with 5-meter contour intervals. Maps have the following symbols:

- Black—used for rock features (boulders, cliffs, stony ground) and for linear features (roads, trails, fences)

- Brown—contour lines, knolls, earth banks, dry ditches

- Blue—water

- Yellow—vegetation (open or unforested land)

- Green—vegetation that will slow the orienteer

- White—forest with little or no undergrowth (easily run through)

- Purple or red—marks the course; also marks out-of-bounds areas

Orienteers may not use any navigational aids other than a compass. Personal aids for sight, such as eyeglasses, magnifying glasses, and flashlights, are permitted.

OFFICIALS

A *meet director* is in charge of the event. A *jury* of at least three people assists the director. These officials act as course planners and organizers.

ORGANIZATIONS

United States Orienteering Federation
P.O. Box 1444
Forest Park, GA 30051
404-363-2110

32

Racquetball

© Terry Wild Studio

Racquetball is a fast-paced game played by two, three, or four players using a hollow rubber ball and strung racquets. It evolved in the late 1940s from paddleball, a slower game played with a solid paddle. The rules are similar to handball and paddleball. The source for the rules in this chapter is the American Amateur Racquetball Association, the national governing body for the sport, which is played by more than 10 million people in the United States.

The objective of the game is to win rallies and score points by serving or returning the ball so that the opponent cannot keep the ball in play. A rally is won when one player or side cannot return the ball before it hits the floor twice, when a player or side returns a ball that hits the floor before it hits the front wall, or when a hinder is called.

PROCEDURES

A match is the best two-of-three games. The first two games are played to 15 points. If a third game is necessary, it is played to 11 points. The player or side winning a coin toss chooses to serve or receive to begin the first game. The player or side beginning the first game as server will begin the second game as receiver. To begin a third game, the player or side that scored the most points during the first two games gets the choice to serve or receive. If the point totals are equal, another coin toss is required.

Points are scored only by the serving side. In singles, the server continues to serve as long as she wins each rally. She earns one point for each rally won. When she loses a rally, her opponent gains the serve; this is called a *sideout*.

In doubles, to begin a game, Server 1 of Team A serves until his team loses a rally. Team B then gains the serve. From there on, when the first server of a team loses the serve, it is called a *handout,* and when the second server loses the serve, it is a *sideout,* and the opponents gain the serve.

Serving

The server has 10 seconds to serve once the score has been called. It is the server's responsibility to make sure the receiver is ready before she serves. A receiver may signal she is not ready by raising her racquet above her head or by turning her back to the server. These are the only two acceptable signals.

The server serves from any place within the *service zone*. Neither the ball nor any part of either foot may be beyond the service zone lines when the server begins her motion. The server may step over the *front service line* if portions of both feet remain on or inside the line until the served ball passes the *short line*.

Once the server begins her motion, she must bounce the ball once and hit it with her racquet. The ball must strike the front wall first and then strike the floor on its first bounce beyond the back edge of the short line. A serve can hit one of the side walls before hitting the floor.

A player may hit a *drive serve* between himself and the side wall nearest to him if he remains

outside of the three-foot *drive service zone.* In doubles, players must maintain their order of serve. That order can be changed between games.

The server's partner must stand with his back to the side wall and with both feet within the service box until the ball passes the short line. A violation results in a *foot fault,*unless the partner enters the *safety zone* (the area between the short line and the *receiving line*); in this case the server loses his serve.

A *dead-ball serve* results in no penalty; the server is given another serve. Dead-ball serves include court hinders (e.g., the ball bounces irregularly because it hit a wet spot or irregular surface) and balls that break on the serve. A server can have one *fault serve;* a second fault results in a handout or a sideout. Fault serves include

- foot faults (for either the server or the partner),
- short serves (hit the floor on or in front of the short line),
- three-wall serves (hit the front wall and both side walls before striking the floor),
- ceiling serves (hit the front wall and then the ceiling, with or without touching a side wall),
- long serves (hit the back wall before hitting the floor or go out of the court),
- bouncing the ball outside of the service zone,
- illegal drive serves (the server must start and remain out of the drive service zone),
- screen serves (rebound so close to the server or the server's partner that the receiver's view is screened),
- serving before the receiver is ready, and
- hitting the server's partner with the ball while the partner is in the doubles box.

Out serves, meaning either a handout or a sideout, may be called after

- there have been two consecutive fault serves;
- the server totally misses an attempted serve;
- a served ball rebounds and touches the server or the server's racquet;
- a served ball is stopped or caught by the server or the server's partner;
- a fake or balk serve occurs (if the referee believes the balk was not to deceive the receiver, he may call a "no serve" and assess no penalty);

- a player hits the ball twice, carries the ball, or hits the ball with the racquet handle or with any part of the body;

- the ball strikes any surface other than the front wall first;

- a player hits a "crotch serve"—one that hits the crotch of the front wall and floor, front wall and side wall, or front wall and ceiling;

- a player serves out of order (any points scored by the player serving out of order are subtracted);

- a serve hits the partner while she is outside the doubles box; and

- the server or his partner enters the safety zone before the served ball passes the short line.

Returning Serve

The receiver may not enter the safety zone until the ball bounces or crosses the receiving line. The receiver may try to return the ball before it strikes the floor, but the ball must pass the plane of the receiving line first. The receiver's racquet or body may break the plane of the receiving line on the follow-through. The plane of the short line may not be broken, however, unless the receiver strikes the ball after it rebounds off the back wall. Any violation results in a point for the server.

A receiver may not intentionally catch or touch an apparently long serve until the referee has made the call or the ball bounces twice. Violation results in a point for the server. A receiver must return a serve before it strikes the floor twice. The return must hit the front wall before it touches the floor. It may hit any combination of walls and ceiling beforehand.

Rallies

During a *rally*—all the play that follows the serve—a player may hit the ball only with the head of the racquet, which may be held in one or both hands. Switching the racquet from one hand to the other, or removing the wrist thong, results in a loss of the rally. Other losses of rally result when a player

- touches the ball more than once on a return,

- carries the ball (slings or throws it, rather than hits it),

- fails to return the ball before it bounces twice,

- fails to hit the front wall on the return, before the return strikes the floor,

- hits himself or his partner with the ball,

- commits an avoidable hinder (see "Hinders"), and

- hits the ball out of the court before the ball has first hit the front wall.

The ball remains in play until it touches the floor a second time, no matter how many walls the ball hits, including the front wall. A player may swing at a ball and miss in a return attempt as long as he hits it before it bounces twice.

In doubles, both partners may attempt to return the ball; no alternating is necessary. Only one player may strike the ball on a return, however. If a return strikes the front wall, bounces once and goes into the gallery or through any opening, the ball is dead, and the server receives two serves. Whenever a rally is replayed, the server begins with two serves.

If a ball breaks during a rally, the rally is replayed. If a foreign object enters the court during a rally, play is stopped and the rally is replayed.

Hinders

A *dead-ball hinder* results in a replay with no penalty; the server receives two serves. The receiver must make a reasonable effort and have a reasonable chance to make a return before a referee will call a hinder. Dead-ball hinders occur when

- a court hinder is called (such as when the ball hits a door knob or bounces irregularly due to rough surface),

- the ball hits an opponent (unless it's obvious the ball would not have reached the front wall),

- body contact occurs (if the contact prevents a player from being able to make a reasonable return),

- an offensive player is screened from the ball passing close to a defensive player,

- a player's backswing hinders an opponent from taking a reasonable swing,

- a player about to make a return stops because she believes that on her return either the ball or her racquet will strike an opponent, or

- there is any other unintentional interference that prevents an opponent from having a fair chance to clearly see and return the ball.

An *avoidable hinder* results in loss of the rally. An avoidable hinder does not necessarily mean the act was intentional. Avoidable hinders occur when

- a player does not move enough to allow her opponent a shot straight at the front wall as well as a cross-court shot;
- a player's movement, or lack of movement, impedes his opponent's swing;
- a player's position blocks her opponent from reaching or returning a ball;
- a player moves in the path of, and is struck by, a ball just hit by an opponent;
- a player deliberately shoves an opponent during a rally;
- a player deliberately distracts her opponent by shouting, waving her racquet, and so on;
- a player moves into his opponent's line of vision just before the opponent strikes the ball;
- the server does not correct a wet ball condition before she serves; or
- a player loses any apparel or equipment (unless the loss of equipment is caused by his opponent, in which case a dead-ball hinder is called).

Timeouts

Each player or team may take up to three 30-second timeouts in games to 15, and two 30-second timeouts in games to 11. If a timeout is called after the serve has begun, or when the player or team has none left, a technical foul (loss of point) for delay of game is called. A player is awarded up to 15 cumulative minutes of injury timeout.

The referee may award a player or team a timeout of up to two minutes, if all regular timeouts have been used, to change or adjust equipment. A two-minute break is given between the first two games; a five-minute break is given between games two and three.

Technicals

One point is deducted from an individual or team's score for a *technical foul*. A technical can be assessed for anything the referee considers unsportsmanlike, such as profanity, excessive arguing, threatening other players or the referee, striking the ball excessively between rallies, slamming the racquet against the wall or floor, delaying the game, not wearing lensed eyewear, or an intentional foot fault to negate a bad lob serve. A *technical warning* may also be issued for less severe behavior; this does not result in point deduction. A warning or a foul has no effect on who will serve when play resumes.

TERMS

An **avoidable hinder**—such as blocking an opponent or impeding an opponent's return—results in the loss of the rally.

A **crotch serve** is one that hits the crotch of the front wall and the floor at the same time. This serve results in an out.

A **dead-ball hinder**—such as when a ball that would have otherwise reached the front wall on the fly hits an opponent or when body contact hinders a return—results in a replay, with no penalty. The server receives two serves after such a hinder.

A **dead-ball serve**—such as from a court hinder or a broken ball—is replayed, but no previous fault serve is canceled.

The **drive serve lines** are 3 feet from and parallel to each side wall, within the service zone. Along with the side walls, they define a 17-foot drive serve zone.

Fault serves result from a variety of violations: foot faults, short serves, three-wall serves, ceiling serves, long serves, and so on. Two consecutive fault serves result in an out.

A **game** is normally played to 15 points.

A **handout** occurs in doubles, when the first server for a team loses the serve. The serve then goes to his partner.

A **match** is the best two-of-three games.

Out serves result from various serves, including consecutive fault serves, missed serve attempts, fakes, and touched serves. The player loses her serve on an out serve.

A **rally** is all the play, beginning with the return of serve.

The **receiving line** is a broken line parallel to, and five feet behind, the short line. The receiver may not break the plane of the receiving line until the serve has done so.

The **safety zone** is the five-foot area between the receiving line and the short line. The receiver may not be in this zone until the served ball has either bounced on the floor inside the zone or else crossed over the receiving line.

Service boxes are at the end of each service zone; they are marked by lines parallel with the side walls. The boxes are 18 inches wide.

The **service line** is parallel with, and five feet in front of, the short line. The space between the service line and the short line is known as the service zone.

The **service zone** is the five-foot area between the short line and the service line.

The **short line** is midway between, and parallel with, the front and back walls.

A **sideout** occurs when a player or side loses the serve to the opponent.

A **technical foul** may be called for a variety of reasons, including profanity, excessive arguing, and slamming the racquet on a wall or floor. A technical warning results in no points deducted; a technical foul results in one point taken away from the offender.

A **tiebreaker** game, to 11 points, is played if the opponents split the first two games of a match.

COURT

The court is 20 feet wide by 40 feet long (see figure 32.2). The court is 20 feet high, with a back

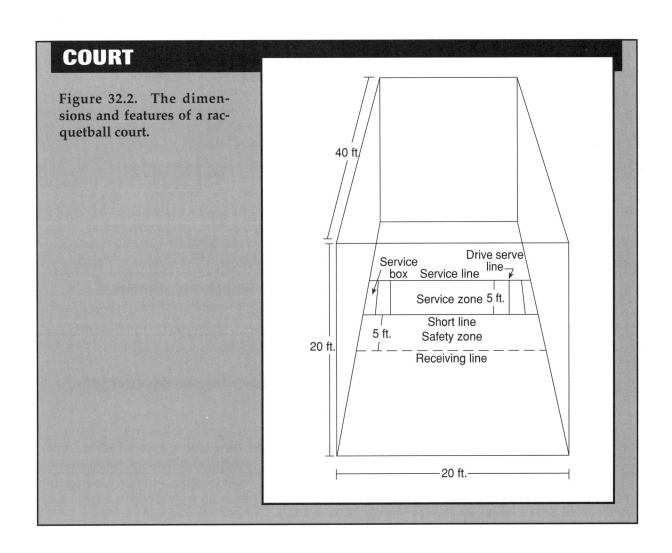

COURT

Figure 32.2. The dimensions and features of a racquetball court.

wall at least 12 feet high. The short line is midway between the front and back walls. The service line is 5 feet in front of the short line. The service zone is the space between these two lines.

Service boxes are on either end of the service zone; they are 18 inches wide. Drive serve lines are marked by lines parallel with the side walls; these lines denote the drive serve zone, which is 36 inches wide. The receiving line is 5 feet behind the short line. The safety zone is that space between the receiving line and the short line.

PLAYERS

Players may play in singles matches (two players) or doubles (four players). A nontournament game consisting of three players—called "cutthroat"—may also be played. In this version the server plays against the other two players; the serve rotates among the three players.

In an adult-age doubles division, the team must play in the age division of the younger player. In a junior-age division, the team must play in the division of the older player. A team with different skill levels must play in the division of the higher-skilled player.

Play is held in various amateur divisions: Skill-Level, Adult-Age, and Junior-Age. Placement in the *Skill-Level Division* is based on the players' skills. The *Adult-Age Division* is determined by the player's age on the first day of the tournament. Divisions are as follows:

- Junior Veterans: 19+
- Junior Veterans: 25+
- Veterans: 30+
- Seniors: 35+
- Veteran Seniors: 40+
- Masters: 45+
- Veteran Masters: 50+
- Golden Masters: 55+
- Veteran Golden Masters: 60+
- Senior Golden Masters: 65+
- Advanced Golden Masters: 70+
- Super Golden Masters: 75+

- Grand Masters: 80+

The **Junior Age Division** is determined by the player's age on January 1 of the calendar year. Divisions include

- 18 and under,
- 16 and under,
- 14 and under,
- 12 and under,
- 10 and under,
- 8 and under, and
- 8 and under Multi-Bounce.

EQUIPMENT

The *ball* is 2.25 inches in diameter and weighs about 1.4 ounces. The *racquet* cannot exceed 21 inches in length; it must have an attached wrist cord. The racquet can be made of any material deemed to be safe; it is strung with gut, nylon, or a combination of materials.

Players are required to wear *protective eyewear* designed for racquetball that meets or exceeds approved standards. *Shoes* must have soles that do not mark or damage the floor.

OFFICIALS

A referee is in charge of the match; two line judges and a scorekeeper may assist the referee. The referee makes all decisions regarding rules.

MODIFICATIONS

This section highlights major rules modifications affecting play for various groups and divisions.

Eight-and-Under Multi-Bounce

The ball is in play until it stops bouncing and begins to roll, with the following stipulations: A player may swing only once at it and must hit it before it crosses the short line on the way back to the front wall. If the ball bounces from the front wall to the back wall on the fly, it may be hit from anywhere on the court, including beyond the short line.

Use tape to mark two parallel lines on the front wall: one line being 3 feet above the floor, and the other being 1 foot above the floor. (Measure from the bottom of the lines.) A ball that hits between the 1-foot and 3-foot lines must be returned before it bounces three times. A ball that hits below the 1-foot line must be returned before it bounces twice. A ball that hits on or above the 3-foot line can be returned on any bounce. All games are played to 11 points.

One-Wall

The wall is 20 feet wide and 16 feet high. The floor is 20 feet wide and 34 feet to the back edge of the long line. The court should extend 3 feet to 6 feet beyond the long line and the side lines for the safety of the players.

The back edge of the short line is 16 feet from the wall. Service markers—lines at least 6 inches long—are parallel with, and midway between, the short and long lines. The service zone is the entire area between and including the short line, side lines, and the service line. The receiving zone is the entire area behind the short line, including the side lines and the long line.

Three-Wall

Three-wall can be played with either a short side wall or a long side wall. With a short side wall, the front wall is 20 feet wide and 20 feet high; side walls are 20 feet long and 20 feet high, tapering to 12 feet high at the end of the court. The rest of the court dimensions are the same as for a four-wall court.

With a long side wall, the court is 40 feet long. The walls may taper from 20 feet high to 12 feet high by the end of the court. All other markings and dimensions are the same as for a four-wall court. A serve that goes beyond the side walls on the fly is an out. A serve that goes long, but is within the side walls, is a fault.

Wheelchair

The standard rules apply, with the following exceptions:

- Body contact includes wheelchair contact. Such contact may be either a dead-ball or an avoidable hinder.
- The ball is not dead until the third bounce.
- If a player intentionally leaves his chair, he automatically loses the rally.
- The serve may take place from anywhere within the service zone.
- Maintenance delays for chair repair may not take more than five minutes. A player may have two maintenance delays per match.
- In multi-bounce play, the ball may bounce any number of times, but the player may swing at it only once. The ball must be struck before it crosses the short line on its way back to the front wall. The receiver cannot cross the short line once the ball hits the back wall.

There are also modifications of rules for visually- and hearing-impaired players.

Men's and Women's Professional Tour

The following modifications apply to competitions in both the men's tour (International Racquetball Tour/Men's) and the women's tour (Women's International Racquetball Tour). Modifications generally are the same, except for screen serves. Matches are the best three-of-five games, which are played to 11 points each. Each game must be won by at least two points. Each player receives a single one-minute timeout per game. The rest period between games is two minutes, except between the fourth and fifth games, when five minutes are allowed.

Players are allowed only one serve to put the ball into play. No court hinders are called. Screen serves are replayed without penalty, except that on the women's tour, two consecutive screen serves result in an out. Line judges are not used.

ORGANIZATIONS

American Amateur Racquetball Association
1685 W. Uintah
Colorado Springs, CO 80904-2921
719-635-5396

International Racquetball Federation
1685 W. Uintah
Colorado Springs, CO 80904-2921
719-635-5396

International Racquetball Tour & Women's International Racquetball Tour
13735 Regency Court
Lake Oswego, OR 97035
503-639-3410

33

Roller Hockey

© Mary Langenfeld

In roller hockey, two teams of five players each attempt to hit a ball or puck into their opponent's goal. The team with the ball or puck attempts to weave its way through the opponent's defense to get a shot on goal. The defenders try to steal the ball, intercept a pass, or block a shot and gain control of the ball or puck. The object is to score the most goals.

Roller hockey is a fast-paced game, employing many of the moves and tactics of ice hockey. Its equipment is also similar to that used in ice hockey. There are, however, two major differences: Roller hockey is a noncontact sport, and it offers hardball, puck hockey, and softball variations. The softball variation is commonly employed in Junior Olympic leagues and leagues for players new to the game.

Hardball hockey was a demonstration sport at the 1992 Summer Olympics. It is played in more than 50 countries. Players use a hard, black cork or rubber ball, and wooden, cane-style sticks. Softball hockey uses a low-impact, lightweight plastic ball and cane-style plastic sticks, adaptable for players of all sizes. Rules for this chapter were supplied by the United States Amateur Confederation of Roller Skating, which is the national governing body for roller skating.

PROCEDURES

A coin toss determines which team has first choice of the goal it wishes to defend. Teams change ends each succeeding period. A game begins with a *face-off*. The referee drops the ball or puck (hereafter referred to as "ball") on the center circle; players must be on their own half of the floor. Play is continuous except for timeouts, injuries, face-offs, penalties, and penalty shots. The offensive team attempts to maneuver the ball into position for a shot on goal; the defensive team tries to gain possession of the ball or stop the shot.

A *goal is scored* when the ball completely crosses the goal line between the two vertical posts of the goal mouth. After each goal, play is resumed with a face-off at center circle.

Players may not play the ball if they are

- skating with a damaged skate or broken stick,

Rule Recommendations

Although each league can develop its own regulations regarding certain procedures, USA Roller Hockey recommends these rules:

- Play two 15-minute halves with a 3-minute halftime.
- Switch sides at halftime.
- Use a commercially available ball suitable for roller hockey.
- Have no more than 10 players and 2 goalkeepers per team.
- A team with less than 4 players at the start must forfeit.
- If a team drops below 3 players during a game, it must forfeit.
- Each team should have two one-minute timeouts per game. A coach or player on the team possessing the ball may call timeout, or one may be called during a stop in the action.
- No timeouts are allowed in overtime.
- In tournament play, a team receives two points for a win, one point for a tie, and no points for a loss.

- holding onto the barrier,
- not using mandatory safety equipment, or
- holding onto the goal cage (except for the goalkeeper).

Various offenses result in a minor, major, or misconduct *penalty* (see "Penalties," page 213). After receiving a warning for their first minor penalty, players committing a penalty must sit out for a specified number of minutes, depending on the severity of the offense.

Except for tournament play, games ending in ties are not continued. In tournament play, teams play a *five-minute overtime*; the first to score wins. If the score is still tied after five minutes, five players from each team each get a shot on goal. If the score remains knotted after this, each team alternates taking a shot until one team scores and the other team fails to score.

TERMS

Boarding is a violation that occurs when a player cross-checks, elbows, body-checks, or trips an opponent, causing him to crash into the boards.

Butt-ending is a violation called when a player uses the shaft of the stick above the upper hand to jab, or attempt to jab, an opposing player. It can be a violation even if the player makes no physical contact.

Charging is a violation called when a player runs or jumps into an opponent.

Chopping is a violation that occurs when a player taking a shot chops the ball by hitting it with the sharp edge of the stick. Players may hit the ball only with the flat part of the blade.

Cross-checking is a violation by a player who checks another by extending his arms with both hands on the stick and makes contact with the opponent above the waist.

Elbowing is a violation called when a player uses an elbow to foul an opponent.

High-sticking is a violation that occurs when a player carries her stick above her shoulder. A player doesn't have to make contact for a referee to call a violation.

Holding is a violation called when a player holds an opponent with his legs, hands, feet, stick, or in any other way.

Hooking is a violation that occurs when a player uses his stick to hook and impede, or attempt to impede, an opponent's progress.

Intentional delay is a penalty called when a player deliberately delays the game (e.g., deliberately holding the ball against the boards, while not being checked). Play is resumed with a face-off at the nearest face-off circle adjacent to the offender's goal.

Interference is a violation resulting in a penalty. Examples of interference include a player who impedes the progress of an opponent who doesn't possess the puck, or a player who deliberately knocks a stick out of an opponent's hand, or one who prevents a player from regaining her dropped stick.

Kicking the ball is legal in all zones, but a goal cannot be scored by an attacking player kicking the ball in (unless it deflects in off a defender other than the goalkeeper).

Lofting the ball is a penalty called when a player intentionally lofts the ball above the height of the goal cage.

Slashing is a violation that occurs when a player slashes with her stick to impede the progress of an opponent. The player doesn't need to make physical contact for this to be a violation.

Spearing, or attempting to spear an opponent, is a violation called when a player stabs at an opponent with the point of the stick blade. The player doesn't need to make contact for the referee to call a foul.

Throwing the stick to stop a goal from being scored is not legal. This results in a penalty shot for the offended team.

Tripping is a violation that occurs when a player uses a stick, knee, foot, arm, hand, or elbow to trip an opponent.

FACE-OFFS

A referee uses a face-off to begin a game and a new period; to restart play after a timeout, after

a player has scored a goal, and after action has displaced a goal cage; and to reset action if he cannot see the play for an extended period. The referee will also call for a face-off if the ball is frozen between two opposing players, if it becomes stuck in the netting outside the goal, and if it goes out of play and the referee is not certain who touched it last. If the referee can identify which team touched it last, the opposing team gets to play the ball from the point it went out of bounds.

Face-offs that are used to begin a game, a period, and to resume play after a goal occur at the center circle. All other face-offs take place at either the center circle or one of the other four face-off spots, depending on where the ball is when the referee calls for the face-off.

Two opposing players, with their backs to their own goal, face each other at the face-off spot, about one stick length apart. The full blade of their sticks must be on the floor, and all other players must be at least 10 feet away and on their own sides of the floor. The referee drops the ball at the face-off circle to resume play.

PENALTIES

A referee can call three types of penalties, depending on the severity of the act: minor, major, and misconduct penalties. A referee will warn a player for the first minor infraction; for each subsequent minor violation, the player will spend two minutes in the penalty box. Players are penalized five minutes for major infractions, and either 10 minutes or expulsion from the game for misconduct penalties.

Goalkeepers do not have to serve minor penalties; the coach appoints a teammate who was on the floor at the time to serve the penalty for the goalkeeper. Goalkeepers are required to serve their own major and misconduct penalties.

A coach may substitute for a player serving a minor or a misconduct penalty, but not for a player assessed a major penalty. A referee will wait until the play has finished before calling a minor penalty on a player whose team possesses the ball. However, a referee will immediately stop play for a major or misconduct penalty.

If the offended team scores on a play where the referee could call a minor penalty, the referee won't call the penalty. He will call major and misconduct penalties, regardless of the play.

The referee uses one of three cards to note the severity of the penalty: a *yellow card* for minor penalties, a *blue card* for major penalties, and a *red card* for misconduct penalties.

Minor penalties may be called for

- chopping,
- displacing the goal cage,
- falling on the ball,
- handling the ball,
- high sticking,
- intentionally delaying the game,
- interference, or
- lofting.

A minor or major penalty, depending on the severity of the act, is called for unnecessary physical contact, including

- boarding,
- butt-ending,
- charging,
- cross-checking,
- elbowing,
- holding,
- hooking,
- kicking,
- kneeing,
- slashing,
- spearing, or
- tripping.

A major penalty is called for fighting and for throwing a stick (unless the referee awards a penalty shot). A minor, major, or misconduct penalty is assessed for abuse of officials and other misconduct, including

- using obscene, profane, or abusive language or gestures;
- showing disrespect for any official;
- banging the boards with a stick or other equipment;

- intentionally shooting the ball out of reach of an official who is reaching for it;
- delaying in going to the penalty box;
- touching or holding an official;
- continuing, or attempting to continue, a fight; or
- throwing anything onto the floor.

Penalty Shot

A referee will award a penalty shot to restore a scoring opportunity that was illegally taken away. The referee designates the player to take the shot; only this player and the goalkeeper are involved in the play. The player begins with the ball in the center circle and attempts to score. She must keep the ball in motion toward the opponent's goal. Once she shoots and either scores or misses, the play is over; she may not play a rebound.

If the player scores a goal, play resumes with a face-off in center circle; if the player doesn't score, play resumes with a face-off at one of the face-off spots in the zone where she attempted the shot.

PLAYING AREA

The size of the *playing surface* is 90 feet wide by 180 feet long, or dimensions that are similar (see figure 33.1). Avoid playing on surfaces longer than 200 feet, and try to maintain the 1:2 ratio of width to length. A *retaining barrier* surrounds the surface to help keep the ball in play.

Goal cages are 15 feet from the end barriers. *Goal lines* are drawn across the mouths of the goals and extend across the width of the floor. The cages are not secured to the floor. They can be any size, but a recommended size is 67 inches wide by 41 inches tall by 36 inches deep. Their frame is covered with netting strong enough to withstand any shot. In front of the cages are *goal creases*, semicircles with a radius of 3.5 feet.

Five *face-off circles* are on the floor, one in the center and four toward the corners, about 20 feet out from each goal line and about one-quarter the distance from the side barriers. The face-off circles have a 10-foot radius, and the circle in the middle, where the referee drops the ball for a face-off, is 1 foot in diameter.

A *center line,* running the width of the floor, separates the floor in equal halves. A *penalty box* is on one side of the court, and two *players' benches* are on either side of the box.

PLAYERS

Local leagues develop divisions based on age, skill level, and size. USA Roller Hockey recommends co-ed play for ages up to 13. It also recommends that team members wear similar shirts, with numbers on the backs of the shirts or on the sides of helmets. A coach may make *substitutions* at any time during play. A team may have no more than five players on the floor at one time.

EQUIPMENT

The *ball* or *puck* must be suitable for roller hockey and commercially available. *Sticks* are made of wood, plastic, aluminum, or other similar material. They cannot have any projections, but players may wrap tape around the blade to reinforce it. A stick may be no longer than 62 inches from heel to end of shaft, and not more than 12.5 inches from the heel to the end of the blade.

The goalkeeper's blade can be no wider than 5 inches at any point, except at the heel where it cannot exceed 5.5 inches. It cannot exceed 15.5 inches in length from the heel to the end of the blade. The widened portion extending up the shaft of the blade cannot exceed 24 inches from the heel and cannot be wider than 5 inches.

When a player's stick breaks, he must retrieve a new one from his bench. When a goalkeeper's stick breaks, he may receive a new one from a teammate, but it may not be thrown on the floor to the goalkeeper; it must be handed to him.

Players wear in-line or quad (conventional) *skates* with no protruding parts. *Protective equipment* that players may use includes helmets with full-protection face masks and chin straps, gloves, shin guards, knee pads, and mouthpieces. Goalkeepers *must* wear approved leg guards, face masks, gloves, chest protectors, pads, and, at the league's discretion, blocker and catching gloves.

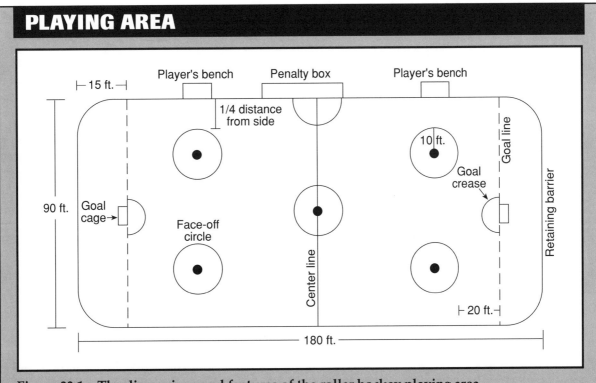

PLAYING AREA

Figure 33.1. The dimensions and features of the roller hockey playing area.
Adapted from U.S.A. Roller Skating.

OFFICIALS

A *referee* is in complete charge of the game. Optional officials include an *assistant referee*, a *goal judge*, a *scorer*, and a *timekeeper*. Referee signals for roller hockey and ice hockey are very similar. For drawings of ice hockey/roller hockey referee signals, please see pages 167-168.

ORGANIZATIONS

United States Amateur Confederation of Roller Skating
4730 South St., P.O. Box 6579
Lincoln, NE 68506
402-483-7551

USA Roller Hockey
4730 South St., P.O. Box 6579
Lincoln, NE 68506
402-483-7551

34

Rowing

© Mary Langenfeld

Rowing races are held over 2,000 meters (1,000 meters for masters competitors) on a course that has no bends or turns. Some boats have a *coxswain*, who steers the boat but does not row, and a crew who rows; other boats have only rowers (a boat may have one, two, four, or eight rowers, not including a coxswain). Rowers sit with their backs to the forward movement of the boat.

Competitions, known as *regattas*, include *sculling events*, in which each rower uses two oars, and *sweep boats*, in which each rower uses one oar. A *head race* consists of crews who start a few seconds apart and race the clock. Events may be categorized by boat (see table 34.1 on page 220), gender, age, weight, or skill level. The rules in this chapter were supplied by US Rowing, the governing body for the sport.

PROCEDURES

This section includes procedures on the start, the race in progress, and the finish. Before the start a crew may practice in its assigned lane, unless prohibited because another race is underway.

Start

Crews are required to be at their starting station two minutes before the start. The aligning judge makes sure that each boat is aligned with the starting line's plane. When alignment is secured, the judge holds aloft a white flag until the start of the race. If alignment is lost before the start, the judge raises a red flag.

Once aligned, crews are polled individually by the starter to make sure they are ready. After the crews are polled, ready, and aligned, the starter raises a red flag overhead and gives the command to begin—a verbal "Attention!" and then "Go!" accompanied by a downsweep of the flag.

A starter also may use a *quick start*, dispensing with the polling procedures. A *countdown start*, in which the starter counts down from five and then gives the normal starting commands, also may be used. During the countdown start, crews must ensure they are ready; the starter will not recognize a crew signaling it is not ready.

Once a crew rows out of the starting area, which is 100 meters long, they may not protest the start as unfair. If a crew's bow crosses the starting line before the signal to begin is given, it is assessed a false start. More than one crew may be assessed false starts on one start. The race is recalled, the offending crews are warned, and the race is restarted. If a crew commits two false starts in one race, it is excluded from the race.

Race in Progress

Crews that row out of their assigned lanes do so at their own risk. If they are out of their own lane and interfere with a crew in its proper lane, the refereee will tell the offending crew to alter its course. If the crew does not alter its course the referee may ask them to stop. If a crew interferes with another crew while out of its lane (clashing oars, washing the opposing crew, or forcing the other crew to alter its course to avoid collision),

the interfering crew may be excluded. If the interference was slight and did not alter the race results, the referee may issue a lesser penalty (see "Paying the Price," below).

A crew must maintain its racing cadence as indicated by strokes per minute. It may be penalized for not maintaining the cadence if so instructed by the referee. A crew may not receive outside assistance or coaching during a race. Such assistance may result in exclusion.

If the referee believes a crew has not had a fair chance to win, place, or advance, due to either interference or unfair course conditions, the referee may elect to advance the crew or to rerow the race with some or all of the participants. The referee may elect to stop a race in progress in such a case.

Finish

A crew finishes a race when its bow or any part of its hull touches the plane of the finish line. If two crews tie in a finals race, they rest and then rerow to determine places. In some cases a tie is awarded without a rerow. If a tie occurs in a race that advances crews, the referee will allow all the crews that tied to advance, if possible; if not, they will rerow after a rest.

Paying the Price

Officials may impose the following penalties on a crew:

- *Reprimand.* This is an informal caution and has no immediate effect upon the crew.

- *Warning.* A crew that is warned twice in the same race is excluded. A false start counts as a warning.

- *Exclusion.* A crew is removed from the event but may compete in other events.

- *Disqualification.* A crew is removed from the event and from all remaining events in the same regatta. This occurs when a crew flagrantly or intentionally breaks the rules.

TERMS

A **coxswain** is a competitor who does not row or physically participate in propelling the boat forward, except to steer.

A **crew** consists of all competitors in the boat, including the coxswain.

A **head race** pits crews who race on a course at different times against one another. Their finish times determine their placement.

A **regatta** is a combination of different events that are considered a single unit.

A **scull** refers to the shell in which rowers use two oars. It also refers to the events in which each rower uses two oars.

The **starting area** is the first 100 meters of the course.

Sweep refers to an event in which each rower uses a single oar.

A crew **washes** another crew when the water turbulence from the oars and the wake of the leading shell affect the progress of the trailing crew.

COURSE

A race course is 2,000 meters long (except for masters courses, which are 1,000 meters long) and is wide enough to hold three to eight lanes. If a buoy system is used, each lane is 12.5 meters to 15 meters wide; without a buoy system, each lane is 15 meters to 20 meters wide; a lane width of 15 meters is recommended. To be part of a registered regatta, the host organization must use licensed USRowing officials, the *USRowing Rules of Rowing*, and follow USRowing safety guidelines.

A *Class A* course has

- no bends or turns on the course or runoff area;
- a current of less than 1 meter per minute;
- at least six lanes, though eight are preferred;
- a water depth of at least 3 meters throughout the course;
- at least 5 meters between the course perimeter and the shore or any obstacle;
- no fixed obstructions on the course;

- use of a buoy system for lanes, with buoys marking the lanes every 10 meters to 12.5 meters (the first 100 meters and the last 250 meters use different-colored buoys);
- a starting station with a platform or stakeboat solidly anchored;
- two steering markers behind the center of each lane; and
- distance markers every 250 meters.

A *Class B* course is the same as a Class A course, with the following exceptions:

- Water current may not exceed 6 meters per minute.
- There must be a minimum of four lanes.
- Water depth must be sufficient to ensure safe racing.
- Obstacles nearer than 5 meters from the perimeter must be marked.
- Fixed obstructions must not interfere with, or create a hazard for, a crew.
- A buoy system is not required, but overhead lane markers every 250 meters define the lane boundaries.
- A single marker may be used for steering markers.
- Distance markers are placed every 500 meters; these may consist of painted stripes on the shore.

A *Class C* course does not meet the standards for a Class A or B course, but does meet the requirements for length, width, and uniform conditions for all crews.

CREWS

Each member of a crew wears identical clothing, although headgear is optional for each competitor. Junior competition is for those 18 and younger; a "Junior B" competition may be held for those 16 and younger. Masters competition is for those 27 and older, broken into the following categories:

- 27 to 35
- 36 to 42
- 43 to 49

- 50 to 54
- 55 to 59
- 60 to 64
- 65 to 69
- 70 to 74
- 75 to 79
- 80 and over

Age for masters competition is determined by averaging the ages of the crew, minus the coxswain. Each rower must be a master but need not fall into the specific age category.

Competitions may also be categorized by skill (intermediate, senior, and elite). In addition, a *lightweight crew* may compete against similar crews, with each men's crew averaging no more than 155 pounds per rower, and with no rower weighing more than 160 pounds. The coxswain is not counted. For women, a lightweight crew must average no more than 130 pounds; the coxswain does not count.

EQUIPMENT

All load-bearing parts of a boat must be firmly fixed to the boat, although the rowers' seats may move along the boat's axis. "Sliding riggers," where the oar's support is not fixed in one place, are forbidden in normal competition. For boat categories, see table 34.1.

Coxswains

In the United States, male coxswains may compete in female events and vice versa. A coxswain for a men's crew must weigh at least 120 pounds; for a women's crew, a coxswain must weigh at least 110 pounds. But coxswains who do not meet the weight requirement may carry dead weight, placed as close to their torso as possible, to meet the requirement.

Each boat must have a *supple* or *plastic ball*, four centimeters in diameter, on its bow, to protect against injury and provide visibility. A *sweep oar* must be at least five millimeters thick, measured three millimeters from the blade's tip; a *scull oar* must be at least three millimeters thick, measured two millimeters from the tip. Each boat must have footgear that allows for quick release, without needing to use the hands, in case the boat capsizes.

To race, each boat has a *numbered card* attached on its bow. The number indicates its race lane. If equipment breaks before a crew passes the 100-meter starting area, the crew may signal the referee, who will stop the race. The referee will restart the race after the crew has had time to repair equipment.

Table 34.1: Boat Categories					
Number of rowers	Boat name/oar	Coxswain	Abbreviation	Minimum weight (lb)	Minimum weight (kg)
1	Single/scull	No	1×	30.86	14
2	Double/scull	No	2×	59.53	27
2	Pair-without/sweep	No	2-	59.53	27
2	Pair-with/sweep	Yes	2+	70.55	32
4	Four-without/sweep	No	4–	110.23	50
4	Four-with/sweep	Yes	4+	112.44	51
4	Quad/scull	No	4×	114.64	52
4	Quad-with/scull	Yes	4×+	116.85	53
8	Eight/sweep	Yes	8+	205.03	93
8	Octuple/scull	Yes	8×	213.85	97

Adapted from U.S. Rowing Association 1996.

OFFICIALS

Officials overseeing rowing competitions include a *chief referee*, a *referee*, a *starter*, a *judge at start*, a *chief judge*, and other judges. A *jury* comprised of the chief referee and four other officials will hear and decide any protests.

Each race is followed by at least one referee (the primary judge), who may be aided by additional referees. These additional referees may withdraw if the primary judge is satisfied with how the race is proceeding. However, the primary judge must remain with the race to keep the total elapsed time.

ORGANIZATIONS

US Rowing
201 S. Capitol Ave., Ste. 400
Indianapolis, IN 46225
317-237-5656 or 800-314-4ROW (4769)

35

Rugby Union

© Claus Andersen

In 1823, a young man named William Webb Ellis of Rugby School in England was playing Foot-the-Ball when he broke the rules by picking up the ball and running with it. About half the players on both sides stopped playing because this clearly was in violation of the rules. But the other half took no heed, and as Ellis recklessly made his way down the field toward his opponents' goal, many defenders became among the first to try to tackle a ball carrier, and many teammates became among the first to move alongside the ball carrier, hoping to catch a pass.

Ellis crashed his way into the soccer net, scoring the game's first try. This rebellious act gave birth to a new sport: rugby. The birth was neither swift nor smooth, however. Cambridge University immediately adopted the new sport, making local rules, but Rugby School itself did not officially consent to play the game until 1841—18 years after Ellis picked up the ball and ran with it. Eton and Harrow went so far as to issue its soccer players white gloves and require them to hold their weekly allowance, a silver piece, between a finger and thumb, to deter them from following Ellis's example by using their hands.

By 1871, however, Laws for Rugby Union were in place, and the game was quickly spreading. Harvard played McGill in Canada in 1874. A derivation of the game, Rugby Leage Football, is also played, but the main body of this chapter contains the Laws of Rugby Union, as put forth by the International Rugby Football Board and as begun by William Webb Ellis in 1823. Rugby School erected a plaque for Ellis, which reads: "THIS STONE COMMEMORATES THE EXPLOIT OF WILLIAM WEBB ELLIS, WHO WITH A FINE DISREGARD FOR THE RULES OF FOOTBALL, AS PLAYED IN HIS TIME, FIRST TOOK THE BALL IN HIS ARMS AND RAN WITH IT, THUS ORIGINATING THE DISTINCTIVE FEATURES OF THE RUGBY GAME. A.D. 1823."

PROCEDURES

The object in rugby is to score the most points. Two teams of 15 players each attempt to score by carrying, passing, kicking, and grounding the ball in *in-goal*. A match lasts 80 minutes—two 40-minute halves with a 5-minute halftime. A team is allowed 1 minute to treat an injured player; if the injury takes longer to treat, he is removed from the match. Playing time lost due to this or any other delay (such as in taking a kick at goal) may be made up at the end of the half in which the delay occurred.

A coin toss decides which team will kick off and which team will begin at which end of the field.

The team that kicks off makes a placekick from the center of the halfway line, while the receiving team stands on or behind its 10-meter line. If the ball doesn't reach the 10-meter line, the receiving team may choose to either field another kickoff or to form a scrummage at the center.

After the kickoff, any player who is *on-side* (whose progress is not ahead of the ball) may

- catch or pick up the ball and run with it,
- pass, throw, or knock the ball to another player,
- kick or otherwise propel the ball,
- tackle, push, or shoulder an opponent holding the ball,
- fall on the ball,
- take part in a scrummage, ruck, maul, or line-out, or
- ground the ball in in-goal.

Tackling

A player is tackled when he is brought to the ground or the ball comes in contact with the ground while the player is holding it. If one or both of the player's knees are on the ground or if he is on top of another player who is on the ground, the ball carrier is considered tackled. Once tackled, a player must immediately release or pass the ball and move away.

Once a player is tackled, the next player to play the ball must be on his feet. A player who goes to the ground to get the ball must immediately get up or pass or release the ball. Failure to do so may result in a penalty. It is illegal to prevent a tackled player from passing or releasing the ball or to impede him from moving away from the ball after he has passed or released it. It is also illegal to pull the ball from a tackled player's possession or to intentionally fall on a tackled player who possesses the ball, or to intentionally fall on other players lying on the ground near the ball.

TERMS

The **dead-ball line** is the line at the end of the in-goal area.

A **drop out** is a drop kick taken on or behind the 22-meter line; the opponents may not cross the line until the kick is made.

A **fair catch** may be made by a player within his 22-meter area or in his in-goal. He must catch the kick and shout "Mark!" He is awarded a free kick for a fair catch.

A **free kick** is awarded to a team after a fair catch or minor infringement. The team may not score a dropped goal from a free kick.

In-goal is the area bounded by a goal line, the touch-in-goal lines, and a dead-ball line. It includes the goal line and goal posts but excludes the touch-in-goal line and dead-ball line.

A **knock-on** (or "throw-forward") occurs when the ball travels toward the opponents' dead-ball line after a player loses possession of it or when a player propels or strikes it with his hand or arm, or the ball strikes a player's hand or arm and touches the ground or another player before it is recovered.

A **line-out** is a set play with a member of one team throwing the ball inbounds between two lines of players with each line defending its own goal. The team throwing in the ball determines the maximum number of players who line up.

A **maul** is formed by players from both teams, on their feet and converging on the ball carrier. It ends when the ball is on the ground or when a ball carrier emerges from the maul, or when the referee calls for a scrummage.

A player is **off-side** in general play when his team is in possession of the ball and he is in front of the ball. He may not take part in the play, but he is not penalized unless he plays the ball or obstructs an opponent, or unless he is within 10 meters of an opponent waiting to play the ball.

A player is **on-side** in general play when he is behind the ball. He may take part in the play when he is on-side.

A **penalty kick** may be taken by any player of the offended team. The kick must be taken at or behind the prescribed mark. When awarded a penalty kick, a team may opt to kick, to drop kick for goal, or to put in the ball in a scrum. The opponents may not interfere with a penalty kick.

A **ruck** occurs when the ball is on the ground and players from each team are on their feet, in physical contact, closing around the ball between them. If the ball becomes unplayable, a scrummage is ordered.

A **scrummage**, or scrum, is a set play where one team puts the ball into play between players from both teams. At least eight players from each team bind together, one team against the other, to form the scrum. Players use their feet to gain control of the ball put in between them.

The ball is in **touch** when it touches on or beyond a touch line (out-of-bounds line) or is carried by a player on or beyond a touch line.

A **touch-down** is scored when a player grounds the ball (touches the ball to the ground) in his in-goal.

A **try,** worth five points, is scored when a player grounds the ball in his opponents' in-goal.

SCORING

Points are awarded as follows:

- Five points for a try
- Two points for a kick scored after a try
- Three points for a goal scored from a penalty kick
- Three points for a dropped goal (drop kick)

A try is scored when a player grounds the ball in his opponents' in-goal. A try may be scored in a scrum or ruck if a team pushes its opponents over its goal line and the ball is grounded in-goal by an attacking player. A try is awarded when the ball is grounded while held on the goal line or when a held ball is in contact with the ground and a goal post. A try may also be awarded if a team probably would have scored a try except for a foul by its opponents.

After a try, a team can take a placekick or drop kick at goal, worth two points. The kick is made anywhere on a line opposite where the try was scored. (Thus, it's an advantage to score near the center of the goal line, so the kick's angle is not too sharp.) The kicker's team must be behind the ball when it's kicked. The opponents must be behind the goal line until the kicker approaches the ball; at that point they may attempt to block the kick.

A penalty kick, taken by any player of the offended team, is taken with the kicker's teammates behind the ball, except for the placer. The kicking team may kick for goal, kick for touch, or kick ahead for possession or territorial advantage. If the kick at goal goes over the crossbar and between the goal posts, it is worth three points. The opponents may not interfere with the kick and must retreat 10 meters from the mark where the kick is being taken.

A drop out is a drop kick taken on or behind the 22-meter line. If the ball is kicked into touch, the opponents may accept the kick, have the ball dropped out again, or have a scrummage formed at the 22-meter line.

SCRUMMAGE

A scrummage, or scrum, is a set play where one team puts the ball into play between two groups of players. A scrum is formed at the place of infringement. At least eight players from each team are involved in a scrum—at least three in the front row and two in the second row. The players must be stationary, and the middle line must be parallel to the goal lines until the ball is put into play.

The middle player in each front row is the hooker; the players on either side of him are the props. Each front row crouches with heads and shoulders no lower than hips and not farther than an arm's length from their opponents' shoulders. The players bind to each other, hooking arms around the bodies of their teammates next to them.

The team not responsible for the infraction puts the ball into play; or, if no infraction occurred, the ball is put into play by the team that was advancing the ball. The player putting the ball into play stands one meter from the scrum, between the two front rows. He holds the ball with both hands between his knees and ankles, and with a single forward movement puts the ball into play between the two front rows. Once the ball enters the "tunnel" between the rows, the front row players attempt to gain possession of it with their feet. If the ball comes out of either end of the tunnel, it is put in again.

LINE-OUT

A line-out is a set play that occurs when a ball has gone *in touch* (out of bounds). The ball is thrown in by a member of the team whose opponents last touched the ball before it went in touch. A member of one team throws the ball inbounds between two lines of players—one line consisting of his teammates and the other of his opponents. The team throwing the ball in determines the maximum number of players on the line. The two lines stand a meter apart.

On the throw-in, the ball must first touch the ground or a player at least five meters from the touch-line. Players may not charge an opponent, except to tackle him or play the ball, and they may not hold, push, or obstruct an opponent not carrying the ball.

The line-out ends when a ruck or maul forms and all the players' feet move beyond the original line on which the ball was thrown in; when a ball carrier leaves the line-out; when the ball is passed, knocked back, or kicked from the line-out; or when the ball becomes unplayable.

RUCK

A ruck occurs when the ball is on the ground and one or more players from each team close in on the ball. Players must be on their feet, and their heads and shoulders must be no lower than their hips. Each player joining a ruck must bind with at least one arm around the body of a teammate; failure to do so results in a free kick for the opponents.

A player in a ruck may not

- return the ball into the ruck,
- pick up the ball with hands or legs,
- handle the ball except to score a try or touchdown,
- intentionally collapse the ruck or jump on other players,
- intentionally fall or kneel in the ruck, or
- interfere with the ball while lying on the ground.

If the ball becomes unplayable in a ruck, a scrum is ordered.

MAUL

A maul is formed by one or more players from each team who surround a ball carrier. The players must be on their feet; they must be in physical contact with each other; and their heads and shoulders must be no lower than their hips. A maul ends when the ball is on the ground, when a ball carrier emerges from the maul, or when a scrum is ordered.

A player in a maul may not jump on top of other players in the maul, collapse the maul, or try to drag a player out of the maul. To be in the maul, a player must be bound to it and not merely alongside it.

FOULS

Fouls may be called for obstruction, unfair play, misconduct, dangerous play, unsportsmanlike behavior, retaliation, and repeated infringements. If the team fouled has an advantage, the referee does not have to whistle for the foul.

Obstruction occurs when a player running for the ball pushes or shoves an opponent also going for the ball; shoulder-to-shoulder contact is not considered obstruction (see figure 35.1). Obstruction is also the call when an off-side player willfully blocks or prevents an opponent from reaching a teammate carrying the ball. A penalty kick is awarded for obstruction.

© Claus Andersen

Figure 35.1.   Players run for the ball during a rugby game. Players cannot push or shove an opponent who is going for the ball.

Unfair play and *repeated infringments* occur when a player deliberately wastes time or knocks or throws the ball into touch, touch-in-goal, or over the dead-ball line. These infractions result in free kicks. The opponents of a player who deliberately plays unfairly or repeatedly breaks the Law of the Game will be awarded a penalty kick.

Misconduct and *dangerous play* include

- striking, kicking, tripping, or trampling an opponent;

- tackling early, late, or dangerously;

- charging or obstructing an opponent who has just kicked the ball;

- holding, pushing, or obstructing an opponent who is not holding a ball, except in a scrum, ruck, or maul; and

- intentionally collapsing a scrum, ruck, or maul.

A player guilty of misconduct or dangerous play is cautioned or ordered off the field. A cautioned player who repeats the offense must be ordered off and may not play anymore in the match.

OFF-SIDE

When a player of the team in possession of the ball is closer to the opponent's goal than the ball is, that player is off-side. This means he may not take part in the play and faces possible penalty. A player can also be off-side in scrums, rucks, mauls, and line-outs.

A player may be penalized while in an off-side position if he plays the ball or obstructs an opponent. He may also be penalized if he comes within 10 meters of an opponent waiting to play the ball and does not retire promptly. He may not move toward an opponent waiting to play the ball or to the place where the ball is pitched until he is put on-side.

A player is off-side in the following situations:

Scrum. A player is off-side during a scrum if he joins the scrum from the opponents' side, if he doesn't retire behind the off-side line or to his goal line, whichever is nearer, or if he doesn't place a foot in front of the off-side line.

Ruck or maul not at line-out. A player is off-side if he joins the ruck or maul from his opponents' side; joins it in front of his hindmost teammate;

doesn't join the ruck or maul, or unbinds from it but fails to retire behind the off-side line without delay; or advances beyond the off-side line but doesn't join the ruck or maul.

Ruck or maul at line-out. When a ruck or maul takes place at a line-out, a player is off-side if he joins the ruck or maul from his opponents' side, joins it in front of his hindmost teammate, or is in the line-out but is not in the ruck or maul and does not retire behind the off-side line.

Line-out. A player participating in a line-out is off-side if he advances beyond the line-of-touch before the ball has touched a player or the ground, unless he is advancing while jumping for the ball. After the ball has touched a player or the ground, a player is off-side if he is not carrying the ball and advances beyond the ball, unless he is attempting to tackle the ball carrier. A player who is not participating in the line-out is off-side if he goes beyond the off-side line before the line-out ends.

ON-SIDE

Except for a player who is within 10 meters of an opponent waiting to catch a kick, a player who is off-side may be made on-side if he retires behind his teammate who last kicked, touched, or carried the ball; when his teammate carrying the ball runs in front of him; or when a teammate runs in front of him after coming from the place, or behind the place, where the ball was kicked.

A player who is off-side may also be made on-side when an opponent carrying the ball has run 5 meters; when an opponent kicks or passes the ball; or when an opponent intentionally touches the ball and does not catch or gather it.

KNOCK-ON AND THROW-FORWARD

A knock-on occurs when the ball is propelled toward the opponent's dead-ball line after a player loses possession of it or strikes it with his hand or arm. A throw-forward occurs when the ball carrier passes the ball forward toward the opponent's dead-ball line. Neither a knock-on nor a throw-forward can occur intentionally; the penalty is a penalty kick at the place of infringe-

ment. If the play is unintentional, a scrummage is formed.

IN-GOAL

In-goal is the area bounded by a goal line, touch-in-goal lines, and the dead-ball line. It includes the goal line and posts but excludes the touch-in-goal lines and dead-ball line. Touch-in-goal occurs when the ball touches a corner post or a touch-in-goal line, or the ground or a person on or beyond the line. The flag is not part of the corner post.

When the ball becomes dead in in-goal, a scrum is formed five meters from the goal line, with the attacking team putting the ball into play. If a player carries the ball into in-goal but is held and cannot ground it, the ball is dead. The ball is also dead if a defender kicks, knocks, or carries the ball into his own in-goal area and the ball becomes dead.

IN TOUCH

The ball is in touch (out of bounds) when it touches on or beyond a touch line or when it is carried by a player who touches on or beyond a touch line. A player may be in touch and kick or propel it with his hand if the ball does not cross the plane of touch. A player may also catch and deflect a ball into the playing area if it has crossed in touch, but the player's feet have not.

BALL OR PLAYER TOUCHING REFEREE

If the ball or a ball carrier touches a referee, play continues unless the referee believes a team has gained an advantage. In this case he orders a scrummage and the team that last played the ball puts it in. If a player carrying the ball touches the referee while in his opponents' in-goal, before he can ground the ball, he is awarded a try.

FIELD

The field of play is rectangular; it is not wider than 70 meters and not longer than 100 meters

FIELD

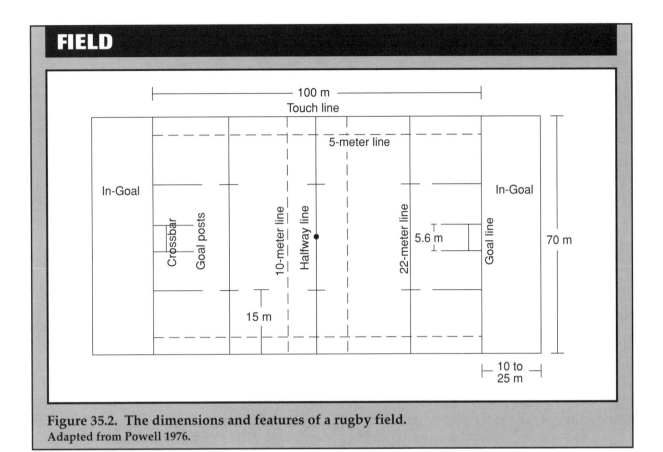

Figure 35.2. The dimensions and features of a rugby field.
Adapted from Powell 1976.

from goal line to goal line (see figure 35.2). The in-goal areas are between 10 meters and 25 meters each. A *halfway line* runs the width of the field at the center of the field. On both sides of the halfway line, *10-meter lines* are marked in broken lines, 10 meters from the halfway line. Broken *5-meter lines* run parallel to, and 5 meters inside, the touch lines. Two *22-meter lines* are on either end of the field, each 22 meters from a goal line.

Solid lines, 15 meters inside the touch lines, intersect the goal lines, the 22-meter lines, and the halfway line. The top edge of the goal's crossbar is 3 meters high; the goal posts are 5.6 meters apart. *Corner posts* are at least 1.2 meters high.

PLAYERS

Players wear appropriate *uniforms*. Players may not wear anything with dangerous projections, such as buckles or rings. They may not wear shoulder pads. They may wear circular studs on their shoes, not exceeding 18 millimeters in length or 13 millimeters in diameter at the base. Players may wear *shin guards* and elastic *knee and elbow pads*. They may also wear soft leather *scrum caps* to protect their ears.

Players normally may only be replaced when injured. No more than six players per team may be replaced.

EQUIPMENT

The *ball* is oval and is 280 millimeters to 300 millimeters long. It is 760 millimeters to 790 millimeters in circumference, from end to end, and 580 millimeters to 620 millimeters in circumference around the middle.

OFFICIALS

A referee is in charge of the match. Two touch judges, one on each side of the field, assist the referee.

MODIFICATIONS

Rugby League Football is similar to Rugby Union Football. The main differences include the following:

- Each side has 13 players per side instead of 15.
- Three points are awarded for a try instead of five.
- A tackled player is allowed to temporarily retain possession of the ball.

- Ground gained by a kick into touch does not count, unless the ball lands in the field of play before it bounces into touch.

ORGANIZATIONS

U.S. Rugby Football Union
3595 E. Fountain Blvd.
Colorado Springs, CO 80910
719-637-1022

36

Shooting

© Claus Andersen

The sport of shooting has a number of events, each with its own detailed technical rules. The International Shooting Union (UIT) recognizes 19 events for men and 11 for women; in Olympic competition, men have 10 medal events, and women have 5.

The object is to score points by hitting targets. Rules for this chapter come from USA Shooting, the national governing body for the sport; for more detailed information on each event, contact USA Shooting (see "Organizations" at the end of this chapter). Only general rules are provided here.

PROCEDURES

Men's and women's events recognized by the International Olympic Committee are shown in tables 36.1 and 36.2.

Table 36.1: Men's Olympic Events	
Event	Shots
50-m free rifle	3 × 40 shots
50-m free rifle	60 shots prone
10-m air rifle	60 shots standing
50-m free postol	60 shots
25-m rapid-fire pistol	60 shots
10-m air pistol	60 shots
10-m running target	30 + 30 shots
Trap	125 targets
Skeet	125 targets
Double trap	150 targets

Adapted from USA Shooting 1995.

Table 36.2: Women's Olympic Events	
Event	Shots
50-m standard rifle	3 × 20 shots
10-m air rifle	40 shots standing
25-m sport pistol	30 + 30 shots
10-m air pistol	40 shots
Double trap	120 targets

Adapted from USA Shooting 1995.

A finals competition consists of 10 shots, fired in a single shot-for-shot format. The shooter has seven minutes of *preparation time,* during which he may take any number of sighting shots. He is given a 30-second warning before his preparation time is up; this is followed by a one-minute pause.

The range officer then gives him the command "Load!" The shooter may not load prior to receiving this command. The next commands are "Attention!" and "Five-four-three-two-one-start!" At this point the shooter has 75 seconds to fire. On the 75th second, if the shooter is still

shooting, the range officer will command, "Stop!" Shots fired before "Start" and after "Stop" will be counted as zeroes.

If a shooter fires more than one shot during the single shot time, all of those shots are scored as zeroes and counted as part of the 10-shot final. Each shot is immediately scored and announced. The procedures for firing are then repeated until all 10 shots are taken.

Aiming exercises between the commands to "Stop" and to "Load" are permitted only in 10-meter and 50-meter rifle and pistol events. Shooters must do such exercises with an open bolt or an uncocked pistol or rifle.

Modifications of these general procedures are as follows:

Smallbore free rifle, prone, men—45-second time limit for shots, rather than 75-second.

Rapid-fire pistol, men—one sighting series of five shots in four seconds during preparation time; two competition series of five shots in four seconds, shot either in two groups of four shooters or four groups of two shooters; on "Attention!" the targets are turned to the edge-on position, and on "Start!" the targets are turned to face the shooters.

10-meter running target—four sighting shots in 2.5 seconds (two shots left, two right); 10 competition shots in 2.5 seconds each (five left, five right at five targets); shots fired in three groups (3 + 3 + 2) or four groups of two; after the sighting shots, competitors have 30 seconds to adjust their position or sights.

Trap, double trap, and skeet—The six best double trap shooters enter the final of 50 targets (25 doubles) for men and 40 targets (20 doubles) for women. For skeet and trap, the six best shooters enter the final round of 25 targets.

The number of targets and number of shots per target are shown in table 36.3.

Scoring and Deciding Ties

Each target has 10 rings on it, with scoring values ranging from 1 on the outside to 10 on the inside. Scoring officials score the targets and call out the results. If shooters are shooting more than

Table 36.3: Targets and Shots

Event	Sighting targets per event	Competition shots per target
10-m air rifle, 10-m air pistol	4	1
10-m running target	1	2 (1 right, 1 left)
50-m rifle events	4	1
50-m free pistol	1	1
25-m sport pistol	1	1
25-m rapid-fire pistol	5 shots in 4 sec	1 per series

Adapted from USA Shooting 1995.

one shot at the same target, officials must mark or score the shots.

Ties are decided in the following manner:

In 10-meter and 50-meter rifle and pistol events and 25-meter sport pistol events, the competitors who are tied participate in a shot-for-shot shootoff.

In 25-meter rapid-fire pistol shootoffs, competitors fire one series of five shots fired in quick succession.

In 10-meter running target events, competitors take two sighting shots (one left and one right) and two competition shots (one left and one right in 2.5 seconds).

In trap events, competitors shoot one shot per target, station after station, until a "lost" target is registered.

In double trap, competitors fire one double from station 3 until a "lost" target is registered.

In skeet, competitors shoot in sequence on the same station until a "lost" target is registered.

TERMS

An **air pistol** is one with a .177 caliber; it is a compressed air or gas pistol that may be loaded with one pellet only.

An **air rifle** is one using compressed air or CO2; its caliber is .177 millimeter.

A **smallbore free rifle** is one with a .22 caliber.

A **smallbore standard rifle** also has a .22 caliber.

A **double** consists of two skeet clay targets thrown at the same time, one from each house; in the case of double trap, a double is two targets thrown from the machines in front of station 3.

Dry firing means the release of the cocked trigger mechanism of an unloaded firearm, or the release of the trigger mechanism of an air gun fitted with a device that allows the trigger to operate without releasing the propelling charge.

A **free pistol** is one with a .22 caliber; it can be loaded with only one cartridge.

An **irregular double** in skeet shooting occurs when one or both targets of a double are irregular (they don't conform to the normal standards) or when only one target is thrown.

A clay target is **lost** when it is not hit in flight, is hit outside the shooting boundaries, or is "dusted" but no visible piece falls from it.

A **"no-bird double"** is called when both clay targets are not thrown according to the rules.

A **rapid-fire pistol** is one with a .22 caliber.

A **regular double** in skeet shooting occurs when regular targets are thrown simultaneously from each house.

Sights are lenses attached to the rifle, or another means of sighting. Sights not containing corrective lenses are permitted.

A **sport pistol** is chambered for long rifle .22 cartridges.

A **standard pistol** is chambered for long rifle .22 cartridges.

RANGE

A range has a *line of targets* and a *firing line*. (For the features of a shooting target, see figure 36.1.) *Firing points* or *shooting stations* are behind the firing line. The firing point is equipped with a removable or adjustable bench. Ranges have walls, backing targets, or bullet traps to provide protection.

Wind flags are placed as close to the bullets' flight path as possible without interfering with the shooting. They aid the shooters in determining the wind's likely effects on the bullet's flight path. Ranges for air gun competitions are located indoors.

Shooting distances are measured from the firing line to the target face.

Targets have 10 rings, with the innermost ring counting 10 points and the outermost, 1 point; the width of the rings depends on the event. For the events specified, the proper heights of the *target centers* are

- 10-meter, 25-meter ranges; 10-meter, 50-meter running targets—1.4 meters;

- 50-meter ranges—0.75 meter; and
- 300-meter ranges—3 meters.

COMPETITORS

In USA Shooting competitions, shooters compete in one of the following categories:

- J1 Juniors—14 years old and under
- J2 Juniors—15 to 17
- Juniors—20 and under
- Scholastic—primary or secondary school students
- Collegiate—undergrad students
- Military—members of U.S. Armed Forces, active or reserve components, National Guard
- Supported Shooters—members of the national team or national development team
- M1 Masters—40 to 49 years old
- M2 Masters—50 to 59 years old
- M3 Masters—60 to 69 years old
- M4 Masters—70 or older

TARGET

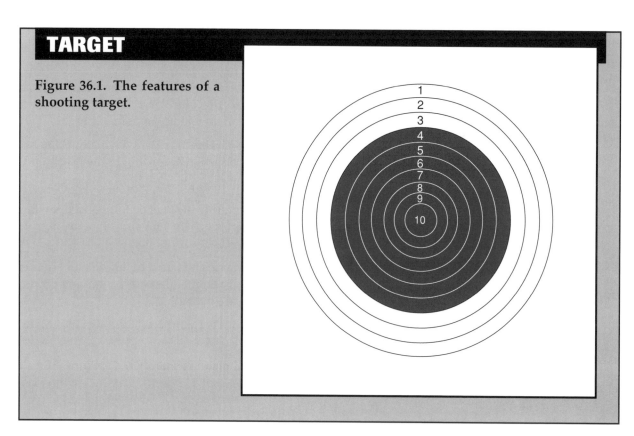

Figure 36.1. The features of a shooting target.

Shooters are further grouped within a shooting discipline by shooting precision classifications, ranging from AA (highest classification) to E (lowest).

EQUIPMENT

Specifications for standard and air rifles are

- length of front sight tunnel—50 millimeters,
- diameter of front sight tunnel—25 millimeters,
- heel-to-toe length of butt plate—153 millimeters,
- weight with sights and hand stop—5.5 kilograms, and
- the front sight may not extend beyond the muzzle.

For pistol specifications, see table 36.4.

OFFICIALS

Competition officials include a *chief range officer* (one appointed for each range), who is in charge of the competition at the range and in charge of the range officers, gives the commands to the shooters, and is responsible for the accurate recording of shots by the *scoring officers.* Scoring officers ensure that targets are rapidly changed, scored, and marked.

ORGANIZATIONS

Amateur Trapshooting Association
601 W. National Rd.
Vandalia, OH 45377
513-898-4638

International Shooting Coaches Association
P.O. Box 1114
Auburn, WA 98071
206-939-7857

National Rifle Association of America
11250 Waples Mill Rd.
Fairfax, VA 22030
703-267-1000

National Skeet Shooting Association *and*
National Sporting Clays Association
5931 Rost Rd.
San Antonio, TX 78253-9261
210-688-3371

Table 36.4: Pistol Specifications			
Pistol	Maximum weight	Maximum barrel length	Caliber
Rapid-fire	1,260 g	Box size only	.22
Center-fire	1,400 g	153 mm	.30 to .38
Sport and standard	1,400 g	153 mm	.22
Free	No restriction	No restriction	.22
Air	1,500 g	Box size only	.177

Adapted from USA Shooting 1995.

37

Soccer

© Claus Andersen

Soccer is based on 17 main laws of the game, which have been refined since its modern beginnings in Great Britain in 1863. The sport was first known in Britain as Association Football; this was shortened to A-soc, and, finally, soccer. The sport's popularity in the United States lagged until the 1970s, when youth leagues began to flourish. The objective of the sport is quite simple: Two teams compete against each other in an attempt to score as many points as possible by putting the ball into their opponents' goal.

The rules in this chapter are from the Fédération Internationale de Football Association (FIFA), the international governing body for the sport. Modifications of these rules are addressed near the end of the chapter.

PROCEDURES

A game is made up of the components shown in table 37.1

Table 37.1:	Components in a Soccer Game			
Teams	Players	Game length	Halftime
2	Up to 11	Two 45-min halves	5 min

The team that wins the coin toss may choose to kick off or defend the goal of its choice. All players must be on their own half of the field before the kickoff takes place. Defensive players must be outside the center circle, at least 10 yards away from the ball, for the kickoff. The referee whistles to begin the game, and the ball is kicked onto the opponent's portion of the field. The player who kicks off may not touch the ball again until another player has.

Players must use their feet, head, or chest to play the ball; with the exception of the goalkeeper—and of making a *throw-in*—players may not use their hands or arms. The game proceeds with each team attempting to control the ball, move it down the field, and score a goal.

The ball is not out of play (out of bounds) until the entire ball has crossed over the touch line or goal line. A player may go out of bounds to keep the ball in play. A ball is in play once it bounces back onto the field after hitting a goal post, crossbar, or corner post, and once it hits an official who is in bounds.

A *goal* (one point) is scored when the ball completely crosses the goal line under the crossbar and between the goal posts. An attacking player may not use his hands or arms to throw, carry, or propel the ball across the goal line.

A goal may not be scored directly from a *kickoff, goal kick,* or *throw-in.* A goal may be scored directly from a *corner kick,* from an opposing goalkeeper's punt, or by an attacker carrying the ball in on his chest or between his knees or feet.

After halftime, the teams change ends of the field, and the team that did not kick off to begin the game does so to begin the second half.

TERMS

An **advantage** refers to a situation in which the referee calls "Play on!" despite a foul—because the team that would be given a free kick already has the advantage of a scoring or passing opportunity.

A **corner kick** is awarded the opposing team when a player kicks the ball over his own goal line. For a corner kick, all opposing players must be at least 10 yards from the ball.

A **direct free kick** occurs after any of nine fouls (see page 240).

A **foul** (see page 240) results in a direct or an indirect free kick for the opposing team at the spot of the foul.

A **goal kick** occurs when a player kicks the ball over the opposing team's goal line. The opposing team is awarded the goal kick. Opposing players must be outside the penalty box; the ball may be kicked by either the goalkeeper or another player. It must be kicked beyond the penalty box area to be put into play. The player who kicks the ball may not touch the ball again until another player has done so.

A player **heads the ball** by hitting it with her head. It is not a foul if a player who jumps and heads the ball bumps into an opponent on the way down.

An **indirect free kick** is awarded for various violations (see page 240).

The **offside** rule is explained on page 239.

A team is awarded a **penalty kick** when an opposing player commits an intentional foul. All players except the kicker and the goalkeeper must stand outside the penalty area, at least 10 yards from the ball (see figure 37.1). The goalkeeper must stand on his goal line and not move his feet until the kick is made. If the ball is stopped by the goalkeeper and rebounds into the field, play continues. If a goal is not scored and the ball goes out of bounds after being touched by the goalkeeper, the attacking team gets a corner kick.

A **shoulder charge** is the only body contact allowed. It occurs when two players press shoulders while attempting to gain possession of the ball. For a shoulder charge to be legal, players must be within playing distance of the ball and have at least one foot on the ground.

A **sliding tackle** occurs when a player slides to kick the ball away from an opponent.

A team is awarded a **throw-in** when the ball goes over the sideline, last touched by an opponent. A player throws the ball in from over her head, with both feet on the ground at the moment of release. At least part of each foot must be on or behind the sideline. If the throw-in is done incorrectly, the opposing team is awarded a throw-in.

A referee may issue a player a **warning** (yellow card) for misconduct, or **eject** a player (red card) for violent conduct, a serious foul, or abusive language.

OFFSIDE, FREE KICKS, AND GOALKEEPING

Many of the rules have been covered under "Procedures" and "Terms," but three—offside, free kicks, and goalkeeping—deserve special attention.

Offside

A player is offside if he is closer to the opponent's goal line than the ball is, unless the player is still in his own half of the field or at least two opponents are closer to the opponent's goal line. Offside is determined by the player's position at the moment of the pass, not at the moment he receives the pass. A player is *not* offside when he receives a ball that

- bounces off a defender who had possession of the ball;
- comes at him directly from a goal kick, corner kick, or throw-in;

© Claus Andersen

Figure 37.1. During a penalty kick, all players except the kicker and goalkeeper must stand outside the penalty area.

- was deflected by the goalkeeper; or
- was shot at the goal and bounces off a defender.

Nor is a player offside when he is in line with a defender at the moment of the pass.

A player is not called offside for merely being in an offside position. The player must be participating in the play to be ruled offside. When a player is offside, the opposing team receives an indirect free kick at the point of the infraction.

Free Kicks

There are two types of free kicks: direct free kicks, awarded for any of nine fouls committed by the other team, and indirect free kicks, awarded for other violations made by the opposing team. Opposing players must be at least 10 yards from the ball during a free kick. Any free kick awarded to the defending team within its own goal area may be taken from any point within the goal area. An indirect free kick awarded to the attacking team within the opponent's goal area will be taken from the goal-area line nearest to the point where the infraction occurred. A goal may be scored on a direct free kick with no other player touching the ball; on an indirect free kick, another player must touch the ball first before a goal can be scored. A direct free kick is awarded to a team's opponents when that team

- kicks, trips, or pushes an opponent;
- jumps into an opponent;
- violently or dangerously charges an opponent, or charges an opponent from behind;
- strikes an opponent with the hand, arm, or elbow;
- holds an opponent's body or clothing; or
- plays the ball anywhere on the arm, from the shoulder to the fingertips (except for the goalkeeper).

An indirect free kick is awarded the opposing team when a player

- is offside;
- obstructs an opponent by deliberately blocking his path, instead of playing the ball;
- kicks too high, thus putting an opponent in danger;

- bends low, putting himself in danger;
- conducts himself in an unsportsmanlike manner;
- charges an opponent when the ball is more than one step away;
- charges into the goalkeeper while in the goal area, preventing the goalkeeper from playing the ball or retaining possession; and when
- a goalkeeper takes more than four steps before releasing the ball.

A goalkeeper is also governed by the following rules.

Goal-Keeping

These rules address the use of hands and of time-delaying tactics:

- After releasing the ball before taking more than four steps, the goalkeeper may not touch the ball again with her hands before another player touches it outside of the penalty area.
- A goalkeeper may use her hands to field a ball that has been deliberately headed or kneed to her by a teammate.
- A goalkeeper may *not* use her hands to field a ball that has been intentionally kicked to her by a teammate.
- A goalkeeper may not delay the game by holding the ball before punting. (Penalty: indirect free kick taken from the spot of the violation, or, if it occurred within the goalkeeper's area, the kick is taken from the goal-area line that runs parallel to the goal line, nearest the spot of the infraction.)

PLAYERS

Each team has up to 11 players; one is the goalkeeper. The other players are known as defenders, midfielders, and forwards, or strikers. In major competitions, a team may not use more than 3 substitutes in a game. In other competitions, up to 5 may be used. Any player, with the referee's approval and when play is stopped, may substitute for the goalkeeper.

A substitute must be summoned onto the field by the referee and must enter the field at the cen-

FIELD

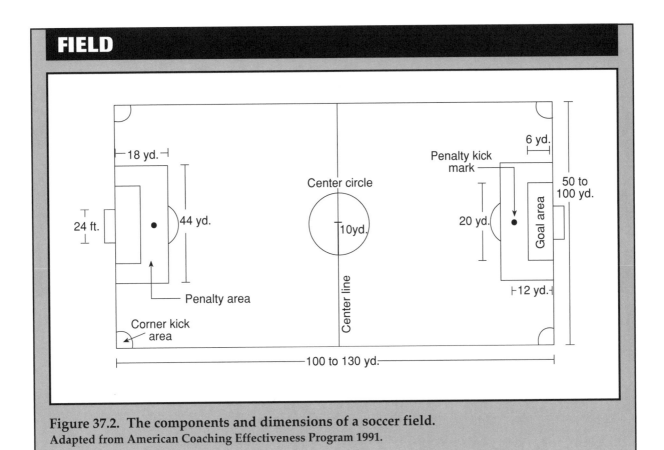

Figure 37.2. The components and dimensions of a soccer field.
Adapted from American Coaching Effectiveness Program 1991.

ter line (see figure 37.2) after the player she is replacing has left the field. Once a player has been replaced, she may not return to the game. (Different soccer associations have variations of this substitution rule for youth, women's, and senior competitions.)

EQUIPMENT

The *ball* is round, covered in leather or a leather-like material, and is between 27 and 28 inches in circumference. It must weigh 14 to 16 ounces and have 14 pounds of air pressure.

Players dress in *team shirts,* shorts, shin guards, and socks. *Shoes* may have studs if they are rounded, no longer than .75 inch, and no less than .5 inch in diameter. Goalkeepers often wear *elbow and knee pads* and *gloves.* The goalkeeper wears a different-colored uniform than his teammates. Any equipment deemed dangerous to players may not be worn. This includes earrings, glasses, necklaces, bracelets, watches, and casts and braces that the referee considers dangerous.

MODIFICATIONS

Soccer is played on various-sized fields with competitions ranging anywhere from 3 on 3 players through 11 on 11. The U.S. Youth Soccer Association (USYSA) mandates 8-on-8 games for their under-10 age group and recommends 4-on-4 for players under 8 and 3-on-3 for players under 6. The concept with the short-sided games is to keep young players more involved in the action. Following is a capsulized version of the USYSA's recommendations for three types of short-sided games.

Three-on-three: No goalkeepers; 8-minute quarters; 25-by-20-yard field; goal 4 feet high, 6 feet wide; No. 3 soccer ball; no score kept.

Four-on-four: No goalkeepers; 12-minute quarters; 50-by-30-yard field; goal 6 feet high, 12 feet wide; No. 4 ball; no score kept.

Eight-on-eight: Goalkeepers are used; 25-minute halves; 70-by-50-yard field; goal 7 feet high, 21 feet wide; No. 4 ball; score can be kept, but it's not recommended.

Note that different organizations have different recommendations; for additional suggestions regarding field dimensions and game length, see tables 37.2 and 37.3. Contact any of the organizations listed at the end of this chapter for specific recommendations for short-sided games.

OFFICIALS

One *referee* and two *assistant referees* control the game. The referee is responsible for enforcing the rules, keeping the time and score, and issuing warnings and ejecting players and coaches. The referee signals the start and end of the game.

The assistant referees indicate when and where a ball goes out of bounds and determine which team is awarded a throw-in, goal kick, or corner kick. They also call offside plays and flag other violations that the referee misses. For various officials' signals, see figure 37.3.

Table 37.2:	Field Dimensions				
Age or level	Length (yd)	Width (yd)	Center circle	Goal area	Goal width (yd)
Under 6 (3 on 3)	20 to 30	15 to 20	3-yd radius	No goal area	6
Under 8 (4 on 4)	40 to 50	20 to 30	5-yd radius	Extends 3 yd out from goal, extends 3 yd beyond both sides of goal	6
Under 8 (up to 11 on 11)	80	60	10-yd radius	6 yd out from goal, 6 yd beyond both sides of goal	8
Under 10	90	60	10-yd radius	Same as above	8
Under 12	100	60	10-yd radius	Same as above	8
Under 14	110	65	10-yd radius	Same as above	8
16 and over	110	70	10-yd radius	Same as above	8

Table 37.3:	Game Length	
Age	Periods	Time between periods
Under 6	Four 8-min quarters	2 min (quarters); 5 min (half)
Under 8	Four 10-min quarters	1 min (quarters); 5 min (half)
Under 10	Four 15-min quarters	1 min (quarters); 5 min (half)
Under 12	Four 15-min quarters	1 min (quarters); 5 min (half)
Under 14	Four 15-min quarters	1 min (quarters); 5 min (half)
16 and over	Four 20-min quarters	1 min (quarters); 5 min (half)
High school	Two 40-min halves	5 min

Penalty kick
(points to penalty area)

Corner kick
(points to corner area)

Goal kick
(points to goal area)

Time out

Misconduct

Charging

(continued)

Figure 37.3. Common soccer official's signals.

Offside

Indirect goal kick

Holding

Charging violently

Striking

Pushing

Handling ball

(continued)

Figure 37.3. *(continued)*

Tripping

Kicking

Figure 37.3. *(continued)*

ORGANIZATIONS

American Youth Soccer Organization
5403 W. 138th St.
Hawthorne, CA 90250
310-643-6455

Cosmopolitan Soccer League
7800 River Road
North Bergen, NJ 07047
201-861-6606

Intercollegiate Soccer Association of America
1821 Sunny Drive
St. Louis, MO 63122
314-822-2814

National Soccer Coaches Association of America
4220 Shawnee Mission Parkway, Ste. 105B
Fairway, KS 66205
913-362-1747

National Soccer League
4534 N. Lincoln Ave.
Chicago, IL 60625
312-275-2850

Soccer Association for Youth
4903 Vine St.
Cincinnati, OH 45217
513-242-4263

United States Soccer Federation
1801-1811 S. Prairie Ave.
Chicago, IL 60616
312-808-1300

United States Youth Soccer Association
899 Presidential Drive, Ste. 117
Richardson, TX 75081
972-235-4499
800-4-SOCCER

38

Softball

© Unicorn/Robin Rudd

Softball was first played in Chicago in 1887, indoors, with a 17-inch ball. An outdoor version of the game was played with a 12-inch ball in Minneapolis in 1895. The game was standardized in 1923, and today there are many variations of the game, including fast-pitch, slow-pitch, 16-inch slow-pitch, and coed play. These variations make softball a widely accessible sport, played by young and old alike.

The bulk of this chapter focuses on slow-pitch rules, compiled by the Amateur Softball Association/USA Softball. Most of these rules apply also to fast-pitch and 16-inch slow-pitch; for differences, see the "Modifications" section near the end of the chapter. The object of the game is to win by scoring more runs than one's opponents.

PROCEDURES

A game of slow-pitch is made up of the components shown in table 38.1.

Table 38.1:		Components in a Game of Slow-Pitch Softball	
Teams	Players per team	Innings	Outs per inning
2	10 (or 11 with extra player)	7	3

The visiting team bats first, in the top half of the *inning;* the home team bats in the bottom half of the inning. A team bats until three *outs* are recorded against it. The batter's object is to reach base and eventually score. Except in special situations, runners advance at their own risk around the bases. A team scores a run when a player safely touches first, second, third, and home before three outs are made. However, a run does not count if the third out is made by the batter or a runner being *forced out* at a base, or by a runner being *tagged out* before another runner touches home plate.

Winning Ways

A win may be recorded in a variety of ways:

- *Seven-inning win for the visitors.* If the visitors are ahead after seven complete innings, the game is over.
- *Seven-inning win for the home team.* If the home team is ahead after the visitors bat in the top half of the seventh inning, the game is over. Or if the home team scores the winning run in the bottom of the seventh, the game is over when the run scores.
- *Extra-inning victory.* A game tied at the end of seven innings goes into *extra innings* and is played until one team has scored more than the other at the end of a complete inning or until the home team scores the winning run.
- *Shortened game.* A game stopped by rain, darkness, or for other reasons is considered complete if after five innings one team has scored

more runs than the other team. The game is considered complete if after four and a half innings the home team has scored more than the visitors.

- *Forfeit.* A forfeit may be called by the umpire for a number of reasons, which include a team's failing to show up or refusing to begin a game, noticeably delaying or hastening the game, or willfully breaking the rules. If an ejected player does not leave within one minute, that, too, is reason to call a forfeit. The score of a forfeited game is always 7-0.

TERMS

Note: The following list includes terms that are specific to fast-pitch as well as slow-pitch.

An **altered bat** is illegal. This includes inserting material inside the bat, applying more than two layers of tape to the grip, or attaching a "flare" or "cone" grip to the bat.

An **appeal play** is one in which the umpire does not have to make a decision unless requested by a coach or player. The appeal must be made before the next pitch or before the pitcher and infielders have crossed the foul line on their way to the bench.

An **assist** is credited to a fielder when her throw leads to the putout of a runner (see figure 38.1). Two or more fielders can receive assists on the same play.

A batter is credited with a **base hit** ("single") when he reaches first base safely on a hit without aid of an **error,** or by way of a fielder's choice or force play at another base.

A batter receives a **base on balls** when the umpire calls four pitches "balls" (outside the strike zone and not swung at by the batter). This allows the batter to reach first base safely. In slow-pitch, the pitcher can notify the umpire if he wants to intentionally issue a base on balls (also called a "walk"); the batter then may go to first base without getting any pitches.

The **base path** extends three feet on either side of a direct line between bases. A runner is out when she runs outside the base path, except to avoid interfering with a fielder fielding a batted ball.

Figure 38.1.   An assist is credited to a fielder when her throw leads to the putout of a runner.

A **catch** means a fielder has secured the ball with his hands or glove. Regarding a catch that results in a putout—such as an outfielder catching a fly ball or a first baseman catching a throw on a forceout from an infielder—the catch is good if the player has complete control of the ball but then drops it in the act of removing it from his glove or throwing it. A fly ball is not considered caught if the fielder simultaneously falls or collides with another player or the fence and the ball is dislodged.

A **chopped ball** occurs in slow-pitch when the batter strikes the ball downward to intentionally bounce the ball high in the air. This is illegal and the batter is ruled out.

A **crow hop** is executed in fast-pitch play by a pitcher who steps or hops off the front of the pitcher's plate, replants her pivot foot, and pushes off from this new starting point as she completes her delivery.

A **dead ball** is a ball that is not in play. A **delayed dead ball** remains live until the play is finished; at that point the proper call is made. A delayed dead ball may be called for

- an illegal pitch,
- catcher's obstruction,
- plate umpire interference,

- obstruction, and
- a batted or thrown ball hit with detached equipment.

A **double play** is recorded by the defense when two outs are made on the same play.

A **double** is a hit in which the batter safely reaches second base.

An **error** is charged to a fielder who misplays a ball (e.g., a dropped fly ball or throw, or a fumbled ground ball) that prolongs an at-bat for the batter or the life of a base runner or that permits a runner to advance one or more bases. An error may be charged even if the fielder does not touch the ball (e.g., a ground ball that goes through the legs).

Fair territory and **foul territory** are marked by two foul lines. Each line extends from home plate. One line creates a third base line and left field line, stopping at the left field fence; the other creates a first base line and right field line, stopping at the right field fence. Anything on or in between the foul lines is considered fair territory; anything outside the foul lines is considered foul territory.

A **fake tag** is a form of obstruction of a runner by a fielder who neither has the ball nor is about to receive it. The umpire will award the runner the base he would have made, in the umpire's judgment, had the obstruction not occurred.

A **force play** occurs when a runner is forced to advance to the next base because the batter becomes a runner. When a batter hits a ground ball with a runner on first, the runner is forced to run to second. If a fielder touches second base with the ball in his possession before the runner reaches second, the runner is "forced out" at second. If a runner is on second when a ground ball is hit, he is not forced to advance, because first base is unoccupied.

A **foul ball** is any ball hit into foul territory.

A **ground rule double** is awarded a batter when his fair ball bounces over or passes through or under the fence.

A **home run** is recorded when a batter hits a fair ball over the fence or circles the bases on an inside-the-park home run without being thrown out.

An **illegally batted ball** occurs when a ball is hit and the batter's entire foot is on the ground completely outside the lines of the batter's box, or when any part of the foot is touching home plate. It also occurs when an illegal bat is used.

The **infield** refers to that portion of the field containing the four bases. In terms of players, the infield is made up of the first, second, and third basemen, and the shortstop. The pitcher and the catcher (called the "battery") also are positioned in the infield.

The **infield fly rule** prohibits an infielder from intentionally dropping a fair fly ball that can be caught with normal effort. This rule is in effect with first and second, or first, second, and third bases occupied before two are out. When an umpire calls an infield fly rule, the batter is automatically out and runners may advance at their own risk. Any defensive player positioned in the infield at the start of the play is considered an infielder for the purpose of this rule.

Interference occurs when an offensive player impedes or confuses a defensive player as she is trying to make a play. Interference can be physical or verbal. Defensive players must be given the chance to play the ball. In fast-pitch, a batter may be called for interference if he impedes the catcher in his throw on an attempted steal. A base runner may be called for interference if she is hit by a batted ball while she is not on a base and the

ball has not passed an infielder, excluding the pitcher. However, it is not interference if the batted ball was first touched by a defensive player or if no infielder had a chance to make an out on the ball.

A runner may **lead off** a base in fast-pitch, once the ball has left the pitcher's hand. In slow-pitch, a runner may not leave her base until the ball is batted, touches the ground, or reaches home plate, but she must return to her base if the ball is not hit.

"**Leaping**" is the term used in fast-pitch when the pitcher goes airborne as he delivers the ball. With this delivery, the ball is released as the pitcher's feet return to the ground. This is legal in male fast-pitch, but illegal in female fast-pitch.

A **legal touch**, resulting in an out, is made by a defensive player who tags a runner with the ball while the runner is not on a base. The ball may not be juggled or dropped by the fielder, unless the runner knocks the ball from the fielder's hands or glove after the tag.

A defensive player can be called for **obstruction** if she hinders a batter from hitting the ball or impedes a base runner while the fielder does not have the ball and is not about to receive the ball.

An **out** may be recorded in a variety of ways, including strikeout, force-out, tag-out, and fly-out.

The **outfield** is that portion of fair territory between the infield and the fence. In terms of players, the outfield consists of the left fielder, the center fielder, the right fielder, and, in slow-pitch, an extra fielder.

A batter-runner may **overslide** first base and not be put out, but a runner oversliding second or third base is in jeopardy of being tagged out.

In fast-pitch, a **passed ball** is charged to the catcher when she fails to control a pitch that should have been caught or contained with normal effort and a base runner or base runners advance.

A **quick return pitch** is one made by a pitcher before the batter is set.

A batter is credited with the appropriate number of **runs-batted-in** (RBIs) when his hit is responsible for one or more runners scoring. RBIs are not tallied for runs scored as a result of **errors** or if a run scores as the batter grounds into a **double play**.

A **sacrifice fly** is credited to a batter whose caught fly ball results in a runner on third base tagging up and scoring. A sacrifice fly does not count as a time-at-bat. A run must score for a sacrifice fly to be recorded.

In fast-pitch, a runner may attempt to **steal** a base during a pitch to the batter. In slow-pitch, no stealing is allowed.

A pitched ball is in a batter's **strike zone** when it is over any part of home plate between his armpits and the top of his knees in fast-pitch play, or between his back shoulder and front knee in slow-pitch play.

A batter is credited with a **triple** when he reaches third base safely on his hit.

A **triple play** is credited to the defense when it records three outs on the same play.

In fast-pitch, a **wild pitch** occurs when a pitch eludes the catcher, allowing one or more runners to advance a base. A wild pitch is judged to be the pitcher's fault, not the catcher's. A ball that bounces in the dirt and allows any base runners to advance is automatically a wild pitch.

FIELD

Figure 38.2 shows the dimensions of a softball field for adult slow-pitch. (See page 257 for dimensions for fast-pitch, 16-inch slow-pitch, and youth softball.)

Home plate is five-sided, 17 inches wide across the edge facing the pitcher, 8.5 inches long on sides parallel to the batter's box, and 12 inches long on the sides of the point facing the catcher.

Bases are 15 inches square, not more than 5 inches thick. A *double base*, 15 inches by 30 inches, can be

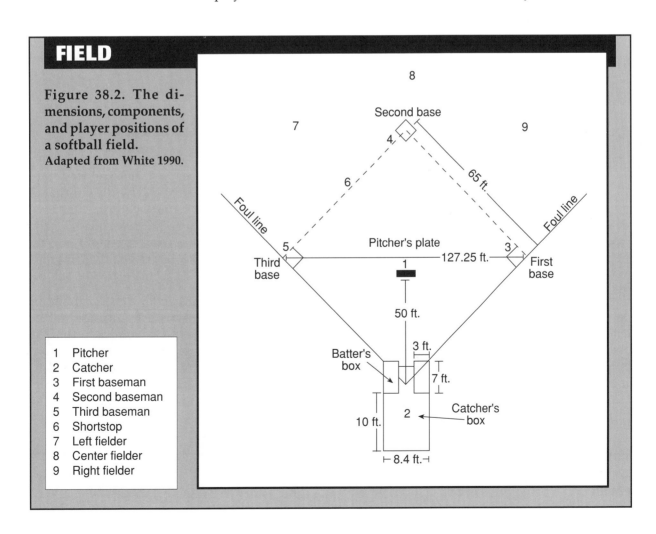

FIELD

Figure 38.2. The dimensions, components, and player positions of a softball field. Adapted from White 1990.

1 Pitcher
2 Catcher
3 First baseman
4 Second baseman
5 Third baseman
6 Shortstop
7 Left fielder
8 Center fielder
9 Right fielder

used at first base. Half the base is in fair territory and is white; the other half is in foul territory and is orange.

The *pitcher's plate* is 24 inches long by 6 inches wide; its front is 50 feet from the back point of home plate.

The *outfield fence* varies in distance, from 265 feet to 275 feet for women to 275 feet to 325 feet for men. In coed play the fences are 275 feet to 300 feet.

A *dead ball area* is drawn with chalk outside the field of play. The line itself is in play, but if a fielder has either foot on the ground completely over the line, the ball is dead and no play can be made. If a fielder intentionally carries a live ball into the dead ball area, each runner is awarded two bases beyond the last base they legally touched. If the act is unintentional, each runner is awarded one base.

PLAYERS

In slow-pitch, a team has 10 fielders:

- pitcher,
- catcher,
- first baseman,
- second baseman,
- third baseman,
- shortstop,
- left fielder,
- center fielder,
- right fielder, and
- extra fielder.

A team may also have an *extra player* (EP) who bats but does not field. The EP is optional, but if one is used, he must be in the starting lineup and must be used for the entire game. With an EP, all 11 players must bat, and any 10 may play defense. Defensive positions may be switched, but the batting order must remain constant.

All players, including the EP, may be replaced and may re-enter the game once. The starting player and the substitute cannot be in the lineup at the same time; each player must oc-cupy his same position in the batting order. A substitute may enter a game only once. A starting pitcher who is removed from the game may re-enter the game once at any position except pitcher.

Under the *short-handed rule*, a team may start with 10 or 11 players and continue with one less player when a player leaves a game for any reason other than ejection. If the player leaving the game is a base runner, she is called out; when her turn at bat comes, an automatic out is declared. The player may not return to the lineup unless she has left for the *blood rule*, which stipulates that a player who is bleeding or who has blood on her uniform must receive appropriate treatment before continuing to play. Play may be momentarily suspended while the player receives treatment, or the player may be required to at least temporarily leave the game.

A player or coach who is ejected may stay on the bench, unless the offense is flagrant, in which case the ejected person must leave the grounds. If an ejected player continues to participate, or re-enters the game, the contest is forfeited to the other team.

EQUIPMENT

The *ball* is smooth-seamed, flat-surfaced, and pebble- or dimple-textured, with concealed stitches. Its core is cork, rubber, or a polyurethane mix, covered with horsehide or cowhide. The 11-inch ball weighs between 5.9 and 6.1 ounces. The 12-inch ball weighs between 6.25 and 7 ounces.

The *bat* is made of hardwood, metal, graphite, or other ASA-approved material. It may not be longer than 34 inches or weigh more than 38 ounces. It may not exceed 2.25 inches in diameter. A safety grip must be between 10 and 15 inches long and not extend more than 15 inches from the bottom of the bat. Metal bats may be angular.

Gloves may be worn by any player, but only the catcher and first baseman may wear mitts, with thumb and body sections. Webbing on any glove or mitt may not exceed five inches.

Uniforms

Pants, sliding pants, and *shirts* should be of the same design. *Caps* are optional; if they are worn, they must be of the same design. Exposed jewelry may not be worn. *Shoes* may have soft or hard rubber cleats, or be smooth. In adult play, metal sole or heel plates may be used if the spikes do not extend more than .75 inch. Shoes with round metal spikes are illegal.

PITCHING

The pitcher must come to a complete stop while facing the batter for at least one second, and release the ball within 10 seconds. One foot must be in contact with the pitcher's plate throughout the delivery. A pitcher may use any continuous windup but must deliver the ball on the first forward swing of the arm past the hip and toward home plate. All pitches must be thrown underhand and must reach an arc between 6 and 12 feet (see figure 38.3). The pitcher may not continue her windup after releasing the ball.

At the beginning of each half inning, and when a relief pitcher enters the game, the pitcher has one

minute to complete not more than three warm-up pitches. A pitcher must be removed on the second conference in an inning. Shouting instructions from the bench is not considered a conference.

A starting pitcher is credited with a win when she has pitched at least four innings and her team has a lead that it does not give up when she leaves the game. In a game shortened to five innings, the pitcher must pitch at least three innings to be credited with a victory. A pitcher is charged with a loss when he leaves the game with his team trailing, and his team fails to tie the score or gain the lead.

Figure 38.3. An underhand pitch is required in softball.

BATTING

Players must hit in the batting order on their lineup card. The batter must stand in the batter's box (the lines are part of the box); no part of her feet may be outside the lines. The batter may not hinder the catcher from throwing while standing in the batter's box. A strike is called when

- a batter swings at a pitch and misses (the ball is dead in slow-pitch),
- a pitch enters the strike zone (see page 251) before touching the ground and the batter does not swing,
- the batter fouls a pitch (in slow-pitch, if this is the third strike, the batter is out and the ball is dead), or
- the ball hits the batter while part of the batter's body is in the strike zone.

A ball is called when

- the pitch does not enter the strike zone and the batter does not swing,
- a pitch is out of the strike zone and the batter swings at it *after* it has bounced (the ball is dead and runners cannot advance),
- an illegal pitch is thrown, or
- a ball out of the strike zone hits the batter.

The batter is out when

- he swings and misses at a third strike, or fouls a third strike;
- her fair or foul fly ball is caught in the air by a fielder;
- on a ground ball, a defensive player who possesses the ball touches first base before the batter does;
- the batter switches boxes after the pitcher begins to pitch;
- an entire foot is on the ground out of the batter's box and the batter hits a fair or foul ball;
- any part of a foot touches home plate and the batter hits a fair or foul ball;
- the batter is caught using an illegal or altered bat;
- the batter bunts or chops the ball;

- after hitting the ball in fair territory, the bat strikes the ball again (unless the umpire rules this contact was unintentional);
- a batted ball in fair territory strikes the batter outside of the batter's box; or
- a base runner interferes with a fielder before the batter reaches first base.

The batter-runner is out when

- he runs outside the 3-foot lane after hitting a fair ball and interferes with the fielder taking the throw at first base (the batter-runner may, however, run outside the 3-foot lane to avoid a fielder attempting to field a ball);
- he interferes with a fielder attempting to field the ball; or
- he rounds first base on a hit, turns toward second, and is tagged.

The classifications in table 38.2 limit the number of over-the-fence home runs that a team may hit. A batter who hits such a ball is out after his team's limit is reached.

Table 38.2: Home Run Limits	
Classification	Over-the-fence home run limit
Super	Unlimited
Major	12
Class A	6
Major coed	5
Class B	3
Class A coed	2
Class C	1
Class D	0

BASE RUNNING

A base runner must touch the bases in legal order. A runner is entitled to an unoccupied base if he reaches it before he is put out. Two runners may not occupy the same base. The runner who arrives first is entitled to the base, unless forced to advance; the other runner may be tagged out with the ball. If the first runner was forced to advance, he may be tagged out.

A runner must *tag up* before advancing on a caught fly ball. The runner may not leave her base until the ball is touched by the fielder. In slow-pitch play, a runner may not steal. A runner hit by a batted ball is out, unless she is on a base when the ball hits her. If the closest defensive player is in front of the base the runner is on, the ball is live. If the closest defender is behind the base, the ball is dead. A runner may advance, without the risk of being put out, when

- he is forced to vacate a base because the batter is walked,
- a fielder is called for obstructing the runner,
- the ball is overthrown (runners advance two bases from where they were when the ball left the thrower's hand),
- the ball is blocked by equipment not involved in the game (unless it is blocked by the offensive team's equipment, in which case the runner closest to home is called out),
- the batter hits an over-the-fence home run,
- the batter hits a ground-rule double,
- a fielder unintentionally carries a live ball into dead ball territory (one base), or
- a fielder intentionally causes a live ball to go into dead ball territory (two bases).

A runner may advance, with the risk of being put out, when

- the batter hits the ball,
- a fly ball is first touched, or
- a fair ball strikes the umpire or another runner after having passed an infielder other than the pitcher.

A runner must return to his base when

- the batter hits a foul ball,
- an illegal hit is declared by the umpire,
- the batter or another runner is called for interference,
- a pitch is not hit by the batter, or
- the umpire rules a fielder intentionally dropped a ball.

The runner is out when

- he runs out of the base line to avoid being tagged out;
- she is tagged with a live ball while not on a base;
- a fielder in possession of the ball touches the base to which the runner is forced to advance;
- he passes a runner ahead of him;
- she leaves her base before a caught fly ball is first touched and the play is appealed;
- he misses a base and the play is appealed;
- she interferes with a fielder attempting to field or throw a ball;
- he is hit by a batted ball while not on base;
- she purposely kicks the ball or runs the bases backward to confuse the defense;
- the third-base coach runs toward home, to draw a throw (the runner closest to home is out);
- a coach or team member intentionally interferes with a thrown ball while in the coach's box;
- the runner stays on his feet and deliberately crashes into a fielder who has the ball;
- she leaves her base before the pitch reaches home plate, touches the ground, or is hit; or when
- he doesn't return immediately to his base when the pitcher receives the ball after a pitch while in the 8-foot radius of the pitcher's mound (fast-pitch only).

A runner is not out when

- she runs out of the base line to avoid interfering with a fielder;
- he is hit by a fair, untouched batted ball and the umpire rules no fielder had a chance to make an out;
- she cannot avoid contact with a fair ball that is touched by any fielder;
- he is tagged with a ball that is not held securely by the fielder;
- she overrruns first base and returns to the base without turning toward second;
- he is on base while hit by a batted ball; or
- she dislodges a base while sliding into it.

PROTESTS

The coach or captain of a team may lodge protests for

- rules misinterpretation (must be made before the next pitch),
- illegal substitution or re-entry (must be made while the illegal player is in the game), and
- ineligible player (can be made anytime).

If a written protest regarding a rules misinterpretation is upheld, the decision will be corrected and the game is replayed from the point of the protest.

If a protest regarding eligibility is upheld, the game is a forfeit, with the offended team winning.

UMPIRES

The *home plate umpire* stands behind the catcher. She controls the game and calls balls and strikes. She also calls plays involving the batter, fair and foul balls, and plays at the plate. The *base umpire* assists the home plate umpire in making calls and makes decisions at the bases.

See figure 38.4 for umpires' signals.

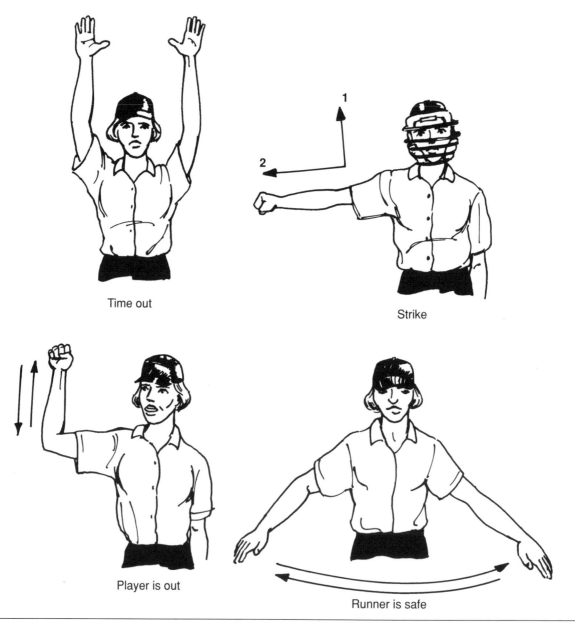

Time out

Strike

Player is out

Runner is safe

Figure 38.4. Common official's signals for softball.

MODIFICATIONS

The following modifications explain the components and rules of junior Olympic, fast pitch, 16-inch slow pitch, coed, and senior softball.

Procedure

Junior Olympic Girls Fast Pitch and Women

If the score is tied after nine innings, this tiebreaker goes into effect: The offensive team begins its half-inning with the batter who had made the last out in the previous inning placed on second base.

Field

Fast-pitch field dimensions are indicated in table 38.3; slow-pitch dimensions are noted in table 38.4.

In Senior Men's slow pitch, a *second home plate* is placed 8 feet from the back tip of home plate, on the first base line extended.

Equipment

The following items are the equipment needed for softball.

16-Inch Slow Pitch

The *ball* weighs between 9 and 10 ounces.

Fast Pitch

Adults must wear *masks* with *throat protectors;* junior Olympic fast pitch catchers must also wear an approved *helmet* with ear flaps, *shin guards,* and a *body protector.* All adult fast pitch and junior Olympic fast pitch batters, including on-deck batters, must wear *batting helmets.*

Men's Fast Pitch

Caps are mandatory and a team's caps must be alike. In women's fast pitch, caps are optional, but if a team wears them, they must all be alike.

Players

The following descriptions explain the pitching rules for the different types of softball.

Fast Pitch

A team has nine players, with an optional *designated player* (DP), who can hit for one of the nine players. If the DP plays defense for the player he's hitting for, that player is considered to have left the game. The DP can play defense for any other player, and that player can still hit.

Table 38.3: Fast-Pitch Field Dimensions			
Level of play	Baselines (ft)	Pitching distance (ft)	Fence distance (min/max) (ft)
Women	60	40	200 to 250
Men	60	46	225 to 250
Girls 18 and under	60	40	200 to 225
Boys 18 and under	60	46	200 to 225
Girls 16 and under	60	40	200 to 225
Boys 16 and under	60	46	200 to 225
Girls 14 and under	60	40	175 to 200
Boys 14 and under	60	46	175 to 200
Girls 12 and under	60	35	175 to 200
Boys 12 and under	60	40	175 to 200
Girls 10 and under	55	35	150 to 175
Boys 10 and under	55	35	150 to 175

Adapted from Amateur Softball Association/USA Softball 1993.

Table 38.4:	16-Inch Slow-Pitch and Youth Slow-Pitch Field Dimensions		
Level of play	Baselines (ft)	Pitching distance (ft)	Fence distance (min/max) (ft)
Women (16SP)	55	38	200
Men (16SP)	55	38	250
Girls 18 and under	65	50	225 to 250
Boys 18 and under	65	50	275 to 300
Girls 16 and under	65	50	225 to 250
Boys 16 and under	65	50	275 to 300
Girls 14 and under	65	46	225 to 250
Boys 14 and under	65	46	250 to 275
Girls 12 and under	60	40	175 to 200
Boys 12 and under	60	40	175 to 200
Girls 10 and under	55	35	150 to 175
Boys 10 and under	55	35	150 to 175

Adapted from Amateur Softball Association/USA Softball 1993.

Coed

The lineup consists of five males and five females, batting in alternating order. Two males and two females play in both the infield and outfield; one male and one female split duties as pitcher and catcher. The lineups can also have two extra players (EPs), one male and one female. Any 10 players may play defense if the proper mix is kept.

Men's Senior

One or two EPs may be used.

Pitching

The following descriptions explain the pitching rules for different types of softball.

Fast Pitch

The pitcher's hand may go past his or her hip twice if there are not two complete revolutions in the windup. In *men's and boys' junior Olympic competition*, the pitcher needs to have only one foot in contact with the pitcher's plate. In *women's and girls' junior Olympic competition*, both feet must be in contact with the pitcher's plate.

One step must be taken forward in releasing the ball. *Male adult and junior Olympic pitchers* may have both feet in the air during this step. *Female adult and junior Olympic pitchers* must drag the foot or push off the pitcher's plate with the pivot foot; the leap is not legal in female competition. For both males and females, the delivery is underhanded, with the hand below the hip and the wrist not farther from the body than the elbow.

After the pitcher has taken her position, she may not throw to a base without stepping back off the pitcher's plate before throwing. Failure to step off the pitcher's plate results in a ball being called and any runners advancing one base. "No pitch" is called when the umpire judges that the pitcher is attempting to "quick pitch" a batter who is not set.

Coed

The 11-inch ball is pitched to women; the 12-inch ball is pitched to men.

Batting

The following descriptions explain the batting rules for different types of softball.

Fast Pitch

The ball is in play when a ball or strike is called. The ball is also live during an intentional walk. A batter is not out on a third strike that is a foul ball, unless it is a bunt. A batter hit by a pitch—even if it bounces—that is not a strike and that he attempts to elude is awarded first base.

In junior Olympic 10-and-under play, the batter is out on the third strike, whether the ball is caught or not.

16-Inch Slow Pitch

A strike is live, but runners cannot advance.

Coed

If a male batter is walked, whether intentionally or not, the following female batter has the option of walking also.

Base Running

The following descriptions explain the base running rules for different types of softball.

Fast Pitch

Runners must maintain contact with their base until the ball leaves the pitcher's hand. Leaving before will result in being called out. Stealing is allowed at all levels except for junior Olympic 10-and-under. In junior Olympic 10-and-under, runners may leave base when the ball leaves the pitcher's hand but must return to their base if the ball is not hit.

A runner off her base after a pitch must advance immediately to the next base or return to her base once the pitcher has the ball within the 8-foot circle. Failure to do so results in her being called out.

Runners advance one base when the umpire calls an illegal pitch. On a wild pitch or passed ball lodged in or under the backstop, runners are entitled to advance one base.

16-Inch Slow Pitch

Runners may lead off their base; they do risk being picked off by the pitcher or catcher. They may not advance on an overthrown pick-off attempt.

Senior

Unlimited *courtesy runners* are allowed; any player in the batting order may be used as a runner. A player may be used as a courtesy runner only once an inning; if it's his time at bat and he is on base, the player is called out.

Runners must touch a second home plate, 8 feet from the tip of home plate and on a line with first base. A runner can be put out at home in a non-force situation without being tagged; if a defensive player steps on the original home plate while holding the ball before the runner touches the second home plate, the runner is out.

If the runner touches the original home plate, he may be called out on an appeal play. Once a runner crosses a line 20 feet from home plate, he may not return to third. He will be called out if he does so.

ORGANIZATIONS

Amateur Softball Association of America/ USA Softball
2801 N.E. 50th St.
Oklahoma City, OK 73111-7203
404-424-5266

Cinderella Softball Leagues
P.O. Box 1411
Corning, NY 14830
607-937-5469

National Softball Association
P.O. Box 23403
Lexington, KY 40523
606-887-4114

United States Slo-Pitch Softball Association
3935 S. Crater Rd.
Petersburg, VA 23805
804-732-4099

39

Speed Skating

© Claus Andersen

Iron skates were first crafted in the 16th century and used in competitions in northern Europe. In America, speed skating competitions began to pop up in the latter half of the 19th century; international racing began in the 1890s. Speed skating events for men became part of the Olympics in 1924; women began Olympic competition in 1960.

Skaters compete in short track and long track events, racing either in packs of four to six skaters (or larger packs for long tracks), or against one other skater. The fastest time wins in metric or Olympic-style racing, where no more than two skaters at a time race against the clock.

Metric or Olympic-style long-track speed skaters reach speeds of up to 35 miles per hour; short-track speed skaters lean into the turns at a 65-degree angle to maintain speeds of up to 30 miles per hour. The world record for 10,000 meters is 27.6 miles per hour. Skaters also compete in relay and marathon competitions.

The U.S. International Speedskating Association governs worldwide metric or Olympic-style, long- and short-track competitions. The Amateur Speedskating Union of the United States governs local, regional, and national age group pack-style competitions in both long- and short-track events. Both organizations have supplied the rules for this chapter.

PROCEDURES

Skaters may compete in *short-track* events, *long-track* events, *relays*, and *marathons*.

Short-track. Individual and relay events are contested on a 111-meter track. In *individual events*, four to six skaters (the pack) start on the line; the first to cross the finish line with her skate wins. International distances for individual competitions are 500 meters, 1,000 meters, 1,500 meters, and 3,000 meters for both men and women. See table 39.1 for national age group championship distances. In *relay events*, teams of four skaters compete. Each member must take part in the race. The touch relay exchange is usually a vigorous push or pull by skaters, so no speed is lost in the exchange. Relay exchanges may take place at any time except during the final two laps. The international distances are 3,000 meters for women and 5,000 meters for men. The national age group championship is 3,000 meters for teams of skaters 12 years and older.

Long-track. Events are contested on a 400-meter oval, using one of two formats: Metric or Olympic-style, or pack-style. In metric or Olympic-style, two skaters compete at once, in separate lanes, racing against the clock; the distances are 500 meters, 1,000 meters, 1,500 meters, 5,000 meters, and 10,000 meters for men; and 500 meters, 1,000 meters, 1,500 meters, 3,000 meters, and 5,000 meters for women. In pack-style, up to six skaters compete at once, not confined to lanes, using drafting and race strategies. See table 39.2 for national age group championship distances.

Relay. Teams of four skaters compete at varying distances; the national championship distance is 3,000 meters. Each member must take part in the race. A skater finishing a portion must touch the team member who is taking over. Relays may take place at any time except during the final two laps.

Marathon. These events are contested over distances of 25 kilometers and 50 kilometers.

Starting and Racing

The starting commands and rules for all styles of speed skating are essentially the same. At the command, "Go to the start," skaters stand motionless at the pre-start line, .75 meter behind the

| Table 39.1: National Championship Distances—Short Track Events ||
Classification (age)	Distances (m)
Midget (through age 11)	333, 500, 666, 777
Juvenile (through 13)	333, 500, 777, 1,000
Junior (through 16)	500, 1,000, 1,500, 3,000
Senior (17 through 35)	500, 1,000, 1,500, 3,000
Master (35 through 50)	500, 1,000, 1,500, 3,000
Grand master (50 through 60)	500, 777, 1,000, 1,500
Veteran (60 and older)	500, 777, 1,000, 1,500

Adapted from *1996-1997 Amateur Speedskating Union Handbook.*

| Table 39.2: National Championship Distances—Long Track Events ||
Classification (age)	Distances (m)
Midget (through age 11)	400, 500, 600, 800
Juvenile (through 13)	300, 500, 600, 800, 1,000
Junior (through 16)	300, 500, 800, 1,000, 1,500
Senior (17 through 35)	500, 800, 1,000, 1,500, 3,000
Master (35 through 50)	500, 800, 1,000, 1,500, 3,000
Grand master (50 through 60)	500, 800, 1,000, 1,500
Veteran (60 and older)	500, 800, 1,000, 1,500

Adapted from Amateur Speedskating Union of the United States 1995.

start line. At the command, "Ready," the skaters assume their start position at the start line and remain motionless. After a pause of one to one and a half seconds, the starter fires a shot to start the race.

If a skater falls within the first 10 meters of a long-track race or the apex of the corner in a short-track race, the starter may recall the race with a second shot. If the fall was not caused by interference and does not impede other skaters, the starter won't recall the race. Falls are not called back in metric or Olympic-style racing. The skater may appeal to the referee for a reskate.

A skater may make one false start, after which the race will be restarted. On the second false start made by the same racer, that racer is disqualified from that event. In races on straight-of-way tracks, racers must stay in their lanes. In races with turns, competitors may not cross to the inner edge of the track, except when they may do so without interfering with other skaters. Skaters must skate in a straight line once they enter the homestretch, unless they are able to change lanes without interfering with another skater.

In metric or Olympic-style racing, the skater who starts on the inner track changes to the outer track at the crossing straight, and the skater starting on the outer track changes to the inner. The change in tracks occurs each time the skaters come to the crossing straight. The skater coming from the inner track may not hinder the skater coming from the outer track on the crossing straight.

In long-track races of 1,500 meters or less, a skater who is lapped by the leader must drop out, unless he is in a position for which a prize is offered. In races longer than 1,500 meters, a skater is not considered lapped unless the leader passes him within the final 1,500 meters. A skater finishes when any part of his skate crosses the finish line.

Speed skating championships traditionally are awarded at different distances. The skater earning the highest point total is the champion. In pack-style racing, skaters earn the following points for each race:

- First place—5 points
- Second place—3 points
- Third place—2 points
- Fourth place—1 point

Passing Rules

In long-track races, a skater with inside or pole position must be passed on the right side, unless she leaves enough room on the left for a skater to pass. It is the responsibility of the skater who is passing to avoid collision, although the skater being passed may not act improperly and intentionally cause a collision.

In short-track races, skaters may pass on the left or right side. Again, the responsibility for avoiding collision falls on the passing skater.

If two skaters tie for a place, the point totals for that place and the next place are added and then divided equally among the two skaters. For instance, skaters tying for second and third would each get 2.5 points (3 + 2 divided by 2) each.

In metric or Olympic-style skating, where the winner is determined by the fastest time, points are the sum of 500 meters' equivalent time, calculated to the third decimal point, for each distance skated. The champion is the skater with the lowest number of points. At the Winter Olympics, medals are awarded for each distance.

Disqualifications

Skaters may be disqualified for

- pushing, impeding, or interfering with another skater;
- intentionally moving, or skating inside, the corner poles or markers;
- skating backward or otherwise ridiculing the other skaters;
- delaying the start of an event;
- deliberately causing danger to another skater;
- unsportsmanlike conduct, including foul language and fighting; and
- not giving honest effort.

TERMS

Charging is a foul that occurs when a skater tries to pass on the inside and makes contact with the skater she's passing, or when a skater skates wide and then attempts to regain her original position and makes contact with a competitor on the left.

Drifting is a foul called when a skater drifts out of his lane, or changes lanes, and interferes with another skater. In straight-of-way races, skaters may not leave their lanes.

Interference will be called if a skater, in passing another competitor, is at fault for obstructing or colliding with the other skater.

Pushing is a foul that occurs when a skater uses his hands, arms, elbows, shoulders, or hips in contacting another skater, causing the skater to fall, lose balance or position, or skate wide.

Tripping is a foul called when a skater drags the rear foot and knocks another skater's foot from under her.

RINK

A *short-track* course is a 111-meter oval. A *long-track* course is a 400-meter oval. *Survey lines* (or points) define track lanes (see figure 39.1). Lines are either snowlines or blocks set on the ice. The *skater's path* is considered to be .5 meter outside the survey line. This path is used in determining the distance.

The tracks have *pre-start, start,* and *finish lines* marked in the ice. Long-track courses also have a *fall-down mark* 10 meters beyond the starting line. Short-track courses have safety padding covering the walls around the entire ends of the rink.

SKATERS

Skaters compete in the following age classes, determined by the skater's age on July 1 preceding the competition:

- Midget—11 years old and younger
- Juvenile—13 and younger

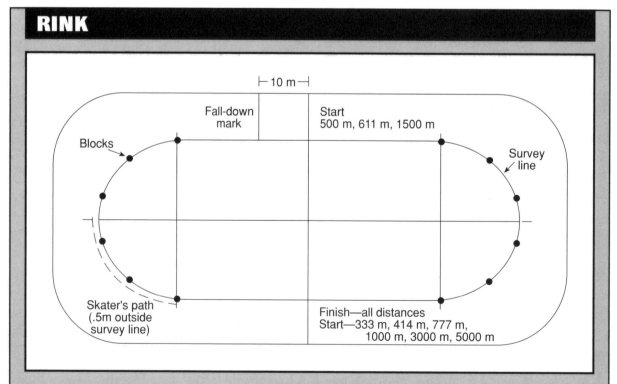

Figure 39.1. The dimensions and components of a speed skating rink.
Adapted from Amateur Speedskating Union of the United States 1995.

- Junior—15 and younger
- Intermediate—18 and younger
- Senior—19 and older
- Master—35 and older
- Grand Master—50 and older

EQUIPMENT

Skaters wear appropriate outfits, *safety helmets, shin guards, neck guards, gloves,* and *skates.* There are no requirements for skates, but the *boots* are usually made of leather and composite materials and have steel blades of 12 inches to 18 inches. Long-track skates have light, low-cut boots with thin blades that are only slightly curved on the bottom. Short-track skates have sturdy, high-cut boots, with thicker, adjustable blades that have more curvature on the bottom to negotiate the sharper turns and more pronounced leans.

OFFICIALS

Large competitions include a *chief referee, assistant referees, clerks, starters, finish judges, timers, scorers,* and a *lap counter.* The chief referee has overall authority, including hearing and deciding all protests.

ORGANIZATIONS

Amateur Speedskating Union of the United States
1033 Shady Lane
Glen Ellyn, IL 60137
630-790-3230

United States International Speedskating Association
P.O. Box 16157
Rocky River, OH 44116
216-899-0128

40

Squash

© Stephen Line

Variations of squash originated in England in the early 1800s; use of a softer ball—one that could be "squashed" by a player's hand—gave rise to the game's name. Squash was introduced in America in the mid-1800s. While there are hard ball and soft ball versions of the game, the soft ball version is much more popular. The main focus of this chapter covers the rules for the soft ball version, which is played internationally. In the "Modifications" section, we point out major differences for the hard ball version.

As with many racquet games, squash may be played by two or four players. Players hit a small rubber ball against the front wall, above the tin and within the out-of-court lines, attempting to score points by hitting the ball in such a way that the opponents cannot return it before it bounces twice. The rules in this chapter were supplied by the U.S. Squash Racquets Association.

PROCEDURES

A singles game is played to nine points; a match is the best of three or best of five games. Players take a 90-second break between games. If the score reaches 8-8, the receiver may choose to call "Set one," which means the next player who scores wins, or "Set two," which means the first player to reach 10 points wins. Before play begins, players may warm up the ball on the court for five minutes. A spin of the racquet determines which side gets first serve.

When a good serve is delivered, the opposing side attempts to return the serve. Hits continue to alternate from side to side until the rally is over. Only the serving side may score a point. When the server wins a stroke, she scores a point. When the receiver wins a stroke, she gains the serve. (In doubles, games go to 15 points, with a point per rally.)

Play is continuous throughout the game, except for equipment changes approved by the referee or for injury. The referee determines what is a reasonable amount of time to resume play after an injury. If a player is unable to continue because of injury, and the injury was deliberately inflicted by the opponent, the injured player is declared the winner. If the injury was accidental or self-inflicted, and the injured player is unable to continue, the opponent wins the match.

Serving

At the beginning of a game and when a receiver becomes a server, the server may choose to serve from either *service box* (see figure 40.1 on page 270). Part of one foot must be on the floor in the service box, with no part of the foot touching the service box line when the server strikes the ball. The server drops or throws the ball to begin the serve. The served ball may not hit any surface before striking the front wall. It must strike the front wall between the *cut line* and the *out line* so that it reaches the floor within the *quarter court* opposite the server's box (unless volleyed by the opponent).

A server who drops or throws the ball and then does not attempt to hit it may serve again. A server continues to serve until he loses a stroke. As long as he holds serve, he alternates boxes. If a rally ends in a *let* (an undecided point), he serves again from the same box.

In singles play, when a player loses serve, the serve then passes to the receiver. In doubles play, the first side to serve in a game gets only one server. Once that rally is lost, the serve switches to the opposing team. From there on, each side gets two servers; when the second server loses serve, the serve goes to the opponents. At the beginning of the second and subsequent games, the winner of the previous game serves first. A server "serves her hand out" (loses her serve) when

- her serve first hits a side wall, floor, or ceiling;
- part of one foot is not on the floor in the server's box, with no part of that foot on the box line, when she strikes the ball; or
- the ball bounces on or outside the short or half-court line of the quarter court opposite the service box.

A serve is also lost when a server

- attempts and fails to hit a serve,
- does not strike the ball correctly (e.g., hits the ball more than once or carries the ball with the racquet),
- serves the ball out,
- serves onto or below the cut line, or
- is struck by his own serve before the opponent can strike at it.

Rallies

Making a return. A good serve may be returned before the ball strikes the ground or after it bounces once. It must hit the front wall above the board before touching the ground. It may not touch any part of the striker's body or clothing, or any part of the opponent's body, clothing, or racquet.

Hitting an opponent with the ball. If a striker hits an opponent with the ball, the striker wins the stroke if the return would have struck the front wall without first touching any other surface. The exception is if the striker has followed the ball around and turned to strike the ball to the right of his body after it has passed to his left, or vice versa—that is, after the ball has passed the striker, struck the back wall, and the striker turns to hit the ball to the front wall. This is an example of "turning," and while the rules do not specifically prohibit turning, it is deemed a dangerous maneuver, because the striker loses sight of his opponent. Players are strongly encouraged to call "let" in this case. If a player does strike a ball while turning and the ball strikes the opponent, it's a let.

If a striker hits an opponent with the ball, and the ball struck another wall before striking the front wall, a let is called, unless the referee believes the return would have won the rally. In the latter case, the striker is awarded the stroke. If the return would not have been good, and it strikes an opponent, the striker loses the rally, or "no let" is awarded to the striker.

Further attempts to hit the ball. A striker may make contact only once on a return but may make any number of attempts to hit the ball before it bounces twice. If a striker swings and misses at a ball, which then hits the opponent, his clothing, or his racquet, the referee will call a let if he believes the striker could have made a good return. The striker loses the stroke if the referee believes he could not have made a good return.

Making every effort. The outgoing striker must make every effort to allow the incoming striker a clear path to the ball. It is also the incoming striker's responsibility to make every effort to get to the ball.

Interference. To avoid interference, a player must make every effort to provide her opponent with unobstructed, direct access to the ball; a fair view of the ball; and freedom to hit the ball directly to the front wall. If interference is called, the play is a let, or a stroke is awarded to the offended player. A let is not allowed if the player would not have made a good return, if he did not make adequate effort to get to and play the ball, if he created his own interference, or if he clearly accepted the interference and played on.

A let is always allowed if one player refrains from striking the ball due to a reasonable fear of striking his opponent with the ball or with the racquet. This is the case even if no interference actually occurred.

The referee will award a stroke to a player if the opponent does not make every effort to avoid interfering and the player would have made a good return. A stroke is also awarded if the player would have made a winning return, even if the opponent makes every effort to avoid interfering. The referee may also award a stroke to a player if her opponent makes unnecessary physical contact with her or endangers her with an excessive racquet swing.

Lets. In addition to previous mentions of lets, rallies are replayed when

- the striker doesn't hit the ball in a manner to ensure the safety of his opponent,
- a player is distracted by an occurrence on or off the court,
- the receiver is not ready for the serve and doesn't attempt to return serve,
- the ball breaks during play, or
- court conditions affect play.

Appeals. A player may appeal a decision that affects the rally by saying, "Let, please." The referee stops play and decides on the appeal.

TERMS

The **board** is the lowest horizontal marking on the front wall, with the tin beneath it stretching the width of the court.

The **cut line** is a horizontal line across the front wall, 6 feet above the floor.

"Down" is the expression used when an otherwise good serve strikes the board or tin or fails to reach the front wall. It is also used when the ball strikes a player before it has bounced more than once.

"Game ball" means that the server needs one point to win the game.

The **half-court line** runs parallel to the side walls, dividing the court into two equal parts, intersecting the short line to form a "T."

A **hand** refers to the time during which a player has the serve.

A **handout** means the serve is changing hands.

"Match ball" means that the server needs one point to win the match.

"Not up" is the term used when the ball has not been struck according to the rules.

The **out line** is a continuous line comprising the front wall line, both side wall lines, and the back wall line. This line marks the top boundaries of the court. If there are no side wall or back wall lines, the boundaries are the tops of the walls. If a ball strikes part of the horizontal top surface of such an unlined wall, it is out, even if it rebounds into the court.

A **quarter court** is one half of the back part of the court, which is divided into two equal parts by the half-court line.

A **rally** is the play that begins with the serve and ends when the ball is no longer in play.

A **service box** is in each quarter court, bounded by the side wall, the short line, and two other lines. The server serves from this box.

The **short line** is parallel to and 18 feet from the front wall.

The **striker** is the player whose turn it is to hit the ball.

A **stroke** is gained by the player who wins a rally. A stroke results in either a point scored for the server or a change of hand.

The **tin** is between the board and the floor, running the length of the floor. It makes a distinctive noise when the ball hits it.

PLAYERS

Players may be coached only during intervals between games. A referee may penalize a player for offensive or intimidating behavior, including

- obscene language and gestures,
- verbal and physical abuse,
- abuse of racquet or ball,
- arguing with the marker or referee,

COURT

Figure 40.1. The dimensions and markings of a soft ball squash court. Adapted from U.S. Squash Racquets Association.

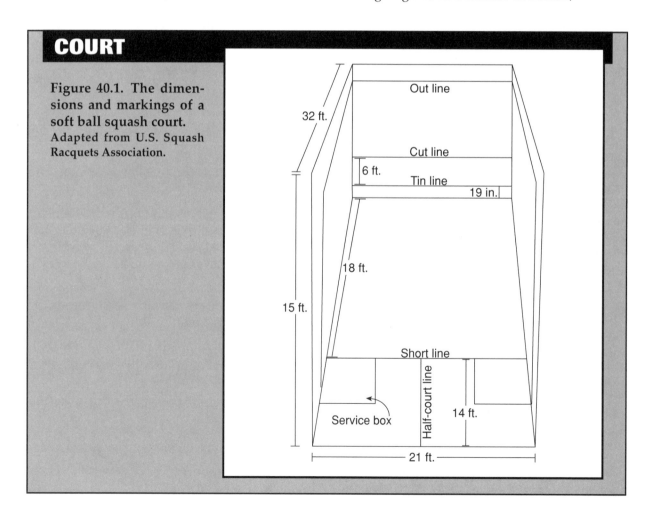

- unnecessary physical contact and excessive racquet swing,
- dangerous play, and
- unfair warmup and returning late to the court.

Penalties that the referee may levy include a warning, and a stroke, game, or match awarded to the opponent.

EQUIPMENT

The *ball* has a diameter of 1.5 inches and weighs 12.7 to 13.4 ounces. It is made of rubber or butyl, or a combination; it's hollow and, appropriately enough, "squashy."

Racquets have a circular head of wood, strung with gut over a handle of wood or metal. They may be no longer than 27 inches; the stringed area may not be larger than 8.5 inches long by 7.25 inches wide. When the ball is not in play, another ball may be substituted for it, upon mutual consent by the players or upon an appeal by one player to the referee.

OFFICIALS

A *referee* controls the match, sometimes assisted by a *marker*. The referee makes all major calls and decisions; the marker calls the play, the score, and calls faults, "downs," "outs," and "handouts."

MODIFICATIONS

Following are major differences in rules for the hard ball (North American) version of squash.

Game. The first player to get 15 points wins, except in the following cases:

At 13-13, the player who first reached 13 must announce either

- "set to five points"—the first person to 18 wins,
- "set to three points"—the first to 16 wins, or
- "no set"—the first to 15 wins.

At 14-14, if the score did not first reach 13-13, the player who first reaches 14 calls the situation, either

- "set to three points"—the first player to 17 wins, or
- "no set"—the first to 15 wins.

Serving. The server loses his serve and the point after making two consecutive faults.

Rallies. Either player who fails to make a good return loses the point.

Let points. The referee may award a let point when a player is deprived of a chance to hit a winning shot, when a player's opponent has caused repeated lets, and when a player's opponent has deliberately pushed off him.

Replaying a let. The server is entitled to two serves, even if she faulted before the let occurred.

Continuity of play. Players may take up to two minutes between games (up to five minutes between the third and fourth game).

ORGANIZATIONS

United States Squash Racquets Association
P.O. Box 1216
23 Cynwyd Rd.
Bala Cynwyd, PA 19004
215-667-4006

World Squash Federation
6 Havelock Court
Hastings, E. Sussex TN34 1BP, England
1424 429245

41

Swimming

© Claus Andersen

Swimming championships were first held in Japan in the early 1600s. Swimming has been an Olympic sport since the inception of the modern Olympics in 1896. Both individual and relay races are contested over varying distances, using one stroke or a combination of strokes. Strokes used are the breaststroke, the butterfly, the backstroke, and the freestyle.

The object is to swim the fastest time. In team competitions, swimmers earn points for their teams according to where they place in finishing. The rules source for this chapter is United States Swimming, the national governing body for the sport.

PROCEDURES

Swimmers are seeded in preliminary heats according to their fastest times. The fastest swimmers in each heat are placed in center lanes of the pool. In finals heats, the slowest swimmers swim first and the fastest swimmers swim last. Swimmers who record the same time tie for that event. Swimmers compete at the distances and strokes shown in table 41.1.

To begin a race, competitors are called to their *starting blocks*. After the referee's whistle, swimmers "take their mark" by moving at least one foot to the front of the starting platform. When they are motionless, the starter signals the start by shooting a gun or sounding a horn.

If a swimmer leaves too early, a false-start recall rope is dropped across the pool, about 11 meters from the start in a short-course pool and 15 meters in a long-course pool. A swimmer who false starts is eliminated from the event. A swimmer is not charged with a false start if it was caused by the motion of another swimmer.

Competitors must stay in their own lanes. Swimmers may be disqualified for swimming out of their lanes or otherwise obstructing other swimmers. Grabbing lane dividers to assist forward motion is prohibited. A swimmer is disqualified for standing on the bottom of the pool, except during a freestyle race. A swimmer may not walk or spring from the bottom of the pool, or leave the pool. A swimmer who is not entered in a race but enters the pool while a race is underway is disqualified from the next event in which he was scheduled to participate. A swimmer may not compete in more than three individual events per day in a preliminaries and finals meet. In a timed finals meet, a swimmer may not compete in more than five events per day.

Breaststroke

Swimmers use a forward start from blocks. In the water, both shoulders must be in line with the water surface, and the arms must move in the same horizontal plane. The hands are pushed forward together from the breast, and brought back under the water's surface; the elbows must be underwater, except for the final stroke. The hands may not be brought beyond the hips, except during the first stroke after the start and af-

Stroke	Short course distance[1]	Long course distance[2] (m)
Freestyle	50, 100, 200, 500, 1,000, 1,650 yd 50, 100, 200, 400, 800, 1,500 m	50, 100, 200, 400, 800, 1,500
Backstroke	100, 200 yd 50, 100, 200 m	100, 200
Breaststroke	100, 200 yd 50, 100, 200 m	100, 200
Butterfly	100, 200 yd 50, 100, 200 m	100, 200
Individual medley	200, 400 yd 100, 200, 400 m	200, 400
Medley relay	200, 400 yd 200, 400 m	200, 400
Freestyle relay	200, 400, 800 yd 200, 400, 800 m	200, 400, 800

Table 41.1:   Distances for Different Events

[1]Made over courses 25 yards or meters long.
[2]Made over courses 55 yards or 50 meters long.
Adapted from United States Swimming 1996.

ter each turn. At least part of the swimmer's head must break the water's surface at least once on each complete stroke cycle, except after the start and turns, during which the swimmer may take one complete arm stroke and leg kick while submerged. The feet should be turned outward during the propelling part of the kick; scissors, flutters, or downward butterfly kicks are not permitted.

At turns, a swimmer must touch the wall with both hands at, above, or below the surface. The swimmer's shoulders must be in line with the surface. Once the touch is made, a swimmer may complete the turn in any way he desires. At the finish, a swimmer must touch the wall with both hands at, above, or below the water surface and with his shoulders in line with the surface.

Butterfly

The swimmer uses a forward start and keeps her shoulders in line with the water's surface and at or past the vertical toward her breast on each stroke. She may use only one arm pull underwater per stroke, but she may use two dolphin kicks. She must bring both arms forward, over the water, and pull them back together. The legs must kick in unison. A swimmer may not use a scissors or breaststroke kick.

At turns, the body should be on the breast and the shoulders in line with the surface. Both hands must touch the wall simultaneously, at, above, or below the surface. After the touch, the swimmer may complete the turn any way she wants. Her shoulders must be at or past vertical toward the breast when she leaves the wall. At the finish, she must touch the wall with both hands simultaneously, at, above, or below the surface, with her shoulders in line with the surface.

Backstroke

The swimmer begins in the pool, using a starting grip, facing the starting end. The feet must be under the water to start. The swimmer pushes off on his back. Part of the swimmer's body must break the water's surface throughout the race, except during the turns. At the start and during turns, a swimmer may be underwater for up to 15 meters.

To make a turn, some part of the swimmer's body must touch the wall. A swimmer may use a single or double arm pull to begin the turn. Upon leaving the wall, the swimmer must return to a position on his back. He finishes the race by touching the wall while on his back.

Freestyle

A swimmer uses a forward start. Any style of stroke may be used. To make a turn, a swimmer must touch the wall; to complete the race, the swimmer must touch the wall at the prescribed distance.

Individual Medley

This event consists of four equal portions, with strokes used in this order: butterfly, backstroke, breaststroke, and freestyle. Swimmers use a forward start and must complete each portion according to the rules for the appropriate strokes. When changing from one stroke to the next, the swimmer follows the turn rules for the stroke just completed. As with the freestyle finish, a swimmer completes this race when any part of her body touches the final wall.

Relays

In a *freestyle relay*, four swimmers each swim one-quarter of the distance, using the freestyle rules. In a *medley relay*, four swimmers each swim one-quarter of the distance, with the first swimmer using the backstroke; the second, breaststroke; the third, butterfly; and the fourth, freestyle.

No swimmer may swim more than one leg in a relay. Each swimmer must touch the touchplate or pad in her lane before her teammate begins. A team is disqualified for violating this rule.

Scoring

In *dual meets*, scoring for individual events is on a 5-3-1-0 basis; that is, the winner gets 5 points, the swimmer placing second gets 3 points, the third-place swimmer gets 1 point, and all other competitors get no points. Scoring for relays is on a 7-0 basis. For *triangular meets*, scoring for individual events is on a 6-4-3-2-1-0 basis; for relays, it's 8-4-0. Scoring for most other meets, with point values doubled for relay events, is as follows:

- 4-lane pools—5-3-2-1
- 5-lane pools—6-4-3-2-1
- 6-lane pools—7-5-4-3-2-1
- 7-lane pools—8-6-5-4-3-2-1
- 8-lane pools—9-7-6-5-4-3-2-1
- 9-lane pools—10-8-7-6-5-4-3-2-1
- 10-lane pools—11-9-8-7-6-5-4-3-2-1

In case of a tie between swimmers, the points for the tied place and the following place are added and divided in two; each swimmer is credited with the same points. For example, in a 10-lane pool, two swimmers tying for first would receive 10 points each (11 for first, 9 for second; divide that total of 20 by 2).

TERMS

Body refers to the torso, including the shoulders and hips.

A **forward start** is a forward entry taken facing the water.

Heats are competitions used to pare the field to a manageable number for a final event.

A **lane** is the area in which each swimmer swims. Lanes are separated by **lane lines,** which are floating markers, and are marked on the bottom of the pool by **lane markings**.

Long-course refers to events held in 50-meter pools.

Short-course refers to events held in 25-meter pools.

Timed finals are competitions in which heats are swum and final placements are determined by times recorded in the heats.

POOL

A *long-course* pool is 50 meters long; a *short-course* pool is 25 meters long (see figure 41.1). The minimum *lane width* is 2.13 meters. The *water depth* is 2 meters.

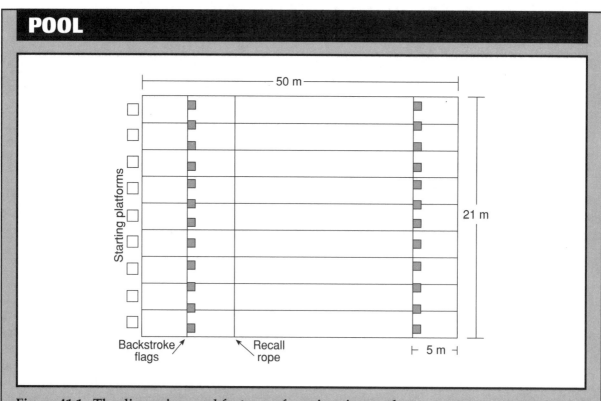

Figure 41.1. The dimensions and features of a swimming pool.

Pool-bottom *lane markers*, 10 inches wide, mark the middle of each lane. These markers terminate in a "T" 2 meters from the pool wall. End-wall targets, in the shape of a "T," are in the center of the wall at the end of each lane, extending at least 1 meter below the surface.

Lanes are numbered from right to left as swimmers stand facing the pool. Lanes are separated by *floating lane dividers* with a diameter of 5 centimeters to 11 centimeters. The color of the floats from the wall to 5 meters out are different than the color for the rest of the course.

The *starting platforms* for a long-course pool are between .5 and .75 meter above the water. For a short-course pool, they're no higher than .75 meter above the water. The front edge of the platforms are flush with the wall. The top surface of the platforms are square, at least .5 by .5 meter, and are covered with a nonslip material.

Backstroke starting grips are between 1 and 2 feet above water. The front edge of the grips is parallel with the water and flush with the face of the end wall.

Three triangular *backstroke flags* are placed 5 meters from each end of the course, anywhere from 1.8 to 2.5 meters above the water.

A *recall rope* is used to recall swimmers after a false start. The rope is dropped about 11 meters from the start in a short-course pool and 15 meters in a long-course pool. Water temperature is to be maintained at 78 to 80 degrees Fahrenheit (26 to 27 degrees Celsius).

ATHLETES

Swimmers wear nontransparent, appropriate *bathing suits.* They may wear *goggles* and *caps.* Competition is held in age groups, with the recommended events shown in table 41.2.

EQUIPMENT

Races are timed with either *automatic, semiautomatic,* or *manual timing systems.* Automatic systems are activated by electric impulse and stopped when the swimmer touches the touch-pad. Semiautomatic systems are activated by electric impulse and stopped by timers pushing buttons when racers finish. Manual timing is usually done with handheld stopwatches.

OFFICIALS

Officials include a *referee,* a *starter,* and a *stroke* or *turn judge.* Three *timers* per lane are used; they are presided over by a *timing judge.* Other officials, in applicable situations, include *place judges* and *relay take-off judges.*

ORGANIZATIONS

Fédération Internationale de Natation Amateur (FINA)
Ave. de Beaumont 9
Rez-de-chaussée
CH-1012 Lausanne, Switzerland
21 3126602

United States Masters Swimming
2 Peter Ave.
Rutland, MA 01543
508-886-6631

United States Swimming
1 Olympic Plaza
Colorado Springs, CO 80909
719-578-4578

Table 41.2: Recommended Events for Different Age Groups

Age group	Events (m/yd)
10 years and younger	Freestyle: 50, 100, 200 Backstroke: 50, 100 Breaststroke: 50, 100 Butterfly: 50, 100 Individual medley: 100, 200 Medley relay: 200, 400 Freestyle relay: 200
11 to 12 years old	Freestyle: 50, 100, 200, 400/500 Backstroke: 50, 100 Breaststroke: 50, 100 Butterfly: 50, 100 Individual medley: 100, 200 Medley relay: 200, 400 Freestyle relay: 200, 400
13 to 18 years old	Freestyle: 50, 100, 200, 400/500, 800/1,000, 1,500/1,650 Backstroke: 100, 200 Breaststroke: 100, 200 Butterfly: 100, 200 Individual medley: 200, 400 Medley relay: 200, 400 Freestyle relay: 200, 400, 800
Senior (short course)	Freestyle: 50, 100, 200, 400/500, 800/1,000, 1,500/1,650 Backstroke: 100, 200 Breaststroke: 100, 200 Butterfly: 100, 200 Individual medley: 200, 400 Medley relay: 400 Freestyle relay: 400, 800
Senior (long course)	Freestyle: 50, 100, 200, 400, 800, 1,500 Backstroke: 100, 200 Breaststroke: 100, 200 Butterfly: 100, 200 Individual medley: 200, 400 Medley relay: 400 Freestyle relay: 400, 800

Adapted from United States Swimming 1996.

42

Synchronized Swimming

© W. Lynn Seldon

Synchronized swimmers compete in solo, duet, trio, and team events, performing routines and figures. *Routines* consist of any figures, strokes, swimming, and propulsion techniques; *figures* are normally performed in a relatively stationary position. The scores earned for figures go toward the total score, which includes the technical merit score of the routine, the artistic impression of the routine, any bonus points, and any penalty points subtracted. The highest score wins. The source for rules for this chapter is United States Synchronized Swimming, the national governing body for the sport.

PROCEDURES

In larger events, preliminaries and semifinals in routine competition are held first, followed by figure competition and then the finals in routine competition. The 10 highest scorers from the semifinal routine competition advance to the finals in figure competition, and the 12 highest combined scorers (figure and routine preliminary scores) advance to the finals in routine competition.

A draw is held to determine the competitors' order of appearance in both figure and routine competition. In figure and preliminary competition, no competitor may start in the number one position more than once (e.g., a solo and a duet). The order of appearance for finals is determined as follows: the highest ranking competitor from the preliminaries draws from the last three positions. Then the position just before the last three positions is added, and the second-ranked competitor draws. This procedure is followed until all starting positions are assigned.

TERMS

Note: Most of these terms refer to figure positions.

In a **back layout position,** the body extends on the back with the face, chest, thighs, and feet at the surface.

In a **ballet leg position,** the body and one leg are extended on a horizontal line either at or beneath the surface, with the other leg extended vertically, and with the water level at the ankle or as high as possible on the thigh.

In a **crane position,** the body and one leg are perpendicular to the surface with the other leg extended parallel to the surface.

In a **flamingo position,** one leg extends perpendicular to the surface and the other draws toward the chest.

In a **front layout position,** the body extends horizontally on the stomach with the head, upper back, buttocks, and heels at the surface.

In a **front pike position,** the hips are bent at 90 degrees, with the legs together and fully extended.

In a **split position,** both legs are fully extended at the surface, evenly split forward and backward, with the shoulders and head on a vertical line directly under the hips.

In a **tuck position,** the body is as compact as possible, heels pressed to buttocks, back rounded, knees to face, legs together.

FIGURES

Figures are combinations of specific and precise movements ranging in degrees of difficulty from 1.1 to 3.9. There are four categories of figures: Ballet Leg, Dolphin, Somersault, and Diverse.

Figure competition is included in the program at all U.S. events, but it is excluded at many international events, including the Olympic Games and the World Aquatic Championships. Figures are performed individually, without music, before panels of trained judges, and are designed to determine the swimmer's ability to control movement and demonstrate balance, coordination, flexibility, and timing.

Each swimmer is required to perform the same 4 of a possible 20 figures. Those 4 figures are drawn 18 to 48 hours prior to the figure competition. Competitors must, therefore, be able to perform all 20 figures. For some competitions the 4 figures are preselected and particular age groups, skill levels, and special programs—such as Novice, 11 and under, Collegiate, and Masters—have specified required figures that are known throughout the season.

Scoring

Judges, seated together in panels, individually award points from 0 to 10, in one-tenth of a point increments, as follows:

- excellent—9.0-10
- good—7.0-8.9
- satisfactory—5.0-6.9
- unsatisfactory—3.0-4.9
- deficient—0.1-2.9

Each individual performance is measured from the standpoint of perfection in design and control, as detailed in the figure description. Design is the assessment of the swimmer's precise definition of positions, the degree of full extension of the body and limbs, and the path of movement from one position to another. Control factors include the swimmer's stability, the support of weight above the water, the water lines achieved, and how smoothly and easily the figure is performed.

To determine the figure score for each competitor, the score for each of the four figures performed is determined by first dropping the highest and lowest scores awarded, then averaging the remaining scores and multiplying the result by that figure's assigned degree of difficulty. The four figure scores are then added together, divided by the degree of difficulty of the group of figures, and multiplied by 10 to obtain the final figure score. For duet, trio, and team events, the figure scores of the competitors performing the routine are averaged to determine the figure score for that routine.

Actions

The following are some commonly-seen actions in figures and routines.

Spins and Twists: The body, remaining on a vertical line, rotates rapidly and descends or ascends for a spin. The body rotates slowly and remains at the same water level for a twist. The degree of the rotation is designated for figure and technical routine elements, but it is not designated for free routines. In routines, the legs may move freely to describe various patterns while spinning or twisting.

Thrust: A rapid and explosive movement from an underwater position to the highest possible level of legs and torso extended above the water. In figure competition the underwater starting position is designated, as is the position to reach above the water. The rate of descent is also described. In routines the positions, timing, and actions at the height of movement upward and on descent are freely created in response to the music.

Walkout: A movement from a split position onto the back or stomach accomplished by lifting one leg in an arc over the surface to meet the other. The timing and the degree of movement toward the feet to complete the action are designated in figure competition and the tech-

nical routine, but are varied greatly when included in the free routine.

Platforms: A table is created by the body or bodies of swimmers in a team routine upon which one or more swimmers stand, pose, or move while being raised from under the water surface by the remaining team members to a position completely above the water. There they are sustained before descending.

Lifts and Throws: One or more swimmers are pushed rapidly upward from underwater on the shoulders, feet, or arms of other team members to high positions above the surface or to be propelled into the air to execute an airborne somersault or flip before re-entering the water.

There are many more positions and actions that are described in the 175 basic figures and their variations. New hybrid figures are created by coaches and athletes for routines every year and they, in turn, inspire new ideas in others.

ROUTINES

There are three routine events recognized internationally: solo, duet (two swimmers), and team (four to eight swimmers). U.S. Championships usually include a trio (three swimmers) event. See figure 42.1.

Figure 42.1. Two synchronized swimmers perform their routine. The time requirement for duets is four minutes.

Routine competition takes two different forms: the free and the technical program. One or both may be included in a competition. The free program has no restrictions concerning music or choreography. The technical program contains at least five required elements, must be performed by all members simultaneously, and is shorter in length. Both are judged by the same criteria.

Scoring

Scores are given for each routine in two categories: technical merit and artistic impression. Judges, seated at various vantage points around the pool, award points from 0.1 to 10.0 in one-tenth of a point increments. There are two panels of five judges, each judging one category, or one panel of five to seven judges, with each awarding scores for both categories.

The technical merit score is based upon

- execution: the perfection of swimming strokes, propulsion, original figures, transitions, and patterns;
- synchronization: the matching of one to the other and to the music; and
- difficulty: the airborne weight, complexity and multiplicity, strength, time (particularly underwater), and placement of the movements and patterns.

The artistic impression score is based upon

- choreography: the variety, fluidity, and spacial use of the pool;
- music interpretation: the use of movement to interpret the musical accompaniment; and
- manner of presentation: the poise and confidence displayed and the ability to communicate with the audience and judges.

The value assigned by the judges to each of the above components varies with the event (solo, team, etc.); see tables 42.1 and 42.2.

The scoring range for routines is as follows:

- excellent—9.0-10
- good—7.0-8.9
- satisfactory—5.0-6.9
- unsatisfactory—3.0-4.9
- deficient—0.1-2.9
- failed—0

The highest and lowest scores awarded in each category are canceled and the remaining scores are averaged. The technical merit average is multiplied by six and the artistic impression average is multiplied by four. The two are added to obtain the routine score.

Table 42.1: Technical Merit Scoring			
Criteria	Solo	Duet/trio	Team
Executing strokes, figures, transitions, propulsion techniques, precision of patterns	50%	40	40
Synchronizing (with partners and with music)	10%	20	30
Difficulty of strokes, figures, and patterns	40%	40	30

Adapted from U.S. Synchronized Swimming 1995.

Table 42.2: Artistic Impression Scoring			
Criteria	Solo	Duet/trio	Team
Choreography, variety, creativity, pool coverage, patterns, transitions	50%	60	60
Music interpretation, use of music	20%	20	20
Manner of presentation	30%	20	20

Adapted from U.S. Synchronized Swimming 1995.

Time Requirements

Time requirements for senior free routines are three and a half minutes for a solo, four minutes for a duet or trio, and five minutes for a team. A variation of 15 seconds over or under the requirement is allowed. Time allowances are reduced for younger and less-skilled competitors; developmental routines have no minimum time. A maximum of 10 seconds is allowed for deck movements, known as "deck work." The timing begins and ends with the accompaniment and the timing of the deck work ends when the last competitor enters the water. The competitors must perform the routine without stopping, and the routine must end in the water.

PENALTIES

Penalties are rarely assessed, but they may be administered by the referee for rules infractions of the particular event, and for deviation from or omission of designated movements. Penalties begin at a half point and can reach a maximum of five points for swimming out of order in a routine or in figures. Following are examples of one-point penalties:

- failing to begin or finish with the accompaniment
- exceeding 10 seconds for deck movements
- exceeding the specified routine maximum or minimum time limits
- interrupting deck movements to begin again (unless of technical nature)
- not ending a routine in the water
- deliberately walking on the pool bottom or using the pool bottom to assist another swimmer (one point per infraction, up to two points possible)
- deliberately touching the pool deck (one point per infraction, up to two points possible)

COMPOSITE SCORE

When only two events are included in the competitive program, the figure *or* the technical rou-

tine score and the free routine score from the preliminary swim are added together to determine who will advance to the finals. The score for the preliminary free routine swim is dropped and replaced by the final free routine swim to determine the winners. The figures or technical routine are weighted 35 percent and the free routine is weighted 65 percent to determine the final score.

When three events (the figures, technical routine, and free routine) are included, the figures are weighted 25 percent, the technical routine 25 percent, and the free routine 50 percent to determine final placement.

Scoring systems for team trophies and for individual high point trophies are shown in tables 42.3 and 42.4.

Table 42.3: Team Trophy Scoring System			
Place	Team	Duet/trio	Solo
1st	16	10	9
2nd	12	8	7
3rd	10	6	6
4th	8	5	5
5th	6	4	4
6th	5	3	3
7th	3	2	2
8th	1	1	1

Adapted from U.S. Synchronized Swimming 1995.

Table 42.4: Individual High Point Scoring System			
Place	Team	Duet/trio	Solo
1st	5.0	5.5	9.0
2nd	4.0	4.5	7.0
3rd	3.0	4.0	6.0
4th	2.5	3.5	5.0
5th	2.0	3.0	4.0
6th	1.5	2.0	3.0
7th	1.0	1.5	2.0
8th	0.5	1.0	1.0

Adapted from U.S. Synchronized Swimming 1995.

COMPETITORS

Competitors may compete in the following classifications:

- senior (14 years old and older)
- junior (14 to 17)
- age groups (11 and under, 12-13, 14-15, 16-17, 18-19)

Competition is also conducted for designated skill levels such as novice and intermediate. Competition is divided geographically (local, regional, zone, and national) to provide progressive opportunities for swimmers to qualify for each succeeding level. The rules for championships conducted at the local level may have minor adjustments to meet the needs of the participants.

OFFICIALS

Up to nine judges score routines. A meet referee has full jurisdiction over the event.

ORGANIZATIONS

U.S. Synchronized Swimming
Pan American Plaza
201 S. Capitol, Ste. 510
Indianapolis, IN 46225
317-237-5700

43

Table Tennis

© Claus Andersen

Table tennis, originally known as ping-pong, was developed in England in the early 1900s. The sport is growing in popularity in the United States, but for decades the players from Asian and European countries have been most dominant.

The object of the game is to score points by hitting the ball across the net and onto the opponent's side of the table without the opponent being able to return the ball. Table tennis may be played in singles or doubles; the first side to score 21 points wins—unless the score is tied at 20. Then the side that gets ahead by 2 points wins. A match is the best two-of-three games or the best three-of-five. Doubles matches are always the best two-of-three. The rules for this chapter are from USA Table Tennis.

PROCEDURES

Before the first game, the winner of a coin toss chooses to serve or receive first, while his opponent chooses which end to play; or the winner may choose an end, while his opponent chooses to serve or receive first.

In doubles, the team that serves first decides which player will serve first; then the opponents choose which player will receive first. In subsequent games, the serving pair chooses who will serve first; the order of receiving for the receiving pair is opposite of what it was in the preceding game.

In singles, the server serves, the receiver returns, and the two continue to alternate hits until a point is scored. In doubles, the server serves, the receiver returns, the partner of the server returns, and the partner of the receiver returns. That sequence continues until a point is scored. In singles, after every five points, the server becomes the receiver, and the receiver becomes the server. In doubles, each player gets five serves at a time, in this repeating order:

- Player 1, Team A (serving to Player 1, Team B)
- Player 1, Team B (serving to Player 2, Team A)
- Player 2, Team A (serving to Player 2, Team B)
- Player 2, Team B (serving to Player 1, Team A)

Play is continuous, although a player may ask for a 2-minute break between games. The referee may stop play for up to 10 minutes for an incapacitated player if the delay does not disadvantage the opposing player or team. Brief pauses at the end of every five points may be taken to towel off or for similar purposes.

Players or teams *change ends* at the end of every game. In the final game, sides change ends when the first side scores 10. At this same point in a doubles match, the receiving team switches receiving order. The player or pair who served first in the preceding game receives first in the next game.

A ball is *in play* until it touches something other than the table, the net assembly, the racket, the racket hand below the wrist, or unless the ball is a *let* (a rally in which no point is scored). A let occurs when

- a serve touches the net or its supports and otherwise is a good serve,
- a serve is made before the receiving team is ready,
- a disturbance outside the receiver's control occurs,
- an error in the playing order or ends occurs, or
- a player changes rackets without notifying the umpire and opponent (the second time this occurs, the player is disqualified).

The *expedite system* is put into effect if a game exceeds 15 minutes, unless both sides have scored at least 19 points. In this system, the serve alternates after each point. If the receiver returns the serve and 12 successive returns, the receiver gains a point. If the receiver cannot make these returns, the server wins the point. Once the expedite system is put into play, it stays in effect for the rest of the match, with the sides alternating serves after every point.

Scoring

A player scores a point when the opponent

- fails to make a good serve,
- fails to make a good return,
- obstructs the ball,
- allows the ball to bounce twice in her court,
- strikes the ball twice in making one return,
- moves the table while the ball is in play,
- touches the playing surface, the net, or its supports while the ball is in play,
- strikes the ball out of sequence in doubles play, or
- fails to return the serve and 12 successive returns under the expedite system.

Serving

The server holds the ball on the open, flat palm of his free hand. The ball must be stationary, above the table, and behind the serving end line. The racket must also be above the table. The server tosses the ball up at least 6 inches, without spinning it. The server strikes the ball on the descent with the racket behind the serving end line, but not farther back than the part of the server's body that is farthest from the net. The ball must touch the server's court first, pass over or around the net, and touch the receiver's court.

In doubles, the served ball must hit on the server's right-hand court and then the receiver's right-hand court. If a player misses the ball while attempting to serve, he loses a point.

Returns

A return is good when it passes over or around the net or its supports and strikes the opponent's court. A return may touch the net or its supports, so long as it lands in the opponent's court. The ball may not bounce twice on the same side, or be hit twice on the same side, before its return.

TERMS

A **let** is a rally that is not scored.

Obstruction occurs when a player or a player's racket or clothing touches the ball in play when it has not passed over his court or over an imaginary extension of his end line and when it has not touched his court since last being struck by his opponent.

A **rally** describes the time during which the ball is in play.

The **receiver** is the player who will strike the ball second in a rally.

The **server** is the player who will strike the ball to begin the rally.

The **stroke counter** is the person who counts strokes under the expedite system.

PLAYING AREA

The *table* is 9 feet long and 5 feet wide (see figure 43.1). The playing surface is 30 inches above the floor. It is made of any material that produces a uniform bounce. Normally the surface is dark green, with a white line along each edge, forming two *side lines* and two *end lines*. For doubles,

a *center line* divides each court in half; the center line is regarded as part of each right-hand court. The *playing surface* includes the top edges of the table, but not the sides below the edge. The *net* is 6 feet long and 6 inches above the playing surface, along its complete length. The *minimum playing space* should be 40 feet long, 20 feet wide, and 11.5 feet high. The *floor* should be of hard, nonslippery wood.

PLAYERS

Players typically wear a *short-sleeved shirt*, shorts or skirt, socks and *soft-soled shoes*. Clothing may be of any color, but the main color must be different from that of the ball in use.

EQUIPMENT

The *ball* is spherical, weighs .1 ounce, and has a diameter of 1.5 inches. It is made of celluloid or similar plastic and can be white, yellow, or orange and matte. The *racket* can be of any size, shape, and weight. The blade must be continuous, of even thickness, flat, and rigid. At least 85 percent of the blade's thickness must consist of natural wood. The color of the blade must be uniformly dark and matte. The sides of the blade used to strike the ball are covered with rubber. The blade should be black on one side and bright red on the other.

OFFICIALS

If available, an *umpire* or *assistant umpire* makes calls during the match.

MODIFICATIONS

Wheelchair competition follows the rules listed elsewhere in this chapter, except for the following modifications:

The table must not have any physical barrier that might hinder the normal and legal movements of a wheelchair. If the receiver does not strike a serve, and the served ball bounces

PLAYING AREA

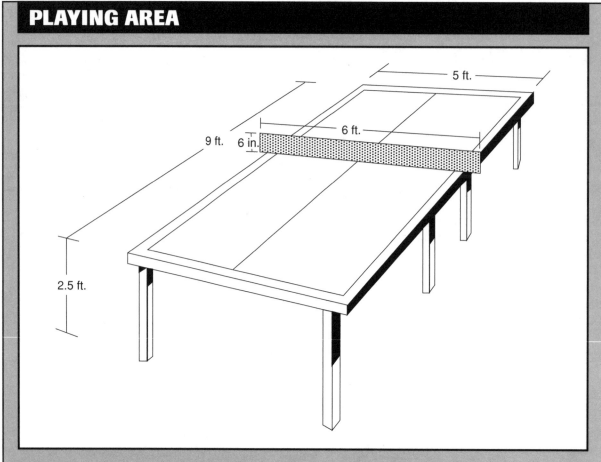

Figure 43.1. The features and dimensions of a table tennis table.
Adapted from USA Table Tennis 1990.

twice on the receiver's court, the serve is a let. Players classified as IA, IB, or IC may toss up the ball up with either hand, and they may touch the playing surface with their free hand while the ball is in play. However, they may not use their free hand for support while hitting the ball.

Competitors' feet may not touch the floor during play, and they may not rise noticeably off their cushions during play. Their cushions may be of any size. Wheelchairs are not required to have back support.

ORGANIZATIONS

USA Table Tennis
One Olympic Plaza
Colorado Springs, CO 80909
719-578-4583

44

Tae Kwon Do

© David Scudder

Tae kwon do originated in Korea and is one of the popular modern martial arts. *Tae* means "to strike with the foot;" *kwon* means "fist" or "to strike with the hand;" *do* means "the way of," or "art of." Thus, *tae kwon do* stands for "the art of kicking and punching."

Competitors use fast, spinning kicks to score points by connecting in legal scoring areas on their opponents. They use no weapons, only their bare hands and feet. The competitor who scores the most valid points wins. The source for rules for this chapter is the United States Taekwondo Union, which is the national governing body for the sport.

PROCEDURES

A contest consists of three rounds, lasting three minutes each, with one minute's rest in between, for both males and females. By prior agreement, rounds may be shortened to two minutes each. Only same-sex competitions are allowed.

Individuals compete in weight divisions and must weigh in one hour before the competition. Three minutes before a competition, the contestants are inspected to ensure that they have nothing in their uniforms that could harm the other contestant.

The contest begins with the referee's call of "shijak," which means "start." Each opponent then attempts to score points in legal scoring areas of his opponent's trunk and face, and to prevent his opponent from scoring (see "Scoring").

At the end of the contest, the competitors bow to each other and then turn and bow to the Head of Court. The referee then raises the hand of the winner.

The referee may suspend a contest for injury to one or both contestants. The injured may be treated for one minute. If a contestant does not demonstrate the will to continue after such an injury, then he or she is the loser, unless the injury was caused by a "gam-jeom" prohibited act (see "Prohibited Acts"). If the prohibited act was a "kyong-go" (one of less severity), then the winner is the one with the most points at the time the contest was suspended.

TERMS

The **alert area** is the area between the outer boundary line and the **contest area** (the inner part of the competition area measuring 8 meters square). The total competition area measures 12 meters on all sides.

A **gam-jeom** penalty is a deduction penalty. It is a more serious penalty than a kyong-go penalty. A contestant who commits a gam-jeom penalty has one point deducted.

Kalyeo means "break." The referee will call "kalyeo" to keep an attacker from a downed opponent.

Keuman means "stop." The referee calls this to end each round.

Keysok means "continue." The referee calls "keysok" when a downed contestant is ready to resume.

A **kyong-go** penalty is a warning penalty. It is less severe than a gam-jeom penalty. Two kyong-go penalties equal one deduction point.

The **permitted area** on a contestant, where attacks using permitted techniques may be delivered, are the trunk and the face.

Permitted techniques include using the fist and the foot to deliver blows.

Shijak means "start." The referee uses this term to begin a contest.

A **valid point** is scored when a permitted technique is scored to a legal scoring area on the trunk or face.

SCORING

A contestant may use the front parts of his forefinger and middle finger of his clenched fist to deliver a *fist technique*. He may deliver a *foot technique* by using his foot.

Legal scoring areas include the midsection of the trunk (the abdomen and both sides of the flank), and the front of the face. A contestant may attack an opponent's trunk with feet or hands but may attack the face only with feet. A contestant scores a point each time he accurately and powerfully delivers a permitted technique in a legal scoring area. Each scoring technique is worth one point. If a contestant knocks down her opponent by delivering an attack to the trunk protector, which covers the back, she earns a point. A point is not valid if, after delivering a legitimate technique, the contestant intentionally falls or commits an illegal act. A point is also not valid if the contestant used any prohibited act in delivering the attack.

PROHIBITED ACTS

There are two types of penalties for prohibited acts: kyong-go (a warning penalty) and gam-jeom (a one-point deduction penalty). Two kyong-go penalties result in a one-point deduction. If a contestant has three points deducted from his score, he loses the contest. If a contestant accumulates an odd number of kyong-go penalties, the last penalty does not result in any point deduction. Examples of each type of prohibited act follow.

Kyong-Go Penalty

Kyong-go penalties may be called for

- grabbing, pushing, or holding an opponent;
- intentionally crossing the alert line;
- evading an opponent by turning the back;
- intentionally falling down;
- feigning injury;
- attacking with the knee;
- intentionally attacking the groin;
- intentionally stomping or kicking the leg or foot;
- hitting the opponent's face with hands or fist;
- gesturing to indicate a scoring or deduction; and
- offensive language or misconduct.

Gam-Jeom Penalty

Gam-jeom penalties may be called for

- attacking a fallen opponent,
- intentionally attacking after the referee calls for a break,
- intentionally attacking the back of the head,
- severely attacking the opponent's face with hands or fists,
- butting,
- crossing the boundary line,
- throwing an opponent, and
- violent or extreme remarks or behavior.

KNOCKDOWNS

A *knockdown* occurs when any part of the body other than the sole of the foot touches the floor, due to an opponent's delivered technique. A contestant is also judged to be knocked down if she is staggering and unable to continue the match.

When a knockdown occurs, the referee calls for a break and counts from 1 to 10 at one-second intervals. If the downed contestant rises, the referee will count up to 8 and, if he believes the contestant is able to continue, he calls for the match to resume. If the contestant does not rise or does not appear able to continue by the count of 8, the referee will declare the opponent the victor.

DECISIONS

If the score is tied at the end of three rounds and one contestant has had more points deducted than the other, the contestant who was awarded the most total points wins. If the score is tied and the point deduction totals are also the same, the referee decides the winner, based on superiority and initiative shown. A contestant may register a win by

- knockout,
- referee stopping contest,
- score or superiority,
- withdrawal or disqualification, or
- referee's punitive declaration.

COMPETITION AREA

The competition area measures 12 meters square. It is covered with an elastic mat and may be on a platform raised 50 to 60 centimeters. The inner part of the competition area measuring 8 meters square is called the contest area; the surrounding area up to the boundary lines is called the alert area. See figure 44.1.

COMPETITORS

Each competitor wears a *uniform* with protective gear, including a *trunk protector, head protector, groin guard,* and *forearm* and *shin guards.* Women

COMPETITION AREA

Figure 44.1. The dimensions and components of a tae kwon do competition area.
Adapted from International Judo Federation 1997.

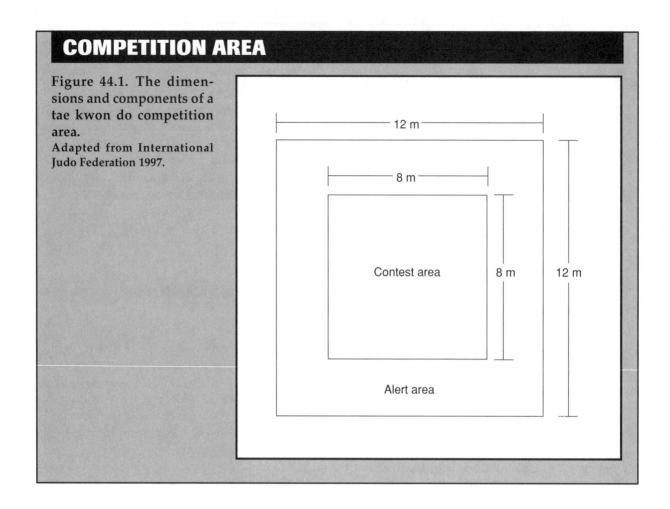

Table 44.1:   Weight Divisions

Category	Men (kg)	Women (kg)
Fin	Up to 50	Up to 43
Fly	Over 50, up to 54	Over 43, up to 47
Bantam	Over 54, up to 58	Over 47, up to 51
Feather	Over 58, up to 64	Over 51, up to 55
Light	Over 65, up to 70	Over 55, up to 60
Welter	Over 70, up to 76	Over 60, up to 65
Middle	Over 76, up to 83	Over 65, up to 70
Heavy	Over 83	Over 70

Adapted from U.S. Taekwondo Union 1993.

also wear *breast guards.* Weight divisions are shown in table 44.1.

OFFICIALS

The *referee* controls the match. *Judges* mark valid points scored by contestants. The *head of court* has overall control of the competition area and confirms the match decision. A *recorder* times the match and records the points scored.

ORGANIZATIONS

Pan American Taekwondo Union
202 Broadway, 2nd Fl.
Lawrence, MA 01840
508-683-3499

United States Taekwondo Union
U.S. Olympic Training Center
One Olympic Plaza, Suite 405
Colorado Springs, CO 80909

Team Handball

Team handball originated in Europe in the 1920s and was introduced to the United States in the late 1920s and early 1930s. The United States formed a team for the 1936 Olympics, at which team handball was a demonstration sport. Interest lagged in the United States until the late 1950s, when the United States Team Handball Federation was formed from a group of clubs in New York and New Jersey. Team handball became an official Olympic sport for men in 1972; women's competition was added in 1976. The sport is now played in 138 nations, with more than 8 million players affiliated with the International Handball Federation. That federation is the source for rules in this chapter.

Team handball is a fast-moving, exciting game that combines running, jumping, catching, and throwing. Elements of soccer, basketball, water polo, and hockey can be seen as players attempt to maneuver past opponents and throw the ball past the goalkeeper and into the goal to score.

PROCEDURES

Seven players per side may be on the court at once. A game consists of two 30-minute halves, with a 10-minute intermission. The clock normally runs continuously but is on occasion stopped (see "When Time Stands Still"). Teams change ends to begin the second half.

When Time Stands Still

The playing clock is always stopped when a referee disqualifies or excludes a player or calls a referee-throw (see "Throws"). Each team also may use a one-minute timeout per half. The clock may also be stopped for

- extraordinary incidents (spectators or objects on the court, goal damaged, and so on),
- consultations between the referees and the timekeeper or scorekeeper,
- injuries,
- delays in executing a formal throw,
- warnings or suspensions,
- goalkeeper substitutions during a 7-meter throw, and
- a player's not giving up the ball or throwing it away.

A coin toss determines which team first gets possession of the ball. The game begins with a *throw-off* at center court. All players must be on their own half of the court when the throw is made, with the opponents at least 3 meters from the thrower. The throw-off to begin the second half is taken by the team that defended the first throw-off.

Advancing the Ball

Players may throw, catch, stop, push, or hit the ball, using their open or closed hands, arms, head, torso, thighs, and knees. A player may hold a ball for a maximum of three seconds. A player may

- take a maximum of three steps with the ball;
- bounce the ball once and catch it while standing or running; and

- dribble the ball and then catch it or roll it on the court and then pick it up.

If a player is holding the ball, she must dribble, pass, or shoot it within three seconds or after taking three steps. She may dribble it continuously an unlimited number of times, but once she has picked up her dribble she may not begin dribbling again unless another player touches the ball. She may take three steps, and then dribble, and then take three more steps; at this point she must pass or shoot the ball within three seconds. Offensive players are not allowed to

- touch the ball with any part of the body below the knee (unless the ball has been thrown at the player by an opponent);
- dive for the ball (except for the goalkeeper);
- play the ball intentionally out of bounds (except for the goalkeeper, in blocking a shot); or
- "stall" without trying to score; this is "passive play" and the defensive team is awarded a free-throw at the point where the ball was when play was interrupted.

Approaching an Opponent

A player may use his arms and hands to try to gain possession of the ball, and he may use his torso to obstruct an opponent either with or without the ball. But he may not

- obstruct an opponent by using his arms, hands, or legs;
- pull or hit the ball with one or both hands out of the hands of an opponent;
- use his fist to hit the ball from an opponent;
- endanger an opponent with the ball, or endanger the goalkeeper; or
- hold, trip, run into, hit, or jump onto an opponent.

Less serious infractions merit first a warning and then a suspension (in which the offending player sits out two minutes). More serious infractions result in disqualification.

Scoring

A team scores a goal when the entire ball crosses the entire width of the goal line and enters the goal, and the scoring team has not committed an

Goalkeeper Rules

The goalkeeper may

- touch the ball with any part of her body while inside the goal area;
- move with the ball inside the goal area, with no restrictions;
- leave the goal area without the ball, at which time she becomes subject to the rules applying to all players in the playing area; and
- leave the goal area with the ball and play it in the playing area, if she has not been able to control it.

A goalkeeper may not

- endanger an opponent;
- intentionally play the ball out over the goal line, after gaining control of the ball;
- leave the goal area while in control of the ball;
- touch the ball outside the goal area after making a goalkeeper throw, unless another player has since touched the ball;
- touch the ball in contact with the floor outside the goal area when he is inside the goal area;
- pick up the ball outside the goal area and bring it inside the goal area;
- touch the ball with any part of his body below his knee, if he's not in the act of defending goal; or
- cross the 4-meter line before the thrower has thrown the ball in taking a 7-meter throw.

infraction on the play. If the game is tied at the end of regulation and a winner must be determined, teams play an overtime period: two halves of five minutes each. A coin toss determines who throws in.

If the score is still tied at the end of the first overtime, the teams play a second overtime period. If a tie exists at the end of the second overtime period, a penalty shoot-out occurs. Each team selects five shooters who alternate shooting from the penalty line. If a tie still exists at the end of each team's five penalty shots, individual penalty shots continue until a winner is determined.

TERMS

The **seven-meter line** is one meter long. It is directly in front of the goal, seven meters away from the rear edge of the goal line.

A **seven-meter throw** is awarded in various situations (see "Throws") and is taken by a player who may not step on or beyond the seven-meter line before he throws the ball.

The **center line** runs the width of the court, dividing the court into equal halves.

A **free-throw** is awarded for goalkeeper infractions and other violations (see "Throws"); the player taking the free-throw takes it from the point of infraction or from the nearest point outside the nine-meter, or free-throw, line, if the violation occurred between the nine-meter line and the goal-area line.

The **free-throw line** is also known as the nine-meter line. It is a broken, nearly semicircular line, drawn three meters from, and parallel to, the goal-area line.

The **goal area** is defined by the goal-area line, which is drawn six meters in front of the goal line. The line is a semicircle, with each end touching the goal line on either side of the goal.

The **goalkeeper's restraining line** is also known as the four-meter line. It is four meters from the rear edge of the goal line, directly in front of the goal.

A **goalkeeper's throw** is awarded to the goalkeeper when the ball crosses the outer goal line. The goalkeeper must throw the ball from the goal area and beyond the goal-area line.

A **referee-throw** is taken at the center of the court. The referee throws the ball vertically between two players from the opposing teams. For situations in which such a throw occurs, see "Throws."

A **throw-in** is taken to put the ball back into play after it has gone out of bounds. It is taken where the ball went out of bounds, or, if it crossed the outer goal line, from the intersection of the goal line and the sideline nearest where it went out of bounds.

A **throw-off** is used to begin each half and to resume play after a team has scored a goal. Each team must be on its own side during a throw-off, which takes place at center court.

THROWS

The following throws may be made during a game.

Throw-Off

When: To begin a half and to resume play after a goal.

Where: From center court.

How: Each team is on its own side of the court. Opponents must be at least three meters from the thrower. The referee whistles; the thrower has three seconds to throw.

Throw-In

When: The ball has gone out of bounds.

Where: From where it went out, or from the intersection of the goal line and side line, if it went out over the outer portion of the goal line.

How: The referee doesn't whistle; a player on the team awarded the ball throws the ball in with one foot on the side line until the ball leaves his hand. He may not play the ball in to himself. Opponents must stand at least three meters away, though they may stand outside their goal line, even if it's less than three meters away.

Goalkeeper's Throw

When: The ball crosses the outer goal line.

Where: From the goal area.

How: The goalkeeper throws the ball over the goal-area line; the referee does not whistle. The goalkeeper may not touch the ball again until another player has touched it.

Free-Throw

When: For numerous violations, including goalkeeper infractions, court player infractions in the goal area, infractions when playing the ball, pas-

sive play, and infractions connected with other throws.

Where: Either where the infraction occurred, or, if the violation occurred between the nine-meter line and the goal-area line, then from the nearest point immediately outside the nine-meter line.

How: Without a whistle, the player takes the throw with opponents at least three meters away. Teammates may not be on the nine-meter line or between it and the goal line before the player takes the throw.

Seven-Meter Throw

When: A clear chance of scoring is destroyed by a defensive player's illegal action or a referee's inadvertant whistle, a goalkeeper enters his goal area with the ball, a court player enters his own goal area while playing defense, a player plays the ball to his goalkeeper in the goal area.

Where: At the seven-meter line.

How: A referee blows her whistle, and the player has three seconds to take a shot on goal from behind the seven-meter line. The player must not touch on or beyond the line before the ball leaves her hand. Just the goalkeeper and the thrower are initially involved; the ball is not played again until it has touched the goalkeeper or goal. All other players must be beyond the nine-meter line or three meters or farther away from the player when she takes the throw. The throw is retaken if a defensive player violates this positioning (unless the player scored a goal); the player may also throw again if the goalkeeper moves beyond the four-meter line before she releases the ball.

Referee-Throw

When: Simultaneous infractions by members of both teams, the ball touches a fixture or the ceiling above the court, the game is interrupted and no team possesses the ball at the time.

Where: Center of the court.

How: The referee throws the ball straight up between a player from each team. Other players must be at least three meters away. Players may play the ball only after it has reached its peak.

PENALTIES

A referee may warn, suspend, disqualify, or exclude a player. *Warnings* result from less serious infractions, such as were noted in "Approaching an Opponent" (page 296). They also may result from violations occurring when a player is executing a formal throw and from unsportsmanlike conduct. The referee indicates a warning by holding up a yellow card.

Suspensions occur for repeated infractions, for faulty substitutions, and for failure to put the ball on the floor when the referee makes a decision. Suspensions last two minutes and are indicated by the referee's holding up her hand with two fingers extended. The team may not replace the player during the suspension.

Disqualifications occur when a player not entitled to participate enters the court; there are serious infractions and repeated events of unsportsmanlike conduct; and when a player receives his third suspension. The team may not replace the disqualified player for two minutes. A referee indicates a disqualification by holding up a red card.

Exclusions result from an assault either on or outside the court, against another player, a referee, any other official, or anyone in the area. Spitting is regarded as assault. The referee indicates an exclusion by crossing his arms in front of his face. The team may not replace the excluded player, although if the excluded player is a goalkeeper, another player may assume goalkeeper duties. But the team will play the remainder of the game short one player.

COURT

The court is 40 meters long and 20 meters wide (see figure 45.1). It has two goal areas and a playing area. The lines marking the boundaries on the sides of the field are called sidelines; the shorter boundary lines are called goal lines for the portion between the goal posts, and outer goal lines for the portions on either side of the goal.

Each goal is netted and is 3 meters wide and 2 meters high. The goal area is marked by a goal area line that fans in a semicircle 6 meters away from the goal line. The free-throw line, or 9-meter

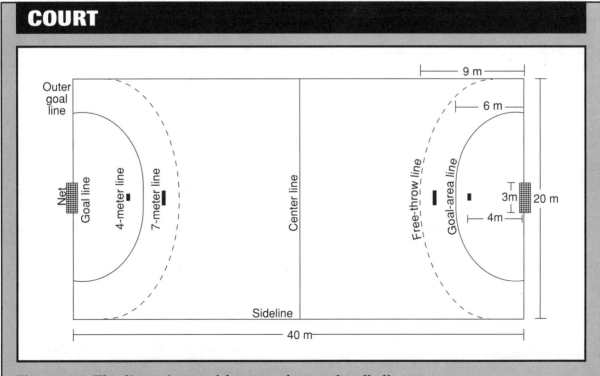

Figure 45.1. The dimensions and features of a team handball court.
Adapted from International Handball Federation 1993.

Goal Area Rules

Only the goalkeeper may be in the goal area. A court player may not play the ball when it is stationary or rolling in the goal area. However, a court player may play the ball when it is in the air above the goal area if she is not in the goal area herself. A free throw is awarded to the opposing team when a court player enters the goal area in possession of the ball; a free throw is also awarded when a court player enters the goal area without the ball but gains an advantage in doing so.

A seven-meter throw is given when a defending court player enters the goal area and gains an advantage over a player with the ball. No throw is awarded if a player enters the goal area without the ball and gains no advantage. If a defending player intentionally plays the ball into his own goal area and the goalkeeper touches it, the opponents are awarded a seven-meter throw. If the goalkeeper doesn't touch it and the ball stops in the goal area or goes out of bounds, the opponents are awarded a free-throw.

line, is a broken line fanning in a semicircle 9 meters from the goal line. The 7-meter line is 1 meter long. It is parallel to, and 7 meters from, the rear edge of the goal line, and directly in front of the goal. The goalkeeper's restraining line (the 4-meter line) is 15 centimeters long and 4 meters from the rear edge of the goal line, directly in front of the goal. The center line runs the width of the court at midcourt, dividing the court into equal halves.

PLAYERS

A team consists of 12 players, 7 of whom may be on the field at one time. A team must have at least 5 players to begin a game, but the game may continue if a team is later reduced to fewer than 5 players on the court. Each team must use a goalkeeper at all times.

Substitutes may enter the game at any time and for an unlimited number of times. They don't need to notify the timekeeper, but the players they are replacing must be off the field before they enter. Substitutes must enter a game at the substitute line, which is near midcourt. A faulty substitution results in a two-minute suspension for the offending player and a free-throw for the opponents. The goalkeeper wears colors distinct from all other players on the court.

Teams use different offensive sets and have different names for positions, but one basic offensive set is to have three players—left backcourt, center, and right backcourt—just beyond the free-throw line, and three others—left wing, circle runner, and right wing—between the free-throw line and the goal-area line. *Wing players* tend to be smaller and quicker players who can shoot from difficult angles. *Circle runners,* who are often directly in front of the goal, are larger and aggressive and can set picks and screens for the backcourt players. *Centers* are like quarterbacks, directing the offense. The other *backcourt players* tend to be taller, with the ability to jump and shoot over the defense from the backcourt.

EQUIPMENT

The *ball* is spherical, made of leather or synthetic material, has an inflated rubber bladder, and has the following dimensions:

Men's—58 to 60 centimeters in circumference, weighing 425 to 475 grams

Women's—54 to 56 centimeters in circumference, weighing 325 to 400 grams

OFFICIALS

Two *referees,* with equal authority, are in charge of the game. A *timekeeper* and a *scorekeeper* assist the referees.

ORGANIZATIONS

United States Team Handball Federation
One Olympic Plaza
Colorado Springs, CO 80909
719-578-4582

46

Tennis

© Claus Andersen

Tennis's roots trace back to 13th-century France, where players hit a ball over a net with their hands. The game was brought to Wales, where it evolved into lawn tennis, with players using rackets. The game became popular in 19th-century England; the first Wimbledon championships were held in 1877.

Tennis also was introduced in America in the 19th century but didn't catch on as a major sport, either professionally or recreationally, until the 1960s. The object in tennis is to hit the ball over the net into the opponent's court either out of the opponent's reach or so that the opponent is unable to return the ball. This is how players score points, which lead to winning *games*, *sets*, and *matches*. The source for rules in this chapter is the United States Tennis Association.

PROCEDURES

A coin toss decides who serves and which player (or doubles team) begins at which end of the court. The player who delivers the ball is called the server; the player receiving the serve is called the receiver. Doubles play is addressed on pages 303-304.

Players alternate serves: Player A serves the first game, Player B the second, and so on. They also alternate the sides of the court they serve from, beginning each game on the right side. The serve is made into the service court diagonally opposite the side the server is standing on. Players switch ends of the court at the end of the first, third, fifth, and subsequent alternate games.

Play is continuous; the receiver must play to the reasonable pace of the server and must be ready to receive serve when the server is ready to serve. When changing ends, a maximum of 1 minute, 30 seconds may elapse from the time the ball went out of play to end the previous game to the time the first serve begins the next game.

Each game begins at 0-0, or *love*. The first point scored is *15*, the second is *30*, the third is *40*, and the fourth is *game point*. Game point wins the game unless the score is a *deuce* (40-40). If the server scores in deuce, she gains the *advantage*, or *ad*; if she scores the next point, she wins. If her opponent scores the next point, it is again deuce. A player must win by two points. When the server has the advantage, it is called *ad-in*; when the receiver has the advantage, it is called *ad-out*.

The first player or side to win six games and lead by two games wins the set. A match is composed of the best two-of-three sets or the best three-of-five.

If a set is 6-6, a *tiebreaker* is often used to determine the winner. Players play 12 points; the first player to reach at least 7 points, who is ahead by 2 points, wins the tiebreaker and the set. If the score is 6-6 after 12 points, the players change ends and resume play until one is ahead by 2 points.

In a tiebreaker, the player whose turn it is to serve serves first. His opponent serves the next two serves. It continues with each player serving twice until the set has been decided. Players change ends every 6 points. An alternative to using a tiebreaker is to continue the set until one player has a two-game lead; which system is used is up to the tournament officials. The points that decide the result of a game, set, or match are called game point, set point, and match point, respectively.

The server's score is always given first.

Serving

The server must stand with both her feet behind the *baseline* (see the court diagram on page 304) and within the imaginary continuations of the *center line* and *sideline*. When the receiver is ready, the server tosses the ball in the air and hits it with her racket before it hits the ground. The ball must pass over the net and hit within the receiver's proper service court.

If the ball strikes the net and lands inside the proper service court, the play is called a *let* and does not count. A let may also be called for an interruption of play. A *service fault* occurs when the server swings and misses, or hits the ball into the net, or hits the ball outside the opponent's proper service court.

A *foot fault* occurs when the server steps on or over the baseline, or over the imaginary extensions of the center line or sideline, while serving. Once the racket strikes the ball, the server may step on or over the baseline, center line, or sideline.

A server is allowed one fault (either service or foot). The player serves from behind the same half of the court on the second serve. If the player faults on his second serve, this is called a *double fault* and he loses a point.

Scoring

The server scores a point if he hits an *ace* (a serve that the receiver cannot return), or if his serve hits his opponent. The receiver scores a point if the server double-faults. A player loses a point if she

- cannot return a ball before it bounces twice on her side,
- returns the ball out of bounds,
- hits the ball into the net,

- carries or catches the ball on her racket or deliberately touches the ball with her racket more than once,
- touches the net or posts,
- hits the ball by throwing her racket, or
- hits the ball before it has crossed the net.

Returning Serve and Playing

The receiver must return the serve on the first bounce, hitting it over the net and into his opponent's court. A ball striking a boundary line is in play. During a *rally*, or series of hits by the players, the ball may hit the net if the ball crosses and lands in bounds in the opponent's court. A let occurs only during the serve.

After the serve is returned, players may *volley* by hitting the ball before it bounces on their side or use *ground strokes* to return the ball after one bounce. A player's racket may cross over the net after she has returned the ball.

If a player intentionally hinders an opponent from making a stroke, the hindered player receives a point. If the action is unintentional, the point is replayed.

TERMS

An **ace** (one point) is scored by a server whose good serve is not touched.

A server commits a **fault** when she hits the ball into the net or outside her opponent's court (service fault) or when she steps on or over the baseline before she hits her serve.

A **game** is won by the first player to score four points and be ahead by two.

Game point is the point that can decide the game.

Hindrance may be called when a player is hindered by either his opponent or a spectator. Depending on the situation, hindrance results in a let, playover, or a point awarded to the player hindered.

A **let** occurs on a serve, when the ball strikes the net and lands in the opponent's proper service court, or when play is interrupted. A let requires that the point be replayed.

A **match** is won by the player who wins the best two-of-three or three-of-five sets.

Match point is the point that can decide the match.

A **rally** is a series of hits between players.

The **serve** is the play that begins each point.

A **set** is won by the player who wins six games and is ahead by two games, or who wins a tiebreaker.

Set point is the point that can decide the set.

A **volley** is a hit before the ball strikes the ground.

COURT

A *court* is 78 feet long by 27 feet wide for singles play or 36 feet wide for doubles play (see figure 46.1). It is divided in half by a *net*, made of cord, 36 inches high in the center and 42 inches high at the two supporting sideposts. Service lines are parallel to and 21 feet from the net. They are 18 feet in front of the baselines, which are also parallel to the net and mark the outer boundary of each side of the court.

A center service line, parallel to the sideline, intersects the net and divides the service courts into two sections on both sides of the net. The center service line connects the two service lines. There are two service courts on each side of the net, covering the area between the net and service line and the center service line and the sideline. Each service court is 21 feet long by 13.5 feet wide. This area is also called the *fore court*.

The *back court* is the area between the service line and the baseline. It is 18 feet long by 27 feet wide for singles play or 36 feet wide for doubles play. The court surface is clay, grass, or a composition.

PLAYERS

Tennis is played in singles matches (two players) or doubles matches (four players). The following rules apply to doubles matches:

- Doubles use the widest portion of the court (36 feet).

COURT

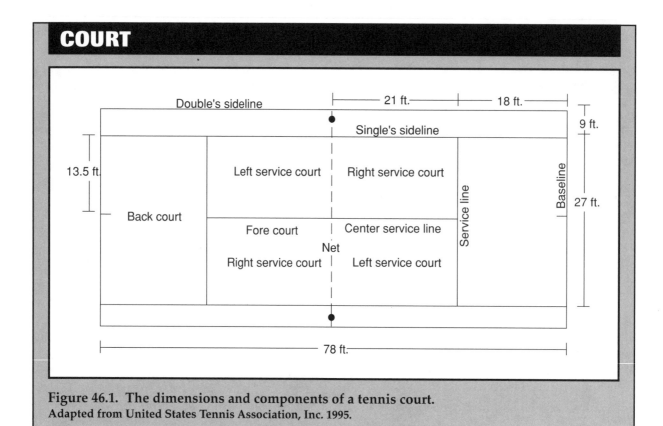

Figure 46.1. The dimensions and components of a tennis court.
Adapted from United States Tennis Association, Inc. 1995.

- For serving, the same size service courts are used as in singles.
- Teams alternate serves after each game, as in singles play; Team A serves the first game, Team B the second, and so on.
- Each team's players alternate serving complete games. Player 1 on Team A would serve game 1; Player 2 on Team A would serve game 3, and so on.
- Players also alternate receiving serves.
- If a player is discovered to have served out of turn, his partner will serve the next point, but all prior points count. If a game is completed before the error is discovered, the play stands as is and the order of service remains as altered.
- If a team is discovered to have changed its receiving order, this order will remain until the end of the game, at which time the team will resume its normal receiving order.
- Doubles partners do not have to alternate hits.
- If both partners hit a ball, either simultaneously or consecutively, it is an illegal hit.

However, if one partner's racket touches the other partner's racket but does not hit the ball, this is legal.

EQUIPMENT

The *ball* is hollow rubber, either white or yellow. It is between 2.5 and 2.63 inches in diameter and weighs between 2 and 2.1 ounces.

The *racket* may be up to 32 inches long and 12.5 inches wide. The strung surface, a pattern of crossed strings, may not be more than 15.5 inches long and 11.5 inches wide. Rackets are made of various materials; they may be of any weight.

OFFICIALS

Matches are typically officiated by an *umpire,* whose decision is final; by *net-cord judges,* who place their fingers on the net to detect lets on serves; by *linesmen,* who make boundary decisions; and by *foot-fault judges,* who call foot faults.

However, in many tournaments where umpires and linesmen are not available, players call their own lines.

MODIFICATIONS

Wheelchair tennis is played the same as regular tennis, except that wheelchair players are allowed two bounces of the ball. The first bounce must be within the court, but the second bounce may be outside the court boundaries and still be in play.

The server may not roll or spin his chair while serving nor have any wheel touching on or beyond the baseline or imaginary extensions of the center line and sideline. A server may not use any part of his lower extremities to brake or stabilize himself while serving. Doing so results in a fault.

If a player is physically unable to serve in a conventional manner, another person may drop the ball to begin the player's serve. The wheelchair is considered part of the body. As such, if the ball touches a chair, that player loses a point. A player also loses a point if

- she hits her own partner with a ball;
- she uses any part of her feet or lower extremities to brake or stabilize while serving, stroking a ball, turning, or stopping; and if

- she fails to keep one buttock in contact with her chair while hitting a ball.

ORGANIZATIONS

American Tennis Association
P.O. Box 3277
Silver Spring, MD 20918-9998
202-291-9893

Peter Burwash International Special Tennis Programs
2203 Timberloch Pl., Ste. 126
The Woodlands, TX 77380
713-363-4707

United States Professional Tennis Association
1 USPTA Centre
3535 Briarpark Dr.
Houston, TX 77042
713-97-USPTA

United States Recreational Tennis Association
3112 Adderley Ct.
Silver Spring, MD 20906
301-598-4820

United States Tennis Association
1212 Avenue of the Americas
New York, NY 10036
914-696-7000

47

Track & Field

© Claus Andersen

Competition in track and field events dates back to the 7th century B.C. Modern track and field (or "athletics," as it is known internationally) sprang from university events in England in the 19th century. Today it is popular worldwide and is one of the headline sports at the Olympic Games.

The object in track and field is to run faster, jump higher or longer, and throw farther than your opponents. In some competitions, team scores are kept; others are geared to individual (non-team) competition.

The source for the rules in this chapter is USA Track & Field, the national governing body for the sport. The rules pertain to the senior classification (16 years old and older). The sport is modified widely for groups of various ages and abilities; toward the end of the chapter some of these modifications are highlighted.

PROCEDURES

USA Track & Field championships include the events shown in tables 47.1 and 47.2. Outdoor competition takes place on and around a 400-meter oval track (see figure 47.1). A track has six to nine *lanes*, measuring between 1.22 meters and 1.25 meters in width. The surface is usually a synthetic composition.

Running events take place on the track; field events take place on the field inside the track, or in a field away from the track. Indoor tracks vary in size; many are 200 meters in length. They usually have banked turns and a board surface.

RUNNING EVENTS

A runner's left hand is always toward the inside of the track; races are run counterclockwise. Many meets have *heats*, or qualifying rounds, through which runners must advance to get to the *finals*. Runners are randomly assigned lanes in the first round; after that, their performance determines in which lane they will run.

Sprinters (competitors in races of 400 meters or less) run in their same lane the whole race. In the 200-meter and 400-meter events, where sprinters must race around curves, the starting

Table 47.1: Championship Track Events				
Event	Indoor	Outdoor	Men	Women
60-meter dash	x		x	x
100-meter dash		x	x	x
200-meter dash	x	x	x	x
400-meter dash	x	x	x	x
800-meter run	x	x	x	x
1,500-meter run		x	x	x
1-mile run	x		x	x
3,000-meter run	x		x	x
3,000-meter walk	x			x
3,000-meter steeplechase		x	x	x
5,000-meter run		x	x	x
5,000-meter walk	x		x	
10,000-meter run		x	x	x
10,000-meter walk		x		x
20,000-meter walk		x	x	
60-meter hurdles	x		x	x
100-meter hurdles		x		x
110-meter hurdles		x	x	
400-meter hurdles		x	x	x
400-meter relay		x		x
800-meter relay		x		x
1,600-meter relay	x		x	x
1,600-meter relay		x		x
3,200-meter relay	x		x	
3,200-meter relay		x		x

Adapted from USA Track & Field 1995.

Event	Indoor	Outdoor	Men	Women
High jump	X	X	X	X
Pole vault		X	X	X
Pole vault	X		X	
Long jump	X	X	X	X
Triple jump	X	X	X	X
Shot put	X	X	X	X
Discus throw		X	X	X
Javelin throw		X	X	X
Hammer throw		X	X	X
Weight throw	X		X	X

Table 47.2: Championship Field Events

Adapted from USA Track & Field 1995.

COMPETITION AREA

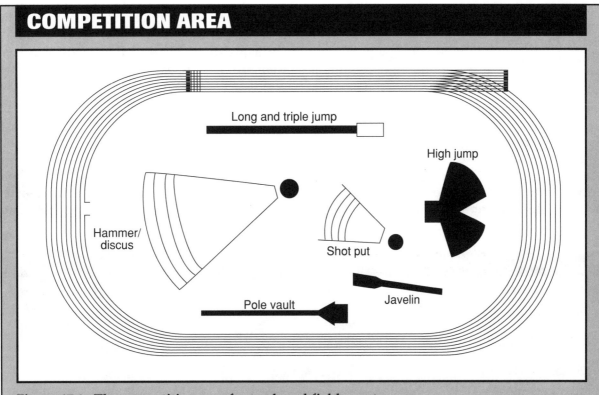

Figure 47.1. The competition area for track and field events.
Adapted from Athletic Congress's Development Committees with Gambetta 1981.

places are staggered so that each runner runs the same distance.

In 800-meter events, runners run in lanes until after the first turn, when they can cut to the inside lane. Races beyond 800 meters are not run in lanes.

The Start

All competitors must be completely behind the starting line, with no part of their bodies touching it or extending beyond it. For races of 400 meters or less, the commands are "on your marks" and "set." When all competitors are set, the starter fires a starting pistol. For races beyond 400 meters, the command is "on your marks," and when runners are ready, the gun is fired. All competitors must immediately follow the commands; delaying in getting set, or resetting once a runner is set, will result in a *false start*.

A runner is allowed two false starts. No false start may be assessed generally to the field; each one must be charged to an individual. In the event a race has to be recalled because of a false start, the starter fires his pistol again. In races where *starting blocks* are used (up to and including the 400-meter), false-start detection apparatus may be hooked up to the blocks.

The Race

Any runner who jostles or impedes another runner may be disqualified. In races run entirely in lanes, competitors must stay in their lanes or be disqualified. In races begun in lanes, runners must remain in their lanes until the break-line mark. A runner who leaves the track (crossing over the inside boundary line of the first lane without being pushed off) is out of the race. An exception to this rule is in races of 20,000 meters, in which a runner may temporarily leave the track if in returning he doesn't shorten his distance. After entering the straightaway of a race with two or more turns, runners are to run in a straight line to the finish, except to avoid other runners.

The Finish

A runner officially ends her race when her torso reaches the finish line. The head, neck, arms, hand, legs, and feet do not count. In case of a tie, one of three things may happen:

- Both runners advance to the next round, if practical.
- If not, the two runners compete again, if practical.
- If not, lots are drawn to determine who advances to the next round.

In a first-place tie, if it's practical, the runners compete again; if not, the tie stands.

Hurdles

Hurdles races are run entirely in lanes. A runner must clear the hurdle with both legs. She is disqualified if her trailing leg dips lower than the height of the hurdle, if she runs around a hurdle, or if she intentionally knocks over a hurdle. Hurdlers are not disqualified, however, for unintentionally knocking over hurdles.

The top bar of the hurdle is made of wood or plastic. The hurdle is durable enough that it is not easily broken by a competitor hitting it. Heights of hurdles and distances between hurdles are shown in table 47.3.

Table 47.3: Hurdle Specifications, Senior Competition			
Hurdle event	Number of hurdles	Height of hurdles (in)	Distance between hurdles (m)
Women's 60-meter	5	33	8.5
Men's 60-meter	5	42	9.14
Women's 100-meter	10	33	8.5
Men's 110-meter	10	42	9.14
Women's 400-meter	10	30	35.0
Men's 400-meter	10	36	35.0

Adapted from USA Track & Field 1995.

Steeplechase

The 3,000-meter steeplechase has 28 hurdle jumps and 7 water jumps (5 jumps per lap, with the water jump as the fourth jump). Runners run the first 200 meters without taking a hurdle; from there on they take 5 hurdles per lap.

The 2,000-meter steeplechase, run in some women's and junior events, has 18 hurdle jumps and 5 water jumps. The height of the men's hurdles is 36 inches; women's hurdles are 30 inches. The hurdles are 13 feet wide and the bar on top of each hurdle is 5 inches square.

The water jump is 12 feet long. The water is 27.5 inches deep at the beginning of the jump, nearest the hurdle; it slopes to the level of the field at the end of the jump.

A runner is disqualified if he doesn't fully take a hurdle. He may not trail a leg or foot lower than the horizontal plane of the top of the hurdle. Runners may clear a hurdle by jumping over it without touching it or by placing a foot on the hurdle and vaulting over it.

Relays

A relay race is made up of teams of four runners each. Each runner runs a set distance before passing a *baton* to a teammate. A baton is a hollow tube, usually made of metal, not longer than 30 centimeters and weighing no less than 50 grams.

The baton handoff must take place in a 20-meter *take-over zone*, with the starting line in the middle of this zone. If the handoff occurs outside of this zone, the team is disqualified. It is the baton's position, and not that of the runners, that determines whether the handoff was legal or not.

For races where lanes cease to be used, waiting runners move to an inside position to receive the handoff as their incoming teammates arrive. After handing off, runners who have finished their leg must remain in their lane to avoid interfering with other runners.

In outdoor relays up to and including the 4 × 200 meters and the 800-meter medley, runners about to receive handoffs may begin running not

more than 10 meters outside the take-over zone. In indoor relays, such a "fly zone" is not used.

In the 4 × 200 meters relay, the first and second legs and part of the third are run in lanes. In the 4 × 400 meters relay, the first leg and part of the second are run in lanes.

JUMPING EVENTS

Jumping events include

- the *high jump,* where competitors attempt to jump over a crossbar;
- the *pole vault,* where competitors use a flexible pole in attempting to vault over a crossbar;
- the *long jump,* where competitors sprint to a take-off board and attempt to leap the farthest into a sand pit; and
- the *triple jump,* where competitors sprint to a take-off board and take a hop, step, and jump into a sand pit.

High Jump

The *apron* surrounding the high jump pit is a 15-meter semicircle. In championship events, a 20-meter *runway* is suggested. The high jump *standards* (the uprights and posts) are rigid. The *crossbar* may be wood, metal, or another approved material; its cross-section is circular and it may be up to three centimeters in diameter. The bar may sag a maximum of two centimeters.

The *landing pit* of cushioned foam rubber is 5 meters long by 4 meters wide. The height of a jump is measured from the ground to the lowest portion of the crossbar. Jumpers may use one or two markers to assist in their runup and takeoff.

Procedure

Jumpers compete in the order drawn. A competitor may choose to pass at any height, but he may not later attempt a jump at that height, except in a jump-off to break a first-place tie.

When more than two or three jumpers are still in the competition, each has about one and a half minutes to take her jump. When only two or three competitors remain, each jumper may take up to three minutes.

If the jumper knocks the bar off the standards, or if she touches an area beyond the uprights before going over the bar, the jump is a failure. Three consecutive missed jumps at any height and the competitor is finished. A jumper may fail at one height and then pass on his next turn, waiting for the next height. See figure 47.2.

At the end of each round the bar is raised at least 2 centimeters. Rounds continue until only one competitor remains in the competition. That jumper may attempt greater heights. If two jumpers are tied, the jumper with the fewest attempts at the winning height wins. If the jumpers are still tied, the competitor with the fewest overall misses wins.

Pole Vault

The suggested runway for the pole vault is 40 to 45 meters. The *take-off box*, where the vaulter plants his pole after his run-up, is about 24 inches wide by 39 inches long, sinking into the ground in front of the standard's uprights, which are rigid. The crossbar is similar to that for the high jump but slightly heavier.

The landing area is cushioned foam rubber, 5 meters square. The *pole* may be of any material, length, and diameter, but its basic surface must be smooth. A vaulter may use one or two layers of adhesive tape on the pole, and can use resin or an adhesive substance on his hands for a better grip. A vaulter may use one or two markers alongside the runway to assist in his run-up and may have the standards moved back toward the landing area by up to 31.5 inches. As with the high jump, the measurement is from the ground to the lowest portion of the crossbar.

Procedure

The procedure is similar to that for the high jump: A vaulter may pass at any height, and he is out of the competition after three consecutive misses. The bar is moved up at least 2 inches after each round. Competition continues until only one vaulter remains. Ties are broken as in the high jump. A jump is a miss if the vaulter knocks the bar off the standards; if the athlete or the pole touches an area beyond the uprights before he clears the bar; and if the competitor, while in the air, moves his lower hand above his upper hand or moves his upper hand off the pole.

Each vaulter has two minutes to attempt his vault. When only two or three vaulters remain, this extends to four minutes. If a pole is broken during an attempt, the attempt does not count against the competitor.

© Claus Andersen

Figure 47.2.   A high jumper can pass on a height and resume jumping at the next height.

Long Jump

There is no maximum limit on the run-up; the minimum run-up is 40 to 45 meters. Competitors may place one or two markers along the runway to assist in their steps on the run-up. On the run-up the jumper approaches the take-off board, made of wood and about eight inches wide by four feet long. The jumper's foot must not mark beyond the *take-off line* at the far end of the board. Beyond this board is a plasticine board, about four inches wide, on which athletes' footprints may be spotted.

A *wind-sock* is placed near the take-off board so jumpers can determine the approximate direction and strength of the wind. The landing area is a sand pit, 3 meters wide by 9 meters long, beginning at least 1 meter beyond the take-off line. The sand must be level with the take-off board.

Procedure

In competitions with more than eight jumpers, each competitor takes three jumps, in rotating order. Each competitor counts his best jump. The eight best marks advance; these eight athletes get three more jumps. The longest legal jump wins. See figure 47.3.

In competitions with eight or fewer athletes, each jumper gets six jumps and counts her best legal jump. Each jumper has one and a half minutes to take a jump. The measurement is taken from the take-off line to the nearest sand broken by the competitor. A jump is a foul when the athlete

- touches the ground beyond the take-off line,
- takes off beyond either side of the take-off board (whether behind the line or not),
- touches the ground outside the landing area closer to the take-off line than to the nearest mark made in the pit, and when the athlete
- walks back through the landing area.

Triple Jump

The jumping area is the same as for the long jump. The placement of the take-off board depends on the caliber of competition. In major competition for men, the distance between the board and the landing area should be at least 13 meters; for women, 10 meters. The recommended distance

Figure 47.3.   During competition for the long jump, each competitor takes three jumps.

between the take-off board and the end of the landing area is 21 meters.

Procedure

The competitor sprints down the runway, takes off on either foot from the take-off board, lands on that same foot, takes a long step and lands on the opposite foot, and jumps into the landing area. It is not a foul if the jumper touches the "off" leg or foot on the ground during the jump. All other rules and procedures for the triple jump are the same as for the long jump.

THROWING EVENTS

Athletes compete against each other to record the longest throw of various implements in

- the *discus throw,*
- the *hammer throw,*
- the *javelin throw,*

- the *shot put*, and
- the *weight throw.*

General Rules

These general rules apply to all throwing events:

In throws from a circle, the athlete must begin from a stationary position. The competitor may touch the inside of the band or stopboard, but not the top. Failing to start from a stationary position and touching the top of the stopboard are fouls. Other fouls include

- touching any surface outside the circle,
- improperly releasing the implement, and
- leaving the circle before the implement lands.

Except in the hammer and weight throws, or to cover an open cut, athletes may not tape their fingers. They may use a substance on their hands to improve their grip, and they may wear belts to protect their backs from injury. Competitors have a minute and a half to begin their trial, once their name is called by the event official.

Except for the hammer and weight throws, no gloves are allowed. No flags or markers may be placed in the landing sector, which fans out in two lines from the throwing circle at a 40-degree angle. A throw is not valid if it does not land within the landing sector marked on the ground.

If a competitor misses his turn, that turn is lost, but he may still use any subsequent turns he has coming to him. In a field of nine or more competitors, each athlete gets three attempts, and the eight individuals with the best attempts advance. In a field of eight or less, all competitors get six throws. The best legal throw for each competitor is used to determine final standings.

For the discus, hammer, shot put, and weight throw, the measurement is made from the inside of the circle's circumference along a line to the nearest point of the mark made by the implement. For the javelin, the measurement is made from the inside edge of the throwing arc on a line to the point where the ground was broken by the tip of the javelin.

Discus

The discus is a smooth implement, usually wood with a metal rim. It is thrown from a circle that is 2.5 meters in diameter. Men throw a discus weighing 2 kilograms (see figure 47.4); women throw a disc weighing 1 kilogram. Contestants may not wear spiked shoes. A cage surrounds the throwing area to protect spectators.

© Claus Andersen

Figure 47.4. A discus thrower concentrates as he prepares to throw the discus.

Javelin

The javelin is a slender metal shaft thrown from behind a curved arc at the end of a runway, which is between 30 meters and 36.5 meters long and 4 meters wide. The arc is white board or metal and has a radius of 8 meters. The men's javelin is 8.8 feet long and weighs 1.8 pounds; the women's javelin is 7.5 feet long and weighs 1.3 pounds.

Tape may not be used on the javelin. The surface and finish must be smooth. A nonslip grip is placed in the middle of the shaft. Competitors may wear spiked shoes.

The javelin is thrown into a landing sector, which begins 8 meters behind the arc and extends out in a 29-degree angle. The javelin must be held with one hand and thrown over the shoulder.

The tip of the javelin must strike the ground first for the throw to be valid. Other fouls are recorded when

- the competitor turns her back to the throwing area after preparing to throw;
- the throw does not land completely in the landing sector;
- the competitor touches the arc, the ground beyond the arc, or the boundary lines; or
- the competitor leaves the runway before the javelin touches the ground.

Javelin throwers may place one or two marks along the runway to assist in their run-up.

Hammer

The hammer consists of three parts: a solid metal head, a wire about 4 feet long, and a single- or double-loop grip. The senior men's hammer weighs 16 pounds; the women's hammer weighs 8.8 pounds.

The hammer thrower may wear gloves. He may rest the head of the hammer either inside or outside the throwing circle. He grips the hammer with both hands.

It is not a foul if the hammer touches the ground or the top of the iron band in the throwing circle as the competitor is making his turns in preparing to throw. However, it is a foul if the hammer touches the ground or iron band and the hammer thrower stops his throw. If the hammer breaks during the throw or while in the air, it is not considered an attempt. The competitor may throw another hammer.

Shot Put

The shot put is a solid metal ball. The men's shot weighs 16 pounds; the women's weighs 8.8 pounds. Contestants "put" (throw) the shot from a circle with a 7-foot diameter.

The shot is put from the shoulder, with one hand. The hand holds the shot close to the chin; it may not be dropped from its position during the put. The shot may not be brought behind the line of the shoulders.

Weight

The weight consists of three parts: a solid metal head, a handle of round metal, and a steel link connection. Men throw a 35-pound weight; women throw a 20-pound weight. In making the throw, a competitor uses both hands, holding the weight by the handle, assuming any position he or she chooses.

COMBINED EVENTS

Men and women have several combined events to compete in, both indoors and out. The most common combined event for men is the *decathlon*, which consists of 10 events over two days:

Day 1
1. 100-meter dash
2. Long jump
3. Shot put
4. High jump
5. 400-meter dash

Day 2
6. 110-meter hurdles
7. Discus throw
8. Pole vault
9. Javelin throw
10. 1,500-meter run

The most common women's combined event is the *heptathlon,* which consists of seven events over two days:

Day 1

1. 100-meter hurdles
2. High jump
3. Shot put
4. 200-meter dash

Day 2

5. Long jump
6. Javelin throw
7. 800-meter run

Rules for combined events generally are the same as for the individual events, with the following exceptions:

- Competitors get three trials each in the long jump, shot put, discus throw, and javelin throw.
- A competitor is disqualified in the hurdles or running events after three false starts.
- An athlete who does not take part in one event is disqualified from the competition.
- Points are awarded for times and distances recorded for each event. Highest score wins.

TERMS

A **false start** occurs when a runner begins a race before the starting pistol is fired. A competitor is disqualified for two false starts.

Some competitions have **heats,** or qualifying rounds, to narrow the field and advance runners to the finals.

A **photo finish** is the term used when a finish is so close that the winner must be determined by a photographic device at the finish line.

A **wind-aided** effort refers to running events, up to and including the 200-meter, and the long jump and triple jump, where the velocity of the wind exceeds 2 meters per second in the direction of the competition. Records set on a wind-aided effort are not allowed.

ATHLETES

Track athletes are classified as follows:

- *Junior*—age 14 to 19
- *Youth*—under age 19
- *Senior*—open (in men's long distance races, athletes must be at least 16; men's race walkers must be at least 14)
- *Sub-masters*—age 30 to 39
- *Masters*—age 40 and over

EQUIPMENT

Runners in events up to and including the 400-meter dash use *starting blocks* to protect the track. Both of a runner's feet must be in contact with the blocks, which often are equipped with a device that helps starters detect false starts. Many races are recorded by *electronic timers,* which register times to a hundredth of a second. Most events allow athletes to wear *spiked footwear,* with up to 11 spikes.

MODIFICATIONS

This section contains rules for Youth, Masters, and Race Walking.

Youth

Youth track is divided into these divisions:

- Bantam (10-and-under)
- Midget (11-12)
- Youth (13 -14)
- Intermediate (15-16)
- Young Men/Women (17-18)

Important modifications of rules for these classifications include the following:

In Bantam, Midget, and Youth competition, starting blocks are not necessary, though runners may choose to use them. In races of 800 meters or more, qualifying rounds are run. In one-day events, all races of 200 meters (656.1 feet) or more are run as finals.

Hurdle distances and heights are as shown in table 47.4. Intermediate Boys and Young Men run a *2,000-meter steeplechase*. In field events, in lieu of three attempts in a preliminary round and three attempts in a final round, competitors may have one round with four attempts. *Implement weights* are as shown in table 47.5.

In the javelin, the measurement is made from the center of the circle to the first point of contact the javelin makes with the ground in the landing sector. The contact may be with any part of the javelin. In the high jump and pole vault, competitors may use more than two marks to assist in their run-up; and if they pass

on three consecutive heights, they are allowed one warm-up jump without the crossbar in place.

Masters

Masters competition is split into 5-year age groups, beginning with 30-34 (sub-masters). No starting blocks are necessary, but competitors may use them. Competitors are disqualified after one false start.

In the high jump and pole vault, athletes who pass on three consecutive heights are allowed one warm-up jump without the crossbar in place. Hurdle distances and heights are shown in table 47.6; implement weights are shown in table 47.7.

Table 47.4: Hurdle Specifications, up to Age 18			
Division	Distance (m)	Hurdles	Height (in)
Midgets (boys and girls)	80	8	30
Youth girls	100	10	30
Youth boys	100	10	33
Youth (boys and girls)	200	5	30
Intermediate and young women	100	10	33
Intermediate and young men	110	10	39
Intermediate and young women	400	10	30
Intermediate and young men	400	10	36

Adapted from USA Track & Field 1995.

Table 47.5: Implement Specifications, up to Age 18			
Division	Shot	Discus	Javelin
Bantam (10 and under)	6 lb	—	—
Midgets (11 to 12)	6 lb	—	—
Youth girls (13 to 14)	6 lb	—	—
Youth boys (13 to 14)	4 kg (8.8 lb)	—	—
Intermediate girls (15 to 16)	4 kg (8.8 lb)	1 kg (2.2 lb)	600 g (21.2 oz)
Intermediate boys (15 to 16)	12 lb	1.6 kg (3.5 lb)	800 g (28.2 oz)
Young women (17 to 18)	4 kg (8.8 lb)	1 kg (2.2 lb)	600 g (21.2 oz)
Young men (17 to 18)	12 lb	1.6 kg (3.5 lb)	800 g (28.2 oz)

Adapted from USA Track & Field 1995.

	Table 47.6: Masters Hurdle Specifications		
Division	Distance (m)	Hurdles	Height (in)
Women 30 to 39	60	5	33
Women 40 to 49	60	5	30
Women 50 and up	60	5	30
Women 30 to 39	100	10	33
Women 40 and up	80	8	30
Women 30 to 49	400	10	30
Women 50 and up	300	7	30
Men 30 to 49	60	5	39
Men 50 to 59	60	5	36
Men 60 to 69	60	5	33
Men 70 and up	60	5	30
Men 30 to 49	110	10	39
Men 50 to 59	100	10	36
Men 60 to 69	100	10	33
Men 70 and up	80	8	30
Men 30 to 49	400	10	36
Men 50 to 59	400	10	33
Men 60 and up	300	7	30

Adapted from USA Track & Field 1995.

Race Walking

Race walking may take place on either road or track. The main rules include the following:

- Unbroken contact must be maintained with the ground (the lead foot must touch ground before the back foot leaves the ground).

- The support leg must be straightened for at least a moment.

One warning is given for a violation; a second occurrence means disqualification.

ORGANIZATIONS

New York Road Runners Club
9 E. 89th St.
New York, NY 10128
212-860-4455

Road Runners Club of America
c/o Henley Gibble
1150 S. Washington St., Ste. 250
Alexandria, VA 22314
703-836-0558

USA Track & Field
One Hoosier Dome, Ste. 140
Indianapolis, IN 46225
317-261-0500

Table 47.7: Masters Implement Specifications						
Division	Shot kg (lb)	Discus kg (lb)	Hammer kg (lb)	Javelin g (oz)	Weight[1] (lb)	Weight[2] (lb)
Women 30 to 49	4 (8.8)	1 (2.2)	4 (8.8)	600 (21.2)	(20)	(20)
Women 50 to 59	3 (6.6)	1 (2.2)	3 (6.6)	400 (14.1)	(16)	(16)
Women 60 and up	3 (6.6)	1 (2.2)	3 (6.6)	400 (14.1)	(12)	(16)
Men 30 to 49	(16)	2 (4.4)	(16)	800 (28.2)	(35)	(35)
Men 50 to 59	6 (13.2)	1.5 (3.3)	6 (13.2)	800 (28.2)	(25)	(35)
Men 60 to 69	5 (11)	1 (2.2)	5 (11)	600 (21.2)	(20)	(25)
Men 70 to 79	4 (8.8)	1 (2.2)	4 (8.8)	600 (21.2)	(16)	(25)
Men 80 and up	4 (8.8)	1 (2.2)	4 (8.8)	600 (21.2)	(12)	(25)

[1]In pentathlon
[2]In individual event
Adapted from USA Track & Field 1995.

48

Triathlon

© H. Armstrong Roberts

The first known triathlon, comprised of a three-part swimming-cycling-running event, was held in 1974 in San Diego, California. John Collins, a U.S. naval officer who competed in this first informal triathlon, brought the sport to Hawaii, helping to create the "Ironman Triathlon" from three separate endurance events already in existence there. The first "Ironman" was held in 1978, with 12 men finishing; the next year, 13 men and 1 woman finished.

The sport began to take off in the early 1980s; now more than a thousand compete in the Ironman event, with thousands more turned away. Triathlons of varying distances are held throughout the United States and internationally. USA Triathlon, the national governing body for the sport and the source for this chapter's rules, estimates there are at least 200,000 active triathletes in the United States. The sport will be included in the 2000 Olympics in Sydney, Australia.

Although the most common events in a triathlon are swimming, bicycling, and running, in that order, USA Triathlon recognizes other forms of the sport, including a different order of events, or even different events (for example, one triathlon in Colorado consists of cross-country skiing, snow shoeing, and speed skating). The rules in this chapter, however, pertain to swimming, biking, and running. The object is to complete the course in the fastest time while keeping within the rules.

PROCEDURES

USA Triathlon recognizes four distance categories. The distances may vary somewhat, but the basic categories are shown in table 48.1.

Table 48.1: Triathlon Distances			
Triathlon type	Swim (mi)	Bike (mi)	Run (mi)
Sprint	.5	12.4	3.1
International	.93	24.8	6.2
Long	1.2	56.0	13.1
Ultra	2.4	112.0	26.2

Depending on the size of the field, a triathlon begins with either a *mass start*, in which all athletes begin at once, or a *wave start*, in which triathletes are grouped and begin at different times. After completing the swim, triathletes enter the transition area, where they don helmets and shoes, get on their bikes, and complete the cycling course. Upon finishing the cycling phase, they again enter a transition area, place their bikes in a designated corral, and begin the running phase. Once they complete the run, their race is over.

TERMS

Banned substances include stimulants, narcotics, anabolic steroids, beta-blockers, diuretics, and peptide hormones and analogues.

Obstruction is the act of intentionally or accidentally blocking, charging, obstructing, or interfering with the forward progress of another athlete. Such a violation results in a variable time penalty.

The **transition area** is set up for the transitions between the swim and the bike, and the bike and the run.

A triathlete may not gain **unfair advantage** by using her body to push, pull, hold, strike, or force her way through other triathletes. Violation results in a variable time penalty.

A **variable time penalty** is assessed for fouls such as obstruction and unfair advantage. The time penalized depends on the race distance:

- Sprint—30 seconds
- International—1 minute
- Long—2 minutes
- Ultra—4 minutes

A **wave start** is one in which groups of athletes begin at different times.

SWIMMING

Swimmers may use any stroke; they may tread water, float, or stand on the bottom to rest. They may also hold on to buoys, boats, ropes, or other objects to rest, but they may not make forward progress while holding onto an object. They may make forward progress while standing on the bottom.

Swimmers may wear *wetsuits* in water temperatures up to and including 78 degrees Fahrenheit (25.6 degrees Celsius). They may wear wetsuits when the water temperature is between 78 and 84 degrees Fahrenheit (28.9 degrees Celsius), but they are not eligible for prizes or awards. When the water temperature is 84 degrees Fahrenheit (28.9 degrees Celsius) or greater, they may not wear wetsuits.

CYCLING

Cyclists must obey all traffic laws, unless directed to do otherwise by a race official. Cyclists must use only their own force in propelling their bikes. They may not use their hands to push or carry their bikes unless their bikes are disabled. Cyclists assume sole responsibility for knowing the course. Officials will not adjust race times if cyclists get off course.

Cyclists who endanger themselves or others will be disqualified. They may not wear or carry headsets, radios, or other items deemed dangerous by race officials. They must wear approved helmets with fastened chinstraps (see "Equipment").

Cyclists may not work together to improve performance or team position. No cyclist may be in the *drafting zone* of another cyclist or of a motor vehicle, except if he is passing. A cyclist's drafting zone is 7 meters long and 2 meters wide, with the length beginning at the front of the front wheel. A motor vehicle's drafting zone is 15 meters wide and 30 meters long. Cyclists must keep to the right of the course unless passing. They may not attempt to pass unless they have adequate space to do so.

A cyclist is generally entitled to a position on the course if he gained it without touching another cyclist. Cyclists who have established the right of way may not obstruct the progress of other cyclists. However, a cyclist who is overtaking another cyclist bears the primary responsibility for avoiding a positioning foul, even if the cyclist ahead decreases speed. A cyclist overtakes another cyclist when his front wheel goes beyond the front wheel of the other cyclist.

When a cyclist overtakes another cyclist, the overtaken cyclist bears primary responsibility for avoiding a positioning foul. An overtaken cyclist must move completely out of the drafting zone of the cyclist who has just passed her before she attempts to pass that cyclist. A cyclist may be in the drafting zone of another cyclist only

- when it takes 15 seconds or less to overtake the cyclist;
- for safety reasons, course blockage, in transition areas, or when making a turn of 90 degrees or greater; or
- when race officials allow it because of narrow lanes.

No cyclist may be directly behind another cyclist, even if she is out of the other cyclist's drafting zone. A cyclist who violates a position foul rule is assessed a variable time penalty (see "Terms") for the first violation and is disqualified for the second violation.

RUNNING

Triathletes must run or walk the run course; they will be disqualified for gaining forward progress by crawling. They are responsible for knowing and following the course. They may not wear or carry headsets, radios, or similar equipment. They may carry nonbreakable containers of liquid.

TRIATHLETES

Triathletes must compete in their appropriate age groups. They will be assessed a variable

time penalty for receiving unauthorized assistance, including food, drink, equipment, support, pacing, a replacement bicycle, or bicycle parts. They may exit a course, but they must re-enter at the point they exited or be assessed a variable time penalty.

EQUIPMENT

Swimmers must wear either the official *race cap* or a brightly-colored *swim cap*. They may wear *goggles* or *face masks*, but these are not required. They may not wear fins, paddles, gloves, floating devices, or any artificial propulsion device.

Cyclists must wear *helmets* that meet or exceed the specifications of the American National Standard Institute (ANSI) or the Snell Memorial Foundation. They must fasten their chinstraps before they mount their bikes and not unfasten them until after they dismount.

Bicycles may not exceed 2 meters in length or 75 centimeters in width. The distance between the center of the chain wheel axle and the ground must be at least 24 centimeters. Bikes may not have any wind resistance shields or devices attached anywhere. The front wheel of the bike must be of spoke construction; the rear wheel may be either spoke or solid. The two wheels may have a different diameter if race officials determine they are safe. Each wheel must have one working brake.

OFFICIALS

Race officials consist of a *head referee, marshals, judges,* and a *head timer.* The head referee has complete charge of the event, except for decisions made by a protest committee.

ORGANIZATIONS

USA Triathlon
P.O. Box 15820
Colorado Springs, CO 80935-5820
719-597-9090

49

Volleyball

© Mary Langenfeld

Volleyball is a popular and diverse sport, having many variations: indoor, outdoor, beach; 2-, 3-, 4-, or 6-player teams; Mixed-Six (co-ed); games to 11 points, to 15 points, or by the clock; and the rally-point system. It is played by young and old and has been an Olympic sport since 1964. It originally was developed as an alternative to basketball by William G. Morgan of the YMCA in Holyoke, Mass., in 1895.

The original game had some baseball-like rules, including innings and outs, with nine players on each side. While many of the rules have changed since then, the object remains the same: to score more points than the other team by hitting the ball over the net so that the opponents cannot return the ball or prevent it from hitting the ground in their court.

The rules in this chapter are from USA Volleyball, the national governing body for the sport. The main body of this chapter refers to indoor, six-player rules. Modifications are noted near the end of the chapter.

PROCEDURES

The winner of a coin toss elects to serve or receive, or selects the end of the court on which he will begin play. The referee blows her whistle for the first serve, which begins play. After the serve, players may move around on their sides of the court, but they may not step completely over the center line.

Players may hit the ball with any part of their body. They may clasp their hands together and strike the ball underhand, overhand, and with either an open hand or closed fist. Only the serving team may score points, except in the deciding game of a match, in which a point is scored on every rally. If the team receiving serve stops its opponents from scoring, they are awarded the serve. A point is scored when

- the ball lands in bounds on the opponents' court,
- the opponents are unable to return the serve within three hits,
- the opponents hit the ball out of bounds, and
- the opponents commit a fault, or foul.

The ball is in when it touches any portion of the court, including the boundary lines. The ball is out when it touches the floor completely outside the boundary lines. It is also out when it touches a person or object outside the boundary lines, when it crosses the net outside the crossing space, and when it touches the net, rope, antenna, or post outside the antenna or side band. (Note: If a player, in pursuing an opponent's serve, goes out of bounds before hitting the ball, the ball is still in play.)

The team that scores 15 points in a game and has a 2-point advantage wins the game. Most matches are the best of three or five games. (For more on the scoring system, see page 329.) Each team may take two 30-second timeouts in a game. When the referee blows his whistle, signaling the end of a game, each team lines up on its end line and then changes playing areas and benches before playing the next game. An interval of 2 minutes, 30 seconds is allowed between games.

TERMS

An **attack hit** is a hit aimed into the opponent's court. Serves, however, are not considered attack hits.

Attack lines separate each side of the court into a front zone and a back zone. Players in the back row may attempt an attack hit when they are behind the attack line, or when they are in front of the line when the ball is lower than the top of the net.

Back-row players are the three who are situated in the back zone when the serve is made.

A **block** occurs when one or more players stop the ball before, or just after, it crosses the net.

A **delay** may be called by a referee when a team takes too long to substitute or otherwise delays play. The first delay results in a warning; the second results in a loss of a rally.

A **dig** is made by a player who first contacts the ball over the net (unless this player is making a block).

A **fault** results in a lost serve or a point awarded to the opposition. For more on faults, see page 328.

A **front-row** player is one who is positioned in the front zone, between the attack line and the net.

A **held ball,** which is a fault, may be called when a player does not contact the ball cleanly.

A **hit** is any contact by a player with the ball. A player may hit the ball once during a play, although if it is the team's first hit and is not a block, the ball may contact the same player on various parts of the body consecutively, provided that the contacts occur in one action.

A **match** is won by the team that wins the most games in the match.

A **playing fault** is any breach of the rules by a player. A fault results in loss of the rally.

A **point cap** is used to end a non-deciding game (one that doesn't determine the winner of the match) that goes beyond 15 points. A team must win by 2 points (15-13, 16-14, 17-15), or by reaching 17 first (17-16).

A **rally** is the exchange of hits between the teams. The team that wins the rally gets the serve.

In the **rally-point scoring system,** a point is scored on every rally. The team that scores the point retains, or gains, the serve.

A team's **rotation order** must be kept when it gains the serve. Each time it gains a serve, players rotate one position clockwise. Failure to do so is a fault.

Sanctions are given for various penalties. A **yellow card** signifies a warning; a **red card** is a penalty for a more serious offense that results either in the serving team losing the serve or the receiving team losing a point. When the referee holds up both a red card and a yellow card in one hand, the offending player is expelled from the game. When the referee holds up a red card in one hand and a yellow card in the other, the offending player is expelled for the match.

Players of the serving team may not **screen** the opponents from seeing the server or the path of the ball. Screening includes arm waving, jumping, and moving sideways as the serve is being made. It also occurs when the server is hidden behind two or more players.

A **serve** puts the ball into play. The server may move freely behind the end line when serving. See page 328 for more on serving.

A **set** is a contact that sets up a spike. The typical order of contacts is dig, set, spike.

A **sideout** occurs when the serving team does not score, and the serve goes over to the other team.

A **spike** is a hard-driven ball that is hit in an attempt to score or sideout.

A player may **tip** a ball with her fingers if she does not throw or hold the ball and the contact is brief.

COURT

The court includes the *playing area* and the *free zone* (see figure 49.1). It is divided into two equal parts by the *center line,* which runs the width of the court under the net. *Attack lines* are on both sides of the net. The *net* itself is made of mesh and is a minimum of 32 feet long and 39 inches wide with a 2-inch canvas band at the top. For men, the top of the net is 2.4 meters high; for

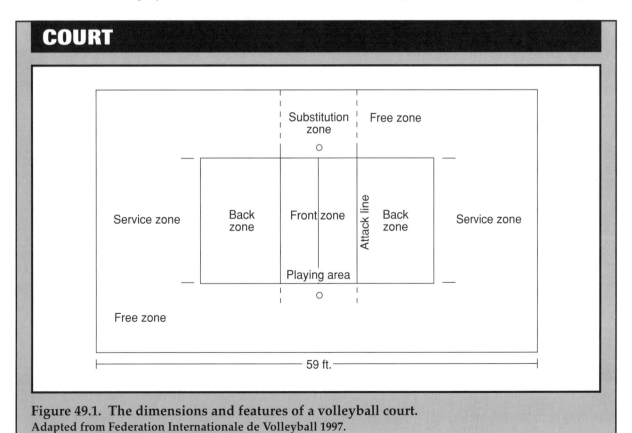

COURT

Figure 49.1. The dimensions and features of a volleyball court.
Adapted from Federation Internationale de Volleyball 1997.

women, it is 2.2 meters high. The top and the bottom of the net are fastened to the posts to remain taut. Two white *side bands* are fastened vertically to the net; they are considered part of the net. *Antennas* are attached to the side bands.

EQUIPMENT

The *ball* is spherical and bound in leather. Its circumference is 25.5 to 27 inches; its weight is 9 to 10 ounces. It has 4.5 to 6 pounds of air pressure per square inch.

Players wear *jerseys* and *shorts*, or *one-piece outfits*; no jewelry may be worn. Players wear *soft-* or *rubber-soled shoes*.

PLAYERS

Each team has six players on the court: three in the front row, three in the back row (left, center, and right in both rows). Each front-row player must have at least part of one foot closer to the center line than both feet of the corresponding back-row player. Outside players in each row must have at least part of one foot closer to their sideline than both feet of the center player in the same row. Player position is determined by the position of the foot last in contact with the floor at the time the ball is served.

Once the ball is served, players may move to any position within their side of the court. When a team gains the serve, its players rotate one position clockwise. In USA Volleyball Open play, a team is allowed a maximum of six substitutions per game. A starting player may leave the game and re-enter once. A substitute player may not re-enter a game after he is replaced, and he may be replaced only by the player he replaced. In all other USA Volleyball play, a team may substitute 12 times per game; a starting player may re-enter a game twice; and a substitute player may enter a game three times.

GAME SITUATIONS

The following rules are split into these categories: Serving, Playing the Ball, Attacking-Hitting, Blocking, Scoring, and Misconduct.

Serving

Players must follow the service order recorded on the lineup sheet. A player retains the serve until the other team wins the right to serve. A player has five seconds to serve once the referee whistles for service. If a player serves before the whistle, the play is canceled and the serve is repeated.

The server may serve from anywhere behind the end line. After completing the serve, the player may step or land inside the court. If the server tosses the ball and it touches the ground without touching the player, this is a service error. One such error is allowed per service; the player may attempt to serve again. A service fault occurs if the ball

- touches a player of the serving team;
- fails to pass through the crossing space over the net;
- touches the net, antenna, or any other object;
- lands out of bounds; or
- passes over a "screen" of one or more players.

Playing the Ball

Each team has three hits, in addition to blocking, to return the ball. A hit is any contact with the ball, whether intentional or not. A player may not contact the ball twice during a rally, unless the

---

Point—Or Fault?

As a player prepares to serve, two of her teammates move sideways to prevent an opponent from seeing the ball. The server, however, does not serve over these players and hits a ball in the opponent's court that is not returned. Does the serving team receive a point?

No, even though the ball was not served over the players making the screen. According to the rules, a sanction may be issued for distracting or moving sideways to prevent an opponent from seeing the serve even if the ball is not served over that player.

first contact is a block or unless two players contact the ball simultaneously. In this case it is counted as one contact, and any player may hit the ball next. A player may not receive assistance from a teammate in trying to hit a ball. However, a teammate may hold back a player who is about to cross the center line or touch the net.

Net Play

If a ball outside the crossing space has not fully crossed the vertical plane of the net, it may be played back to a teammate. A ball is "out" when it completely crosses under the net. A ball may touch the net and still be in play, except during the serve. If a ball is driven into the net, it may be recovered if the team hasn't used its three hits.

A blocker may contact the ball beyond the plane of the net but may not interfere with an opponent's play. A hitter's hands or arms may cross the net if the contact was made on his side of the net or within the net's plane (see figure 49.2). However, if any part of a player touching the floor (hands, knees, feet) crosses completely over the center line into the opponent's court, a fault is called regardless of whether it interfered with the opponent's play.

© Frances M. Roberts

Figure 49.2.   A volleyball player attacks the ball at the net.

A player may not touch the net. The only exceptions are incidental contact by a player's hair or an insignificant contact by a player not involved in the play. If a driven ball causes the net to touch a player, this is not a fault.

Attacking–Hitting

An attack-hit is any action directing the ball toward the opponent's court, except for serves and blocks. Front-row players may make an attack-hit when the ball is at any height. Back-row players may make an attack-hit at any height as long as they are behind the attack line at take-off; they can land beyond the line. A back-row player may also make an attack-hit from the front zone if the ball is below the top of the net.

Blocking

A block occurs at the net as a player or players attempt to block the ball from entering their side of the court. At least one blocker must have a portion of his body above the net at some point during the block. A block is not counted as one of the team's three hits.

A player who blocks the ball may be the first to contact the ball after the block. A player may place her hands and arms beyond the net in an attempt to block if she does not interfere with her opponents' play. An example of interference is when an offensive player is setting a pass and a defensive player touches the ball with her hands or arms over the net. It is not interference if the defensive player touches the ball beyond the net when the offensive team is attacking.

Consecutive contacts with the ball are permitted in blocking if the contacts are quick and continuous and made during one action. A serve cannot be blocked.

Scoring

Matches are usually the best of three or best of five games; games are usually played to 15 points. Points are scored only by the serving team except in the deciding game of a match, where the rally-point system is used. In this system, a point is scored on each rally; if the receiving team scores a point, it gains the serve and continues to serve as long as it keeps scoring.

In a non-deciding game, the first team to score 15 and lead its opponent by 2 points wins. If the margin is 1 point, play continues until the margin is 2 points or until a team reaches 17.

If one team is penalized, the other team receives the serve and a point. If the receiving team faults, the serving team gets a point. If the serving team faults, the receiving team gets a point and the serve.

Misconduct

Misconduct is classified as unsportsmanlike conduct, rude conduct, offensive conduct, or aggression. It may be directed at officials, players, coaches, or fans. Depending on the degree of the misconduct, a player may be warned (yellow card), penalized (red card), expelled for the game (red card and yellow card in one hand), or expelled for the match (red card in one hand, yellow card in the other).

MODIFICATIONS

The two main variations of the sport allow for co-ed play and for outdoor play. A third variation employs a time clock. The net heights suggested by USA Volleyball are indicated in table 49.1.

Table 49.1: Net Heights		
Age groups	Females/ reverse mixed six (ft, in)	Males/ mixed-six (ft, in)
55 and above	—	7, 9 5/8
45 and above	7, 2 1/8	—
18 and under	7, 4 1/8	7, 11 5/8
16 and under	7, 4 1/8	7, 11 5/8
14 and under	7, 4 1/8	7, 4 1/8
12 and under	7, 0	7, 0
10 and under	6, 6	7, 0

Adapted from USA Volleyball 1995.

Mixed-Six Play

The rules for Mixed-Six (co-ed) play are the same as for indoors, except for the following:

- Males and females alternate serves and court positions.
- When the ball is played more than once by a team, at least one hit must be made by a female. A block does not count as a hit. Females may make all three hits; a male is not required to hit.
- An illegally hit ball by an illegal blocker becomes a double fault and the opponent is awarded the point or serve.
- When only one male is in the front row, one back-row male may, after beginning in the back row, come forward of the attack line in order to block.
- No female back-row player may block.
- The net height is 2.4 meters (same as in men's play).

Reverse Mixed-Six Play

The rules for Reverse Mixed-Six play are the same as for Mixed-Six play, with the following exceptions:

- When only one female is in the front row, one female in the back row may be in the attack zone in order to block.
- No male may block.
- Males may not spike. They may contact the ball above the net and send it into the opponent's court, but the trajectory of the ball upon their contact must be upward.
- The net height is 2.2 meters (same as for women's play).

Timed Play

Occasionally, games are governed by time, rather than a certain point total. In such cases, a game consists of eight minutes of live-ball action. The clock starts with each serve and stops with each dead ball. As in other competitions, a team must win by two points; the same scoring rules apply as detailed in the "Scoring" section in this chapter.

Outdoor Play

The popularity of volleyball is evidenced by outdoor participation on beach or grass (see figure

49.3). The rules for outdoor play are the same as for indoor play, with these exceptions:

- Brightly-colored boundary lines (flat bands or tape) mark the boundaries; if they move during play, play continues. If it can't be determined whether the ball was in or out, the rally is replayed. It is the players' responsibility to correct the boundary lines if they are moved.

- Attack lines are marked, but the center line is not.

- Teams may consist of 2, 3, 4, or 6 players, either of the same sex or co-ed.

- In doubles competition, no substitutions are allowed. Rosters are as follows for other play: triples competition—5 players; 4-player competition—6 players; 6-player competition—12 players. Unlimited subsitution is allowed in triples, 4-player, and 6-player competition, as long as each player plays within his or her serving position during a single game.

- Players may wear jewelry, caps, visors, casts, eyewear, etc., at their own risk. Rubber-soled shoes may be worn on grass, but nonflexible cleats or spikes are not allowed.

- The deciding game of a best-of-three games match may be a game to 15, played by rally-point rules (a point scored on every serve), or a game to 7 played by "regular" scoring rules (only the serving team can score).

- In doubles, triples, and 4-player competition, players may position themselves anywhere on the court, and the server may serve from anywhere beyond the end line.

- In doubles and triples play, the first contact after a hard-driven ball (a spike or block) may be a lift or push, as long as the motion is continuous and does not change directions.

- In doubles and triples play, if a ball is intentionally set into the opponent's court, the shoulders of the player setting the ball must be square to the direction of the ball.

- In doubles play, if a player serves out of turn, the play is allowed and that player holds serve until the opponents gain the serve. When the out-of-turn player's team regains the serve, her teammate will serve.

- In doubles, triples, and four-player competition, players may not "dink" or tip an attack hit with the fingers.

- In doubles and triples competition, a player may not make an attack-hit using an overhand set that puts the ball on a sideways trajectory with the player's shoulders.

- In six-player competition, a back-row player may not participate in a block.

- In 15-point games, teams switch sides each time the total score reaches a multiple of 5. In 11-point games, teams switch sides each

Figure 49.3. **Beach volleyball has become a popular sport among volleyball players.**

time the total score reaches a multiple of 4. In 7-point games, switches occur on multiples of 2.

OFFICIALS

The officials include the *first referee*, the *second referee*, the *scorekeeper*, and two or four *line judges*. The first referee sits or stands at one end of the net and has final authority over all decisions. He or she may overrule other officials. The second referee stands near the post outside the playing court, opposite the first referee. He or she signals faults, including net, center line, and back faults, and assists the first referee. The second referee authorizes game interruptions, substitutions, and timeouts.

The scorekeeper sits facing the first referee and records points, timeouts, and checks that substitutions are legal. Line judges stand at opposite corners of the court, opposite the service zones (if two judges are used), or at each corner (if four judges are used). They stand one to three meters outside the court and rule whether balls are in or out, signal when a ball crosses the net outside the crossing space, and when a server foot-faults. Officials' signals are shown in figure 49.4.

ORGANIZATIONS

USA Volleyball
3595 E. Fountain Blvd.
Colorado Springs, CO 80910-1740
719-637-8300

Side out

Ball in bounds or line violation

Double hit

Four hits

(continued)

Figure 49.4.   Common volleyball official's signals.

Ball out

Crossing center line

Ball contacted by a player
when going out-of-bounds

Carried ball, thrown ball,
held ball, or lifted ball

Ball contacted below the waist

Substitution

(continued)

Figure 49.4. *(continued)*

Ball served into net or
player touching net

Over the net

Double fault or
play over

Illegal block or
screen

Point

Figure 49.4. *(continued)*

50

Water Polo

© Claus Andersen

Water polo originally drew its rules from rugby, and in the 1860s it was being played in rivers and lakes. By 1870 the sport had moved indoors, and by the late 1880s water polo was introduced to America. By that time the game had become more similar to soccer with its passing and its caged goals. Water polo became an Olympic sport in 1900.

The object of the game is to score points by putting the ball into the opponent's goal. Each team has seven players in the water, a goalkeeper and six field players. A game consists of four seven-minute periods; time stops when the ball is out of play. There is a two-minute break between periods. Each team is entitled to two one-minute timeouts in a game, including extra time.

If the score is tied at the end of four periods, *extra time* goes into effect: The teams play two three-minute periods with a one-minute break in between. If the score is still tied, a third overtime period is played until a team wins by scoring a goal. The rules in this chapter were supplied by U.S. Water Polo Inc.

PROCEDURES

The winner of a coin toss chooses the end on which her team will begin play. To begin a game, players line up on their goal lines at least one meter apart and at least one meter from the goal posts. No more than two players may be between the goal posts, and no part of a player's body at water level may be beyond the goal line. A referee blows a whistle to begin play and tosses the ball on the half-distance line, near the edge of the field of play. The clock begins when a player touches the ball. Each team attempts to advance the ball by passing and dribbling it to get into position to score. A team has 35 seconds to shoot at its opponent's goal.

Scoring

A player scores a goal when the entire ball passes fully over the goal line and into the goal (between the posts and under the crossbar). A team may score a goal from anywhere within the field of play, although a goalkeeper may not touch the ball beyond the half-distance line or go beyond that line himself.

A field player may score a goal with any part of his body except a clenched fist. (A goalkeeper may score a goal with a clenched fist.) At least two players, excluding the defending goalkeeper, must have intentionally touched the ball on the play for a goal to count. A player may score a goal by obtaining a goal throw or free throw from the goalkeeper and throwing the ball into the goal; it doesn't have to touch another player first.

A player may score a goal by immediately shooting from outside the seven-meter line after his or her team has been awarded a free throw outside seven meters. The player may not score after putting the ball into play unless the ball has been touched intentionally by another player other than the defending goalkeeper.

A goal is legal if the 35-second clock or the period clock expires after the ball has left a player's hand but before the ball enters the goal. If the ball floats over the goal line in this circumstance, the goal is good if the ball floated over the goal due to its own momentum.

Restarting After a Goal

After a goal, once the players are in their respective halves of the pool, the referee whistles the ball into play. A player of the team just scored upon puts the ball into play by passing to a teammate; the teammate may be forward, backward, or to the side of the passer. The clock begins when the player releases the ball.

TERMS

A **corner throw** is taken by the attacking team from the 2-meter mark on the side nearest where the ball crossed the goal line.

An **exclusion foul** results in a free throw for the team fouled and in the temporary or permanent exclusion of the offending player.

Extra time is used to break a tie score at the end of regulation. Extra time consists of two three-minute periods; if the score is still tied, a third period is played in "sudden death" style: the first team to score wins.

A **free throw** is awarded for ordinary and exclusion fouls.

A **goal throw** is a free throw awarded to the goalkeeper and taken within the 2-meter area.

A **neutral throw** is made by the referee to put the ball back into play after players from each team have committed simultaneous fouls, or when the ball hits an overhead obstruction and rebounds into the field of play.

An **ordinary foul** results in a free throw for the offended team.

A **penalty foul** results in a penalty throw for the offended team.

A **penalty throw** may be taken by any player of the team awarded the throw, except for the goalkeeper. The throw is made from the opponent's 4-meter line as a direct shot on goal.

A **personal foul** is assessed against a player who commits an exclusion or penalty foul. A player who commits three personal fouls is excluded from the game.

FOULS

The three types of fouls and their penalties are shown in table 50.1. A player committing three personal fouls is eliminated from the contest. Free throws and penalty throws are described in "Throws."

Table 50.1: Fouls and Penalties		
Foul	Penalty	Personal foul charged
Ordinary	Free throw	No
Exclusion	Free throw	Yes
Penalty	Penalty throw	Yes

Ordinary Fouls

An ordinary foul is called for

- advancing beyond the goal line at the start of a period, before the referee gives the signal to start;
- assisting a player;
- holding onto or pushing off from the goal posts or sides or ends of the pool;
- standing on the floor of the pool while taking an active part in the game;
- holding the ball underwater while being tackled;
- striking the ball with a clenched fist (except the goalkeeper, within the four-meter area);
- touching the ball with two hands at once (except the goalkeeper);
- impeding the movement of an opponent who is not holding the ball;
- pushing, or pushing off from, an opponent;
- being within two meters of the opponent's goal, except when behind the line of the ball;
- unduly delaying a free throw, corner throw, or goal throw;
- goalkeeper's going beyond the half-distance line, or touching a ball beyond that line;
- maintaining possession of the ball for more than 35 seconds without shooting at the opponent's goal; or
- sending the ball out of the pool.

Exclusion Fouls

An exclusion foul results in a free throw for the team offended and in the exclusion of the player who committed the foul. This player can re-enter the game at the earliest of these occurrences: 20 seconds of playing time has elapsed; a goal has been scored; the excluded player's team has regained possession of the ball; or play is stopped and then restarted, with possession in favor of the excluded player's team. An exclusion foul is called for

- leaving the water or sitting or standing on the steps or side of the pool during play, except for injury or illness (this exception must be allowed by the referee);
- intentionally splashing water in an opponent's face;
- holding, sinking, or pulling back an opponent who does not have the ball;
- intentionally kicking or hitting an opponent, or attempting to do so;
- using foul language or violent or persistent foul play;
- interfering with a free throw, corner throw, or goal throw;
- goalkeeper's failing to take position for a penalty throw after being told to do so by the referee;
- interfering with a penalty throw (exclusion from game);
- committing an act of brutality (exclusion from game); or
- refusing to obey, or disrespecting, an official (exclusion from game).

When players from both teams simultaneously commit an exclusion foul or a penalty foul, both players are excluded and a neutral throw is made.

Penalty Fouls

A penalty foul, resulting in a penalty throw for the team offended, is called for

- committing any defensive foul within the four-meter area when a goal likely would have resulted;
- defending player's kicking or striking an opponent within the four-meter area;
- an excluded player's intentional interference with the goal alignment or other aspects of play;
- pulling over the goal to prevent a likely score; or
- any player's entering the game improperly.

THROWS

One of these throws may be awarded, according to the foul: goal, corner, neutral, free, or penalty.

Goal Throw

A goal throw is awarded when the entire ball has passed the goal line, outside of the goal posts (i.e., it hasn't scored), and was last touched by an attacking team player. The throw is taken by the defending goalkeeper within the two-meter area. If the goalkeeper is out of the water, it is taken by another defender.

Corner Throw

A corner throw is awarded when the ball has passed the goal line but has not gone between the goal posts and was last touched by a defender. The throw is taken by an attacking team player from the two-meter mark on the side where the ball crossed the goal line. The throw may be taken by any attacking player if undue delay does not occur.

Neutral Throw

A neutral throw is awarded when players from each team commit a foul at the same time and when, at the start of a period, the ball falls into a position of definite advantage for one team. The referee throws the ball into the water or up into the air at the same lateral position where the event occurred, so that players of both teams have an equal chance to gain possession. Players may touch the ball before it touches the water. The goalkeeper is excluded from taking a neutral throw.

Free Throw

A free throw is awarded for ordinary and exclusion fouls. The throw must be made so that the other players can see the ball leave the thrower's hand. The thrower may carry or dribble the ball before throwing. The ball is in play when it leaves the hand of the player passing it to another player.

Penalty Throw

A penalty throw is awarded for a penalty foul and may be taken by any player except the goalkeeper, from any point on the opponent's four-meter line. No player other than the defending goalkeeper may be in the four-meter area, and no player may be within two meters of the player taking the penalty throw. On the referee's signal, the player must immediately throw, with an uninterrupted motion, toward the goal. If the ball rebounds off the goal or the goalkeeper, it is in play, and another player does not need to touch it before a goal can be scored.

FIELD OF PLAY

The *field of play* is between 20 and 30 meters long from goal line to goal line, and between 10 and 20 meters wide (see figure 50.1). Boundaries beyond each goal line measure .30 meters. For women's matches, the maximum dimensions are 25 meters long and 17 meters wide.

The pool has a *half-distance line,* dividing the width of the pool in half. It also has *7-meter, 4-meter,* and *2-meter lines,* which are 7 meters, 4 meters and 2 meters from each goal, respectively. *Goal lines* run the width of the pool. A *re-entry area* is marked at each end of the pool, 2 meters from the corner, on the side opposite the official table.

The *goals* consist of white, rigid goal posts, a crossbar, and a net. Goals are rectangular; they are

3 meters wide and centered between the sides of the pool.

PLAYERS

A team consists of seven players in the pool and no more than six reserves. Substitutes may enter between periods, before extra time, after a goal has been scored, or during a timeout. If a player is bleeding, he must immediately leave the water. The game is not stopped; a substitute may immediately replace the injured player, who may return after the bleeding has stopped.

Age classifications for competition include

- 13-and-under,
- 15-and-under,
- 16-17,
- 18-20,
- Open, and
- Masters.

EQUIPMENT

The *ball* is round, weighs between 400 and 450 grams, and has a circumference between 68 and 71 centimeters for men and between 65 and 67 centimeters for women. One team wears *white caps;* the other team wears *caps of a contrasting color* (other than solid red or the color of the ball). Goalkeepers wear *red caps.* The goalkeeper's cap is numbered 1; the rest of the caps are numbered 2 through 13.

OFFICIALS

Games are controlled by up to eight officials: *referees, goal judges, timekeepers,* and *secretaries.* The referee is in absolute control of the game. Goal judges make calls and signals on goals and corner and goal throws. Timekeepers keep the time and keep track of excluded players and re-entries. Secretaries maintain records of the game.

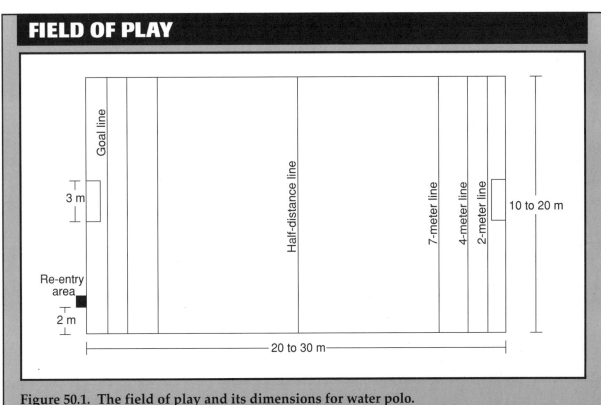

FIELD OF PLAY

Figure 50.1. The field of play and its dimensions for water polo.
Adapted from White 1990.

MODIFICATIONS

The following modifications are made for Junior Olympic competition (17-and-under) and for Masters competition (30-and-over).

Junior Olympics. A game lasts four five-minute periods. Each team is allowed one two-minute timeout per half. Substitutes may be made during a timeout.

Masters. Age groups are in five-year intervals (30-34, 35-39, and so on). A team is placed in the age group of its youngest player; there are no age limits for older players playing in younger age groups. The distance between goal lines is 23.5 meters minimum, and the minimum width of the field of play is 17 meters. A game lasts four five-minute periods. Each team receives two one-minute timeouts.

ORGANIZATIONS

United States Water Polo Inc.
1685 West Uintah
Colorado Springs, CO 80904-2921
719-634-0699

51

Water Skiing

© Photophile/Arthur Fox

Water skiing is a sport that combines strength, dexterity, grace, and precision at high speeds. Skiers perform in three events: Jumping, Slalom, and Tricks. Places are determined in each event, based on scores, with highest being best.

Competitions are held in various divisions, beginning with boys' and girls' divisions for 9 years old and younger, and ending with mens' and womens' divisions for 75 years old and older. Within each division, skiers are rated and compete according to their performance levels; there are six performance levels in each division. The rules for this chapter are provided by the American Water Ski Association (AWSA), a division of USA Water Ski.

PROCEDURES

Competitions may be held for individuals and for teams. At national tournaments, skiing order is based on seedings, with the highest-rated skier going last. At other tournaments, order may be based either on seedings or on a draw.

Boys I and Girls I divisions (nine years old and younger) are the only divisions that do not complete all three events. These divisions do not take part in the Jump competition.

Overall Scoring

Each event has a standard of 1,000 National Overall Performance Standards (NOPS) points. (The American Water Skiing Association provides formulas for each event.) Each contestant receives points in proportion to the standard. For example, a trick skier with 1,130 points compared to a 2,560 NOPS would get 441 overall points: $1,130/2,560 \times 1,000 = 441$.

A jumper receives points in proportion to the square of his distance to the square of the NOPS distance. For example, if the NOPS standard is 150 feet, and the jumper jumps 130 feet, he scores 751 points: $[(130 \times 130)/(150 \times 150)] \times 1,000 = 751$.

Points are carried to the first decimal (one-tenth of a point), if necessary, to break a tie. If a tie still exists, the winner is the one with the highest single-event NOPS score.

TERMS

A **balk** occurs when a skier refuses to take a ramp in a jumping event.

A **fall** occurs when a skier loses possession of the tow line, does not have at least one ski on, or does not have his weight primarily supported by one or both skis and is not able to regain skiing position.

A **handle throw** occurs when a skier refuses to enter a jump, slalom, or trick course by throwing her handle in the air before reaching the entry point. She is not penalized for this if the majority of judges agree that she had reason to refuse to enter the course.

A **pass** is registered if a skier in skiing position passes the 180-meter buoy mark on the jump course and does not make a jump, if he falls, or if his handle throw is not acceptable to the judges. Once the boat moves past the ramp, the skier must jump or pass.

A **reride** request may be made by the contestant or by a judge. A reride is allowed for unfair conditions or for faulty equipment. The reride must be taken before the next contestant starts.

A skier has **skiing position** when she has possession of the tow line; is riding on the water with a ski or skis on her feet; and, supported by her ski or skis, is able to regain control.

A judgment of **unfair conditions** can result in a reride for a competitor. Unfair conditions include malfunctioning equipment, fast slalom times, slow jump times, and short trick times.

A **wake** is the area of water disturbed by the towboat, lying at the rope's length, with the crest of the wave as the wake's nominal boundary.

JUMPING

Each contestant gets *three passes* through the jump course. The course begins with a 180-meter buoy and ends with 100-meter buoys.

If the towboat passes the ramp, the skier must *pass* or *jump*. If the skier passes because of hazard or interference, he is allowed another pass. A skier is considered to have passed a jump if he falls within or outside the course, or if his handle throw is not acceptable to the judges. He is considered to have made a jump when he passes over the ramp, lands, and skis to the ride-out buoys without falling. The skier must regain skiing position to be credited with a scoring jump. A skier must be on his skis within three minutes of a fall, or he passes his remaining jumps.

The jumper may tell the boat driver what speed to use; the maximum speed ranges from 28 miles per hour for Boys II, Girls II, and Women VI and VII divisions to 35 miles per hour for Open Men, Men I, and Men II divisions. The jumper may tell the boat driver at what distance to pass the ramp. The driver must drive straight and parallel to the right side of the ramp.

A jumper may petition for a reride due to unfair conditions or for the boat going either too fast or too slow. The boat is timed in two segments to ascertain accurate speeds. A jumper may refuse to enter the course by *throwing her handle* before she reaches the course entry buoy. If the judges agree with her decision not to enter the course, she is not penalized. If they don't agree, the jumper is charged with a pass. If the jumper's handle is damaged after a throw, she is granted three minutes to repair or change the handle. If she is not ready to ski after three minutes, she may not continue that round.

Jump distances are measured from the end of the jump ramp to the point where the skier's heels reach their maximum depression in the water (usually where the plume of water rises upon landing). Distances are calculated to the nearest whole foot; a half foot or more is rounded up.

A jumper's single longest jump is her *official score* for the event. If two jumpers tie, then the one with the longest second jump places higher. If all three of their jumps are equal, then each tied contestant gets two more passes through the course.

SLALOM

The skier skis through the entrance gate of the slalom course and must pass around the outside of the six buoys and proceed through the far-end gate. If she has not missed any buoys or end gates, she may continue making runs through the course until she falls or misses a buoy or gate. The sponsoring club may choose to make rules exceptions or format changes if approved by the AWSA.

A *miss* is defined as riding inside a buoy or outside an end gate, or riding over, straddling, or grazing a buoy. A skier is not penalized for grazing a buoy. A fall inside or outside the course ends the run at that point.

Boat speeds range from a minimum and maximum of 16 and 30 miles per hour, respectively, for Boys I and Girls I divisions, to 30 and 36 miles per hour, respectively, for Open Men. Speed increases by 2 miles per hour on each pass, until the maximum speed for that division is reached. A skier may select his starting speed and rope length, which ranges from 10.25 to 18.25 meters.

Once maximum speed is attained, the rope length is shortened on each subsequent pass, anywhere from 2.25 meters when the rope is between 18.25 and 16 meters long, to .5 meter, beginning when the rope is 11.25 meters long.

The boat is driven in a straight line through the center of the course. A reride may be granted for unfair conditions or when the boat speed is either too slow or too fast. A skier may refuse to enter the course by throwing her handle before she reaches the entry gate. If the judges agree with her decision not to enter the course, she is not penalized. If they don't agree, the skier is scored "0." Once she enters the course, she may not refuse to enter the course on subsequent passes.

If the skier's handle is damaged after a throw, she is granted three minutes to repair or change the handle. If she is not ready to ski after three minutes, she may not continue that round.

Judges mark scores for each pass. Any disagreement is decided by the majority of judges before the next pass. Skiers earn full, half-, or quarter-points for not missing a buoy or gate. In case of a tie, the skier with the most consecutive points scored wins. If skiers are still tied after this, the skier with the fastest boat speed at the shortest rope length where the miss occurred is the winner.

TRICKS

Each contestant gets two 20-second passes through the trick course. He may perform as many tricks as he can during each pass. A trick is any activity that occurs between two hesitations. To receive credit for tricks, a skier must perform tricks listed in the rules and return to skiing position. At larger tournaments the skiers must turn in their declared trick lists before they compete and perform tricks in the order listed to earn points.

A pass begins when the skier makes his first move to do a surface trick after reaching the entrance buoy, when the skier crosses a wake to attempt a wake trick, or when the skier makes no movement to do a trick as he passes the second entrance buoy. A pass ends when 20 seconds have elapsed, when the skier falls, when three minutes have elapsed while the skier is repairing or replacing equipment, or when the skier falls twice while practicing. If the skier falls at the end of the first pass and the 20 seconds have already elapsed, it is not considered a fall.

The skier may choose her boat speed, which must be maintained within one-half mile per hour. She may request a speed change by hand signal in the 50 meters before she enters the course, but if she does this she must accept whatever speed the boat attains and not ask for a reride, assuming that the speed is constant in the course.

The boat path is specified by the judges before the event; the second path is in the opposite direction of the first. The path is reasonably straight throughout the course. A skier may request a reride for unfair conditions, for boat speed that varies beyond the limit allowed, for a boat that does not follow the path, and for timing device malfunctions.

A skier may throw the handle before entering the course. He is not penalized for this if the judges agree with his reasoning for not entering. If the judges do not agree, he is charged with a fall while practicing. If a skier's handle is damaged after a throw, he may be given three minutes to repair or fix it. If he is not ready after that time, he may not continue that round. Trick skiers may use only one line; they may not use a helper line.

In executing a *toe turn trick,* where the skier is towed by one foot, the towing foot may not touch water.

Judges score each trick; if five judges are scoring, at least three must credit a skier for a trick for the skier to receive points. The American Water Ski Association recognizes 55 tricks, with point values ranging from 20 for a sideslide on two skis to 1,000 for a wake double-flip.

If two trick skiers are tied, the skier with the highest-scoring single pass wins. If they are still tied, they get one more pass through the trick course to break the tie.

COURSES

Courses for the Jump, Slalom, and Trick events are marked with buoys and have the following specifications:

Jump Course. This has a 15-meter runup to the ramp, which must be parallel to the course. The ramp is 3.7 to 4.3 meters wide and 6.4 to 6.7 meters long out of the water. It has an apron that extends to 8 inches below the water. See figure 51.1a.

Slalom Course. This is 259 meters long, with buoys set up throughout. See figure 51.1b.

Trick Course. This measures between 157.5 and 192.5 meters long by 12 to 18 meters wide, with an additional 13.5 to 16.5 meters at each end of the course. Buoys set approximately 200 meters apart mark the course.

COMPETITORS

Skiers compete in the following age divisions:

- Boys I/Girls I: 9 years old and under
- Boys II/Girls II: 12 and under
- Boys III/Girls III: 13-16
- Men I/Women I: 17-24
- Men II/Women II: 25-34
- Men III/Women III: 35-44
- Men IV/Women IV: 45-54
- Men V/Women : 55-64
- Men VI/Women VI: 65-74
- Men VII/Women VII: 75 and over
- Open Men/Open Women: any age

Boys I/Girls I divisions do not compete in jumps. Skiers are rated according to ability as follows: 2nd class, 1st class, Expert, Master, Exceptional Performance, and Open. Ratings standards are available from the American Water Ski Association.

EQUIPMENT

Towboats must be able to maintain required speeds. They are equipped with a *towing pylon* that has an area integrated in its design for a trick release mechanism. *Tow lines* are .24 inch thick and 23 meters long. An event also should have one or two *safety boats* in use.

Skiers must wear approved *flotation devices* or suits or vests designed to provide flotation. Maxi-

COURSES

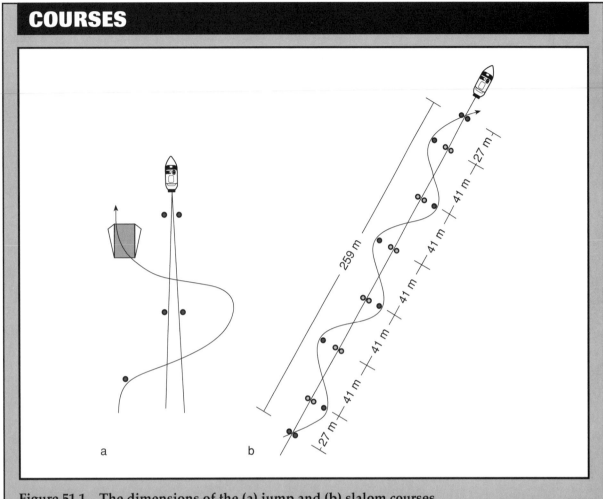

Figure 51.1 The dimensions of the (a) jump and (b) slalom courses.
Adapted from Kistler 1988.

mum *ski* width must not be greater than 30 percent of the length; skiers may use any type of foot binding and fixed fins.

Boat-guide buoys may be spherical, cylindrical, rectangular, or bullet-shaped. *Skier buoys* are usually spherical, 22 to 28 centimeters in diameter, with 11 to 7 centimeters showing out of the water. Buoys are fastened to anchor lines.

OFFICIALS

Officials include a *chief judge*, an *assistant chief judge*, and a *qualifications judge*, as well as *appointed judges*, *boat drivers*, and *scorers*. In case of disagree-ment among judges, the majority rules. An issue is settled before the next contestant begins. Judges are separated, when possible, to ensure independent opinions.

ORGANIZATIONS

American Water Ski Association
799 Overlook Drive
Winter Haven, FL 33884
941-324-4341

International Jet Sports Boating Association
1239 E. Warner Ave.
Santa Ana, CA 92705
714-751-4277

52

Weightlifting

© Claus Andersen

In weightlifting, participants execute two lifts, in this order: the snatch, and the clean and jerk. Each participant gets three attempts at both lifts. Competitions are held in weight divisions, beginning from 46 kilograms for women and 54 kilograms for men. In international competitions, teams of 10 competitors compete in the different divisions, earning points through 15 places (16 points for first place, 14 for second, and down to 1 point for 15th place).

The object is to successfully lift the most weight. As soon as the participant successfully executes the movement and becomes motionless, the referee signals completion of the lift, and the participant may lower the barbell. The source for rules for this chapter is the United States Weightlifting Federation.

PROCEDURES

Lots are drawn for each athlete before a competition. This determines the order of both weigh-in and lifting. Weigh-ins begin two hours before the competition. An athlete who is underweight for his category is eliminated from the competition. An athlete who is overweight for his category may move up to the appropriate category.

When a competitor's name is called, she has one minute to begin her attempt. If she does not begin her attempt within one minute, "No lift" is ruled, and the competitor has one less attempt left for that lift. If a competitor is attempting two lifts in a row, he has two minutes between attempts.

Before each attempt, the athlete or the coach writes the weight required for the attempt. The weight must be in multiples of 2.5 kilograms. The exception is when a record is being attempted; then the weight must be in multiples of 500 grams. An athlete may notify the officials before her name is called if she wishes to decrease or increase the weight she originally selected.

General Rules

These rules apply to both the snatch, and the clean and jerk:

- *Hooking*—covering the thumb joint with the fingers when gripping the bar—is allowed.
- If the competitor lifts the bar to her knees, and then doesn't finish the attempt, it is a *no lift*.
- On the referee's signal to lower the bar, the athlete must not release the bar until it has passed his waist.
- The lifter may swing and rock his body to aid recovery while snatching or cleaning.
- A lifter may not use lubricant or any other substance on the legs.

Snatch

The lifter stands with the barbell on the platform in front of his legs. He grips the barbell, palms down, and in a continuous movement pulls the barbell from the platform to above his head, with his arms fully extended. He may not pause during the lift or touch the bar to his head while lifting it above his head.

He may either split or bend his legs while lifting the bar, and the bar may slide along his thighs and lap as he moves it upward. He may not turn over his wrists until the bar passes the top of his head. He may recover in his own time from a split or squat position. He must hold the weight motionless with his arms and legs fully extended and his feet in a line. When the referee signals that he has executed the lift, he may lower the barbell to the floor.

Clean and Jerk

This lift has two parts. For the *clean*, the athlete stands with the bar on the platform in front of her legs. She grips the bar, palms down, and in a continous movement pulls the bar from the platform to her shoulders. Her elbows or upper arms may not touch her thighs or knees. She may either split or bend her legs as she executes this lift, and the bar may slide along her thighs and lap. The bar may not touch the chest before the final position. It should rest on the clavicles or on the chest above the nipples or on the fully bent arms. She returns her feet to the same line, straightens her legs, and recovers in preparation for the second part, the *jerk*. She and the barbell must be motionless before she begins the jerk.

When the athlete begins the jerking motion by lowering her body or bending her knees, she must complete the movement. To execute the jerk, she bends her legs and extends them and fully extends her arms vertically. She returns her feet to the same line and waits with her arms and legs fully extended for the referee's signal, which will come when she is motionless in this fully extended position. She may then lower the barbell to the platform.

TERMS

A **barbell** is the apparatus containing the bar, the **discs**, and the **collars**.

A **clean** is the first part of the clean and jerk lift. It comprises lifting the barbell from the platform to the shoulders.

Incorrect Movements

In either lift, the athlete may not

- touch the platform with any part of the body other than the feet,
- unevenly or incompletely extend the arms to finish a lift,
- pause while extending the arms,
- finish with a "press-out,"
- bend and extend the arms during recovery,
- touch any area outside the platform during the lift,
- lower the bar to the platform before the referee's signal,
- drop the bar after the referee's signal,
- finish with the feet out of line and not parallel to the plane of the trunk, or
- replace the bar outside the platform.

Collars are used to hold the discs on the barbell.

Discs are of various weights (ranging from .25 kilogram to 25 kilograms) and colors.

Hooking describes the technique of covering the thumb joint with the fingers while gripping the bar.

The **jerk** is the second part of the clean and jerk lift. It involves lifting the barbell from the shoulders to above the head.

"No lift" is called when an athlete commits a fault during a lift or fails to begin a lift in the allotted time.

The **snatch** is a lift that involves lifting the barbell from the platform to above the head.

COMPETITION AREA

All lifts take place on a *platform*, which is square, four meters on each side. The platform is between 50 and 150 millimeters high, is made of wood, plastic, or any solid material, and has a nonslip surface.

ATHLETES

Athletes compete at the junior level (up to and including 20 years old) and at the senior level (no age limit). Men and women compete in the weight categories shown in table 52.1.

Table 52.1: Weight Categories		
Category	Men (kg)	Women (kg)
1	54	46
2	59	50
3	64	54
4	70	59
5	76	64
6	83	70
7	91	76
8	99	83
9	108	>83
10	>108	—

Adapted from USA Weightlifting Federation 1994.

Competitors must wear *costumes* that are one-piece, close-fitting, and collarless. The costumes may not cover the elbows or knees. Lifters may wear a T-shirt under the costume, but it may not cover the elbows. Similarly, they may wear leotards under or over the costume, but these may not touch the knees.

Lifters must wear *weightlifting shoes*, which may have a strap over the instep. The maximum height on the shoes is 130 millimeters from the top of the sole to the top of the shoe. Competitors may wear a *belt*, up to 120 millimeters wide, around the waist to provide support. It must be worn outside the costume.

An athlete may wear bandages, tape, or plaster on the wrists, knees, hands, fingers, and thumbs. The plasters or bandages may not be fastened to the wrist or the bar. Fingerless gloves are allowed. No bandages or similar materials may cover the elbows, the torso, the thighs, the shins, or the arms.

EQUIPMENT

The barbell consists of the bar, the discs, and the collars. The bar weighs 20 kilograms and is 2,200 millimeters long. Its diameter is 28 millimeters on the smooth part of the bar. See table 52.2 for disc weights and colors.

Table 52.2: Disc Weights and Colors	
Weight (kg)	Color
.25	Chrome
.5	Chrome
1.25	Chrome
2.5	Black
5	White
10	Green
15	Yellow
20	Blue
25	Red

Adapted from USA Weightlifting Federation 1994.

The collars, which fasten the discs to the bar, weigh 2.5 kilograms each. The bar is loaded with the heaviest weights toward the inside, and the weights must be fastened with the collars.

OFFICIALS

Referees judge the lifts. At larger competitions, a *secretary* is responsible for running the competition, and *technical controllers* assist the secretary. A *timekeeper* operates the competition clock.

ORGANIZATIONS

United States Weightlifting Federation
1 Olympic Plaza
Colorado Springs, CO 80909
719-578-4508

53

Wrestling

© Mary Langenfeld

The two main styles of international wrestling are *Greco-Roman* and *freestyle*. In Greco-Roman, wrestlers may not attack their opponent's legs or use their own legs to trip, lift, or execute any holds. In freestyle, wrestlers may use their legs to execute holds and to defend against attacks.

While the styles differ, the requirements for scoring points and for winning are the same. A wrestler's goal is to win by pinning his opponent's shoulders to the mat (a *fall*), or to win by scoring more points. Many recent rules changes are geared to making the sport more exciting and the wrestlers more aggressive. The rules discourage passivity and encourage all-out, risk-taking wrestling.

The rules in this chapter are from USA Wrestling, the national governing body for the sport. USA Wrestling follows the rules of the International Wrestling Federation (FILA—Fédération Internationale des Luttes Associées), with modifications for age group competition. Near the end of the chapter is a section on NCAA (National Collegiate Athletic Association) rules.

PROCEDURES

Wrestlers weigh in before their competition to ensure they are not over their weight limit. Participants are then paired off by drawing lots. Lengths of bouts are shown in table 53.1.

Wrestlers are called by name and take their place at the corner of the mat to which they've been assigned (the corners correspond with their singlet colors: either red or blue). The referee calls the wrestlers to the center of the mat and makes sure that the wrestlers' bodies have no greasy or sticky substances on them, that they are not perspiring, and that their fingernails are cut short. The wrestlers shake hands and when the referee blows a whistle, the bout begins. Both wrestlers are standing at the beginning. A bout may be stopped for injury, but if the wrestler cannot continue within two minutes, the bout is over and the opponent wins.

The referee may warn one or both wrestlers regarding *passivity,* which is against the aims and spirit of all-out wrestling. After a verbal warning, if a wrestler is still passive, the referee may stop the bout and give the wrestler a formal warning. The referee then gives the more active wrestler the choice of resuming the action standing or in the *par terre* position (on the mat).

Winning the Bout

A wrestler may win a bout by

- scoring a fall (pinning his opponent's shoulders to the mat long enough for the referee to say "tombé");
- scoring a technical fall (10-point difference; the bout is stopped when any immediate attack or counterattack is finished);
- the opponent's injury, forfeit, withdrawal, or disqualification;
- scoring more points than the opponent; and by
- an official's decision at the end of overtime, if no winner could be declared earlier (see figure 53.1).

Overtime happens when neither wrestler has scored three points or when the score is tied at the end of regulation. The overtime period is not longer than one regulation period. Wrestlers begin in the standing position.

The *minimum victory rule*—where a wrestler must score at least three technical points—is still in effect in overtime. The bout is over when a wrestler achieves a fall or when one competitor scores a technical point that raises his total to at least three technical points.

Table 53.1: Bout Length			
Division	Periods	Time per period	Rest between periods
Bantam (7 to 8)	2	90 sec	30 sec
Midget (9 to 10)	2	90 sec	30 sec
Novice (11 to 12)	2	2 min	30 sec
Schoolboy/girl, USA (13 to 14)	2	2 min	30 sec
Schoolboy/girl international (13 to 14)	1	4 min	—
Cadet (15 to 16)	1	4 min	—
Junior (17 to 18)	1	5 min	—
Espoir (19 to 20)	1	5 min	—
University (18 to 24)	1	5 min	—
Senior (19 and up)	1	5 min	—

© Frances M. Roberts

Figure 53.1.   A wrestler wins a bout by scoring points on his opponent.

If neither wrestler has scored three or more technical points at the end of overtime, the wrestler with the most points wins. If the score is tied, the wrestler with the least cautions and warnings for passivity wins. If a winner can't be determined this way, officials choose a winner.

Scoring Points

Various moves and holds are given point values of 1, 2, 3, or 5 points. Following are examples of how wrestlers may score points. Wrestlers score *one point* when they

- execute a *takedown* (bring their opponent to the mat but do not put him in danger of a fall),
- execute a *reversal* (move out from underneath an opponent and gain control),
- force their opponent down on one or two outstretched arms or on his back,
- compete against an opponent who flees a hold or the mat,
- hold their opponent in a position of danger for five seconds or longer, and when they
- break free while in the par terre position and rise to a standing position to face their opponent.

Wrestlers score *two points* when they

- place their opponent in a position of danger or in an *instantaneous fall* situation (when both the opponent's shoulders touch the mat at the same time),
- roll their opponent onto her shoulders,
- face an opponent who flees a hold while in danger,

Scoring a Fall

Both shoulders must be simultaneously pinned against the mat long enough for the referee to observe total control. When the fall takes place at the edge of the mat, both shoulders must be completely in contact with the passivity zone; the head may not be touching the protection area. A fall in the protection area is not valid. The fall is valid when the judge or mat chairman agrees with the referee's decision. The referee strikes the mat and blows a whistle to signify a fall.

- face an opponent who goes into an instantaneous fall or rolls onto his shoulders while executing a hold, and when they
- block the opponent's execution of a hold while in the standing position and in a danger position.

Wrestlers score *three points* when they

- execute a hold (a *short-amplitude* move), while standing, that brings their opponent to a position of danger on the mat;
- raise a wrestler off the ground and place him in danger (this can happen with one or both of the attacking wrestler's knees on the ground and even if the defending wrestler maintains contact with the ground with a hand); and when they
- execute a *grand amplitude* hold that does not place the opponent in immediate danger.

Wrestlers score *five points* when they

- execute a grand amplitude hold from a standing position that places the opponent in immediate danger, and when they
- lift their opponent off the ground in executing a grand amplitude hold that places them in immediate danger.

Classification Points

The points awarded at the end of a bout are indicated in table 53.2.

TERMS

Most organizations have a **blood rule** that guides the course of action when a participant is bleeding. See the sidebar, "Blood Rule."

A **bout** is the competition, or match, between two wrestlers.

Blood Rule

USA Wrestling regulations state that an athlete known to be infected with the HIV/HBV virus may not compete; likewise, health care attendants known to have AIDS may not attend to bleeding athletes. When a wrestler is bleeding in competition, the bout is stopped and the athlete may not continue unless the bleeding and spread of blood is stopped within five minutes. Blood must be cleaned from the mat and from uniforms and bodies with a bleach solution, which must be dried before competition resumes.

A wrestler creates a **bridge** to support himself on his head, elbows, and feet, to keep from touching his shoulders to the mat.

Brutality is unnecessary roughness with intent to injure the opponent. A wrestler may be disqualified for such an act.

A wrestler receives a **bye** in tournament play when he has no opponent in a given round.

A **caution** may be issued for an illegal hold, fleeing a hold or the mat, or refusing to take the proper starting position. A wrestler is disqualified after three cautions.

The **center circle** is one meter in diameter in the center of the mat. It is the starting area.

The **central wrestling area** is the middle of the mat, seven meters across, where most of the action should be taking place.

A **correct hold** refers to a well-executed throw that doesn't result in a **takedown** or in putting the opponent in danger. A wrestler may be awarded a point for such a throw.

Table 53.2: Classification Points		
4 points for victory by . . .	3 points for victory by . . .	1 point in loss where . . .
Fall, technical fall, injury default, withdrawal, forfeit, disqualification	Points	At least one technical point is scored by the losing wrestler

A **counter move** is one that stops or blocks an opponent's attack. A wrestler may score on a counter move.

A wrestler is in the **danger position** when the line of his shoulders or back forms an angle with the mat that's less than 90 degrees, and when he resists with the upper body to avoid a fall.

A **decision** refers to a victory on points, with a margin of one to nine points.

A **default** occurs when a bout is determined by injury.

A wrestler is **disqualified** after three cautions, or for misconduct.

A wrestler is awarded an **escape point** when he escapes from the bottom position and rises to a standing position to face his opponent.

A **fall** is scored when a wrestler pins his opponent's shoulders to the mat.

A wrestler **flees a hold** when he refuses contact to prevent the opponent from executing a hold. This may result in a **caution**, a penalty point, and choice of position for the opponent.

Fleeing the mat to elude an opponent's attack may result in a **caution**, a penalty point, and choice of position for the opponent. If the fleeing occurred from a danger position, two penalty points are awarded to the opponent.

A **forfeit** occurs when a wrestler fails to show for his bout.

A **grand amplitude** hold is a high, sweeping throw during which the opponent is lifted off the mat.

A **gut wrench** is a hold applied to a wrestler's torso in order to turn him to score points.

Two points are awarded for a gut wrench when executed in the **danger position**, one point when not in the danger position. However, a wrestler must score at least one technical point after scoring a gut wrench before he can score on another gut wrench.

An **illegal hold** is one prohibited by the rules (see "Illegal Actions and Holds," page 356). A wrestler is cautioned for an illegal hold, and the opponent may be awarded one or two points.

Par terre position is a starting position in which one wrestler begins with hands and knees on the ground and the other wrestler begins with his hands on the back of the wrestler on the ground.

The **passivity zone** is the outermost part of the mat that is in bounds. When wrestlers reach the passivity zone, the referee calls "Zone!" and they must attempt to return to the center of the mat while not interrupting their action.

Positive points are the classification points awarded to a wrestler to determine his position in his group (see "Classification Points," page 354).

The **protection area** of the mat borders the **passivity zone** (see figure 53.2 on page 356). It is out of bounds.

A **red card** signals the expulsion of a coach for unsportsmanlike behavior. A red card is preceded by a **yellow card**, which is a warning.

A **reversal** (one point) is executed by a wrestler who comes out from underneath the other wrestler and gains control of his opponent.

A **slam** occurs when a wrestler throws an opponent down with unnecessary force without accompanying him to the mat. A slam is illegal in Kids competition.

A **slipped throw** is an unsuccessful attempt at a throw from either a standing position or from the **par terre position**.

A **takedown** (one point) occurs when a wrestler takes his opponent to the mat in a position not in danger.

A **technical fall** occurs when a wrestler wins by 10 or more points.

Technical points refer to points scored for holds and moves. Penalty points may also count as technical points.

Tombé is the French word for "fall." The referee says this word to count time during a fall.

COMPETITION AREA

The *mat* is cushioned canvas or synthetic material with a diameter of 9 meters (see figure 53.2). The center circle is in the center of the mat, 1 meter in diameter. It has a thin red border. The central wrestling area is 7 meters in diameter.

COMPETITION AREA

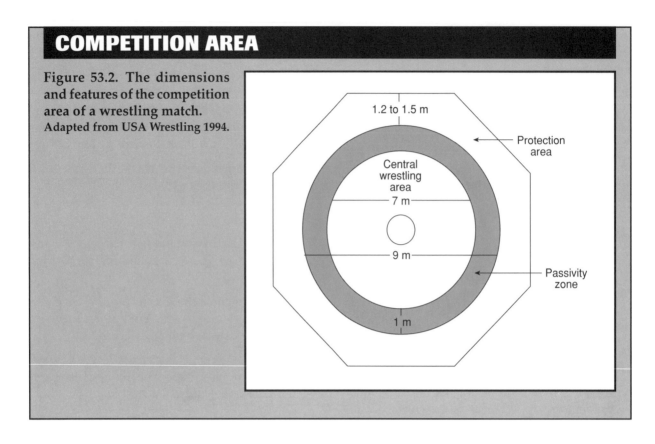

Figure 53.2. The dimensions and features of the competition area of a wrestling match. Adapted from USA Wrestling 1994.

The passivity zone is red and encircles the central wrestling area. It is 1 meter wide. The protection area surrounds the passivity zone and is 1.2 to 1.5 meters wide.

For greater visibility, the mat can be set on a platform not more than 1.1 meters high.

No ropes or posts are allowed. Diagonally opposite corners of the mat are marked in red and blue.

ATHLETES

Wrestlers compete in age divisions categorized by weight, as shown in table 53.3.

EQUIPMENT

Wrestlers wear *singlets* (tight-fitting, one-piece uniforms), either red or blue, corresponding to their corner of the mat. *Headgear* to protect the ears is prohibited in international competition but is allowed in the United States at the junior and younger levels.

Knee pads are permissible. Wrestlers must wear *shoes* with soft, pliable soles. Except in case of injury, bandages on wrists, arms, and ankles are not allowed.

ILLEGAL ACTIONS AND HOLDS

Wrestlers are not allowed to pull hair, ears, or genitals; pinch, bite, kick, or head-butt; strangle; twist fingers; use a hold that may fracture or dislocate a limb; or act in any way to intentionally injure an opponent.

Wrestlers may not cling to the mat, talk during the bout, or grab the sole of the opponent's foot. (Grabbing the upper part of the foot or the heel is allowed.) Wrestlers may not flee a hold or flee the mat. (See "Terms" section for penalties.) *Illegal holds* include

- holding the throat;
- twisting an arm more than 90 degrees, including behind the back;
- applying a forearm lock;

	Table 53.3: Age Divisions and Weight Classes	
Division	Weight classes	Heavyweight difference no more than . . .
Bantam (7 to 8)	9 classes: 40 to 75 lb, plus heavyweight	15 lb
Midget (9 to 10)	15 classes: 50 to 130 lb, plus heavyweight	20 lb
Novice (11 to 12)	18 classes: 60 to 165 lb, plus heavyweight	25 lb
Schoolboy/girl (13 to 14)	19 classes: 70 to 175 lb, plus heavyweight	30 lb
Cadet (15 to 16)	13 classes: 83.5 to 242 lb	—
Junior (17 to 18)	12 classes: 98 to 275 lb	—
Espoir (19 to 20)	10 classes: 105 to 286 lb	—
University (18 to 24)	10 classes: 105 to 286 lb	—
Senior (19 and up)	10 classes: 105 to 286 lb	—

Adapted from USA Wrestling, Inc. 1995.

- executing a three-quarter nelson or double nelson (unless executed from the side, without using the legs on any part of the opponent's body);
- stretching the opponent's spinal column;
- using two arms on an opponent's head or neck (one arm may be used);
- breaking a "bridge" by pushing in the direction of the opponent's head;
- lifting an opponent in a bridge position and throwing her to the mat; and
- holding an opponent upside down and then falling on top of her (a "header").

If a wrestler uses any of these holds, the action is void, and the wrestler is either warned or cautioned. If a defending wrestler executes an illegal hold in an attempt to prevent the attacking wrestler from executing his hold, he will be cautioned, and his opponent will be given two points.

OFFICIALS

Three officials work competitions: a *referee*, a *mat chairman*, and a *judge*. Referees work the mat and are in charge of the bout. They wear a red cuff on their left arm and a blue cuff on their right arm, and raise the appropriate arm and fingers to indicate points for the wrestlers.

The mat chairman is the head official and settles any disagreements between the referee and the judge. The judge marks points on a scoresheet, consults with the referee, and verifies and signals a fall. He or she may indicate a passive wrestler. Doctors and other medical attendants may declare a wrestler unfit to continue. Officials' signals are shown in figure 53.3.

NCAA MODIFICATIONS

Modifications are categorized in the following sections: Mat, Weight Classifications and Rules, Match Length and Procedures, and Scoring.

Mat

The wrestling area may be either square (no less than 32 feet and no greater than 42 feet on all sides) or circular (no less than 32 feet in diameter and no greater than 42 feet in diameter). A *mat area* or *apron*, at least 5 feet wide, encompasses the wrestling area.

Indicating no control

Awarding points

Reversal

Near fall

Stalling

Unsportsmanlike conduct

(continued)

Figure 53.3.   Common official's signals in wrestling.

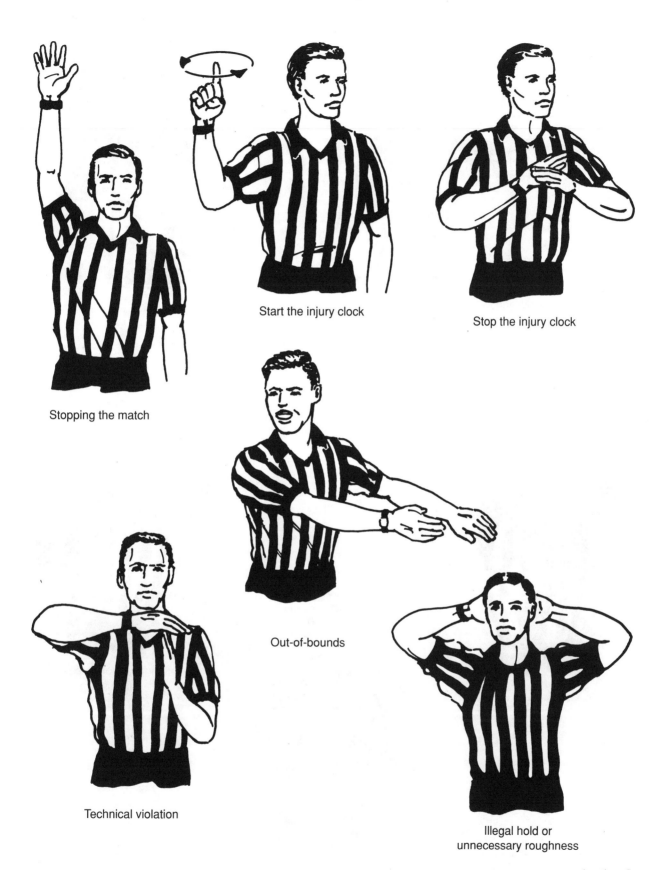

Stopping the match

Start the injury clock

Stop the injury clock

Out-of-bounds

Technical violation

Illegal hold or
unnecessary roughness

(continued)

Figure 53.3. *(continued)*

Indicating wrestler
in control

Stalemate

Time out

Neutral position

Potentially dangerous

Figure 53.3. *(continued)*

At the center of the mat is a circle, 10 feet in diameter. Inside this circle are two 1-inch *starting lines;* they are 3 feet long and 10 inches apart. One starting line is green and located closest to the home team; the other is red, and nearest the visitors.

Weight Classifications and Rules

Wrestlers are divided into 10 weight classifications, including

- 118 pounds,
- 126 pounds,
- 134 pounds,
- 142 pounds,
- 150 pounds,
- 158 pounds,
- 167 pounds,
- 177 pounds,
- 190 pounds, and
- Heavyweight (177 pounds to 275 pounds).

For dual, triangular, and quadrangular meets, wrestlers *weigh in* between 5 hours before and 30 minutes before the meet. For tournaments, wrestlers weigh in each day.

Wrestlers are allowed the following *weight allowances* (excess weight), except for qualifying tournaments, which must be wrestled at scratch weight:

- November—3 pounds
- December—3 pounds
- January—2 pounds
- February—1 pound

In all tournaments, wrestlers may weigh one pound more each day, above the weight limit of the previous day (up to two pounds more). Wrestlers may not forfeit in one weight class and wrestle in another, or compete in more than one weight class in any meet. A wrestler may, however, weigh in at one weight and then shift to a higher weight class.

Match Length and Procedures

Matches last seven minutes, split into periods of three, two, and two minutes. Multiple dual meet matches and tournament matches may last less than seven minutes.

Each match is begun with both wrestlers standing. A premeet coin toss determines which team has the *choice of position* (top, bottom, neutral) at the start of the second period. The winner may choose the odd- or even-numbered weight classes.

The wrestler with the choice of position may either make his choice or defer until the third period. If he defers, his opponent chooses the position to begin the second period. In a tournament, choice of position is determined for each match by a coin toss by the referee at the beginning of the second period. The other wrestler has the choice for the third period.

An injured or ill wrestler has up to one and a half minutes of *injury timeout* throughout the match. This time is cumulative, and only the referee may call such timeouts. Timeout for excessive bleeding does not count against the wrestler's one and a half minutes of injury timeout.

If the match score is tied at the end of regulation, one sudden-death *overtime* period, with a two-minute maximum, immediately follows. Wrestlers begin in the neutral position; the first to score wins.

If neither wrestler scores in the overtime, a 30-second *tiebreaker* is wrestled. A coin toss determines which wrestler is up and which is down. The wrestler who scores first wins. If neither wrestler scores in the tiebreaker, the offensive wrestler is declared the winner. At the end of the match, the wrestlers shake hands and the referee declares the winner.

Scoring

As mentioned earlier, wrestlers may score by *takedown, escape,* and *reversal.* They may also score a *near fall,* where a wrestler has his opponent in a controlled pinning situation for at least two seconds (two points) or at least five seconds (three points). Points may also be awarded for an *imminent score,* when a wrestler is injured and action is stopped just before successful completion of a scoring move appeared imminent.

If a wrestler accumulates one minute or more of *time advantage,* he receives one point. Both shoulders of a wrestler must be pinned to the mat for one second for a *fall* to occur. Part of both shoulders must be in bounds. A *technical fall* occurs when a wrestler gains a 15-point advantage. (A time advantage cannot be counted toward a technical fall until regulation time expires.)

A *major decision* occurs when the margin of victory is between 8 and 14 points, inclusively. A *decision* is a victory with the margin less than 8 points. Individual and team scoring are shown in table 53.4.

ORGANIZATIONS

Amateur Athletic Union Wrestling
c/o Bob Johnson
328 22nd Ave.
Brookings, SD 57006
605-692-6765

National Wrestling Coaches Association
Iowa State University
10 State Gym
Ames, IA 50011
515-294-4642

USA Wrestling
6155 Lehman Drive
Colorado Springs, CO 80918
719-598-8181

Table 53.4: Individual and Team Scoring			
	Individual points	Team points, dual	Team points tourney
Takedown	2	—	—
Escape	1	—	—
Reversal	2	—	—
Near fall	2 or 3	—	—
Time advantage	1	—	—
Fall, forfeit, default, disqualification	—	6	1
Technical fall	—	5	3/4
Major decision	—	4	1/2
Decision	—	3	—
Bye followed by a win, championship bracket	—	—	1
Bye followed by a win, consolation bracket	—	—	1/2

54

Yachting

© Photophile/Frank Grundman

Yachting began as recreation in Holland in the 1600s and later caught on in England. The word *yacht* is a Dutch term for "ship for chasing." Modern racing began in the early 1800s; by the mid-1800s, rules for *regattas,* or sailing races, were in use in England, Scotland, and Ireland.

Yachting in the United States began in the early 1800s; racing takes place inshore for smaller boats and offshore for larger yachts. There are many types of yachts, including *dinghies,* which are open crafts without ballast (added weight); *keel boats,* which have ballasts; and *catamarans,* which have two hulls connected by beams, a deck, or a trampoline. There are also various classes of races and types of courses (see "Course"). The object is to complete the course in the shortest time. The rules for this chapter were provided by the United States Sailing Association, by permission of the International Yacht Racing Union.

PROCEDURES

A race starts with three flag and sound signals. Each yacht must pass each mark on the course on the required side, in correct sequence, so that a line representing its wake falls on the required side of each mark (see figure 54.1). Yachts may be propelled only by sailing; the crew may not use their bodies to propel the craft, except to exaggerate the rolling through a *tack* or a *gybe* (see "Terms"). Rigging may be adjusted and operated by manual power only. A yacht finishes a race when any part of its hull, or of its crew or equipment in normal position, crosses the finish line, in the direction from the last *mark*.

TERMS

A yacht is **clear astern** of another craft when its hull and equipment are behind the other craft's hull and equipment. The other yacht is **clear ahead**.

A yacht is said to be **close-hauled** when it is sailing as close to the wind as it can lie, which is about 45 degrees off the direction of the wind.

A yacht **gybes** when the foot of its mainsail crosses its center line and the mainsail fills on the other **tack** (either starboard or port side).

The **leeward side** is the side on which the yacht is carrying its mainsail, or the side on which the yacht was carrying its mainsail when head to wind.

A yacht **luffs** when it alters its course toward the wind.

A **mark** is an object that a yacht must round or pass on a required side.

An **obstruction** is any object that requires a yacht, when more than one overall length from it, to substantially alter its course to pass it.

A yacht is **on a tack** except when it is **tacking** or **gybing**. The tack, either starboard or port, corresponds to the windward side.

Yachts **overlap** when neither is **clear astern**.

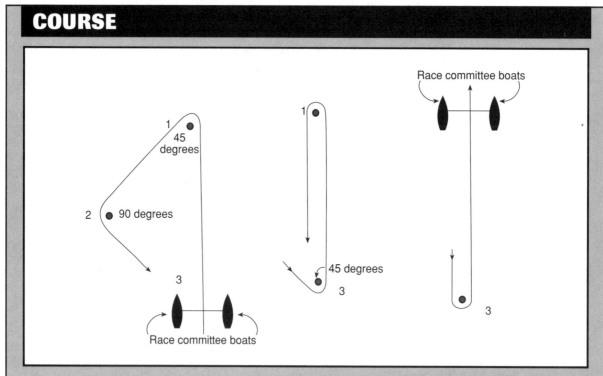

COURSE

Figure 54.1. A typical course used in yachting. The boat starts by going through two race committee boats and then follows the numbered path and ends by going through two race committe boats again.

Adapted from International Sailing Federation 1997.

A yacht **tacks** from the time it is beyond head to wind until it has borne away to a close-hauled course on its new tack.

Windward side is opposite the leeward side.

MARKS AND OBSTRUCTIONS

Yachts must pass each mark on the prescribed side. They may neither touch a mark nor shift it to avoid touching it. If a yacht touches a mark, it must promptly complete a 360-degree penalty turn before continuing the race. It must keep clear of other yachts while doing so.

When two yachts are close-hauled on the same tack and about to meet an obstruction, and the yacht clear ahead or to leeward cannot tack without colliding with the other yacht, it may hail the other yacht for room to tack. The hailed yacht shall then either tack promptly or tell the hailing yacht to tack, in which case it shall give room for the hailing yacht to tack and clear it. A yacht must keep clear of another yacht that is rescuing a person overboard or that is anchored, aground, or capsized.

RIGHT-OF-WAY

A yacht may not hinder another yacht that is in the process of exonerating itself (see "Marks and Obstructions"). A yacht with the right-of-way may not alter course to prevent another yacht from keeping clear, except while

- luffing (to prevent another yacht from passing it to windward and taking its wind);
- assuming a proper course to start, when it is on the starboard tack and the other yacht is on the port tack; and while
- rounding a mark.

A port-tack yacht (i.e., one with the boom over the starboard, or right, side) must keep clear of a starboard-tack yacht (i.e., one with the boom over the port, or left, side). When boats are on the same tack and they are overlapped, a windward yacht must keep clear of a leeward yacht. If they are not overlapped, the yacht that is clear astern must keep clear of the yacht that is clear ahead.

A yacht that is either tacking or gybing must keep clear of a yacht on a tack. When two yachts are both tacking or both gybing, the one on the other's port (left) side must keep clear. When one yacht is tacking and the other is gybing, the one that is tacking must keep clear.

SCORING

The two scoring systems most often used are the bonus-points scoring system (formerly the Olympic system) and the low-point scoring system. In both systems, lower point totals are better.

The bonus-points system uses a "curved" points schedule that provides additional rewards for the top six finishers. The bonus-points system is used for a series of seven races, five of which must be completed. A yacht's total score is the sum of its score for all races, excluding its worst score. Lowest total score wins.

The low-point system uses a "straight" schedule that awards points in direct proportion to finish place. The number of races scheduled and the number required to constitute a series depend on the event. A yacht's total score is the sum of its scores for all races, excluding its worst score. Lowest total score wins. See table 54.1 for points awarded in each system.

Ties are broken in favor of the yacht with more first places. If a tie still remains, the nod goes to the yacht with more second places, and so on, until the tie is broken. An alternative scoring system for a long series, spanning several weeks, is the corresponding point total for each finishing place (one point for first place, two points for second, and so on).

PROTESTS

A yacht may file a protest if it is directly involved in or witnesses an incident. A yacht protesting another yacht must hail that yacht its intentions to do so and display a code flag for protest. The protest committee may hold a hearing if it accepts the protest and make a decision based on the finding of facts. If a protest is upheld, a yacht will be disqualified and may be

Finish place	Bonus-points system points	Low-point system points
First	0	.75
Second	3	2
Third	5.7	3
Fourth	8	4
Fifth	10	5
Sixth	11.7	6
Seventh and thereafter	Place + 6	Place

Table 54.1: Scoring Systems

Adapted from International Sailing Federation 1997.

penalized beyond disqualification for gross infringement of rules or misconduct.

COMPETITORS

Competitors must wear life jackets for adequate personal buoyancy when conditions warrant. They may not carry clothing or equipment to increase their weight. The total weight of clothing and equipment cannot be capable of exceeding either 15 kilograms or 20 kilograms, depending on the class rules. When in a position to do so, yachts must render assistance to any yacht or person in peril.

EQUIPMENT

Sails, anchors, and other equipment vary according to the class and event. Yachts must carry lifesaving equipment for all persons on board, unless otherwise prescribed by class rules.

OFFICIALS

Officials include *race* and *protest committees.* Competitors, however, may protest other yachts and are required to note their own violations.

ORGANIZATIONS

United States Sailing Association
Box 1260
Portsmouth, RI 02871-6015
401-683-0800

Credits

Table 1.2: Adapted from International Ski Federation, 1992, *The international ski competition rules* (Switzerland: Author), 22.

Figure 3.1, Table 3.2: Adapted, by permission, from Fédération Internationale de Tir à l'Arc, 1994, *F.I.T.A. constitution and rules* (Milan, Italy: Author) 76, 77.

Figures 4.1 and 4.2: Adapted, by permission, from T.D. Jacques, 1994, *Australian football: steps to success* (Champaign, IL: Human Kinetics), 2-3.

Figure 5.1: Adapted, by permission, from The International Badminton Federation, 1990, Badminton. In *Sports rules encyclopedia*, 2d ed., edited by J.R. White (Champaign, IL: Leisure Press), 17.

Table 6.2: Adapted, by permission, from PONY Baseball and Softball, 1995, PONY baseball and softball annual rules and regulations (Washington, PA: Author), 12-13.

Figure 6.2: Adapted, by permission, from J.R. White, 1990, *Sports rules encyclopedia*, 2d ed. (Champaign, IL: Leisure Press), 27.

Figure 7.1: Adapted, by permission, from J.R. White, 1990, *Sports rules encyclopedia*, 2d ed. (Champaign, IL: Leisure Press), 38.

Tables 8.1 and 8.2: Adapted from Union Internationale de Pentathlon Moderne et Biathlon, 1994, *Event and competition rules* (Austria: Author), 37, 65.

Figure 9.1: Adapted, courtesy of American Bowling Congress/Women's International Bowling Congress/Young American Bowling Congress, 1995, *1995-96 playing rules book* (Greendale, WI: American Bowling Congress), 6.

Table 10.2: Adapted, by permission, from United States Amateur Boxing, Inc., 1995, *USA boxing: official rules 1995-1997* (Colorado Springs: Author), 57, 59.

Table 11.1: Adapted, by permission, from International Canoe Federation, 1993, *Slalom and wildwater racing competition rules* (Budapest: Author), 6.

Figure 12.1: Adapted, by permission, from T. Melville, 1993, *Cricket for Americans: Playing and understanding the game* (Bowling Green, OH: Bowling Green State University Popular Press), 5.

Table 13.1: Adapted, by permission, from United States Ski and Snowboard Association, 1993, *Cross country rulebook* (Park City, UT: Author), 64-65.

Figure 14.1: Adapted, courtesy of, USA Curling ™, 1995, *U.S. Curling Association rules for play 1995/96* (Stevens Point, WI: Author), 2.

Figure 15.1: Adapted, by permission, from The Diagram Group, 1983, *The rulebook* (New York, NY: St. Martin's Press), 74.

Tables 17.1, 17.2, 17.3, and 17.4: Adapted from American Horse Shows Association, 1995, *The American Horse Shows Association rulebook 1996-1997* (New York: Author), 164-165.

Figures 18.1 and 18.2: Adapted, by permission, from United States Fencing Association, 1994, *United States Fencing Association rulebook* (Colorado Springs: author), 4.

Figure 21.2: Adapted, by permission, from National Football League, 1994, *Official rules of the NFL* (Chicago, IL: Triumph Books).

Tables 22.1 and 22.2 Adapted, by permission, from U.S. Golf Association, 1994, *1995 Official Rules of Golf* (Chicago, IL: Triumph Books), 141, 195.

Figures 23.1 and 23.2 Adapted, by permission, from American Coaching Effectiveness Program in cooperation with the United States Gymnastics Federation, 1992, *Rookie coaches gymnastics guide* (Champaign, IL: Human Kinetics), 34-35.

Figure 24.1: Adapted, by permission, from U.S. Handball Association, 1991, *The new and official United States Handball Association rulebook* (Tucson, AZ: Author), 38.

Figure 25.1: Adapted, by permission, from USA Hockey, 1990, Ice hockey. In *Sports rules encyclopedia*, 2d ed., edited by J.R. White (Champaign, IL: Leisure Press), 343.

Table 25.2: Adapted, by permission, from USA Hockey, 1993, *Official playing rules 1993-95* (Colorado Springs: Author), 12.

Figure 26.1: Adapted, by permission, from International Judo Federation. *Home page*. [Online]. Available WWW (World Wide Web): http://www.ijf.org/24.gif (April 1997).

Figure 27.1: Adapted, by permission, from USA Karate Federation, 1995, *USA Karate rules and regulations for competitions including the World Karate Federation rules for competition* (Akron, OH: Author), 2.

Figure 28.1: Adapted, by permission, from U.S. Women's Lacrosse Association, 1996, *Official rules for women's lacrosse* (Chevy Chase, MD: Author), 11, 15.

Figure 28.2: Adapted, by permission, from National Collegiate Athletic Association, 1996, *NCAA lacrosse men's rules* (Overland Park, KS: Author), 10.

Tables 29.1 and 29.2: Adapted from Union Internationale de Pentathlon Moderne et Biathlon, 1996, *Modern pentathlon competition rules* (Budapest: Author), 75, 81.

Table 30.1: Data from International Federation of Netball Associations, 1991, *Official rules* (Mosman, Australia: Author); J. Magnay, 1991, *8ᵗʰ world championship—Sydney 1991* (Hornsby, Australia: Chevron Publishing Group); and M. Thomas, 1994, *Know the game: netball* (London: Black).

Figure 30.1: Adapted, by permission, from Wilma Shakespear, 1997, *Netball: steps to success* (Champaign, IL: Human Kinetics), 3.

Table 31.1: Adapted, by permission, from U.S. Orienteering Federation, 1990, Orienteering. In *Sports rules encyclopedia*, 2d ed., edited by J.R. White (Champaign, IL: Leisure Press), 399.

Figure 33.1: Adapted, by permission, from USA Roller Skating, *USA roller hockey rules*, 2d ed. (Lincoln, NE: Author), 7.

Table 34.1: Adapted, by permission, from U.S. Rowing Association, 1996, *1996 rules of rowing* (Indianapolis, IN: Author), 36.

Figure 35.2: Adapted, by permission from J.T. Powell, 1976, *Inside rugby: the team game* (Washington, D.C.: Regnery Publishing, Inc.), 7.

Tables 36.1, 36.2, 36.3, and 36.4: Adapted, by permission, from USA Shooting, 1995, *Official rules for international shooting* (Colorado Springs: Author), GR26, GR27, F4, P48.

Figure 37.2: Adapted, by permission, from American Coaching Effectiveness Program, 1991, *Rookie coaches soccer guide* (Champaign, IL: Human Kinetics), 39.

Figure 38.2: Adapted, by permission, from J.R. White, 1990, *Sports rules encyclopedia*, 2d ed. (Champaign, IL: Leisure Press), 27.

Tables 38.3 and 38.4: Adapted, by permission, from Amateur Softball Association/USA Softball, 1993, *'94 ASA guide and playing rules* (Oklahoma City, OK: Author), 56.

Tables 39.1 and 39.2: Adapted, by permission, from Amateur Speedskating Union of the United States, 1997, *Speedskating handbook* (Glen Ellyn, IL: Author).

Figure 39.1: Adapted, by permission, from Amateur Speedskating Union of the United States, 1988, *1988-1989 Amateur Skating Union handbook* (Glen Ellyn, IL: Author), 70.

Figure 40.1: Adapted, by permission, from U.S. Squash Racquets Association, *International rules of squash* (Bala-Cynwyd, PA: Author), 23.

Tables 41.1 and 41.2: Adapted, by permission, from United States Swimming, 1996, *United states swimming 1996 rules and regulations* (Colorado Springs, CO: author), 17.

Tables 42.1, 42.2, 42.3, and 42.4: Adapted, by permission, from United States Synchronized Swimming, 1995, *1995-1996 United States Synchronized Swimming official rules* (Indianapolis, IN: author), 17, 23.

Figure 43.1: Adapted, by permission, from United States Table Tennis Association, 1990, Table tennis. In *Sports rules encyclopedia* 2d ed., edited by J.R. White (Champaign, IL: Leisure Press), 543.

Table 44.1: Adapted, by permission, from United States Taekwondo Union, 1993, *United States Taekwondo Union: school/club handbook* (Colorado Springs, CO: Author), B4.

Figure 44.1: Adapted, by permission, from International Judo Federation. *Home page*. [Online]. Available WWW (World Wide Web): http://www.ijf.org/24.gif (April 1997).

Figure 45.1: Adapted, by permission, from International Handball Federation,1993, *International handball federation: rules of the game* (Switzerland: Author), 7.

Figure 46.1: Adapted, by permission, from United States Tennis Association, Inc., 1995, *1995 rules of tennis and cases and decisions* (White Plains, NY: Author), 2.

Figure 47.1: Adapted, by permission, from The Athletics Congress's Development Committees and V. Gambetta, 1981, *The Athletic Congress's track and field coaching manual* (Champaign, IL: Leisure Press), 1.

Tables 47.1, 47.2, 47.3, 47.4, 47.5, 47.6, and 47.7: Adapted, by permission, from USA Track and Field, 1995, *Competition rules 1995* (Indianapolis, IN: Author), 18-19, 23-24, 97, 154, 152, 176, 177-178.

Table 49.1: Adapted, by permission, from USA Volleyball, 1995, *United States Volleyball official rules* (Lynn, MA: H.O. Zimman, Inc.), 13. For a copy of the latest rulebook, contact Volleyball Informational Products at 1-800-275-8782.

Figure 49.1: Adapted, by permission, from Federation Internationale de Volleyball, 1997, *Official 1995 United States Volleyball rules as approved by USA Volleyball*, edited by J.B. Blue (France: Author), 81.

Figure 50.1: Adapted, by permission, from United States Water Polo, Inc., 1990, Water polo abridgment of official water polo rules. In *Sports rules encyclopedia*, 2d ed., edited by J.R. White (Champaign, IL: Human Kinetics), 659.

Figure 51.1: Adapted, by permission, from B. Kistler, 1988, *Hit it: your complete guide to water skiing* (Champaign, IL: Leisure Press), 124.

Tables 52.1 and 52.2: Adapted, by permission, from United States Weightlifting Federation, 1994, *Official rulebook 1994 edition* (Colorado Springs, CO: Author), 53-53, 57.

Figure 53.2: Adapted, by permission, from USA Wrestling, 1997, *International rulebook and guide to wrestling 1997 edition* (Colorado Springs, CO: Author), 15.

Table 53.3: Adapted, by permission, from USA Wrestling, 1995, International rulebook and guide to wrestling: freestyle and greco-roman, 1995 edition (Colorado Springs, CO: Author), 59.

Table 54.1; Figure 54.1: Adapted, by permission, from International Sailing Federation, 1997, *Racing rules of sailing for 1997-2000* (London, England: Author).

References

Amateur Softball Association/USA Softball (1993). '94 ASA guide & playing rules. Oklahoma City: Author.

Amateur Speedskating Union of the United States (1995). Speedskating handbook. Author.

American Amateur Racquetball Association (1995). 1995-96 official rules of racquetball. Colorado Springs: Author.

American Horse Shows Association (1995). The American Horse Shows Association rule book 1996-1997. New York City, NY: Author.

American Water Ski Association (1996). Official tournament rules. Winter Haven, FL: Author.

Babe Ruth Baseball (1995). Bambino division rules and regulations. Trenton, NJ: Author.

Bass Anglers Sportsman Society (1997). 1996-97 official rules of bass anglers sportsman society bassmaster tournaments. Montgomery, AL: Author.

Broido, B. (1992). Spalding book of rules and 1993 sports almanac. Indianapolis: Masters Press.

East, A. Frequently asked questions (FAQ) for rec.sport.football.australian. [Online]. Available WWW (World Wide Web): http://www.ozsports.com.au/Football/FAQ.html (April 30, 1977).

Fédération Internationale de Football Association (1994). Official rules of soccer. Chicago: Triumph Books.

Gullion, L. (1993). Nordic skiing: steps to success. Champaign, IL: Human Kinetics.

Jacques, Trevor D. (1994). Australian football: steps to success. Champaign, IL: Human Kinetics.

International Archery Federation (1994). Constitution and rules: FITA. Milan, Italy: Author.

International Biathlon Union (1994). Event & competition rules. Wals-Himmelreich, Austria: Author.

International Canoe Federation (1993). Flatwater racing competition rules. Budapest: Author.

International Canoe Federation (1993). Slalom and wildwater racing competition rules. Budapest: Author.

International Federation of Netball Associations (1991). Official rules. Mosman, Australia: Author.

International Gymnastics Federation (1989). Code of points: artistic gymnastic for men. Switzerland: Author.

International Gymnastics Federation (1989). Code of points: artistic gymnastic for women. Switzerland: Author.

International Handball Federation (1993). Rules of the game. Basel, Switzerland: Author.

International Hockey Federation (1995). Rules of hockey 1995. Surrey, England: Author.

International Rugby Football Board. The laws of the game of rugby football. [Online]. Available WWW (World Wide Web): http://rugby.phys.uidaho.edu/rugby/Rules/LawBook/contents.html (April 30, 1997).

International Ski Federation (1992). The international ski competition rules. Berne, Switzerland: Author.

Magnay, J. (1991). 8th world netball championship—Sydney 1991. Hornsby, Australia: Chevron Publishing Group.

Major League Baseball (1994). Official baseball rules (1994 edition). St. Louis: The Sporting News.

Melville, T. (1993). Cricket for Americans: playing and understanding the game. Bowling Green, OH: Bowling Green State University Popular Press.

National Collegiate Athletic Association (1996). 1996 NCAA men's lacrosse rules. Overland Park, KS: Author.

The National Collegiate Athletic Association (1995). 1995 offical rules of basketball. Chicago: Triumph Books.

The National Collegiate Athletic Association (1992). 1993 NCAA wrestling: rules and interpretations. Overland Park, KS: Author.

National Federation of State High Schools (1995). High school soccer rules book. Kansas City, MO: Author.

National Football League (1994). Official rules of the NFL. Chicago: Triumph Books.

National Hockey League (1994). *1995 official rules of the NHL*. Chicago: Triumph Books.

National Off-Road Bicycle Association (1995). *1995 competition guide: national off-road bicycle association*. Colorado Springs: Author.

NBA Properties (1994). *1994-95 official NBA rules*. St. Louis: The Sporting News.

PONY Baseball (1995). *Pony baseball 1994-95 rules and regulations*. Washington, PA: Author.

Pop Warner Football (1994). *The complete set of official rules: 1994, 1995, 1996*. Langhorne, PA: Author.

Professional Publications, Inc. (1994). *Soccer: do you know the rules?* Belmont, CA: Blue Moose Press.

Soccer Association for Youth (1995). *SAY soccer rules*. Cincinnati: Author.

Thomas, M. (1994). *Know the game: netball*. London: Black.

Union Internationale de Pentathlon Moderne et Biathlon (1996). *Modern pentathlon competition rules*. Budapest: Author.

United States Amateur Confederation of Roller Skating (no date). *USA roller hockey rules*. Lincoln, NE: Author.

United States Badminton Association (1995). *Official rules of play & court officials handbook*. Colorado Springs: Author.

United States Curling Association (1995). *Rules of play 1995-96: club and bonspiel use*. Stevens Point, WI: Author.

United States Diving (1995). *United States diving rules & regulations 95-96*. Indianapolis: Author.

United States Fencing Association (1994). *United States Fencing Association rule book*. Colorado Springs: Author.

United States Figure Skating Association (1995). *The 1996 official USFSA rulebook*. Colorado Springs: Author.

United States Flag & Touch Football League (1994). *1994-95 official rule book & constitution: United States flag & touch football league*. Mentor, OH: Author.

The United States Golf Association and the Royal and Ancient Golf Club of St. Andrews, Scotland (1994). *1995 official rules of golf*. Chicago: Triumph Books.

United States Handball Association (1991). *The new and official United States Handball Association rulebook*. Tucson: Author.

United States Judo Association (1994). *1994 contest rules of the international judo federation*. Colorado Springs: Author.

The United States Rowing Association (1996). *1996 rules of rowing*. Indianapolis: Author.

United States Sailing Association (1994). *1993-96 international yacht racing rules*. Newport, RI: Author.

United States Ski Association (1993). *Cross country rulebook*. Park City, UT: Author.

United States Squash Racquets Association (1993). *The international rules of squash*. Bala Cynwyd, PA: Author.

United States Squash Racquets Association (1987). *The rules of squash*. Bala Cynwyd, PA: Author.

United States Swimming (1996). *United States Swimming 1996 rules and regulations*. Colorado Springs: Author.

United States Synchronized Swimming (1995). *1995-1996 United States Synchronized Swimming official rules*. Indianapolis: Author.

United States Taekwondo Union (1993). *United States Taekwondo Union: school/club handbook*. Colorado Springs: Author.

United States Team Handball Federation (1996). *Basic rules of team handball*. Colorado Springs: Author.

United States Tennis Association (1995). *1995 rules of tennis & cases and decisions*. White Plains, NY: H.O. Zimman.

United States Water Polo, Inc. (1996). *1996 water polo playing rules*. Colorado Springs: Author.

United States Weightlifting Federation (1994). *Official rulebook 1994 edition*. Colorado Springs: Author.

United States Women's Lacrosse Association (1995). *Official rules for women's lacrosse: 1995*. Hamilton, NY: Author.

U.S. Cycling Federation (1995). *1995 rules of bicycle racing*. Colorado Springs: Author.

U.S. Youth Soccer (1995). *The official U.S. youth soccer 8 v 8 program under ten*. Richardson, TX: Author.

U.S. Youth Soccer (1995). *The small sided game: the official U.S. youth soccer 3 v 3 program under six.* Richardson, TX: Author.

U.S. Youth Soccer (1995). *The small sided game: the official U.S. youth soccer 4 v 4 program under eight.* Richardson, TX: Author.

USA Boxing (1995). *USA boxing: official rules 1995-1997.* Colorado Springs: Author.

USA Hockey (1993). *Official playing rules 1993-95.* Colorado Springs: Author.

USA Karate Federation (1995). *USA karate rules and regulations for competitions.* Akron: Author.

USA Shooting (1995). *Official rules for international shooting.* Colorado Springs: Author.

USA Table Tennis (1994). *The law of table tennis.* Colorado Springs: Author.

USA Track & Field (1995). *Competition rules 1995.* Indianapolis: Author.

USA Triathlon (1996). *Tri-Fed/USA competitive rules.* Colorado Springs: Author.

USA Volleyball (1995). *1996 United States volleyball official rules.* Lynn, MA: H.O. Zimman.

USA Wrestling (1995). *International rule book & guide to wrestling: freestyle and greco-roman, 1995 edition.* Colorado Springs: Author.

White, J.R. (1990). *Sports rules encyclopedia (second edition).* Champaign, IL: Human Kinetics.

Williams, H. *Orienteering homepage.* [Online]. Available WWW (World Wide Web): http://www.williams.edu:803/Biology/Orienteering/O~index.html (April 30, 1977).

Women's International Bowling Congress and American Bowling Congress (1994). *Playing rules 1994-95: ABC/WIBC.* Greendale, WI: Authors.

Yacenda, J. (1992). *Alpine skiing: steps to success.* Champaign, IL: Human Kinetics.

Human Kinetics

Human Kinetics began in 1974 on a ping-pong table in the basement of Rainer and Marilyn Martens's house in Champaign, IL, when Rainer—then a professor at the University of Illinois—decided to publish the proceedings of a sport psychology conference he had organized.

Now publishing annually more than 100 books, 23 journals, and a rapidly growing number of audio, video, software, and on-line resources, Human Kinetics has become the world's largest producer of information in the physical activity field. Fueling this growth has been a commitment to developing quality resources in such areas as the sport and exercise sciences, physical education, fitness, sports, and coaching.

Needless to say, the company has long since outgrown the Martens's basement! With 9 divisions and 12 departments, Human Kinetics employs nearly 180 people at the home office—a sprawling 85,000 square foot office-warehouse complex in Champaign, IL—and another 16 at subsidiaries in Canada, Europe, Australia, and New Zealand.